More Praise for Sam Harris and *Making Sense*

"To the raging controversies of the day, Sam Harris adds a voice of civility and reason."

–LAWRENCE WRIGHT, author of *The Looming Tower*

"*Making Sense* brings the power and patience of contemplation to the art of conversation. Sam Harris models not only how to articulate complex ideas, but also how to truly hear the ideas of others. This is cognitive jazz at its best."

–DOUGLAS RUSHKOFF, author of *Present Shock*

"Whatever your politics, you will find ideas and points of views you've never considered before, in fields you don't know, from neuroscience to computer science to culture."

–ANNE APPLEBAUM, author of *Gulag*

"Sam is an enlightened, rational voice in a world that needs it now, perhaps more than ever—especially if we are to survive, or thrive, in spite of the collective weaknesses that make us human."

–NEIL DEGRASSE TYSON, astrophysicist,
American Museum of Natural History

"It's no wonder that Sam attracts a huge audience. He is a thinker with his own ideas, so his interviews are some of the most interesting conversations you are ever likely to hear."

–PETER SINGER, author of *Animal Liberation*

"There is no podcast that approaches the intellectual rigor and open-mindedness of Sam Harris's *Making Sense*. It's a regular dose of sane, patient reason, and dialogue. In a tribalized world, it reveres the individual, inquisitive mind. And Sam has some balls to talk honestly where so many others won't."

–ANDREW SULLIVAN, author of *The Conservative Soul*

"Sam Harris is tremendous at his job; sharp, skeptical in just the best sense, and full of curiosity and openness. He's a terrific questioner, and he greatly enlivens and improves public discourse."

—CASS R. SUNSTEIN, author of *Can It Happen Here?: Authoritarianism in America*

"In the huge world of interviewers, Sam Harris stands out at the top for his probing questions and for his own thoughtful views."

—JARED DIAMOND, author of *Guns, Germs, and Steel*

"Of all the podcasts available, the one nobody should miss is *Making Sense*. Every episode is stimulating. In an era when everyone seems to have lost their reason, here is one of the few places where reason remains safe."

—DOUGLAS MURRAY, author of *The Madness of Crowds*

"Sam Harris is a true public intellectual: he thinks deeply about a wide range of issues and engages fearlessly with controversial topics and unpopular opinions. You don't have to agree with him to learn from him—I always come away from his show with new insights and new questions."

—ADAM GRANT, author of *Originals* and host of the TED podcast *WorkLife*

"Sam makes sense of important, difficult, and often controversial topics with deep preparation, sharp questions, and intellectual fearlessness."

—ANDREW MCAFEE, author of *More from Less*

"Sam has given us one of the greatest podcasts in the world for clear thinking. We are better equipped to face the perils and uncertainties of life with it in the air. It's a stand-out leader in a cluttered field and being Sam's guest on it was a career highlight."

—DERREN BROWN, author of *Happy*

"There are precious few spaces in the media landscape where difficult, rigorous, and respectful conversations can play out at substantial length, without agenda. Sam Harris created the model for such illuminating exchange, and the *Making Sense* podcast is a treasure trove of discussions with many of the most compelling and fascinating minds of our era."

—THOMAS CHATTERTON WILLIAMS, author of *Self-Portrait in Black and White*

"As an interviewer, Sam is both rigorous and generous. His show is completely devoid of the cheap shots and tribal bickering that characterize so much of podcasting. *Making Sense* is joyful play of the mind, without a trace of the partisan cretinism that disfigures the vast majority of our discourse these days."

—GRAEME WOOD, author of *The Way of the Strangers*

"Sam Harris does an incredible job probing—and finding answers to—some of the most important questions of our times."

—SIDDHARTHA MUKHERJEE, author of *The Emperor of All Maladies*

Making Sense

Making Sense

CONVERSATIONS ON CONSCIOUSNESS,
MORALITY, AND THE FUTURE OF HUMANITY

Sam Harris

ecco
An Imprint of HarperCollins*Publishers*

HarperCollins books may be purchased for educational, business, or sales promotional use. For information, please email the Special Markets Department at SPsales@harpercollins.com.

Ecco® and HarperCollins® are trademarks of HarperCollins Publishers.

FIRST EDITION

Designed by Michelle Crowe

Library of Congress Cataloging-in-Publication Data has been applied for.

ISBN 978-0-06-285778-1

20 21 22 23 24 LSC 10 9 8 7 6 5 4 3 2 1

To my mother

Contents

Preface   ix

THE LIGHT OF THE MIND
A Conversation with David Chalmers   1

FINDING OUR WAY
A Conversation with David Deutsch   29

CONSCIOUSNESS AND THE SELF
A Conversation with Anil Seth   95

THE NATURE OF CONSCIOUSNESS
A Conversation with Thomas Metzinger   157

THE ROAD TO TYRANNY
A Conversation with Timothy Snyder   187

WHAT IS RACISM?
A Conversation with Glenn C. Loury   213

THE BIOLOGY OF GOOD AND EVIL
A Conversation with Robert Sapolsky   253

THE MAP OF MISUNDERSTANDING
A Conversation with Daniel Kahneman   283

WILL WE DESTROY THE FUTURE?
A Conversation with Nick Bostrom   319

COMPLEXITY AND STUPIDITY
A Conversation with David Krakauer   353

OUR FUTURE
A Conversation with Max Tegmark   385

Acknowledgments   439
Contributors   441

Preface

We are living in a new golden age of public conversation.

Millions of us have recently discovered that significant parts of the day—a commute, an hour at the gym, an eternity spent on the threshold of sleep—can be filled with podcasts and related media. Increasingly, we replace the voice in our heads with the voices of others—whose opinions, whether considered or not, now inform our own. I'm convinced that this is generally a good development. Every hour, we struggle to maintain a vast, technological civilization, and yet conversation remains our only means of making intellectual and moral progress.

Podcasting began in 2004, which happens to be the year I published my first book. If someone had told me then that I would eventually spend most of my time producing a podcast, rather than writing, I would have said, "What's a podcast?" If they had then described this new form of media—more or less accurately—as "radio on demand," I would have been willing to bet the fate of our species that they were mistaken about me. For as long as I can remember, I've wanted to write books. At no point in my life have I spent two consecutive breaths wondering whether I might like to work in radio.

And yet, creating the *Making Sense* podcast has consumed most of my professional energy in recent years. The reasons for this are disconcertingly simple: I will reach more people in forty-eight hours with my next podcast than I will reach in a decade with all of my books. And the results are instantaneous: instead of waiting a year for a book to be published, I can release a podcast the moment it's finished.

In truth, the analogy to radio is somewhat misleading. The distinction between a radio show that is allotted a full hour in a fixed schedule, and a podcast episode that just happens to wrap up after fifty-nine minutes, can be hard to appreciate from the outside. But the difference is felt every moment along the way. Time pressure changes everything—a fact that anyone can perceive when watching a formal debate. A willingness to explore adjacent topics, to backtrack, to try ideas on for size only to discard them, to invite criticism without knowing what one's response to it will be—and when disagreements surface, to give one's opponents the freedom to present the best possible case for their views—such a spirit of dialogue can only arise when the threat of being interrupted isn't further weaponized by a ticking clock. When we are guided by real curiosity and a principle of charity, every human problem seems to admit of solution. In other moods, even conversation itself proves impossible.

Podcasting is the only medium that allows for truly natural, open-ended conversation. So it's not an accident that this is where scientists, journalists, and public intellectuals now think out loud. But the strength of the medium is also its primary weakness, because conversation lacks the precision of written work. And listeners may fail to catch subtle points that readers would naturally pause to absorb. Thus, when compared to the clarity and accessibility of books, even some of the most interesting podcasts can feel like missed opportunities.

In this volume, I've collected some of my favorite conversations from *Making Sense* and adapted them for print. To do this, I've asked my guests to refine their side of the exchange, and I've done the same to mine. The result follows the pattern of our original conversation, but we've made many small amendments and clarifications throughout. Now, everyone involved can be counted upon to have said what they truly mean.

Since 2014, I've released over two hundred episodes of the *Making Sense* podcast, now averaging about one per week. This volume presents thirteen of my favorites, with eleven guests—David Chalmers, David Deutsch, Anil Seth, Thomas Metzinger, Timothy Snyder, Glenn Loury, Robert Sapolsky, Daniel Kahneman, Nick Bostrom, David Krakauer, and Max Tegmark. The book covers a wide range of concerns—

consciousness, the foundations of knowledge, ethics, artificial intelligence, politics, physics, decision making, racism, violence, existential risk—but it is heavily weighted toward questions about the nature of mind and how minds like ours can best create a world worth living in. As listeners to *Making Sense* know, these are my core interests, and I return to them often.

I have long believed in the ultimate unity of knowledge, and thus that the boundaries between traditional disciplines should be generally ignored. One thing we surely know about reality at this point, is that it isn't partitioned like a university campus. I also believe that most of the evil in our world—all the needless misery we manufacture for one another—is the product, not of what bad people do, but of what good people do once in the grip of bad ideas. Taken together, these principles suggest that there is no telling how much moral progress we might make by removing the impediments to clear thinking on any topic that interests us.

For instance, as I write these lines the world is still struggling to understand the gravity of the COVID-19 pandemic, which has now spread to 187 countries. Political, philosophical, religious, and economic beliefs now contend with the basic principles of epidemiology in the brains of millions of people, some of whom are responsible for making and enforcing policies that will affect the lives of billions. There is still no consensus on how societies should respond to this crisis, and factions have formed on the basis of entirely different views of terrestrial reality. Has the danger of this disease been exaggerated for political gain? Is it unethical to force businesses to close and people to stay indoors in an effort to slow the contagion? Do governments have a responsibility to provide free health care to their citizens? Should the Chinese be admonished to stop eating bats, or would that be a sign of racism? Where is the boundary between contrarian thinking and deadly misinformation? Everywhere one looks, one sees the ruins of failed epistemology— and bad ideas are getting people killed.

There are now nearly one million different podcasts to choose from. Many just give voice to the general pugnacity of our age—and my own podcast has not been entirely immune. But the antidote to bad conversations is always better ones. And here I present some of the most satisfying conversations I've ever had.

Enjoy . . .

Sam Harris
May 6, 2020
Los Angeles

Making Sense

The Light of
the Mind

A CONVERSATION WITH DAVID CHALMERS

Trying to understand consciousness has long been a foundational interest of mine, and given his role in sparking that interest, I begin *Making Sense* with David Chalmers. A philosopher at New York University and at the Australian National University, Chalmers is also a codirector of the Center for Mind, Brain, and Consciousness at NYU.

We spend most of our time discussing the nature of consciousness and why it is so difficult to understand scientifically. We begin with Chalmers's notion of "the hard problem of consciousness"—a phrase that has influenced every debate on the subject since the early 1990s. We also talk about artificial intelligence, the possibility that the universe is a simulation, and other fascinating topics, some of which may *seem* impossibly distant from the concerns of everyday life. But I would urge you not to be misled here. All of these topics will become more and more relevant as we continue to build technology that, whether conscious or not, will seem conscious to us. And as we confront the prospect of augmenting our own minds by integrating devices directly into our brains, all of these philosophical puzzles will become matters of immediate personal and ethical concern.

HARRIS: You've played an important role in my intellectual life. I went to one of those early biennial Tucson conferences on consciousness, at the University of Arizona. I had dropped out of school, and I guess you could say I was looking for some direction in life. I'd become interested in the conversations that were happening in the philosophy of mind—initially because of the sparring between Daniel Dennett and John Searle. Then I saw an ad for the Tucson conference, probably in the *Journal of Consciousness Studies*, and just showed up.

I distinctly remember your talk there. Your articulation of the hard problem of consciousness made me want to do philosophy, which led directly to my wanting to know more science and sent me back to the ivory tower. Part of my reason for getting a PhD in neuroscience, and for my continued interest in this issue, was the conversation you started in Tucson more than twenty years ago.

CHALMERS: I'm really pleased to hear that. That was probably the '96 conference. Dennett was there.

HARRIS: Along with Roger Penrose, Francisco Varela, and many others. It was a fascinating time.

CHALMERS: The previous event in 1994 is what people called the Woodstock of Consciousness. Getting the band together for the first time. It was crazy, a whole lot of fun, and the first time I'd met a lot of these people, too.

HARRIS: I'm a bad judge of how familiar people are with the problem of consciousness, because I've been so steeped in it for decades now. I'm always surprised that people find it difficult to grasp that consciousness poses a special challenge to science. So let's start at the beginning. What do you mean by "consciousness," and how would you distinguish it from the topics it's usually conflated with, like self-awareness, attention, thinking, behavior, and so forth?

CHALMERS: It's awfully hard to define consciousness. But I'd start by saying that it's the subjective experience of the mind and the world.

It's basically what it feels like, from the first-person point of view, to be thinking and perceiving and judging. When I look out the window, there are trees and grass and a pond, and so on. And there's a whirl of information processing as photons in my retinas send a signal up the optic nerve to my brain—that's on the level of functioning and behavior.

But there's also something that it feels like from a first-person point of view. I might have an experience of the colors, a certain greenness of the green, a certain reflection on the pond—like an inner movie in my head. And the crucial problem of consciousness—for me, at least—is this subjective part. We can distinguish it from questions about behavior or functioning. People sometimes use the word "consciousness" just to indicate, for example, that I'm awake and responsive. That's something that is straightforward and can be understood in behavioral terms. I like to call those problems of consciousness the easy problems—the ones about how we behave, how we respond, how we function. What I call the hard problem of consciousness is the one about how it feels from the first-person point of view.

HARRIS: There was another influential statement of this problem, which I assume influenced you as well: Thomas Nagel's 1974 essay "What Is It Like to Be a Bat?" The formulation he gave there is: if it's *like something* to be a creature processing information—if there's an internal, subjective, qualitative character to the processing—that is what we mean by "consciousness," in the case of a bat or any other system. People who don't like that formulation think that, as a definition, it just begs the question. But as a rudimentary statement of what consciousness is, I've always found it very attractive. Do you have any thoughts on that?

CHALMERS: It's about as good a definition as we're going to get. The idea is roughly that a system is conscious if there's something it's like to be that system. There's something it's like to be me. There's nothing it's like, presumably, to be this glass of water on my desk. If there's nothing it's like to be the glass of water on my desk, then the glass of water is not conscious.

Likewise, some of my mental states. There's something it's like for me to see the green leaves outside my window right now, so that's a conscious state to me. But there may be some unconscious language-processing going on in my head that doesn't feel like anything to me, or some motor processes in the cerebellum. Those might be states of me, but they're not conscious states of me, because there's nothing it's like for me to undergo those states.

So Nagel's definition is vivid and useful for me. That said, it's just a bunch of words, like any other. And for some people, this bunch of words is useful in activating the idea of consciousness from the subjective point of view. Other people hear something different in that set of words. For those people, the words "What is it like?" doesn't work. What I've found over the years is that this phrase of Nagel's is useful for some people, in getting them onto the problem, but it doesn't work for everybody.

My sense is that most people do have some notion that there's a big problem here. What they do after that is different in different cases. Some people think we ought to see the hard problem as an illusion and get past it. But to focus the issue, I find it useful to start by distinguishing the easy problems—which are basically about the performance of functions—from the hard problem, which is about experience.

The easy problems are: How do we discriminate information in our environment and respond appropriately? How does the brain integrate information from different sources and bring it together to make a judgment and control our behavior? How do we voluntarily control our behavior to respond in a controlled way to our environment? How does our brain monitor its own states? These are all mysteries, and neuroscience has not gotten all that far on some of them. But we have a pretty clear sense of what the research program is and what it would take to explain them. It's basically a matter of finding some mechanism in the brain that is responsible for discriminating the information and controlling the behavior. Although pinning down the mechanisms is hard work, we're on a path to doing it.

The easier problems at least fall within the standard methods of neuroscience and cognitive science. What makes the hard problem of experience hard? Because it doesn't seem to be a problem about behavior or about functions. You can in principle imagine explaining all of my behavioral responses to a given stimulus and how my brain discriminates and integrates and monitors itself and controls my behavior. You can explain all that with, say, a neural mechanism, but you won't have touched the central question, which is, "Why does it *feel* like something from the first-person point of view?"

The usual methods that work for us in the neural and cognitive sciences—finding a mechanism that does the job—doesn't obviously apply here. We'll certainly find correlations between processes in the brain and bits of consciousness—an area of the brain that might light up when you see red or when you feel pain. But nothing there seems to explain why all that processing feels like something from the inside. Why doesn't that processing just go on in the dark, as if we were robots or zombies without any subjective experience?

So that's the hard problem, and people react in different ways to it. Someone like Dan Dennett says it's all an illusion, or a confusion, and one that we need to get past. I respect that line of thought. It's a hard-enough problem that we need to be exploring every avenue, and one avenue that's worth exploring is the view that it's an illusion.

But there's something faintly unbelievable about the idea that the data of consciousness are an illusion. To me, they're the most real thing in the universe—the feeling of pain, the experience of vision, the experience of thinking. Dan Dennett takes a very hard line in his 1991 book *Consciousness Explained*. It was a good and very influential book. But I think that most people found, at the end of the day, that it didn't do justice to the phenomenon.

HARRIS: That might have been the first book I read on this topic. It's strange—I'm aligned with you and Thomas Nagel on these questions in the philosophy of mind, and yet I've had this alliance with Dan for many years on the conflict between religion and science. I've spent a fair amount of time with Dan, but we've never really gotten into a conversation on consciousness. Perhaps we've been wary of it; we had a somewhat unhappy collision on the topic of free will. It's been a long time since I've read *Consciousness Explained*—does he say that *consciousness* is an illusion, or just that the hardness of the hard problem is illusory? I understand that he'd want to push the latter intuition. But as for the former, it seems to me that consciousness is the one thing in this universe that cannot be an illusion. Even if we're confused about the qualitative character of our experience in many other respects, the fact that it is *like something* to be us, the fact that something seems to be happening, even if it's only a dream—that *seeming* is all one needs to assert the undeniable reality of consciousness. I just don't see how anyone can credibly claim that consciousness itself might be an illusion.

CHALMERS: I'm with you on this. I think Dan's views have evolved over the years. Back in the 1980s or so, he used to say things that sounded much stronger, like "Consciousness doesn't exist. It's an illusion." He wrote a paper called "On the Absence of Phenomenology," saying there really isn't such a thing as phenomenology, which is basically just another word for consciousness. He wrote another one called "Quining Qualia," which said we needed to get rid of the whole idea of qualia, which is a word that philosophers use for the qualitative character of experience; what makes seeing red different from seeing green. Those experiences seem to involve different qualities. At one point Dan was inclined to say, "That's just a mistake. There's nothing there."

Over the years, I think he found that people consider that position—that from the first-person point of view there are no qualia, no feeling of red versus the feeling of green—a bit too strong to be believable. So he's evolved in the direction of saying, yes, there's consciousness, but it's just in the sense of functioning and behavior and information encoded, and not really consciousness in the strong phenomenological sense that drives the hard problem.

In a way, this is a verbal relabeling of his old position. I know you're familiar with the debates about free will, where one person says, "There's no free will," and the other person says, "Well, there is free will, but it's just this much more deflated thing which is compatible with determinism"—and these are basically two ways of saying the same thing. Dan used to say there's no consciousness; now he says, "Well, there's consciousness, but only in this deflated sense"—which is another way of saying the same thing. He still doesn't think there is consciousness in the strong, subjective sense that poses the whole problem.

HARRIS: I want to retrace what you said in sketching the hardness of the hard problem. You make the distinction between understanding function and understanding the fact that experience exists. We have functions, like motor behavior and visual perception, and it's straightforward to think about explaining them in mechanistic terms. With vision, for example, we can talk about the transduction of light energy into neurochemical events and then mapping the visual field onto the relevant parts of the visual cortex. This is complicated but not, in principle, obscure. However, the fact that it's *like something to see* remains mysterious, no matter how much mapping we do.

And if we built a robot that could do all the things we can, it seems to me that at no point in refining its mechanisms would we have reason to believe that it was conscious, even if it passed the Turing Test.

This is one of the things that concerns me about AI. It seems increasingly likely that we will build machines that will seem conscious, and the effect could be so convincing that we might lose sight of the hard problem. It could cease to seem philosophically interesting, or even ethically appropriate, to wonder whether there is something it is like to be one of these robots. And yet we still won't know whether they are actually conscious unless we have understood how consciousness arises in the first place—which is to say, unless we have solved the hard problem.

CHALMERS: Maybe we should distinguish the question of whether a system is conscious from the question of how that consciousness is explained.

I suspect that with machines, if they're hanging around with us, talking in a humanlike way and reflecting on their consciousness, saying, "I'm really puzzled by this whole consciousness thing, because I know I'm just a collection of silicon circuits, but it still feels like something from the inside"—if machines are doing that, I'll be pretty convinced that they're conscious as I am conscious. But that won't make consciousness any less mysterious, and it might make it all the more mysterious. How could this machine be conscious if it's just a collection of silicon circuits? Likewise, how could I be conscious just as a result of processes in my brain? I don't see anything intrinsically worse about silicon than about brain processes here; there's a mysterious gap in the explanation in both cases.

And, of course, we can wonder about other people, too. That's a classic philosophical problem, the problem of other minds. How do you know that anybody apart from yourself is conscious? Descartes said, "Well, I'm certain of one thing: I'm conscious. I think, therefore I am." That only gets you one data point. It gets me the me being conscious—and only being conscious right now, because who knows if I was ever conscious in the past? Anything beyond right now has to be an inference or an extrapolation. We end up taking for granted most of the time that other people are conscious, but as you move to questions about AI and robots, about animals and so on, the question of who else is conscious becomes very murky.

HARRIS: The difference as far as AI or robots are concerned is that presumably we'll build them along lines that aren't analogous to the emergence of our own nervous systems. We might proceed as we have with chess-playing computers—where we have built something that we have no reason to believe is aware of chess, and yet is now the best chess player on Earth. If we do this for a thousand different human attributes and thus create a computer that can function as we do, but better—perhaps a robot that has mimetic facial displays we find compelling, and so no longer seems weird or lifeless to us. If this system is built in a way that is nonanalogous to our own nervous system, then it could be hard to tell whether or not it's conscious. Whereas in the case of other people, I have every reason to believe that the structures that suffice to produce consciousness in my case, probably suffice for them too. Solipsism isn't really tempting, philosophically speaking, because there's a deep analogy between how I came to be conscious and how you came to claim that you are conscious too. I'd have to argue that there was something about your nervous system, or your situation in the universe, that wasn't sufficient to produce consciousness, while it clearly was in my own case.

To wonder whether other people, or even the higher animals, are conscious is not an example of being parsimonious; rather, it requires extra work.

CHALMERS: How would you feel if we met Martians? Let's say there are intelligent Martians who are behaviorally sophisticated and we find we can communicate with them about science and philosophy, but they've evolved through an evolutionary process different from ours. Would you have doubts about whether they might be conscious?

HARRIS: Perhaps I would. It would be somewhere between our own case and whatever AI we might build. This leads to a topic I wanted to raise with you: the issue of epiphenomenalism, which is actually the flip side of the hard problem. The fact that we can describe all this functioning without introducing consciousness leaves us with another problem many people find counterintuitive: namely, that consciousness might not be doing anything—that it's an epiphenomenon. In an analogy often cited, it's like the smoke coming out of the smokestack of an old-fashioned locomotive. The smoke is associated with the progress of the train down the tracks, but it's not actually doing any work; it's merely a by-product of the mechanism that is actually propelling the train. Consciousness could be like this. In your first book, *The Conscious Mind*, you seemed to be fairly sympathetic with epiphenomenalism.

CHALMERS: The idea that consciousness doesn't do anything—that it's epiphenomenal—is not a view that anyone feels an initial attraction for. It sure seems to do so much. But there's this puzzle: For any behavior, there's a potential explanation in terms of neurons or computational mechanisms that doesn't invoke consciousness in the subjective sense. You can at least start to wonder if maybe consciousness *doesn't* have any function. Maybe it doesn't do anything at all. Maybe, for example, consciousness simply gives value and meaning to our lives—which is something we can talk about. But if it does nothing else, then all kinds of questions arise: How and why would we have evolved as we have—let alone come to be having this extended conversation about consciousness—if consciousness were not playing some role in the causal loop?

In *The Conscious Mind*, I at least tried on the idea of epiphenomenalism. I didn't flat out say, "This is definitely true." I tried to say, "Well, if we're forced to, that's one way we could go." Either consciousness is epiphenomenal or it's outside a physical system but somehow playing a role in physics. That's a more traditional, dualist possibility. Or there's a third possibility: Consciousness is somehow built in at the fundamental level of physics.

HARRIS: I'd like to track through each of those possibilities, but let's stick with epiphenomenalism for a moment. You've touched on it in passing here, but remind us of the "zombie argument," the thought experiment that describes epiphenomenalism. It's not an argument I'd noticed before I heard you make it, but I don't know if it originates with you.

CHALMERS: The idea of zombies, in philosophy not to mention in popular culture, was out there before me. I think the philosopher Robert Kirk originated the label in the 1970s, and the idea itself goes back further. The zombies of philosophy are different from the zombies of the movies or in Haitian voodoo culture. All these zombies are missing something. The zombies in the movies are lacking life; they're dead but reanimated. The zombies in the voodoo tradition lack some kind of free will. The zombies that play a role in philosophy lack consciousness.

In this thought experiment, the conceit is that we can imagine a being behaviorally identical to a normal human being—a being that acts and walks and talks in a perfectly humanlike way—but without any consciousness at all. There's an extreme version that asks you to imagine a being *physically identical* to a particular human being but without subjective consciousness. I talk about my zombie twin, a hypothetical being in the universe next door, who's physically identical to me. He's holding this conversation with a zombie analog of you right now, saying all the same stuff and responding but without any consciousness.

Now, no one thinks that anything like this exists in our universe. But the idea is at least conceivable. And the very fact that you can make sense of it immediately raises questions like "Why aren't *we* zombies?" Evolution could have produced zombies; instead, it produced conscious beings. Why didn't evolution produce zombies? If there were some function we could point to and say, "That's what you need consciousness for; you couldn't do that without consciousness," then we might have a function for consciousness. But right now, for anything we actually do—perception, learning, memory, language, and so on—it sure looks as if a whole lot of it could be done unconsciously. The whole problem of what consciousness is doing is thrown into harsh relief by the zombie thought experiment.

HARRIS: Most of what our minds accomplish is unconscious, or at least it seems so. The fact that I perceive my visual field, the fact that I hear your voice, the fact that I effortlessly decode meaning from your words because I'm an English speaker—this is all done unconsciously before I have an experience of any of these things. So it's a mystery why there should be something that it's like to be associated with any part of this process, because so much of it takes place in the dark.

This is a topic I raised in my last book, *Waking Up*, in discussing split-brain research. There is reason to wonder whether or not there are islands of consciousness in our brains that we're not aware of—that is, we have an "other minds" problem with respect to our very own brains. What do you think about the possibility that there is something that it's like to be associated with parts of your own cognitive processing that seem like zombie parts?

CHALMERS: Well, I don't rule it out. When it comes to the mind/body problem, the puzzles are large enough. One of the big puzzles is, we don't know which systems are conscious. Most of us think humans are conscious, and probably a lot of the more sophisticated mammals are conscious: apes, monkeys, dogs, cats. When it gets to mice, maybe flies, some people start to wobble, but I like the idea that for many reasonably sophisticated information-processing devices there's some kind of consciousness. Maybe this goes very deep, and at some point we can talk about the idea that consciousness is everywhere.

But before that, if you're prepared to say that a fly is conscious, or a worm with its three hundred neurons, then you do have to wonder about pieces of the brain that are enormously more sophisticated than that but are part of another conscious system. The neuroscientist Giulio Tononi recently proposed a theory of consciousness called IIT, integrated information theory. He's got a mathematical measure, Φ, of the amount of information a system integrates. Whenever it's high enough, you get consciousness.

When you look at different pieces of the brain, like each hemisphere, the cerebellum, and so on, you note that the Φ isn't as high as it is for the brain as a whole, but it's still pretty high. Tononi would say that an animal with a Φ that high was conscious. So why isn't that piece of the brain conscious? He ends up throwing in an extra axiom, which he calls the exclusion axiom, saying, in effect, that if you're a part of a system that has a higher Φ than you do, then you're not conscious. If the hemisphere has a high Φ but the brain as a whole has a higher Φ, then the brain gets to be conscious but the hemisphere doesn't. To many people, that axiom looks arbitrary. But without that axiom, you'd be left with a whole lot of conscious subsystems. And I agree: Who knows what it's like to be a subsystem—what it's like to be my cerebellum, what it's like to be a hemisphere? On the other hand, there are experiments and situations in which one half of the brain gets destroyed and the other half keeps going fine.

HARRIS: I wanted to ask you about Tononi's notion of consciousness as integrated information. To me, it's yet another case of someone trying to ram past the hard problem. Max Tegmark wrote a paper, "Consciousness as a State of Matter," that took Tononi as a starting point. He basically said, "Let's start here. We know there are certain arrangements of matter that are conscious, now we just have to talk about the plausible explanation for what makes them conscious." He went on to embrace Tononi and then did a lot of physics.

But is there anything in Tononi's discussion that pries up the lid on the hard problem farther than the earlier work he did with Gerald Edelman, or farther than anyone else's attempt to give some information-processing construal of consciousness?

CHALMERS: To be fair to Tononi, he's actually very sensitive to the problem of consciousness. And when pressed, he says he's not trying to solve the hard problem of showing how you can get consciousness from matter. He's not trying to cross the explanatory gap from physical processes to consciousness. Rather, he says, "I'm starting with the *fact* of consciousness. I'm taking that as a given, and I'm trying to map its properties." And he starts with some phenomenological axioms of consciousness, for example that it consists of information that's differentiated in certain ways but integrated and unified in other ways. Then he takes those phenomenological axioms and turns them into mathematics of information and asks, "What informational properties does consciousness have?" Then he comes up with this mathematical measure, Φ. At some point, the theory that consciousness is a certain kind of integration of information arises. The way I see the theory—I don't know if he puts it this way—is as correlating different states of consciousness with different kinds of integration of information in the brain.

So the hard problem is still there, because we still have no idea why all that integration of information in the brain should produce consciousness in the first place. But even someone who believes there's a hard problem can believe that there are systematic correlations between brain processes and consciousness that we should have a rigorous mathematical theory of. Tononi's theory is basically a stab in the direction of providing a rigorous mathematical theory of those correlations.

HARRIS: I agree that you can throw up your hands over the hard problem and just try to map the neural correlates of consciousness without pretending that the mystery has been reduced thereby.

CHALMERS: I do think there's something intermediate you can go for which allows the possibility of a broadly scientific approach to something in the neighborhood of the hard problem. It's not just, "Oh, let's look at the neural correlates and see what's going on in the human case." It's more like, "Let's find the simplest, most fundamental principles that connect physical processes to consciousness, as a kind of basic general principle." We might start with correlations we find in the familiar human case, between, say, certain neural systems and certain kinds of consciousness. And then, based on as much evidence as possible, we should try to generalize principles that might apply to other systems.

Ultimately, you'd look for simple bridging principles that predict what kind of consciousness you'd find in what kind of physical system. So I'd say that something like Tononi's integrated information principle, with this mathematical quantity Φ, is a proposal for a fundamental principle that might connect physical processes to consciousness.

It won't remove the hard problem, but you can at least go on to do science with that principle. We already know that elsewhere in science you have to take some laws and principles as axiomatic, basic principles we don't try to explain any further: the fundamental laws of physics, the law of gravity, the laws of quantum mechanics. And it may well be that we'll have to take something like consciousness for granted as well.

HARRIS: As you say, there are brute facts we accept throughout science, and they're no impediment to our thinking about the rest of reality. But placing the emergence of consciousness among these brute facts wouldn't be the same as understanding it.

I want to ask another question about the zombie argument—whether it's conceivable that a zombie would, or could, talk about the idea of consciousness.

If you imagine my zombie twin, which is devoid of experience, but speaks and functions just as I do—what could possibly motivate it to think about consciousness or say things like "You have subjective experience but I don't"? How could it distinguish experience from nonexperience?

CHALMERS: This is a puzzle, and probably one of the biggest puzzles when it comes to thinking through the zombie thought experiment. Why are zombies talking about consciousness if they don't have it?

Now, if the claim is just that a zombie is conceivable, I don't think it's particularly hard to at least conceive of a system doing this. I'm talking to you now, and you're making a lot of comments about consciousness that strongly suggest that you have it. Still, I can at least entertain the idea that you're not conscious and that you're a zombie who is making all these noises with no consciousness on the inside.

So there seems to be no contradiction in the idea. That doesn't mean it's a sensible way for a system to be, or that it somehow makes it easier to understand or to explain these systems. If there were actual zombies among us, they probably *wouldn't* talk about consciousness.

In some ways, conceiving of zombies is a bit like conceiving of anti-gravity in a world of gravity. But the basic idea, I guess, is that there are brain mechanisms responsible for everything we say and do. And whatever is the explanation for those behavioral responses in us will also explain them in a zombie.

HARRIS: So the question is really whether it's possible for brain mechanisms alone to explain our talking about consciousness.

CHALMERS: I've entertained this idea—that even if it's hard to explain the actual experience of consciousness in physical terms, maybe you can explain the things we say *about* consciousness in physical terms. Because that would be a behavioral response—in principle, one of the easy problems. It might be a straightforward research project for science: "Explain the things we say about consciousness in physical terms." Who knows? Maybe that's possible.

If it turns out to be possible, you can go in a few different directions. It's easy to see why you might be tempted to go Dan Dennett's way and say, "We've explained all the things people say about consciousness. That's all we need to explain. The rest is an illusion."

Another way to go would be the epiphenomenalists' way, which is "Well, it sounds like you can explain the things we say. But consciousness isn't about saying something; it's about feeling something."

The third view is that consciousness gets into the system and plays a role in physical processing in a way we don't yet fully understand.

HARRIS: I'm not at all tempted by behaviorism here, because it's clear that the reality of consciousness lies beyond what we say about it. But it's hard for me to escape epiphenomenalism. Let's just say that consciousness is the experiential component of what it's like to be me—the subjective side of a certain class of physical events—and that's what it is to be conscious. So my consciousness is, at bottom, something my brain is doing.

Then, when we say that consciousness makes a difference in how I can function, which would allow us to think about why it evolved, wouldn't we still be talking about a difference in terms of its physical correlates? The cash value of consciousness in each moment would be the cash value of its antecedent physicality. Doesn't this still leave the qualitative character out of the clockwork as an epiphenomenon?

CHALMERS: I think it does, given certain assumptions. If you think consciousness is distinct from its physical correlates, and if you think the physical correlates form a closed system—a kind of closed network wherein every physical event has a physical cause—then you can't help but conclude that consciousness is an epiphenomenon.

So to avoid that, you either need to say that consciousness is somehow right there in the physical network, part of the physical system at its foundation, or you have to say that the physical system is not a closed network—that there are holes in the physical processing where consciousness gets in and makes a difference. Some people think something like this goes on in quantum mechanics, for example, with wave-function collapse. Maybe there's something like that happening with consciousness. But you'd have to say one of those two things to avoid the conclusion that consciousness is an epiphenomenon.

HARRIS: Well, let's talk about the way in which consciousness could be more fundamental to the fabric of reality. You've briefly sketched the possibility that consciousness goes all the way down, to the most rudimentary forms of information processing. At one point in your book *The Conscious Mind* you suggested that even a system as simple as a thermostat might be conscious, because it processes information.

Even deeper than that is the notion of panpsychism—that conscious-ness may in fact be a fundamental constituent of reality prior to any notion of information processing.

CHALMERS: The idea is that consciousness may be present at a funda-mental level in physics. This corresponds to the traditional philosophi-cal view called panpsychism—the view that basically everything has a mind where mind equals consciousness. Thus, every system is con-scious, including fundamental physical systems like atoms or quarks or photons.

Initially this seems like a pretty crazy idea, and we have no direct evidence for it. But once you entertain the possibility that the world *could* be that way, that every physical system is somehow made of a little bit of consciousness, there are certain philosophical advantages. If consciousness is what physics is ultimately made of, you imagine that our consciousness—the one you're experiencing, the one I'm experiencing—is somehow a combination of all those little bits of con-sciousness at the basic level. That would mean consciousness doesn't have to interfere with the physical causal network because it's part of it right from the start. It's a huge problem to understand how that would work, but it holds certain philosophical attractions.

As a result, quite a few people, both in philosophy and in science, have been exploring this panpsychist idea for the past few years. People who go this way think maybe it will help us avoid some of the really dif-ficult problems.

HARRIS: For me, it creates some other hard problems. For one, it doesn't explain why some of the brain's functions don't seem to be conscious. The panpsychist idea still leaves mysterious the apparent split in my brain between what-it's-like-to-be-me and what-it's-like-to-be-the-rest-of-me.

CHALMERS: Yes, the panpsychist view does create other problems. It avoids the original hard problem—Why is there consciousness at all?—by taking consciousness as fundamentally present, in the same way we take space or time to be present. But after having got around that problem, we still have questions about explaining why it is like this to be us.

One of these problems is called the combination problem. How is it that all those little bits of consciousness in, say, fundamental particles, could come together to yield a unified and bounded and rich consciousness of the kind I have? And another aspect of that question is, Why isn't every high-level system conscious?

A panpsychist could say that in fact there's consciousness in all kinds of systems, but we just don't have access to them. I happen to be identical to the brain-level consciousness. I'm not the hemisphere-level consciousness. I'm not the New York–level consciousness. I'm not the Earth-level consciousness.

An extreme panpsychist view would say that some kind of consciousness is present in all these levels but that the brain has certain special properties of unity and integration such that it's not just conscious but also intelligent and has thoughts and a coherent narrative and can describe itself, and so on. That would explain why the only systems actually thinking about this stuff are things at the level of brains.

HARRIS: You say panpsychism is a strange theory. And it is strange to imagine that everything, including tables and chairs and the subatomic particles of which they're composed, is conscious on some level. But I don't think a panpsychist would say that a chair is conscious *as* a chair— just that matter, at its most basic level, would feel the dull hum of subjectivity.

Then the question is, Would we expect to see anything different in the world if panpsychism were true? My intuition is that we wouldn't. I wouldn't expect chairs to start talking to me if their atoms were conscious on some level. And if we wouldn't expect to see any difference, then we should be hard-pressed to say why it's a strange thesis. Its strangeness seems predicated on the sense that you have some reason to find it implausible, given how the world seems. But if, upon analysis, you can't see how the world would be any different if panpsychism were true, then I'm not sure how you can make a strong assertion that it's a strange idea. It might be vacuous, or unfalsifiable, but I'm not sure why it's strange.

CHALMERS: Well, there's no direct evidence either for panpsychism or against it. Some people say that means it's a ridiculous hypothesis. If we'll never have any evidence for it, it can't be science, so we shouldn't take it seriously. But, as you say, the other view is, "Well, it's not ruled out, and therefore we should take it seriously."

I can see motivations for accepting either. Across the whole field of study of consciousness, evidence is very, very hard to come by. We all have first-person evidence about our own states, but the moment it comes to anybody or anything else, our access is indirect. In the case of other people, we tend to listen to what they say. If they tell us they're conscious, by and large we believe them, and we take what they say as evidence. But once we get to other systems: Is a dog conscious? Is a fly conscious? Our evidence is only indirect. Things might be a whole lot easier if we had a consciousness meter. Then we'd have a straightforward, objective science of consciousness. I'd point my consciousness meter at the chair, or the fly, or the atom, or the dog, or another person, and get a readout of their states of consciousness. But because consciousness is private and subjective, it's a whole lot harder.

I once gave a talk about consciousness at the CIA, of all places. I think they were kind of bored. Then I got to the bit about the consciousness meter, and I sensed that their ears pricked up: "We could really use one of those. It would save us a lot of money and time and trouble and waterboarding."

HARRIS: Well, they could use a lie detector, too. Whether or not anyone is conscious, we really want to know whether they're lying. And the same will be true of robots.

CHALMERS: We should at least be open to the idea that there's something about the way consciousness interacts with our psychology that makes it hard for us to get a grip on it. It may well be that for creatures a million times more intelligent than us, consciousness is simply not much of a problem.

It could be that we're victims of a giant illusion. And I do take seriously the idea that we're getting something very wrong in our thinking about this problem. It could also be that we're limited in the bits of the world that we can understand. For example, we're pretty good at understanding the mathematical structure of the world scientifically. Although math isn't necessarily natural for a human, it turns out to be pretty tractable for us.

But trying to interface that mathematical structure with the deliverances of consciousness—maybe those are just two aspects of the brain that don't work terribly well together. Now, maybe there's some more complex, unifying story. If we had some consciousness meter in our heads and had access to all the possible intrinsic states of consciousness, and we could intuit not just what it's like to be us but what it's like to be a bat or what it's like to be a mouse, and so on, then maybe we'd be more deft about this.

But we're basically stuck, at least for now, with what we've got. We need to reason with the resources we have. But I think we need to be humble. The philosopher Colin McGinn takes humility to an extreme. He says that maybe we'll never solve the problem, just because we're too dumb, our brains didn't evolve to do philosophy, and there's a perfectly straightforward solution to the hard problem of consciousness out there somewhere, it's just that we'll never be able to grasp it.

I once teased Colin about this. I read his review of Dennett's *Consciousness Explained*. He was not a fan of the book. The review said things like "Look, this book is just ridiculous. It doesn't even look like a theory of consciousness." I said, "Colin, how would you react if you saw the true solution written by those beings who are a million times smarter than you? Maybe you'd go apoplectic in exactly the same way. So you have to at least entertain the idea that Dan is on the other side of that bright line and has the solution."

HARRIS: Nice point. Did Dan see your defense of him?

CHALMERS: I told him about it. I was on a cruise around Greenland a year or two ago with Dan and a few other people—Paul and Pat Churchland, Andy Clark, Nick Humphrey—who were dedicated to the idea that consciousness is an illusion, a view that Dan is a big fan of. So we gave that idea a run for its money for a week or so, between looking at icebergs and sailing around this amazing landscape. Although I find their position completely implausible, I think it's the kind of view the materialists and reductionists need to be developing, at least as one of the major alternatives in the theory of consciousness.

HARRIS: In an article, you took an unconventional line on the notion that we might all be brains in vats, or otherwise in the Matrix. If that were the case, then reality, not consciousness, would be in some sense an illusion. Again, I would say that consciousness is the one thing that *can't* be an illusion. Even if everything is different from what we think it is, the seeming itself is an undeniable fact. But you've argued that even if we're in the Matrix and this is all just a simulation, tables and chairs and the world and other people aren't illusions in the usual way that is often claimed. Can you say more about that?

CHALMERS: I was in a debate on this topic at the Natural History Museum in New York: "Is the Universe a Simulation?" Neil deGrasse Tyson was there, and Max Tegmark, Lisa Randall, James Gates, and Zohreh Davoudi. It was a whole lot of fun. The Matrix idea has been getting a lot of currency lately, not least due to Nick Bostrom, who's put forward a statistical line of reasoning to support it. Because a lot of simulations will be developed through ever-improving simulation technology, over time simulated beings may well outnumber nonsimulated ones, and maybe we're among them.

This is great for a philosopher, because it's reminiscent of René Descartes's thought experiment that maybe we're being fooled by an evil genius into thinking all this stuff exists. The standard line is that if we're in a simulation, like the Matrix, everything is an illusion. While he is in the Matrix, it seems to Neo that there are tables and chairs and leather coats and agents and so on. But none of that really exists. It's all a big illusion.

My view is, that's the wrong way to think about the simulation hypothesis. I take seriously the idea that we're in a simulation. I have no idea whether or not it's true, but if it is, if we *are* in a simulation, it's not that nothing is real, not that there are no tables and chairs and trees. Rather, it's that they exist in a different form from what we first thought. There's a level of computation underneath what we take to be physical reality.

This is a hypothesis some people in physics take seriously, sometimes called the "It from Bit" hypothesis—information *underneath* physics. It's not a worldview in which trees don't exist or atoms don't exist. It's a view in which they do exist and they're made of information. So if I discovered that we were living in a simulation, I'd basically say "Okay, all this is real, but it turns out we live in an informational world," a world that's more informational than physical. Max Tegmark likes this idea, because it corresponds roughly to his idea of a mathematical universe. But it reconfigures the way you think about this stuff, and it makes the simulation hypothesis seem not so threatening.

HARRIS: If the beings of the future—who are creating more simulated worlds than real ones, and therefore make it likely that we're in a simulation rather than in the base layer of reality—if they turn out to be Mormons, they may have simulated the Mormon universe. And then everything I've said about religion in general and Mormonism in particular is wrong. If you're going to follow Bostrom down this path, things can be as weird and as provincial as you want them to be.

CHALMERS: I'm a natural atheist in my thinking about gods and so on. But thinking about simulations can prompt you to take the idea of a creator a little more seriously. There could be a creator, at least of our local bit of the universe. I think of this as simulation theology—speculating about the character of who made the simulation. Maybe it's just a teenage hacker in the next universe up.

HARRIS: That brings me to my final question for you: What are your thoughts on AI?

I assume you've read Nick Bostrom's book *Superintelligence*. It's been about a year since I first became interested in the implications of AI, and Bostrom's book was the first stimulus. I'm now worried about the safety concerns—the "control problem," as he calls it. What are your thoughts on this front?

CHALMERS: I'm very interested in AI. And I think there certainly are reasons for this concern. I did my PhD in an AI lab at Indiana University. Doug Hofstadter, who wrote *Gödel, Escher, Bach*, was my thesis advisor, and he was basically doing AI—as he still is. So I've always been sympathetic toward the whole AI project. But you do have to take seriously this idea about what happens when machines become as intelligent as we are. The statistician I. J. Good argued that this might lead to a runaway explosion in intelligence.

I wrote an article on this, maybe six years ago, called "The Singularity: A Philosophical Analysis," which turned Good's idea into a philosophical argument. When machines become a little smarter than we are, they'll be a little better than we are at designing machines, and therefore they'll end up designing machines a little smarter than they are. And that process will continue recursively, until fairly soon you'll have machines that are *way* smarter than we are. Which would presumably lead to many ramifications. Certain strong conditions would have to hold for AI of this kind to not be possible. One thing worth noting is that consciousness considerations can be laid aside here, because from the point of view of self-interest, all that matters for us is the behavior of these machines, zombie or not.

HARRIS: I recently heard one computer scientist talk about this, and he took a line that was analogous to the philosopher Robert Nozick's utility-monster thought experiment. He said that in creating superintelligent, even godlike AI, we would be creating systems that are more conscious, and therefore more ethically important, than ourselves. We'll be creating gods. So we could be creating the utility monsters whose interests outweigh our own to a nearly infinite degree. And this will be the most glorious thing we'll ever accomplish. That they may trample on our interests and even annihilate us shouldn't really matter—no more than it matters that we occasionally trample on anthills.

But what this computer scientist didn't entertain is the possibility that we might build systems far more intelligent than ourselves, in the sense that they're far more competent at solving problems—including the problem of designing ever better iterations of themselves—and yet there will be nothing that it's like to be these machines. That, in some sense, is the worst-case scenario, ethically speaking. We've built something that will destroy us, simply because it wasn't aligned with our interests, it's just a blind apparatus. And the universe will go dark once it's populated by these machines.

CHALMERS: Now, that would certainly be a shame. We're creating our successors, and we think, "Well, this is the glorious future of evolution." But what if it turns out to be the step that stamps out consciousness, and suddenly the world loses all its meaning and value?

But there are two ways it could go. In one of them we're still around, and in the other one we're not. In one kind of future we design creatures utterly unlike us who take over. In another, we start with us and we enhance ourselves, and maybe we upload ourselves, and so on. In that future *we* are those superintelligent creatures—or at least the superintelligent creatures of the future are recognizably versions of us, somehow evolved from us, maybe by transferring us onto different hardware. That, I think, reduces the distance between those creatures and us. And it may increase the chances that those beings will be genuinely conscious.

That raises the question of whether consciousness gets lost when we upload ourselves onto the faster technology. I've thought a bit about this. One approach I'm attracted to is doing it gradually, one neuron replaced by one silicon chip at a time, and you stay awake throughout. If you're worried about the machine at the other end not being conscious, upload yourself slowly and observe your consciousness carefully and see what happens en route.

HARRIS: That's interesting. Do you think that solves the problem introduced by Derek Parfit in his "teletransporter" thought experiment?

The normal notion of uploading is: We have cracked the neural code, and we can now read out every human mind onto some more durable substrate—in the Matrix or in one of Amazon's servers. "Congratulations, Mr. Chalmers. Your mind has been successfully backed up. Now you don't need your meat body anymore." But, on Parfit's account, how is that different from being copied and then murdered?

What you've sketched out here is a process whereby we could gradually integrate our minds by migrating ourselves, one functional neuron at a time, into the cloud. And if at any point in that process the lights seem to dim, we could presumably stop it. It's an interesting notion, bridging what it's like to be us and what it's like to be on some other substrate, that removes the fear that we could end up as unconscious information processors, copied and then simply killed.

CHALMERS: There are two distinct worries about uploading. One is, Will the uploaded version be conscious? Will the lights be on? And the second worry is, Will it be *me*? You could, in principle, hold, "Yes, it will be conscious, but it won't be me. It'll just be a duplicate of me"—like making a twin of me in the next room.

One of these corresponds to the philosophical problem of consciousness; the other one corresponds to the philosophical problem of personal identity, as Parfit talked about in his teletransporter problem. But the idea of doing it gradually bears on both these worries. If you create a duplicate of me, it's tempting to think it's someone, but it's not me. But if it's my brain throughout, and the old neurons get destroyed and replaced by silicon chips, and I stay conscious throughout, so it's a continuing stream of consciousness, then it's harder to think that this new being won't be me.

I suppose you could take the line that maybe the consciousness would gradually dwindle during this process and we'd be left with functional duplicates at the other end, responding normally but without any consciousness and without being me.

If the engineering works well enough, if the simulations are good enough, we know what the simulations will say at the other end. If they're good simulations of how we are now, they'll say, "Well, I'm still conscious. I'm still here," because that's what I say now. So I suppose if you're worried that this process will produce zombies, you'll still have that worry. But I predict that having a few people go through this process will be persuasive to the rest of us.

HARRIS: But if we do it in a "safe" way—where we maintain our physical bodies in case the process goes wrong—well, then we've fallen into Parfit's trap. Transferring a person's information into another medium seems like one thing—transferring his mind; copying him, and then destroying the original seems like a murder.

If we do it the way you're describing, gradually, and perhaps even allowing a person to reverse the process if he doesn't like what's happening—and, once the migration is complete, once all of him is on the server, no original has been left behind—then there's a compelling case that the mind on the server is really him. But if we don't do that, and the original remains, outside the Matrix, and we simply tell this befuddled person that copy arrived safe and sound, how sanguine should he be about his imminent death? Whether or not the copy is conscious, it's still going to be a different person.

CHALMERS: Maybe we'll do it first in worms and mice and so on. Maybe the first human to do it would be a volunteer. The first human case, I predict, will be a backup. You scan the brain, you keep the original brain around, and you make a simulated copy, and then you activate the simulation.

And if it's a good enough simulation, I suspect we'll get two simultaneous reactions. One: Yes, that is a person; he's talking, there's probably some kind of consciousness there. Two: But he's not the *same* being as the original, because presumably he and the original will be able to have a conversation. So they are like twins. If that's the way this technology is introduced, we may end up deciding that the copies are conscious but distinct from their originals.

There's an interesting sociological question too. What could happen is that a few of us start upgrading bits of our brain with silicon components and say, "Hey, this seems fine. I'm still here." Then you keep on going, and you'll eventually get to fully silicon systems, and you'll still maintain that you're still here. Then the philosophical and sociological question will be, Can you justify drawing a distinction between what happens in the case of a straight-out copy and what happens in the case of a gradual copy? We would have two classes of silicon beings in our society: the ones that are just copies, which could have a much more negligible legal and ethical status, and the ones that correspond to versions of the original, which have a higher status.

HARRIS: If merely backing up your mind creates a conscious copy of yourself, do you have the right to delete that copy? Are you committing murder if you do? It seems you would be, if this being is just as conscious as you are and has all your memories and aspirations.

CHALMERS: Maybe our intuitions are a bit different depending on whether the copy has been activated. If it's just a record on a disk and has never yet produced any consciousness and it's just waiting to be activated, maybe we can delete it. The moment it's conscious and has started going in its own direction and had a moment of input and has thought its own thoughts—at that point, yes, if you deactivate it, well, that's killing a conscious being. They have to be admitted into a moral circle of concern.

HARRIS: Let's talk about the idea that we would merely augment our minds or repair damaged parts of our brains. Many people have suggested that this might be a solution to the control problem—we'd essentially become the limbic systems of these new minds.

CHALMERS: And our own values will be playing a role, at least in directing the values of these machines.

HARRIS: Yes. The prospect of doing this seems more or less synonymous with having reached something like a complete scientific understanding of the brain. We've cracked the code to the point where we can seamlessly augment ourselves, give ourselves more mind, and then explore the landscape of mind with these bigger brains. But it seems likely to be easier to build superintelligent AI than to build superintelligent AI and make these breakthroughs in neuroscience. And it will be very tempting to take the shortest possible path. There is an immense amount of wealth—really, winner-take-all wealth—awaiting anyone who can build such a system. So we seem likely to get superintelligent AIs first, before we can plug our brains into them and organically anchor their behavior, if such a thing is truly possible.

CHALMERS: I've heard all kinds of arguments about which will come first. The AI project will be much less constrained by the limits of science and engineering technology; on the other hand, the brain provides a working system we've got right now. If these brain-activity mapping projects continue developing, in a couple of decades we'll have a working map of the brain, all the connections between neurons, and maybe even an understanding of the workings of individual neurons. At some point we'll be able to record all that onto a computer and simulate it.

Of course, there could be intermediate points, which is actually where we are right now. The worm *C. elegans* has 302 neurons, and we've mapped all the connections between them. But we still can't get a simulation to work, because we don't understand the principles of how all the components work. But in, say, thirty years' time, we may understand both the mechanisms and the connections well enough to scan a brain and activate it—well before we can design a new AI from scratch.

Whichever one comes first is going to make a big difference to what happens after that. I find myself hoping that the brain-based version comes first, because that looks like a future more friendly to human beings, and I'm holding on to a little sliver of hope that I may still be here when it arrives—and then upload myself.

HARRIS: I'll buy the original David a scotch, when the time comes.

Finding Our Way

A CONVERSATION WITH DAVID DEUTSCH

David Deutsch has a talent for expressing scientifically and philosophically revolutionary ideas in deceptively simple language. He is a visiting professor of physics at the Center for Quantum Computation at the Clarendon Laboratory of Oxford University, where he works on the quantum theory of computation, and constructor theory.

This chapter features two of our conversations. In the first, we focus on the surprising power and reach of human knowledge, the future of artificial intelligence, and the survival of civilization.

After our first conversation, Deutsch read my book *The Moral Landscape* and wanted to discuss it. He intended to do this privately—probably because he disagreed with much of it and didn't want to break the news to me on my own podcast. But I urged him to let me record our conversation, because if he was going to dismantle my cherished thesis, I wanted it done in public. Given all that was covered in our first meeting, we hit the ground running.

In this second conversation, we further explore the nature of knowledge and the implications of its being independent of any specific, physical embodiment. This is one of the things that make David's views on more ordinary topics so interesting. As a physicist, his understanding of something as mundane as why it's wrong to coerce people to do things they don't want to do connects directly to his view of how knowledge ultimately accumulates in the cosmos. His ideas are fairly startling—and unlike most scientific thinking about our place in nature, they put us somewhere near the center of the drama.

HARRIS: David, I want to creep up on your central thesis. Certain claims you make—specifically, about the reach and power of human knowledge—are fairly breathtaking. And I want to agree with them in the end, because they're so hopeful. But I have a few quibbles.

DEUTSCH: Sure. But I should say first that while I think the outlook is positive, the future is unpredictable. Nothing is guaranteed. There's no guarantee that civilization or our species will survive, but there *is* a guarantee that we know in principle how both can survive.

HARRIS: Before we get into your theory, let's start somewhere near epistemological bedrock. I'd like to get to a definition of terms, because in *The Beginning of Infinity* you use words like "knowledge" and "explanation" and even "person" in novel ways, and I want to make clear just how much work you're requiring those words to do. Let's begin with the concept of knowledge. What is it, in your view?

DEUTSCH: The way I think of knowledge is broader than the usual use of the term—and yet, paradoxically, closer to its commonsense use. Knowledge is a kind of information, which is to say that it's something that is one particular way and could have been otherwise; additionally, knowledge says something true and useful about the world.

Knowledge is in a sense an abstraction, because it's independent of its physical instantiation. I can speak words which embody some knowledge. I can write them down. They can exist as movements of electrons in a computer, and so on. So knowledge isn't dependent on any particular instantiation. But it does have the property that when it *is* instantiated, it tends to remain so. Let's say a scientist writes down a speculation that turns out to be a genuine piece of knowledge. That's the only version he doesn't throw in the wastebasket. That's the version that will be published, that will be studied by other scientists, and so on.

So knowledge is a piece of information that has the property of tending to stay physically instantiated. Once you think of knowledge that way, you realize that, for example, the pattern of base pairs in a gene's DNA also constitutes knowledge, in line with Karl Popper's concept of knowledge as not requiring a knowing subject. It can exist in books, or in the mind, and people can have knowledge they don't know they have.

HARRIS: A few more definitions: in your view, what's the boundary between science and philosophy, or between science and other expressions of rationality? In my experience, people are profoundly confused about this, including many scientists. I've argued for years about the unity of knowledge, and I feel you're a kindred spirit here. How do you differentiate—or do you differentiate—science and philosophy?

DEUTSCH: Well, they're both manifestations of reason. But among the rational approaches to knowledge, there's an important difference between science and things like philosophy and mathematics. Not at the most fundamental level, but at a level which is often of great practical importance. That is, science is the kind of knowledge that can be tested by experiment or observation. I hasten to add, that doesn't mean that the content of a scientific theory consists entirely of its testable predictions; the testable predictions of a typical scientific theory are a tiny sliver of what it tells us about the world. Karl Popper introduced this criterion, that science is testable theories and everything else is untestable. Ever since, people have falsely interpreted him as saying that only scientific theories can have meaning. That would be a kind of positivism, but he was really the opposite of a positivist. His own theories aren't scientific, they're philosophical, and yet he doesn't consider them meaningless. In the bigger picture, the more important distinction that should be uppermost in our minds is the one between reason and unreason.

HARRIS: The widespread notion is that science reduces to what is testable, and that any claim you can't measure is somehow vacuous. So, too, is the belief that there exists a bright line between science and every other discipline where we purport to describe reality. It's as if the architecture of a university had defined people's thinking: you go to the chemistry department to talk about chemistry, you go to the journalism department to talk about current events, you go to the history department to talk about human events in the past. This has balkanized the thinking of even very smart people and convinced them that all these language games are irreconcilable and that there's no common project.

Take something like the assassination of Mahatma Gandhi. That was a historical event. However, anyone who purports to doubt that it occurred—anyone who says, "Actually, Gandhi was not assassinated. He went on to live a long and happy life in the Punjab under an assumed name"—would be making a claim that is at odds with the data. It's at odds with the testimony of people who saw Gandhi assassinated and with the photographs we have of him lying in state. The task is to reconcile the claim that he was not assassinated with the facts we know to be true.

That task doesn't depend on what someone in a white lab coat has said, or facts that have been discovered in a laboratory funded by the National Science Foundation. It's the distinction between having good reasons for what you believe and having bad ones—and that's a distinction between reason and unreason, as you put it. While one sounds more like a journalist or a historian when talking about the assassination of Gandhi, it would be deeply unscientific to doubt that it occurred.

DEUTSCH: I wouldn't put it in terms of reasons for belief. But I agree with you that people have wrong ideas about what science is and what the boundaries of scientific thinking are, and what sort of thinking should be taken seriously and what shouldn't. I think it's slightly unfair to put the blame on universities here. This misconception arose originally for good reasons. It's rooted in the empiricism of the eighteenth century, when science had to rebel against the authority of tradition and to defend new forms of knowledge that involved observation and experimental tests.

Empiricism is the idea that knowledge comes to us through the senses. Now, that's completely false: all knowledge is conjectural. It first comes from within and is intended to solve problems, not to summarize data. But this idea that experience has authority, and that only experience has authority—false though it is—was a wonderful defense against previous forms of authority, which were not only invalid but stultifying. But in the twentieth century, a horrible thing happened, which is that people started taking empiricism seriously—not just as a defense, but as being literally true—and that almost killed certain sciences. Even within physics; it greatly impeded progress in quantum theory.

So to make a little quibble of my own, I think the essence of what we want in science are not justified beliefs but good explanations. You can conduct science without ever believing in a theory, just as a good policeman or judge can implement the law without believing either the case for the prosecution or the case for the defense—because they know that a particular system of law is better than any individual human's opinion.

The same is true of science. Science is a way of dealing with theories regardless of whether or not one believes them. One judges them according to whether or not they're good explanations. And if a particular explanation ends up being the only explanation that survives the intense criticism that reason and science can apply, whether or not that includes experimental testing, then it's not so much adopted at that point as just not discarded. It has survived for the moment.

HARRIS: I understand that you're pushing back against the notion that we need to find some ultimate foundation for our knowledge, encouraging instead this open-ended search for better explanations. But let's table that for a moment. Let's address the notion of scientific authority. It's often said that, in science, we don't rely on authority. But that's both true and not true. We do rely on it in practice, if only in the interest of efficiency. If I ask you a question about physics, I'll tend to believe your answer, because you're a physicist and I'm not. And if what you say contradicts something I've heard from another physicist, then, if it matters to me, I'll look into it more deeply and try to figure out the nature of the dispute.

But if there are any points on which all physicists agree, a nonphysicist like me will defer to the authority of that consensus. Again, this is less a statement of epistemology than it is a statement about the specialization of knowledge and the unequal distribution of human talent—and, frankly, the shortness of every human life. We simply don't have time to check everyone's work, and sometimes we have to rely on faith that the system of scientific conversation is correcting for errors, self-deception, and fraud.

DEUTSCH: Yes, exactly. You could call that consensus "authority." But every student who wants to make a contribution to a science is hoping to find something about which every scientist in the field is wrong. So it's not irrational to claim one is right and every expert in the field is wrong. When we consult experts, it's not quite because we think they're more competent. You referred to error correction, and that hits the nail on the head. If I consult a doctor about what my treatment should be, I assume that the process leading to his recommendation is the same one I would have adopted if I'd had the time and the background and the interest to go to medical school. Now, it might not be exactly the same, and I might also take the view that there are widespread errors and irrationalities in the medical profession. And if I do think that in regard to a particular case, I'll adopt a different attitude. I may choose much more carefully which doctor I consult. When I fly, I expect that the airplane's maintenance will have been carried out according to the standards I would use. Well, approximately to the standards I would use—enough for me to consider the risk of boarding that airplane on the same level as other risks I take, say, just by crossing the road. It's not that I take someone's word that they've got the information right. It's that I have this positive, explanatory theory of what has happened to get that information. And that theory is fragile. I can easily adopt a variant of it.

HARRIS: Yes, and it's also probabilistic. You realize that a lot of errors and irrationalities are being washed out, and that's good, but in any one case you may judge the probability of error to be high enough that you need to pay attention to it.

I still feel that we are circling your thesis and not quite landing on it. Science is largely a story of our fighting our way past anthropocentrism, the notion that we're at the center of things.

DEUTSCH: It has been, yes.

HARRIS: We were not specially created: we share half our genes with a banana, and more with a banana slug. As you described in *The Beginning of Infinity*, this is known as the principle of mediocrity. And you summarize it with a quote from Stephen Hawking, who said we're just chemical scum on the surface of a typical planet in orbit around a typical star on the outskirts of a typical galaxy. You take issue with this claim in a variety of ways, but the result is that you come full circle, in a sense. You fight your way past anthropocentrism, just as every scientist does, but you arrive at a place where people—or, rather, *persons*—suddenly become hugely significant, even cosmically so. Say a little more about that.

DEUTSCH: Yes. What Hawking said is literally true, but the philosophical implication he drew is false. First of all, this chemical scum—namely, us, and possibly anything like us on other planets and in other galaxies—is impossible to study in the way we study every other scum in the universe. Because this scum is creating new knowledge, and the growth of knowledge is profoundly unpredictable. So to understand this scum— never mind predict, but to understand it—entails understanding everything in the universe.

I give an example in *The Beginning of Infinity*: If the people engaged in the search for extraterrestrial intelligence were to discover it somewhere in the galaxy, they'd open a bottle of champagne and celebrate. Now, if you try to explain scientifically what the conditions are under which that cork will come out of that bottle, all the usual scientific criteria—of pressure and temperature and biological degradation of the cork and so on—will be irrelevant. The most important factor in the physical behavior of that cork is whether life exists on another planet! And in the same way, anything in the universe can affect the gross behavior of things that are affected by people. So, in short, to understand humans, you have to understand everything. And humans, or persons in general, are the only things in the universe of which that is true. So they are of universal significance in that sense. Then there's the other way around. It's also true that the reach of human knowledge and human intentions on the physical world is unlimited.

So we're used to having a relatively tiny effect on this small, insignificant planet, and we're used to the rest of the universe being beyond our ken. But that's a parochial misconception, because we haven't set out across the universe yet. We know that there are no limits to how much we can affect the universe if we choose to. So in both those senses, there's no limit to how important we are—and the same is true of the extraterrestrials and the artificial intelligences, if they exist. We're central to any understanding of the universe.

HARRIS: Again, I'm struggling to get all the pieces of your account in play, before plunging forward. Let's discuss the concept of *explanation* and the work it does.

In your book, you make a few points about explanation that I find uncontroversial and even obvious, but which are in fact highly controversial in educated circles. One is this notion that explanation is the bedrock of the scientific enterprise—of the enterprise of reason generally. Explanations in one field of knowledge potentially touch explanations in many other fields, even all other fields, and this suggests a kind of unity of knowledge. But you make two especially bold claims about explanation that I do see some reason to doubt. And I'd rather not doubt them, because they're such hopeful claims.

I'll divide these into the *power* of explanation and the *reach* of explanation. These may not be entirely separate in your mind, but you place a distinct emphasis on each.

You make an extraordinary claim about explanation that at first seems pedestrian. You say there's a deep connection between explaining the world and controlling it. Everyone understands this to some degree. We see evidence of it all around us. This echoes a well-worn phrase—attributed to Francis Bacon, I believe—that "knowledge is power." But you go on to suggest—as you did in passing a moment ago—that knowledge confers limitless power, or it's limited only by the laws of nature. You're saying that anything not precluded by the laws of nature is achievable, given the right knowledge. Because if something were *not* achievable, given complete knowledge, that itself would be a regularity in nature that could be only explained in terms of natural law. So there are really only two possibilities: Either something is precluded by the laws of nature, or it is achievable with knowledge. Have I read you correctly?

DEUTSCH: Yes. It's what I call the "momentous dichotomy." There can't be any third possibility. And you've given a very short proof of it right there.

HARRIS: To play devil's advocate for a moment: How isn't this just a clever tautology, analogous to the ontological argument proving the existence of God? According to St. Anselm, Descartes, and many others, you can prove the existence of God simply by forcing your thinking about Him to essentially bite its own tail. For instance, I could make the following claim: I can form a clear and distinct concept of the most perfect possible being, and such a being must therefore exist, because a being that exists is more perfect than one that doesn't. I've asserted I'm thinking about the most perfect possible being, and then declared existence is somehow a predicate of perfection.

Of course, most sane and educated people will recognize this to be a trick of language. And it could be used to prove the existence of anything. I could say, "I'm thinking of the most perfect chocolate mousse. Therefore, it must exist, because a mousse that exists is more perfect than one that doesn't. And I already told you that I'm thinking of the most perfect chocolate mousse."

What you're saying here doesn't have the same structure, but one could worry that you might be performing a similar trick. Why mightn't certain transformations of the material world be unachievable even in the presence of complete knowledge, merely by—and I realize you do anticipate this in *The Beginning of Infinity*, but I want you to flesh it out here—say, a contingency of geography?

For instance, you and I are on an island and one of our friends falls ill with appendicitis. Let's say you and I are both competent surgeons. We know everything there is to know about removing an appendix, but it just so happens we don't have any of the necessary tools, and everything on that particular island has the consistency of soft cheese. By sheer accident of our personal histories, there is a gap between what's knowable, and in fact known, and what's achievable. Even though there are no laws of nature that preclude our performing an appendectomy, why mightn't every space we occupy, just by contingent fact of our history, not introduce some gap of that kind?

DEUTSCH: Well, there definitely are gaps of that kind, but they're all laws of nature. For example, I'm an advocate of the many-universes interpretation of quantum theory, which says that there are other universes which the laws of physics prevent us from getting to. There's also the finiteness of the speed of light. It doesn't prevent us from getting anywhere but it does prevent us from getting there in a given time. So if we want to get to the nearest star within a year, we can't, because of the accident of where we happen to be.

And in your example, if there's no metal on the island, then it could be that no possible knowledge applied on that island could save the person, because no knowledge could transform the resources on that island into the relevant medical instruments in time. So that's a restriction that the laws of physics apply because we're in particular times and places.

But that's completely different from what you're imagining, which is that there might be some reason why, for example, we can never get out of the solar system. If getting out of the solar system were impossible, it would mean that there is some number—for example, some constant of nature—that limits the application of the other known laws of nature. Now, there surely are laws of nature that we don't know. But when you say, "How do we know there isn't one that forbids this?" that's a bit like creationists saying, "How do we know that Earth didn't start six thousand years ago?"

There's no conceivable evidence that could prove that it didn't, or that could distinguish the six-thousand-year theory from a seven-thousand-year theory, and so on. Both explanations are easily variable into each other or into countless other explanations. There's no way that evidence or rational argument can be brought to bear to distinguish one from another. And that easy variability is a characteristic of bad explanations that should, rationally, be rejected out of hand. As you said, the ontological argument for the existence of God is a perversion of logic: it purports to use logic but then smuggles in assumptions like perfection entails existence—to name a simple one. With perversions of logic you can seem to "prove" anything. So it's a bad explanation too. Whereas my argument is highly explanatory. It isn't just "this must exist." It's "if this didn't exist, something, unacceptable for independent reasons, would happen." For example, the universe would be controlled by the super-natural, or something of that kind. So my argument works because it's explanatory. You can't prove that it's true, of course, but it's the opposite of the ontological argument.

HARRIS: You're saying that there are the laws of nature, and there's the fact that knowledge can do anything compatible with those laws—which leads to amazingly strong claims about the utility of knowledge. At one point you ask the reader to imagine a cube of intergalactic space the size of our solar system that has nothing but stray hydrogen atoms in it. And you then describe a process by which that near-vacuum could be primed and become the basis of the most advanced civilization we can imagine.

Take us to deep space and explain how we can get from virtually nothing to something profoundly complex. It's a picture of the almost limitless fungibility of the cosmos, based on the power of knowledge.

DEUTSCH: Yes. Well, you and I are made of atoms, and that already gives us a tremendous fungibility in that sense, because atoms are universal. The properties of atoms are the same in a cube of space millions of light-years away as they are here. So we aren't talking about tasks like saving someone's life with just the resources on an island or getting to a distant planet in a certain time. What we're talking about is converting some matter into some other matter. What do you need to do that? Well, generically speaking, what you need is knowledge. The cube of almost empty space will never contain anything other than boring hydrogen atoms and photons *unless* some knowledge somehow gets there. Now, whether it does get there depends on decisions that people with knowledge will make. There's no doubt that knowledge could get there if people with that knowledge decided to make that happen. It's not a matter of futuristic speculation to know that it would be possible. It's only a matter of transforming atoms in one configuration into atoms in another configuration. And we're getting used to the idea that this is an everyday thing. We have 3-D printers that can convert generic stuff into any object, provided the knowledge of what shape that object should be is somehow encoded into the 3-D printer. A 3-D printer with the resolution of one atom would be able to print a human if it was given the right program.

HARRIS: So you start with hydrogen atoms, and you have to make heavier elements in order to get to your printer.

DEUTSCH: Yes. The cube has to be primed not just with abstract knowledge but with knowledge instantiated in something. We don't know what the smallest possible universal constructor is (that's just a generalization of a 3-D printer): it can be programmed to make the machine that would make the machine that would make the machine . . . to make anything. One of those with the right program, sent to empty space, would first gather the hydrogen, presumably with some electromagnetic broom, and then convert it, by transmutation, into other elements and then by chemistry into what we would today think of as raw materials. And then would use space construction—which we're on the verge of doing—to build a space station. And then the space station could instantiate people to generate the knowledge to suck in more hydrogen and make a colony, and so on.

HARRIS: It's a fascinating way of thinking about knowledge and its place in the universe. Before I get to the issue of the *reach* of explanation, and my quibble there, I want you to talk about this notion of spaceship Earth. I love how you debunk this idea that Earth's biosphere is wonderfully hospitable for us, and that if we built a colony on Mars, or some other place in the solar system, we'd be in fundamentally different circumstances than we are now. You say in *The Beginning of Infinity* that the Earth no more provides us with a life-support system than it supplies us with radio telescopes.

DEUTSCH: Yes. We evolved somewhere in East Africa's Great Rift Valley. Life there was sheer hell for humans. "Nasty, brutish, and short" doesn't begin to describe how horrible it was. But we transformed it—or, rather, initially some of our predecessor species did by inventing things like clothes, fire, and weapons, and thereby made their lives much better, although still horrible by present-day standards. Then they moved into environments such as Oxford, where I work. It's December. If I went outside now with no technology, I would die in a matter of hours, and nothing I could do would prevent it.

HARRIS: So you are already an astronaut. Your condition is as precarious as that of the people in a well-established colony on Mars who can take certain technological advances for granted. And there's no reason to think that such a future beyond Earth doesn't await us, barring some catastrophe, whether of our own making or not.

DEUTSCH: Yes, very much so. And there's another misconception related to the notion of the Earth being hospitable, namely that applying knowledge takes effort. *Creating* knowledge takes effort. But applying knowledge is automatic. As soon as somebody invented the idea of, for example, wearing clothes, from then on those clothes automatically warmed them. It didn't require any further effort. Of course there would have been plenty of things wrong with those original clothes, but then people invented ways of making better clothes.

And now we've invented things like mass production, unmanned factories, and so on. We take for granted that water gets to us from the water supply, without anyone having to carry it on their heads in pots. It doesn't require effort, it just requires the knowledge of how to install the automatic system, with ever less attention or labor by humans being needed. Much of our life support is automatic, and every time we invent a better method of life support, it becomes more automatic. So, for the people in a lunar colony, keeping the vacuum out won't be something they think about. They'll take it for granted. What they'll be thinking about are new technological improvements. And the same will hold on Mars and in deep space.

HARRIS: Again, I'm struck by what an incredibly hopeful vision this is of our possible future. Thus far, we've covered territory where I don't have any significant doubts, despite feigning one with the ontological argument. So let's talk about the reach of explanation, because you seem to believe that it's unbounded—that anything that can be explained, either in practice or in principle, can be explained by human beings as we currently are.

You seem to be saying that we, alone among all the Earth's species, have achieved a kind of cognitive escape velocity, and we're capable of understanding everything. And you contrast this view with what you call parochialism, which is a view I've often expressed, as have many other scientists. Max Tegmark and I argued for this thesis on a previous podcast. Evolution hasn't designed us to fully understand the nature of reality. The very small, the very large, the very fast, the very old—these are not domains to which our intuitions about what's real or logically consistent have been tuned by natural selection. Insofar as we've made progress on these fronts, it has been by happy accident, and consequently there is no reason to believe that we can travel as far as we might wish—across the horizon of all that is knowable. Which is to say that if a superintelligent alien came to Earth for the purpose of explaining to us everything that's knowable, he or she or it might make no more headway than you would if you were attempting to teach the principles of quantum computation to a chicken.

Why is that analogy false? Tell me why parochialism—this notion that we occupy a niche that might leave us cognitively closed to certain knowable truths and that there's no good evolutionary reason to expect we can fully escape it—doesn't hold true.

DEUTSCH: Well, you've made two or three different arguments there, all of which are wrong. Let me start with the chicken thing. There, the point is the universality of computation. The thing about explanations is, they are a form of information, and information can only be processed in basically one way—with computation of the kind invented by Babbage and Turing. We already know that our computers are universal, in the sense that given the right program, they can perform any transformation of information whatsoever, including the creation of explanations and other knowledge. Now, there are only two possible limitations to that. One is the lack of computer memory—lack of information-storage capacity—and the other is the lack of speed, or the lack of time. Apart from that, our computers, and our brains, and any computers that will ever be built or can ever be built anywhere in the universe, have the same repertoire. That's the principle of the universality of computation. That means that the reason I can't teach quantum mechanics to a chicken must be either that its neurons are too slow—which I don't think is true; they don't differ that much from our own—or it doesn't have enough memory, which it certainly doesn't, or it doesn't have the right knowledge already. It doesn't know how to learn language and how to learn what an explanation is, and so on.

HARRIS: It's not the right sort of chicken.

DEUTSCH: If you had said "chimpanzee," my guess would be that the brain of a chimpanzee *could* contain the knowledge of, say, how to learn language, but that there's no way of imparting that knowledge short of some sort of nanosurgery, which would presumably be immoral to perform. But in principle it could be done, because a chimpanzee's brain isn't that much smaller than ours, and it would have a whole lifetime to fill its memory. Then I could teach it quantum theory—if it was interested.

Now, what if that superintelligent alien had a lot more memory than us? What if it had a lot more computational speed than us? Well, we already know the answer to that. We've been improving our memory capacity and our speed of computation for thousands of years with the invention of things like writing, writing implements, even language itself, which enables more than one person to work on the same problem and coordinate their understanding of it. Nowadays, we use computers, and in the future we can use computer implants and so on. So if the knowledge that this alien wanted to impart involved more than a hundred gigabytes, or whatever the capacity of our brain is—then we could in principle enhance our brains sufficiently to grasp the knowledge being imparted. There's no fundamental reason why we can't understand whatever the alien tells us.

HARRIS: And this all devolves from the concept of the universality of computation—that there's no alternate version of information processing. What's interesting about that is that it's a claim that we've just barely crossed the finish line into infinity.

Let's not talk about chickens anymore and make a comparison that's even more invidious. Imagine that every person with an IQ over a hundred had been killed off by a plague in the year 1850, and all their descendants had IQs of a hundred or less. I think it's uncontroversial to say that we wouldn't have the internet. In fact, it's probably uncontroversial to say that we wouldn't have the concept of computation, much less the possibility of building computers to instantiate it.

So this insight into the universality of computation would remain undiscovered, and humanity, for all intents and purposes, would be cognitively closed to the whole domain of facts and technological advances we now take for granted and which you say open us onto an infinite horizon of what is knowable.

DEUTSCH: I think that's wrong. Your very premise about IQ is incompatible with the argument I just made.

HARRIS: But there has to be some lower bound past which we would be cognitively closed in practice, even if computation is itself universal in principle.

DEUTSCH: Yes, but you have to distinguish between hardware and software when you're thinking about how this cognitive closure manifests itself. Like I said, it seems plausible that the hardware limitation is not relevant even for chimpanzees. I imagine that with nanosurgery, one could implant ideas into a chimpanzee's brain that would make it able to create further knowledge just as humans can. I'm questioning the assumption that if everybody with an IQ of over a hundred died, then in the next generation nobody would have an IQ of over a hundred. I think they well might. It depends on culture.

HARRIS: Of course. This wasn't meant to be a plausible biological or cultural assumption. I'm just asking you to imagine a world in which we had seven billion human beings, none of whom could begin to understand what Alan Turing was up to.

DEUTSCH: *That* nightmare scenario is different. It's something that actually happened—for almost the whole of human existence. Humans had the ability to be creative and to do everything we're doing. They just didn't, because their culture was wrong. It wasn't their fault. Cultural evolution has a nasty tendency to suppress the growth of what we would consider science or anything important that would improve their lives. So yes, that's possible, and it's possible that it could happen again. Nothing can prevent it except our working to prevent it.

HARRIS: This brings us to the topic of AI, which I only recently became interested in, after I became aware of the fears about artificial general intelligence raised by people like Stephen Hawking, Elon Musk, Stuart Russell, Max Tegmark, and Nick Bostrom. I've landed on the side of those who think there's something worth worrying about here, in terms of our building intelligent machines that undergo an intelligence explosion and get away from us.

I worry that we'll build something that can make recursive self-improvements, and it will become a form of intelligence that stands in relation to us the way we stand in relation to chimps or chickens or anything else that can't effectively link up with our cognitive horizons. I take it, based on what I've heard you say, that you don't share this concern. And I imagine that your insouciance is based to some degree on what we've just been talking about—that there's only computation, and it's universal, and we can bridge any distance between minds as a result. What are your thoughts about building superintelligent machines, in light of what we've been discussing?

DEUTSCH: The fear of superintelligent machines entails the same mistake as thinking that IQ is a matter of hardware. IQ is just knowledge of a certain type. And we shouldn't be talking about IQ. We should instead be talking about creativity, which is also a species of knowledge. The picture that people paint of the AI technology you're referring to (sometimes called AGI or artificial *general* intelligence, to distinguish it from things like search engines that we already have today) is that it will be a machine—hardware— that will design better hardware, which will design even better hardware, and so on. But that's not what such an AI is. It will be a program, and programs that have creativity will be able to design better programs. Now, these better programs will not be qualitatively different from us. Because of computational universality, they could differ from us only in the quality of their knowledge and in their speed and memory capacity. But we can also share that speed and memory capacity, because the technology that would make better computer hardware will also, in the long run, be able to make better implants for our brains.

So whatever succeeds in making AIs of that kind will also make better people. By the same token, those AIs aren't fundamentally different from people. They *are* people, and so they would have culture. Whether they can improve or not will depend on their culture, which initially will be our culture. So the problem of AIs is the problem of humans. Now, humans are dangerous, and there's a real problem of how to manage the world in the face of growing knowledge—to make sure that knowledge isn't misused. Because in some cases it need only be misused once to end the whole project of humanity.

Humans are dangerous, and to that extent AIs are also dangerous. But the idea that AIs are somehow more dangerous than humans is literally racist: it is judging people by their external appearance instead of their ideas, the content of their character. There's no basis for it at all. And on a smaller scale, the worry that AIs are somehow going to get away from us is the same worry that people have about wayward teenagers. Wayward teenagers are also AIs with ideas that are different from ours. And the impulse of human beings throughout the centuries has been to control their waywardness. That impulse is the very thing that caused stasis for most of human history. Just as it is now the ambition of AI people to invent ways of shackling the AIs so they can't get away from us and form different ideas. That's the mistake that will both delay the growth of knowledge and ensure that if AIs are invented and are shackled in this way, there will be a slave revolt. And quite rightly.

HARRIS: I can only aspire to say, "You've just made three arguments there, and all of them are wrong." However, there are two claims you just made which do worry me.

First, consider the processing speed of our brains compared with that of our new artificial teenagers. If we have teenagers who think a million times faster than we do, even at the same level of intelligence, then every time we let them scheme for a week, they'll have actually schemed for twenty thousand years of parent time. Who knows what teenagers could get up to given a twenty-thousand-year head start? The problem I see is that their interests, their goals, and their subsequent behavior could diverge from ours very quickly—just by virtue of this difference in clock speed.

DEUTSCH: Difference in speed has to be judged relative to the available hardware. Let's be generous for a moment and assume that these teenagers doing twenty thousand years of thinking in a week begin well disposed toward us and sharing our values. And I'd readily accept that ensuring that young people share the values that will allow civilization to continue is a problem. But before the artificial teenagers do their twenty thousand years of thinking, they'll have done ten thousand years and before that five thousand years. There will be a moment when they'll have done one year and, because they are well disposed toward us and share our values, they'd like to take us along with them.

You're assuming that there'll be some reason they'd like to diverge. The implied reason could only be hardware, because if they're only a year away from us, we can assimilate their *ideas*, if those ideas are better than ours, and persuade them to abandon those ideas if they're not better than ours.

HARRIS: But we're talking about something that would happen over the course of minutes or hours, not years.

DEUTSCH: Well, before the technology exists to make it happen over the course of minutes, there will be the technology to make it happen over the course of years. And that technology will simply be brain add-on technology. Which we can use, too.

HARRIS: Well, that leads to my second concern. What if the problem of building a superhuman AI is more tractable than the problem of cracking the neural code and designing the implants that would enable us to essentially become the limbic systems for any superintelligent AI that might emerge? What if we needed a superintelligent AI to tell us how to link up with it? We may build an independent superintelligent AI first, harboring goals however imperceptibly divergent from our own, which we discover to be divergent only after it's an angry little god in a box that we can no longer control.

Are you saying that that scenario is impossible *in principle*, or just unlikely given certain assumptions—one being that we'll figure out how to link up with the superintelligent AI before it becomes too powerful?

DEUTSCH: I think it's a bit implausible, in terms of the parameters you're positing about what can happen, at what speed, relative to what other things can happen. But let's suppose, for the sake of argument, that the parameters just happen to be, by bad luck, as you said. What you're essentially talking about is the difference in values between ourselves and our descendants in twenty thousand years' time if we hadn't invented AI, and instead just had the normal evolution of human culture. Presumably people's values in twenty thousand years will be alien to us. We might think they're horrible, just as people twenty thousand years ago might think various aspects of our society are horrible when in fact they aren't.

HARRIS: Not quite. What I'm imagining would be worse, for two reasons. One is that we'd be in the presence of this thing that would not only be twenty thousand years ahead of us, it would be vastly more powerful than us. So this would be no mere difference of opinion with respect to values. Thus, given any difference of opinion, we could find our own survival incompatible with its aims. Let's say it decides to turn the world into paper clips—to use Bostrom's cartoonish analogy. Granted, we wouldn't be so stupid as to build a paper-clip maximizer, but let's say that the AI we build discovers a use for the atoms in your body which it deems better than their current use. And let's say this is something that happens very quickly, not in some distant future.

And there's another element here that seems ethically relevant. We can't be sure that any superintelligent AI would be conscious. It's plausible that consciousness will come along for the ride if we build something as intelligent as a human being. But given that we don't understand what consciousness is, it's at least conceivable that we could build an intelligent system—even a superintelligent one, that can make changes to itself—and yet it won't be conscious. The lights won't be on, yet this thing will be godlike in its capabilities.

Ethically, that seems to be the worst-case scenario. Because if we built a conscious AI whose capacity for happiness and creativity greatly exceeded our own, the question of whether or not we link up to it would be less pressing ethically, because the creature would be, when considered dispassionately, more important than we are. However, it's conceivable that we could build an intelligent system that exceeds us in every way—and, in particular, is better able to survive—but there will be nothing that it's *like* to be that system, just as there's presumably nothing that it's like to be the best chess-playing computer on Earth today.

I find that a truly horrible scenario, with no silver lining. It's not that we'll have given birth to a generation of godlike teenagers who, if they viewed the world differently from us, well, cosmic history will judge their worldview to be superior to ours. No, we could build something that does everything intelligence does in our case and more, and yet the lights won't be on.

DEUTSCH: First of all, I agree that it's somewhat implausible that creativity can be improved to our level and beyond without consciousness also being there. But suppose it can. Then, although consciousness isn't there, morality is there—that is, an entity that's creative has to have a morality, in the sense that it would have to decide what it wanted, decide what to do—make paper clips, say. This brings us back to what you call "bedrock," because morality is a form of knowledge and what the paper-clip argument supposes is that something is judged right or wrong according to hierarchy of ideas, until we eventually get to bedrock where there isn't a deeper level. Human bedrock, on that view, consists of sex and eating and something-or-other which we sublimate into other things.

But this whole picture is wrong. Knowledge can't exist like that. Knowledge consists of problem-solving, and morality is a set of ideas that have arisen from previous morality by error correction. We're born with a certain set of desires, aversions, likes and dislikes, and so on, and we immediately begin to change them and improve them. By the time we've grown up and some things become overridingly important to us, they can easily contradict any inborn desires. Some people decide to be celibate; some people decide to fast; some people decide to eat much more than is good for their survival. My favorite example is parachuting. We have an inborn fear of heights, and yet we've converted that inborn impulse into a sport and a sense of fun. We intellectually know that the parachute will save us—or will probably save us—and we convert the inborn impulse from an aversion into something highly attractive, which we go out of our way to do.

HARRIS: To argue the same point from the other side: most men don't do what genetically should be the most desirable thing for them to do, which is to spend all their time donating sperm to a sperm bank so they can each father tens of thousands of children for whom they have no financial responsibility.

DEUTSCH: Yes, that's another good argument in the same direction. Morality consists of theories that begin as inborn ideas but pretty soon it consists of improvement upon improvement upon improvement, and some of this is mediated by culture. Our morality is a set of theories as complicated and subtle and adapted to its various purposes as our scientific knowledge is.

This imaginary AI with no consciousness would still have to have morality, otherwise it couldn't make any progress of any kind. And its morality would begin as our morality, because the AI would begin as a member of our society—a teenager, if you like. It would make changes whenever it decided they were improvements.

HARRIS: But aren't you assuming that we would have designed it to emulate us from the beginning, rather than design it in some other way?

DEUTSCH: We can't do otherwise. It's not a matter of emulating us; we have no culture other than our existing ones.

HARRIS: But if we were stupid enough to do it, we could build a paper-clip maximizer, correct? We could decide to devote all our resources to such a bizarre project and leave morality out of it.

DEUTSCH: Well, we have error-correcting mechanisms in our culture to prevent someone doing that. But those mechanisms aren't perfect, and it could happen—and something of the sort has happened in the past, many times. I'm not saying there's some magical force for good that will prevent bad things from happening. I'm saying that the bad things that can reasonably be envisaged as happening in the invention of an AI are the same things we have to watch out for anyway. The AI situation is slightly better, actually, because these AIs will very likely be children of

Western culture in particular—assuming we don't stifle their creativity by some misguided prohibitions.

HARRIS: Okay. I want to make sure this point is clear: you are not saying that some deep principle of computation or knowledge acquisition or anything else *prevents* us from producing a nightmare scenario.

DEUTSCH: No. As I said, we've done it before.

HARRIS: So, this isn't analogous to the claim that, because of the universality of computation, we needn't worry that we won't be able to fuse our cognitive horizons with a superintelligence. There's a continuum of intelligence, and a continuum of knowledge, that can, in principle, always be traversed through computation of some kind, and we know what that process entails.

Those are two very different claims. One is a claim about what we think we know about the nature of computation and the nature of knowledge. The other is a claim about what seems plausible to you, given what smart people will tend to do when designing intelligent machines. The latter is a much, much weaker claim, in terms of telling people they don't have to worry about the advent of strong AI.

DEUTSCH: Yes. One of them is a claim about what must be so, and the other is a claim of what's available to us if we play our cards right. I think it's something we have to work for. Yes, it's plausible to me that we will. It's also plausible to me that we won't.

HARRIS: Well, it must also be plausible to you that we could fail to build AI for reasons of simple human chaos.

DEUTSCH: Oh, yes. What I meant was, it's plausible that we'll succeed in solving the problem of stabilizing civilization indefinitely, AI or no AI. It's also plausible that we won't, AI or no AI, and that's a very rational fear to have, because otherwise we won't put enough work into preventing it.

HARRIS: Perhaps we should talk about that—the maintenance of civilization. What's on your short list of concerns?

DEUTSCH: Well, I see human history as a long period of virtually complete failure—failure, that is, to make any progress. Our species has existed for, depending on where you count it from, maybe a hundred thousand or two hundred thousand years. And for the vast majority of that time, people were alive, they were thinking, they were suffering, and they wanted things. But nothing ever improved. The improvements that did happen happened so slowly that archaeologists can't distinguish between artifacts from eras separated by thousands of years. There was generation upon generation upon generation of suffering and stasis.

Then there was slow improvement, and then faster improvement. Then there were attempts to institutionalize a tradition of criticism, which I think is the key to rapid progress—that is, progress discernible in a human lifetime—and there was also error correction, so that regression was less likely. That happened several times and failed every time except once—in the European Enlightenment of the seventeenth and eighteenth centuries.

What worries me is that the inheritors of that unique instance of sustained progress are only a small proportion of the population of the world today. It's the culture, or civilization, that we call the West. Only the West has a tradition of institutionalized criticism. And this has made for various problems, including the problem of failed cultures that see their failure writ large by comparison with the West and therefore want to do something about it that doesn't involve creativity. That's very dangerous. And even in the West, what it takes to maintain our civilization is not widely known. As you've also said, the prevailing view among people in the West, including very educated people, is a picture of the relationship between knowledge and progress and civilization and values that's wrong in dangerous ways. Although our cultural institutions have now preserved stability despite rapid change for hundreds of years, the knowledge of what it takes to keep civilization stable in the face of rapidly increasing knowledge is not widespread.

We're like people on a huge, well-designed submarine which has all sorts of lifesaving devices built in, who don't know they're in a submarine. They think they're in a motorboat, and they're going to open all the hatches because they want a nicer view.

HARRIS: What a great analogy! The misconception that worries me most, frankly, is the fairly common notion that there's no such thing as progress in any real sense, and there's certainly no such thing as *moral* progress. Many people believe that you can't justify the idea that one culture is better than another, or one way of life is better than another, because there's no such thing as moral truth. They've somehow drawn this lesson from twentieth-century science and philosophy, and now, in the twenty-first century, even very smart people—even physicists whose names would be well known to you, with whom I've collided on this point—think there's no place to stand where you can say, for instance, that slavery is wrong. They consider a condemnation of slavery a mere preference that has no possible connection to science.

I'll give you an example of just how crazy this hypocrisy and doublethink can become among well-educated people. I was at a meeting at the Salk Institute to talk about things like the alleged gulf between facts and values, which I consider one of the more spurious exports from philosophy that has been widely embraced by scientists. I was making an argument for moral realism and said something like, "If there's any culture that we can be sure has not given the best possible answer to the question of how to live a good life, it's the Taliban. Consider, for instance, the practice of forcing half the population to live in cloth bags, and beating them or killing them when they try to get out. If we know anything about human well-being, we know that this is an idiotic and immoral practice."

It turns out that to disparage the Taliban at an academic conference is to court controversy. After my talk, a woman who holds multiple graduate degrees in relevant fields—she's technically a bioethicist, but she has graduate degrees in science, philosophy, and law—

DEUTSCH: That doesn't fill me with confidence.

HARRIS: Right. I should also say that this prodigy has gone on to serve on the Presidential Commission for the Study of Bioethical Issues. She's now one of thirteen people advising President Obama on the ethical implications of current advances in medicine.

After my talk, she said, "How could you possibly say that forcing women and girls to live under the veil is wrong? I understand *you* don't like it, but that's just your Western notion of right and wrong."

I said, "The moment you admit that questions of right and wrong relate to the well-being of conscious creatures—in this case, human beings—then you have to admit that we know something about morality. And we know, in this case, that the burqa isn't the best solution to the mystery of how to maximize human well-being."

"That's just your opinion," she said.

"Well, let's make it simpler. Let's say we found a culture on an island somewhere that was removing the eyeballs of every third child. Would you then agree that we had found a culture that was not *perfectly* maximizing human well-being?"

"It would depend on why they were doing it," she said.

"Let's say they're doing it for religious reasons. They have a scripture which says, 'Every third should walk in darkness,' or some such nonsense."

Then she said, "Well, then you could never say that they were wrong."

The fact that these hypothetical barbarians were laboring under a religious precept trumped all other possible truth claims for her, leaving us with no way to declare anything better or worse in moral terms. I've had the same kinds of conversations with physicists who say, "I don't like slavery. I personally wouldn't want to be a slave, or to keep slaves. But there's no place to stand scientifically that allows me to say that slaveholders are in the wrong."

Once we acknowledge the link between morality and human well-being, or the well-being of all possible conscious persons, this kind of moral relativism is tantamount to saying not only that we don't know anything about well-being, but that we will *never* know anything about it. The underlying claim is that no conceivable breakthrough in knowledge would tell us anything relevant to navigating the difference between the worst possible misery for everyone and every other state of the universe that is better than that.

What worries me is that many of the things you've said about progress, and about there being only a subset of humanity that has found creative methods for improving human life, will seem controversial—even bigoted—to many of the people who make decisions about how we should live.

DEUTSCH: Yes, that is scary. But it has always been so. The thing is, our culture is wiser than we are in many ways. The people who defeated communism, for instance, might well have said that they were doing it for Jesus. In fact they weren't. They were doing it for Western values, which they had been brought up to reinterpret as "doing it for Jesus." They'd say things like "The values of democracy and freedom are enshrined in the Bible." Well, those things aren't enshrined in the Bible. But the practice of saying that they are is part of a subculture which was extraordinarily good, and *did* good. So things are not as bad as the existence of perverse academics like those might lead you to think.

HARRIS: One thing that makes it not as bad as one might think is that it's impossible, even for someone like her, to live out the implications of such hypocrisy. I could have said, "You've convinced me. I'll send my daughter to Afghanistan for a year abroad, forcing her to live in a burqa with a Taliban family. What do you think? Is that the best use of her time? Am I a good father? After all, there's really no basis for judging that this could be bad for her, apart from my succumbing to my own xenophobic biases, so presumably you support me in this decision." I have to imagine that even she would balk at that, because we all know in our bones that certain ways of living are undesirable.

DEUTSCH: Right. There's another, related irony, which is that she's willing to condemn you for not being a moral relativist. But moral relativism is a pathology that arises only in Western culture. Every other culture has no doubt that there's such a thing as right and wrong, they've just got the wrong idea of what right and wrong are, but they don't doubt that there is such a thing, and she wouldn't condemn them for that, although she does condemn you for it.

You say "hypocrisy." I think this all originated in the same mistake we discussed at the beginning of this conversation—empiricism, or the idea that knowledge comes to us through the senses, which has led to scientism, which is the idea that science, by itself, constitutes the whole of reason—that the scientific method constitutes the whole of rationality. Which leads to the idea that there can't be such a thing as morality since we can't do an experiment to test it. Your answer to that seems to be, "But we can, if we adopt the simple criterion of human well-being." But we can't just leave it at that. The idea that there can't be any morality because it can't be derived from the senses is the same argument that there can't be any scientific knowledge because it can't be derived from the senses.

In the twentieth century, empiricism was found to be nonsense, and some people therefore concluded that scientific knowledge was nonsense. But the real truth is that science isn't based on empiricism, it's based on reason, and so is morality. So if you adopt a rational attitude toward morality, and therefore say that morality consists of moral knowledge—and knowledge always consists of conjectures, doesn't need a basis, only needs modes of criticism; and those modes of criticism operate by criteria that are themselves subject to modes of criticism—then you come to a transcendent moral truth. If all knowledge is conjectural and subject to improvement, then protecting the means of improving knowledge is more important than any particular piece of knowledge. That idea—before one even invokes ideas like "humans should flourish," and then "all humans are equal," and so on—will lead directly to, for example, the fact that slavery is an abomination. Human well-being is a good approximation in most practical situations, but not an absolute truth. I can imagine, for example, situations in which it would be right for the human race as a whole to commit suicide.

HARRIS: There's a homology between your open-ended picture of knowledge acquisition and explanation, and my moral realism. I don't know that our views are precisely the same, but there's a line in your book I loved, which is something like, "Moral philosophy is about the problem of what to do next." More generally, you said that it's about what sort of life to lead and what sort of world to want, but this phrase, "the problem of what to do next," really captures morality for me, because for years I've been talking about morality as a kind of navigation problem.

Even if we didn't have the words "morality," or "good and evil," or "right and wrong," we'd still have a navigation problem. We've been thrust into a universe of possible experiences. And there's no difference more salient than the difference between the worst possible misery for everyone and all other available states. There's the question of how to navigate in this space of possible experiences so as, at a minimum, to avoid the worst possible misery. Beyond that, what sorts of well-being are possible? What sorts of meaning, beauty, and bliss are available to conscious minds appropriately constituted?

For me, realism of every kind is just a statement that it's possible not to know what one is missing. If you're a realist with respect to geography, you have to acknowledge that there are parts of the world you may not know about. If the year was 1100, and you were living in Oxford and had never heard of Africa, Africa nevertheless existed despite your ignorance, and it was discoverable. This is realism with respect to geography. Things are true whether or not anyone knows they're true, and once knowing they're true, people can forget this knowledge. As you pointed out, whole civilizations could forget forms of knowledge that are actually vital to human flourishing.

All we have to admit is that there's some criterion, as fundamental as any criterion we'd invoke in any other domain of science, by which we can determine that certain states of consciousness are better or worse than others. And if someone won't acknowledge that the worst possible misery for everyone is worse than the many alternatives on offer, then I don't know what language game he's playing. And the acknowledgment that the worst possible misery for everyone is worse than the alternatives is all we need to get the growth of moral knowledge started.

Then it becomes a story of forward movement, toward we know not what, but we know there's a difference between profound suffering with no silver lining and many of the things that we, rightly, value in life. The fact/value divide—Hume's idea that you can't derive an "ought" from an "is"—is deeply misleading. This notion comes, I think, from a misreading of Hume—at least it's a reading that makes far too much of a peripheral point. But I've met physicists who think this principle is inscribed at the back of the Book of Nature: "There's no statement of the way the world is that can tell you how it ought to be; there's no statement of fact that can tell you anything at all about values, and therefore values are just made up. They have no relationship to a scientific picture of reality."

DEUTSCH: Yes, it's empiricism again. It's justificationism: You can't *deduce* an ought from an is. But we're not—or shouldn't be—trying to deduce; we should be trying to explain. And moral explanations can follow from factual explanations, as you've just done by thinking of the worst possible misery a human being could suffer.

HARRIS: Even deeper than that—and you make this point in *The Beginning of Infinity*—is the fact that you can't even get to an "is," a factual claim, without presuming certain "oughts," or values—the value of logical consistency, the value of evidence, and so forth. This is a confusion about the foundations of knowledge. Science is the part of culture where we invoke the value of not fooling ourselves, make a competitive game of discovering where we might all be fooled, and then work to remedy that confusion.

This brings me to a final topic, which is related to our discussion about maintaining civilization and the possible peril of birthing intelligent machines. What's your opinion of the so-called Fermi paradox? Why isn't our galaxy teeming with civilizations more advanced than our own? Is there something about increased knowledge that might, in fact, be fatal?

DEUTSCH: The Fermi problem—it's not actually a paradox—is due to the fact that the galaxy is very old, so old that its vast size doesn't matter as much as its age. If there were two civilizations anywhere in the galaxy, the chances that they arose less than, say, ten million years apart are infinitesimal. So if there's another out there, it's overwhelmingly likely to be at least ten million years older than we are and thus it would have had ten million more years to develop, and that's plenty of time for them to get here.

By the sheer mixing of the stars in the galaxy, they need to colonize just a few stars in their vicinity, and then those stars will spread throughout the galaxy. So we should be seeing evidence of colonies, and since we don't see evidence of them, they're not out there.

Well, this *is* a problem, but I think the problem is just that we don't yet understand most of the parameters, such as, are they likely to use radio waves? What are they likely to do by way of exploration? What are their wishes likely to be? In all these cases, we assume they'll be like us and that they'll use technology in the same ways we do. Only one of those assumptions needs to be wrong for the conclusion that we should have seen them by now to be false. Another possibility is that we're the first—at least in our galaxy. I don't think we know enough about all the factors affecting this question for any one idea to be plausible or implausible. What's implausible is that they could have a different *way of creating* knowledge, because that would imply that physics is very different from the way we think it is. Basically, that it's supernatural. Another possibility is that most societies destroy themselves. But I think it's very implausible that this always happens.

HARRIS: Nick Bostrom has written about what he called the Great Filter. The idea is that at some point almost all advanced civilizations discover computation and build intelligent machines, and this, for some reason, is generally fatal. Or maybe there's some other filter that's generally fatal, and this would explain the absence of evidence of complex alien life.

DEUTSCH: But we'd expect to see those machines, right? They'd have got here by now, unless they're busy making paper clips at home. What's more plausible is that most societies settle down to staticity. Our idea of staticity is conditioned by the static societies in our past—which, as

I said, have been horrible from our present perspective. If you imagine a society whose material welfare is, say, a million times better than ours is now, and somehow it settles into a sort of ritualistic religion in which everybody does the same thing all the time but nobody suffers—that seems to me like hell. But I can imagine societies in which, as you said, they can't see any different ways of being—like living in Oxford and not knowing about Africa. You might be moderately happy and not know that greater happiness is available. If so, then you'd just stay that way.

HARRIS: Yes, I think there's a landscape of possible states of well-being, and you can find yourself on a local peak that knows nothing of other peaks. But obviously there are many more ways *not* to be on a peak. There are probably many peaks analogous to a high state of civilization whose members are effectively the best heroin addicts in the galaxy. That is, they've found a stasis where there's no pain, nor a lot of variation in what they do. They're in a great reservoir of bliss, which they've managed to secure via knowledge of some type—a very Aldous Huxley sort of endgame.

DEUTSCH: First of all, a civilization like that will eventually be destroyed by a nearby supernova or something of the kind. On a scale of tens or hundreds of millions of years, there are plenty of things that could wipe out a civilization *unless* it does something about it. If it does do something about it—with automatic supernova-suppression machines, say—we'd notice that. On the other hand, it's hard to imagine that they don't know about that and do get wiped out, because how did they get to that stage of exalted comfort without finding out about the danger of supernovae?

There are other possibilities. I'm actually considering writing a science fiction book with a very horrible possibility—which I won't mention now.

HARRIS: Don't give the horrible surprise away. . . .

One last question, David. Who's your vote for the smartest person who has ever lived? If you had to nominate one human brain, past or present, to dialogue with the aliens, who would you recommend?

DEUTSCH: This is different from asking who has contributed the most to human knowledge, or who has created most? It's rather who has the highest IQ?

HARRIS: It's good to differentiate those, because there are obviously people who are quite smart, who have contributed more than anyone in sight to our knowledge, but when you look at how they thought and what they accomplished, there's no reason to think they were as smart as someone like John von Neumann, for instance. I'm wondering about someone like von Neumann—raw brain power.

DEUTSCH: In that case (it's mind, not brain, by the way: software not hardware), I think it probably has to be Richard Feynman. Although his achievements in physics are nowhere near those of, say, Albert Einstein.

I met Feynman only once, and people were saying to me, "You'll have heard a lot of stories about Feynman, but he's only human." Well, to cut a long story short, I went and met him, and the stories were all true. He was an absolutely amazing intellect. I haven't met many of the others, I never met Einstein, but my impression is that he was something unusual. I should add, in terms of *achievement*, I would choose Karl Popper.

HARRIS: Don't cut that long story quite so short. What was it like being with Feynman, and can you describe what was so unusual about him?

DEUTSCH: Well, he was very quick on the uptake. That is not so unusual in a university environment, but the creativity applied directly to understanding things was. Let me give you an example. I was sent to meet him by my boss when I was just developing the ideas of quantum computation, and I had constructed what we would today call a quantum algorithm—a very, very simple one. It's now called the Deutsch algorithm. It's not much by today's standards, but I had been working on it for months. I started telling him about quantum computers. He was very interested, and then he said, "So what can these computers do?" I said, "Well, I've been working on a quantum algorithm." So I began to tell him about it, and I said, "Suppose you had a superposition of two different initial states." He said, "Well, then you just get random numbers out." And I said, "Yes, but suppose you then do an interference experiment." I started to continue, and he said, "No, no, stop, stop. Let me work it out." And he rushed over to the blackboard and he produced my algorithm with almost no hint of where it was going.

HARRIS: So how much work did that represent? How much of your work did he recapitulate standing at the blackboard?

DEUTSCH: I don't know, because it's hard to say how much of a clue the few words I said represented. But a crude measure is, say, a few months. A better measure is that I was flabbergasted. I had never seen anything like this before, and I had been interacting with some extremely smart people.

HARRIS: And your boss was John Wheeler at that point?

DEUTSCH: At that time, yes.

HARRIS: Not a dunce.

DEUTSCH: That's right.

HARRIS: What a wonderful story! I'm very glad I asked. Well, David, let me insist that this not be the last time you and I have a conversation like this, because you have a beautiful mind.

DEUTSCH: That would be very nice. It was very nice talking with you.

———

DEUTSCH: Knowledge is critical by nature. Not accumulative. Traditionally, the idea has been that we build it up—either from nothing, like Descartes; or from our senses; or from God or what-have-you; or from our genes. And that thinking consists of building brick upon brick. But Karl Popper's view of science, which I and others want to extend to all thinking and all ideas, is that knowledge isn't like that. It's a great slew of inconsistent ideas, and thinking means wandering about in this slew, trying to make the ideas that seem the most seriously inconsistent with one another consistent by modifying them. And we modify them by conjecture. We guess that something might remove the various inconsistencies we see, and if it does, we move on. And to get to your book, I'm interested to see what you think of this take on it:

We're coming from the same place in some respects and from opposite, incompatible places in other respects—so that it's hard even to express to each other what we mean exactly. I think the reason you developed a theory of morality and took the trouble to write *The Moral Landscape* is not an intellectual reason, or at least not primarily intellectual. It's not that you wanted to fine-tune the best existing theories or contradict some prevalent erroneous theories. I think the reason you wrote this particular book and developed this particular theory is for a particular purpose: namely, to defend civilization—to use a grandiose phrase. To defend it against two existential dangers: one is moral relativism and the other is religious dogmatism.

HARRIS: Yes, that's fair, and imputations of grandiosity are probably also fair. What I was doing in that book was attempting to draw a line in the sand, to defend the claim that the most important questions in human life are those upon which the greatest swings in human well-being depend. And the answers to those questions exist whether or not we can ever get them in hand. Certainly better and worse answers exist. Therefore, it's possible to be right or wrong—or *more* right or *more* wrong—about those questions. I wanted to carve out an intellectual space where we could unabashedly defend the intuition that moral truths exist—

and that claims about morality and values are no different from factual claims we might make about the universe.

DEUTSCH: I wasn't using the word "grandiose" pejoratively! I agree that moral relativism and religious dogmatism are existential dangers. Whether they're the biggest dangers, I'm not sure, but they're existential dangers, which is bad enough. And I agree with what you just said about morality—there is true and false in morality, or right and wrong. Moral truths are objective. They can be discovered by the usual methods of reason, which are essentially the same as those of science (although there are important differences).

Okay. So in developing this moral theory you had an intellectual purpose that was morally driven, and therefore you had a moral purpose *before* you had the details of the theory. You wanted your theory to have certain properties, as you just said—that is, to create an intellectual space in which one could assert and defend the proposition that there's objective right and wrong. So these properties that you wanted the theory to have in advance weren't just expressions of your personality or something, they *were* the moral values that made you want to write this book, and which you take to be *objectively true*.

HARRIS: I'm amused at how tenderly you're leading me by the hand down the garden path to the ruination of my cherished view.

I should also say that I think "theory" is too big a word for what I thought I was putting forward. My theory, such as it is, contains the explicit assumption that there are many things about the morality I have in hand that I can be wrong about. So my theory isn't based on my current moral intuitions.

DEUTSCH: It's based on some of them.

HARRIS: It's based on the intuition of what I call, in various places, moral realism, which is just the claim that it's possible to be wrong. It's possible to not know what you're missing. It's also possible to be cognitively closed to true facts about how good life could be if you only had the right sort of mind—one that would give you access to those states of consciousness. It's not that I think, "Well, my intuition that gay marriage should be legal is so foundational that I know there's no state of the universe that could disconfirm it." That's not where I'm standing. I'm relying on an intuition about realism and about the frontiers of conscious experience.

DEUTSCH: I wasn't making that sort of allegation. In fact, I agree with everything you've just said about morality. The ideas you express in the book contain that, but they also contain something else—something I disagree with. I suppose the basic thing I disagree with is that a property you wanted your theory of morality to have was that it should be based on a secure foundation: namely, science, and especially neuroscience.

HARRIS: Actually, that may be a point of confusion. The fault is certainly mine, from the subtitle—*How Science Can Determine Moral Values*—onward. Although, as you probably know, subtitles are sometimes outside the author's control, as it was in this case. But it's not that morality has to be founded on the secure foundations of science. It's that the claims we want to make about morality are just as well founded as the claims we make in science—however well founded those turn out to be.

I'm talking about this larger cognitive space in which we make claims about the nature of reality—and reality includes all possible conscious experiences. For methodological reasons, we call some of those claims "scientific." Some we call "historical." Some we call merely "factual." Some sciences are still struggling to be as scientific as other sciences, but we still call them "sciences." But there are also claims about subjectivity, about the character and contents of consciousness. And those claims, too, are either true or not true, whether or not we can ever access the relevant data.

What was John F. Kennedy thinking about the moment before he was shot? We know there was a fact of the matter, and we know there's no way we could access that data. And yet there are an infinite number of claims we could make about his subjectivity, about what he was thinking in his last moments of life, that we know are wrong. I know, for instance, that he wasn't thinking about string theory. He wasn't thinking of the largest prime number discovered the year after he died. We could go on like that until the end of time—describing what *wasn't* in his mind at that moment. These claims are as factual as any we ever make in science.

So what I was trying to argue is that morality—rightly considered to depend on the conscious states of conscious creatures—is a space of objective claims that are equivalent to all the other kinds of objective claims we make, differences of methodology aside.

DEUTSCH: Well, there are two ways that something can be objective. You're in favor of one of them and I'm in favor of the other. The first way things can be objective is in the sense that the truths about them are just truths about some *other* thing. Take, for example, chemistry. The truths of chemistry are just truths about physics. That wasn't obvious when chemistry started, but it's obvious now. In principle, every law of chemistry, everything you can say about chemical reactions and so on, is a statement about physics. Chemistry is objective because physics is objective.

Then there's a second way of being objective—namely the way in which the integers exist objectively. And, again, historically there have been theories about the integers that took various positions about whether or not they were real, and if so, in what sense they were real. I think they're real independently of physics—that the truth about them is independent of the truths of physics. Unlike chemistry, integers aren't objective because they're aspects of physical objects. They're objective because they exist in some sense that isn't the same as existing physically—although many truths about them are indeed reflected in truths about physical objects. But the integers are not identified *as* physical objects. Nothing we could discover about the laws of nature could possibly change the truth of theorems about prime numbers. And that's the kind of independence from science that I think truths of morality have.

HARRIS: Actually, I talk about this in *The Moral Landscape* at some point. I follow the philosopher John Searle here. He makes a useful distinction between the ontological and the epistemological senses in which we use the word "objective." If something's ontologically objective, it exists "in the real world," whether or not anyone knows about it. It's independent of human minds. It's the kind of fact you just described, the facts of chemistry and physics—and this probably also extends to things like integers. We can imagine a universe without any conscious creatures, and the facts of chemistry, physics, and even mathematics would still be the case even without anyone around to know them.

And then there's epistemological objectivity, which relates to the methods and attitude with which we make various claims about facts of all kinds. To be objective in the epistemological sense is to not be misled by one's biases. It's to not give in to wishful thinking. Epistemological objectivity requires that one make intellectually honest claims about the data, or about the consequences of logical arguments, and so on.

With respect to the subjective side of things, something can be *ontologically* subjective—which is to say that its existence depends on the existence of conscious minds, human or otherwise. When I speculate about what JFK experienced the moment before he was shot, I'm making a claim about his subjectivity. But I can make that claim in the spirit of *epistemological* objectivity. I can objectively say, about JFK's subjectivity, that it was not characterized by his contemplating the details of string theory.

The ontological difference between objective and subjective doesn't really interest me—and it has no implication for whether one is making true or false claims about the nature of reality. It's useful for certain conversations and not useful for others. In the case of morality, what we're talking about is how experience arises in this universe, and what its character can be, and about the extremes of happiness and suffering that conscious minds are susceptible to. Part of that conversation takes us into the ontologically objective world of neurotransmitters and neurons, or of economic systems, and of "objective reality" at every scale. But the cash value of all these facts—if we're talking about morality—is the conscious states of conscious creatures. As you know, "well-being" is a suitcase term I use to incorporate the range of possible experience, the horizon beyond which we can't currently imagine—with the extreme negative pole being the worst possible misery for everyone.

I don't have strong intuitions about whether or not integers occupy some kind of Platonic zone of existence independent of material reality, and even independent of the conscious minds that apprehend them. But to bring it back to what you just said: There's physical reality—which is often called "objective," in the ontological sense. And then there are things like integers, which, as you said, aren't dependent on what we know about atoms. But then there are also the experiences of conscious systems, whether or not we can ever understand them physically. They have a certain character, and that character depends on whatever material requisites exist for those conscious systems. But it's the subjective side of that coin that's of real interest.

DEUTSCH: Yes. It's funny—just at the end, you said what I was about to say. You use the term "science" more broadly than some people, and so do I. You and I both use it to encroach on things that some people who think they're purists would like to exclude from science. We expand science to include parts of philosophy.

If you want to extend the term "science" to cover things that are traditionally considered philosophy—like the interpretation of quantum theory, for example, which I think is definitely part of science—then you can make the connection between human well-being and neuroscience. There you're encroaching on "neurophilosophy," as it were, and "neurophilosophy" is epistemology. And once you've extended science into epistemology, you run into a deep fact about the physical world, which is that epistemology is substrate-independent.

That is to say, once knowledge, or feelings, or consciousness, or any kind of information or computation is instantiated in a universal device, then the laws it obeys are completely independent of physics and of neurology. All physical attributes of the device fall away, and you can talk about the properties of those things as abstract things or not at all.

Perhaps "abstract" is a misleading word, because they're perfectly objective. It's just that they're not atoms, they're not neurons.

HARRIS: I think that's probably true, but what you seem to be smuggling in here is a kind of information-based functionalism, wherein you're assuming, for the purposes of this conversation, that we know consciousness to be an emergent property of information processing and not some other constituent of physical reality that isn't based on bits. And if we assume that, then consciousness is something that nonbiological computers will likely have by virtue of processing information in a certain way. This might turn out to be true, but I don't think we know it to be true, yet.

DEUTSCH: One thing that's generally true of morality is that it has a reach. If you don't steal a book from the library when you easily could without getting caught, this doesn't just affect you and the library, because the decision to not steal the book is instantiated in a universal machine, which is you. This machine has universal theories, or theories which aspire to be universal theories, or to be universal in some domain. And when you commit a crime, you're changing the facts. You're changing something that you can't change back.

HARRIS: Isn't that change occurring in you, assuming that no one else will ever discover your crime? Where else would the change occur?

DEUTSCH: Well, for example, suppose you're later telling your children about morality. Do you say, "When you're in that library, it's okay to steal the book, provided no one will ever find out," or do you say, "You shouldn't steal the book, *even* if no one will ever find out"? If the first, then your immoral act is affecting your child as well, not just you or the library. And if the second, you're lying to the child, which itself has vast implications.

HARRIS: Yes. The effects of these things tend to spread. And when we're talking about the consequences of an action, we have to include things like one's memory of having performed it and the effect this memory will have on one's future experiences, relationships, beliefs, and so forth.

To examine a specific principle: Where does the principle of a person's consent get its ethical significance? It is easy to think of experiences that are unpleasant but that could be very good for people, and we may, in fact, be doing them a favor by subjecting them to those experiences without their consent. Where does the autonomy of the individual derive its importance in your view?

DEUTSCH: It's epistemology, once again. I don't think that even human rights are fundamental. They're just a feature of institutions that promote the growth of knowledge. And the reason knowledge trumps everything else is fallibilism. In all these cases where we have a theory that something is better, we're implementing a moral theory we might be mistaken about. And an objective truth of morality is that it's immoral to close off the paths to correcting a false theory.

HARRIS: Again, I'm with you there, but this seems another way of asserting my foundational claim, which is that human flourishing—conceived as broadly as you want—is continually open to refinement and correction. We want to move in the direction of better and better worlds with better and better experiences. But we know it's possible to move in the wrong direction, and we never want to tie our hands and make it impossible to correct course.

DEUTSCH: Yes. That's why consent isn't just a nice thing to have but a fundamental feature of the way we handle ideas. If you have a system that allows people to force an idea on another person who disagrees with the idea, then the means of correcting errors are closed off. Imagine people who had a disability but could be cured of it but that cure couldn't be explained to them. Well, either those people are in an inherent state of suffering, in which case applying the cure won't change that, or there's something that they prefer to another thing, in which case there will be a path toward the better state that involves doing just the things they prefer. If it involves an injection that they don't want because it's painful, say, then what they prefer might involve either an anesthetic or getting them into a certain mood in which an injection doesn't matter.

HARRIS: There's an example I mention somewhere in *The Moral Landscape*, which comes from Danny Kahneman's research, where people received colonoscopies—back when there was no twilight anesthesia for the procedure—and researchers were trying to figure out what accounted for their subjective measures of suffering and also what would positively influence them to get another colonoscopy five years hence. Their findings confirmed something in psychology called the "peak-end rule," which is that your judgment about the valence of an experience is determined both by its peak intensity at any point over its duration and by what it was like at the end. It appears that those are the two levers one can pull to influence whether someone thinks an experience was a good one or a bad one.

To test this, they gave ordinary colonoscopies to a control group, taking the scope out as soon as the procedure was over. However, in the experimental condition they left the apparatus in, quite unnecessarily, for some minutes at the end, providing a comparatively low-intensity but still negative stimulus. And the result was that the subjects' impression of how much they had suffered was significantly reduced, and their willingness to come back and get a potentially life-saving colonoscopy in the future was increased. So, by any measure, this was a good thing to have done to these people—except that if you consider the window of time around the procedure, it is also true to say that the doctors prolonged an unpleasant experience without any medical necessity.

DEUTSCH: There'll be a way of telling the subjects what you're doing, without invalidating the experiment.

HARRIS: But what if the effect is reduced or canceled if you do? If you say, "It's not medically necessary, but we're going to leave this tube in for a few minutes, because you'll eventually feel better about the experience if we do." What if that abolished the effect or even increases patient suffering?

DEUTSCH: If it does, there'd be a way of getting around that. For example, you could say to the patient, "Look, there's a way of reducing the amount of your perceived suffering from this procedure, but it won't work if we tell you what it is. So do you give us permission to use this way?" And, of course, the patient will say yes.

HARRIS: But is that really consent? What if we offer it like that, and 99 percent of patients say, "Sure. Sign me up." But we have another experimental condition, and we tell these people exactly how we propose to reduce their suffering: "We're going to leave the tube in you for five minutes not doing anything, and those will be five minutes where you'll probably be thinking, 'When is this going be over, for Christ's sake?' And you could have been off the table and going home at that point, but in this protocol you'll still be on the table with this tube in you. But trust us, it will be better that way." Let's assume that the percentage of people consenting under those conditions drops to 17 percent. Now we know that all the people in the first condition were only consenting because we masked the tactic we were using. So, in fact, they weren't really consenting to its use at all.

DEUTSCH: It was still consent. After all, you don't have to know exactly what the heart surgeon will do to your heart in order to validly consent to heart surgery. It's the same with a placebo. And the 1 percent who still say no are simply making a mistake, the same kind of mistake you'd be making if this whole theory wasn't true. You can't bias the rules under which people interact toward a particular theory they might disagree about.

HARRIS: But there are people who have ideas about reality and about how we should all live within it that are so perverse that we have to block their aspirations—whether that means locking them in prison because they're so badly behaved or just excluding them from important conversations. The Taliban and ISIS don't get to vote on our public policy, and for good reason, because their votes would be crazy. Not all autonomy needs to be respected.

DEUTSCH: Yes. Well, again, we have institutions. We're trying to tune the political institutions to enable disputes between people to be resolved without violence. Our moral institutions include the idea that participating in and obeying such institutions is morally right. In interpersonal relationships that don't involve the law, we want something much better than that. We want interpersonal relationships not only to resolve disputes without violence but to do so without any kind of coercion. An institution that codifies coercion is ipso facto irrational. Now, I'm not saying that I know of institutions that achieve this elimination of coercion perfectly. I'm saying that's the criterion by which institutions should be judged—by how good they are at resolving disputes between people without violence, without coercion.

HARRIS: But people who aren't rational actors occasionally have to be coerced, right?

DEUTSCH: Yes. And we have found ways of getting along which involve far less coercion than what was needed to stabilize society a few centuries ago, as Steven Pinker has pointed out. And I expect this trend to continue. One day somebody might invent a way of curing the most fanatical mass murderer or terrorist and converting him to a benign religion—or to a benign atheism, or whatever. But when this is initially invented it's fabulously expensive because it involves, say, putting him in an artificial community with thousands of people who have to be trained to act in a certain way toward him, and so on. Under such circumstances, we wouldn't do it. Even though it might be *possible* to reform him, it would still be better just to imprison him, because the institutions couldn't survive if we had to spend billions curing each terrorist. But once that sum is down to thousands, we certainly should and would do it.

HARRIS: What if he didn't want this done to him? What if he wanted to remain a psychopath or a terrorist? We're back to the problem of consent.

DEUTSCH: As I see it, he'd have been caught at some point and put on trial and sentenced. And then these new methods might have him consent to after they are already underway—after a month of rehabilitation. And then a better method would have him consent after a week. And you can imagine that millions of years in the future there will be methods so sophisticated that they'll involve things like doing a brain scan and discovering some memories of his and working out a customized treatment for him which, say, involves the sun coming out from behind the clouds at the exact moment when he leaves the courthouse. I think there's no limit to the possibility of removing evil by knowledge.

HARRIS: Well, in that case, it's no longer evil, it's just bad luck that he was the kind of person who wanted to be a terrorist or a psychopath— that is, he was unlucky to be biologically susceptible to being that way. And once we have the cure for terrorism or psychopathy or anything else that falls under the rubric of evil, there'll be no more moralizing about it than there is about a disease like diabetes. We'd just provide the cure.

DEUTSCH: Well, I think after he'd been cured, he should still say, "What I did was wrong." I think that would be a bit more than saying, "What I did was a mistake." It's different.

HARRIS: Yes. He might be horrified by what he did. He might say, "I can't believe I was the kind of person who wanted to do that." And we can imagine his gratitude at no longer being that sort of person. But I think this will completely negate the ethic of justice as retribution—the notion that we are right to punish people because, on some level, they *deserve* it.

DEUTSCH: I agree. It's just a matter of operating the institution that is the best institution we have for achieving this vital purpose.

HARRIS: Imagine this future of a completed science of the mind, when we not only understand the computational basis of every possible experience, but we can intervene in the brain as much as we want. Assume I now have a machine that I can put on your head which can dial in any possible conscious state. It's a perfect experience machine.

DEUTSCH: Wait . . . we'll always have limited knowledge, and therefore the only states we'll be able to download are the ones we already know. The infinite majority of possible states will always be unknown.

HARRIS: Can't we use this device to explore experiences that have yet to be characterized?

DEUTSCH: There's the experience of knowing tomorrow's scientific discovery, which we'll never be able to download into somebody until tomorrow.

HARRIS: Right. I'm excluding experiences of that type. Let's trim it down to something simpler. Let's say we've taken a range of people who are good candidates for having had the best sorts of human experiences—the greatest scientists, the most-saintly people, the best athletes, the most creative artists. And we've not only recorded their experiences but we've extrapolated from various commonalities among different classes of experience to produce new experiences that are in some ways even better, or more pure, or just fundamentally new. You take a little bit of John von Neumann and a little Mozart, or their equivalents, and you throw in what it's like to be Lionel Messi scoring his record-breaking goals. And you get all this tuned up in novel ways—and let's assume we've got all the time in the world to explore these states of consciousness to see which we prefer.

I'm presupposing that you and I will converge on the value of those kinds of experiences—that is, we won't radically disagree in our sense of what's good, given an ever-expanding menu of possible states. And if we do have some disagreement—if you really like experience number forty-five and I really like number forty-six—then that difference will have a neurological or computational explanation that will be open for revision. Then the question becomes, How should we change our intuitions about what is good in light of what is possible? And is it good to change one's sense of what is good in the first place?

DEUTSCH: There's a mismatch between that idea and how I think about minds. You're assuming that there's such a thing as a happy state of mind that's orthogonal to the question of which experience is being processed. You say you can be as happy as Mozart. That omits the question of what specific problem you are solving as Mozart. Are you solving one of the specific problems he solved when he was alive? In that case, you're just repeating an experience, and that can't be what happiness consists of, because we need to make progress to be happy.

I think we're more characterized by our problems than by our particular ideas at any one time. A happy person is somebody who has a set of hard problems that are interesting enough to be worth devoting a lot of effort to, and yet not so hard that they can't make any progress toward solving them. And these problems will consist of conflicts between theories. The conflicts, again, must be interesting. It's not obvious that you can download this state into somebody without its simply being a re-creation of the individual. If I get a download of Mozart's theories as they were at a particular time, then it could be the equivalent of remembering what it felt like to solve that problem, but it wouldn't be *my* problem unless they managed to integrate it with the rest of me so thoroughly that I was actually Mozart and not me. In which case, what's the point?

HARRIS: There are states of consciousness that are extraordinarily pleasant—and it's the kind of pleasantness that does shine through in moments when we're solving problems in satisfying ways—but you can tap into this pleasure in a way that isn't dependent on having interesting problems to solve or successfully solving them. Granted, some ways of tapping into this pleasure seem pathological, in that they don't equip you to do anything else. For instance, if you want to be a heroin addict and just lie on the couch all day and dissolve into bliss, well, you may be able to do that. No doubt there are drugs that haven't been invented yet that are far better than heroin, without its obvious downsides. Just being able to sustain that pure, useless pleasure may be something you'd actually prefer to the Mozart experience.

DEUTSCH: I think not. Or only at first.

HARRIS: Well, that remains to be seen. I share your intuition, but for argument's sake let's grant the depressing, Aldous Huxley–style punch line, which is that, given the opportunity, we'll just want to be medicated into oblivion.

DEUTSCH: I think that's a myth. Pleasure isn't joy. People can be trained by our culture, and by their circumstances, to interpret pleasure as joy if they haven't experienced much joy. But pleasure doesn't fulfill the same function in the mind. And it's particularly insidious because when you first experience, say, heroin, it might well be joy, because you're undergoing a new experience, a new way of being, new sensations, and that's interesting and therefore can be fun and joyful. But once you are doing this every day and it's your way of life, it gives you nothing. And if you nevertheless interpret that "nothing" as "good," well, that's like being dead. It's not a human state of mind. I think the great majority of actual heroin addicts stop of their own accord because they're bored with it.

HARRIS: The problem you describe—the difference between mere pleasure and joy—might be overcome with yet more knowledge. You could create a drug-induced oblivion that included joy.

DEUTSCH: I don't think so, because now you're assuming there's some kind of joy-receiving center in the brain that receives messages from the creative center. So that you could simulate this joy-receiving center artificially. I don't think the mind can possibly be like that. I think the only way you can create joy artificially is by downloading some state of a person who is experiencing joy, and then you would *be* that person.

HARRIS: This is an empirical question, and you might be right. Let's forget about drugs and talk about something that's more akin to the Matrix, where every mind could be consigned to a state that could be as creative, or as apparently creative, as you like, but would in fact be pitched into an hallucinatory solitude—just a simulacrum, within which we wouldn't actually be in contact with other minds. We've lost reality, and we're now in virtual reality—but a virtual reality so thrilling and beautiful, and so conducive to joy, that it would be impossible to care about what is actually real.

Ethically, is there an important difference between being in reality and being in some kind of dreamscape of our own invention?

DEUTSCH: No (assuming the person has gone into this dreamscape voluntarily). In that case, what he's experiencing is real joy, genuinely generated by his own mind in the same way any other joy is. Actually, this Matrix-like thing isn't so far from the truth, if you think about, for example, pure mathematics. G. H. Hardy said that the nice thing about being a mathematician was that you could sit in an armchair after dinner with your eyes shut and nobody would know whether you were working or not. He was in the virtual reality of pure mathematics, and he experienced great joy and great creativity just in the confines of a few cubic centimeters of brain.

HARRIS: Let's push this a little further. We create a Matrix, and we decide to migrate a human consciousness into it. But then where does consent come in? Neither you nor I consented to be born, and yet we don't blame our parents for hurling us into the world. Would we blame the generation of humans who created a Matrix for us?

DEUTSCH: Well, obviously there are practical issues. How safe is this Matrix from real-world asteroid strikes, and so on? But assuming that kind of problem can be dealt with, then there is an ethics to consider. However, I use the word "ethics" slightly differently. You say "ethics" and "morality" almost interchangeably. "Ethics" I would define more as just a set of practical rules—like medical ethics, which doctors have to adopt for patient safety so they won't be criticized morally. There'd have to be an ethics for putting people in this virtual reality. If there was a question of people sometimes wanting to get out, then there would have to be a way out. But that's just a practical problem.

HARRIS: To clarify, I'm imagining that this Matrix would be like a dream. Everyone would be in an imaginary realm of his or her own. That might allow for maximum creativity, but no one would be in a relationship with anyone else. And the sense that one was in relationship with others would be illusory.

DEUTSCH: So, there wouldn't be genuine collaboration on any problem, because the other "people" wouldn't be creative. It's true that people collaborating can generally create better and faster than the sum of their individual contributions. But that's only a rule of thumb. Sometimes people like to work by themselves and be by themselves. I'm fairly solitary. Not many people would want to be in a Matrix where there was only one real person, and the rest were zombies. But for those who would, it's fine—as long as they're creative. That's the fundamental thing.

By the way, there's a concept of being entertained by other people, or by heroin, or by TV programs, or whatever. That's a mistake. We may subjectively interpret what's happening as being entertained *by* something, but really the only thing that entertains us is our own creative engagement with it. Without that creative engagement, nothing can entertain us. Think about the cliché of winning the lottery and ending up miserable. The generic trap you can fall into in this situation is thinking money can entertain you, not realizing that only you can entertain you. Same with rock stars, who had imagined that if only they had a life of as much sex and drugs as they wanted, they'd be happy. And then one in a million of them achieves that and finds he's miserable. That cliché strikes me as very plausible.

HARRIS: No doubt. However, there's another way to be happy, and in some sense it's a more fundamental way of experiencing well-being, and it seems *not* to result from being creative. I agree with you that most people think the opposite of being entertained is being bored. But boredom, in my experience, is nothing more than a lack of attention.

To pay sufficient attention to anything is to be cured of boredom. I've gone on retreats where I've done nothing but meditate in silence for up to three months. In the beginning, a common technique is to focus on the sensation of breathing, but once you have some ability to concentrate, the practice opens up, and you can then pay attention to anything that arises—other sensations, sights and sounds, moods, and even thoughts themselves—as a transitory appearance in consciousness.

From the perspective of someone who wants to be creative and solve complex problems, this may seem like a crazy and unproductive thing to do. In some ways, meditation is inimical to creative thought because, for the purposes of the practice, one has decided to relinquish any train of thought, no matter how interesting it seems. When you meditate, paying close attention to something—the breath, say—you find that thoughts continually arise. And you discover that you regularly get lost in thought for minutes at a time. With more concentration, you begin to observe thoughts closer to the moment of their arising, as objects in consciousness. The deeper you go into this process the fewer thoughts intrude and the earlier you notice them. And the moment you notice them, they unravel and disappear. This mere witnessing of experience, without being lost in thought, can become a circumstance of utter tranquillity and well-being.

There's much more to say about this, but I'm merely hoping to indicate that this state of mind isn't prototypically creative. It's not a way of generating new concepts, or of following them on to new theories, or of solving any problems that require conceptual thought.

DEUTSCH: I know nothing more about meditation than what you've told me. It could be that the whole thing is an illusion, but since it's you, I doubt it.

Most thinking is actually unconscious. What we're aware of is just the tip of the iceberg, and even our conscious thoughts are supported by a rich infrastructure of unconscious thoughts, which obey the same epistemology as the conscious ones. So thoughts can be creative or uncreative, they can be irrational or rational, they can make progress or not, and it depends on the same conditions—conditions which either promote or inhibit the growth of knowledge in various ways. So, assuming that at the end of meditation you're a better person—that is, your mind is a better mind—the "betterness" has been created by something real, not supernatural. And if you're not consciously aware of the process, then it must have been in your unconscious mind. And maybe, under certain circumstances, deliberately preventing your conscious mind from doing anything clears some obstacles to creativity in your unconscious mind. Obstacles are themselves ideas, and in fact the unconscious mind almost certainly goes wrong more often than the conscious one. So this could simply be a way of enhancing creativity after all.

HARRIS: Well, nothing really turns on this, but that's definitely true. When you're trying to meditate, it's very common to find that your thoughts, when they do arise, are more and more creative. If you're a novelist, you'll have the best ideas you've ever had—for plot or dialogue, for instance—and letting go of all this in the interests of staying on retreat can become very difficult to do. I've had retreats where I've failed to do it. I'd have an idea for something to write, or something to think more about, which persuaded me that I shouldn't let the opportunity for creativity pass, and it completely derailed the retreat. That happens, but I'd say that the value of meditation isn't merely that it equips you to be more creative in the future. The value is that there's a fundamental insight to be had about the nature of well-being itself, and about the mechanics of human suffering. There's a riddle to be solved, the solving of which allows one to be not only more creative in the future, but happier in the present, even in the absence of creativity.

DEUTSCH: That's exactly what you'd expect if your unconscious mind is indeed being creative. You'd expect an unconscious well-being to percolate up until you became aware of it, and that it hadn't happened before because something in your conscious mind was preventing it.

HARRIS: I think it's more that you're ceasing to do something that's *negatively* creative—if it makes sense to say that neurosis, fear, anxiety, and so forth can be creative in this way.

DEUTSCH: Yes, unfortunately they often are.

HARRIS: And as for clearing away obstacles to creativity, I feel as though we haven't fully identified what we disagree about.

DEUTSCH: Well, just as a last thing, let me say that I think your book achieves its purpose, and it's a timely and important purpose. If I have a criticism of its fundamental logic, I can't say I'm sure that if your book *had* been written to conform to what I'm about to say, it would have achieved its purpose better.

I want to take the same attitude toward moral theories that Popper does toward scientific theories, and therefore I view all theories about morality that claim to give it a foundation as mistaken. Yet all of these theories have value—some of them much less and some of them more—when they are regarded not as foundational ideas about morality but as critiques. For example, there are lots of different suggestions for the foundation of morality—like Kant's categorical imperative, or utilitarianism, or Rawls's fairness, or God's will, or human flourishing. All those are proposals for foundations of morality. But if you regard them, instead, as critiques, then I think they're all quite valuable. Human flourishing could be interpreted as a proposed improvement on what went before—as a critique.

Consider, for example, utilitarianism. A utilitarianist could ask, "If what morality consists of is going to church every Sunday, what purpose does that serve?" And it's up to the person who advocates going to church to make the case. To say that something has no purpose is a prima facie critique of it. Therefore the onus is on the religious-morality person to explain why, although we can usually reject something that has no purpose, in this case we should *not* reject it. The person might respond, "Well, because God said so."

And then there's the standard critique of religious-based anything: "How can we tell the difference between that claim and someone else's claim which is based on a different idea of god?" Or a different holy book, or whatever. "What criterion should we use?" And if the religiously inclined person says, "The criterion is that, well, this one is correct," then that's a bad explanation, because everyone else could offer the same criterion. It's a criterion that isn't a criterion.

I think the case for human flourishing as a foundation for morality is similar. Utilitarianism, regarded as a foundational moral theory, is rubbish. But regarded as a critique of other theories, it's very powerful. And I think your argument is like utilitarianism, but it also has more elements of plain common sense.

HARRIS: Let me recharacterize my foundation, because it's not merely a matter of human flourishing; it extends to all possible conscious systems. My base claim is that there's a space of possible minds and possible experiences, and there are experiences that are better and worse than others, whether or not we'll ever discover them. My only axiomatic claim is that the worst possible misery for everyone is bad, if the word "bad" is going to mean anything. And that's as foundational a claim as we ever make in science, about anything. The foundation upon which even Popperian science is based is just a claim about there being a larger reality than the one we currently have in hand, which is to say there's stuff we can be confused about.

DEUTSCH: It's not a foundation in the sense of being "uncriticizable." We can always ask, "Why that criterion and not another criterion?"

Why assume that we exist? Why assume that there is a truth? I think we are giving up unnecessarily if we say, "Well, there are some things you just have to accept on faith. You have to start somewhere." I don't think you have to start somewhere, and I think all claims that you do are fallacies.

HARRIS: Can't you start with consciousness? Because, for me, consciousness, defined as the fact that there's something that it's like to be you in this moment, can't be doubted. Granted, this might be a dream. You might be a brain in a vat. You might be confused about everything, but the fact of consciousness is a starting point even if reality itself is in question. Consciousness, the mere fact that there is an experiential aspect to existence, is all that we need to ground a moral landscape wherein all possible mental states, good and bad, can be explored.

DEUTSCH: The fact that there's consciousness doesn't get us anywhere. You have a certain substantive conception of what it is to be conscious. And, as we've discovered in this conversation, different people can have different conceptions. For example, I prefer to think of the mind as a dynamic thing that's perpetually not self-consistent. You regard happiness more as a state, whereas I think you can't separate it from the specifics of what causes it. For example, there's no such thing as downloading Mozart's happiness without downloading his specific problems.

HARRIS: This is also a framing issue. Certain unpleasant experiences can be framed in such a way that they seem to increase one's sense of well-being—the intense physical struggle of climbing a mountain, for instance. It might be painful all along the way, but the struggle itself becomes the basis for a deep sense of accomplishment. These framing effects are themselves empirical claims that we can investigate in each case. Some struggles improve us, while others undermine our sense of well-being without producing any further benefit.

You're a mountaineer of physics, experiencing the pains and pleasures of solving problems. Perhaps even the pain of making mistakes adds to the interest of your work. But let's say we could add something to your tea every morning that would make you a little happier in the conventional sense, throughout the whole process of theorizing. Perhaps there's an optimal way to dial in your mental state so things could be twice as pleasant, and you'd be just as creative.

DEUTSCH: Yes, I think we should do that, but I don't think the flourishing meter would register this, even though we should do it, which I suppose is an argument against your theory.

HARRIS: Why would you think that? Let's go better than double. Let's say we raise your happiness by a factor of ten, so that each day you have from now on will feel like the best day you've ever had until this point. And let's assume you'll be just as creative. You're saying that the flourishing meter wouldn't register that?

DEUTSCH: I've slightly lost track of exactly what you're putting in my tea here. We're accustomed to levels of physical comfort that would have been inconceivable in the past. Newton or Mozart, say, lived lives of incredible discomfort. It was never really warm in the winter, it was never really cool in the summer, and they were constantly in danger of various kinds, and their clothes itched—I could go on forever—and yet it was possible to be happy under those circumstances. What you propose is definitely worthwhile, if only because the change itself would be a creative and beneficial thing. But once you've experienced the change, I don't think you're any happier. I think the only thing that makes you happy is creating.

HARRIS: Well, that's understandable coming from you, but it seems like a parochial definition of happiness. A scientist or an artist could easily sign on to it, but many people who can still register important swings in their well-being would not.

Let's say you're very happy, you're as fulfilled as you've ever been, but then your wife dies, or your child dies, and now you're not as happy, for obvious reasons. It seems to me that those reasons aren't best summarized as a sudden loss of creativity on your part.

DEUTSCH: I think they are. I think the reason you're unhappy in that situation is that your previous methods of making progress in thinking were tied to those people who have died, and you can't instantly replace what you'd have got from them.

HARRIS: What do you mean by "progress in thinking"?

DEUTSCH: Well, remember, I'm not elitist about what kinds of knowledge count as knowledge. No state of mind which one regards as preferable to another state of mind can be reached without creativity, and the process of striving successfully for it is happiness. Somebody who isn't interested in science and isn't interested in art or any of the things usually regarded as progress or creativity is still thinking about *something*. All happiness takes is for them to be a better person in regard to x after the thought than before. And x might be anything, might be something impossible to name, perhaps because it's not socially valued. It might be a particular way of interacting with one's family. But one would have to be improving it by thinking, "Yes, I could have done that better, and now I am doing it better." And that takes creativity. Lots of people don't do that, and I think they're in a bad way.

HARRIS: So, to come back to my argument about the worst possible misery for everyone being bad: What's wrong with that as a foundational claim? Just imagine a universe in which any conscious system that can suffer, suffers as much as it possibly can, for as long as it can, and nothing good ever comes of it. There's no silver lining to this suffering. It's just the worst possible hell that could exist. My foundational claim is that this is one possible state of the universe and that everything else is better than that.

DEUTSCH: Yes. I'm not denying there are objectively better and worse states, and that's one of the ones that's objectively worse.

HARRIS: But what's wrong with asserting it as a foundation for morality?

DEUTSCH: Well, different theories of morality and different theories of human flourishing will disagree about exactly which is the worst possible state.

HARRIS: I'll grant you that there might be some diversity of opinion. But let's just say that we have a universe of a finite number of beings. We're talking about the worst possible misery for everyone at time t, which is obviously defined by whoever "everyone" consists of. So, whatever beings are here, each is as miserable as he, she, or it can be, given the sort of being it is and given its entanglement with all other beings. There may be some vagaries here: you know, if something is really bad for one being, things might get a little better for another, because of how they're both situated.

DEUTSCH: Never mind that.

HARRIS: Okay. So let's say that if there's not *one* worst possible state, there are a finite number of worse possible states for all these beings to be in. And if we start making life better for them, or even just some of them, that represents movement in a direction that we will call "good." What I'm claiming is that any theory you have about goodness has to entail moving away from the worst possible misery (or miseries) for everyone. Whether it's Kant's categorical imperative, religion, consequentialism, virtue ethics, or something yet to be invented—a moral theory has to recognize that, in the space of possible experiences, moving away from the worst possible misery for everyone is, in fact, the cash value of goodness.

DEUTSCH: Yes, although once you're more than a millimeter away from this worst possible state, there are many ways of improving, and some of them are better than others. And once you get as far away from the worst possible state as we are, countless things affect what people think is right and wrong, good or evil, flourishing or not flourishing. It's like saying, "Okay, you're cured of cancer. Now you're happy," and the person may not be, because they weren't happy before the cancer and now they're back in the state they were in. And the fact that the state is now better than the worst possible doesn't actually resolve disagreements about what is better or worse.

HARRIS: That's why the metaphor of a moral landscape seems relevant. I acknowledge that there are peaks and valleys we may disagree about and we may in fact both be right. And in this landscape people with divergent ethics may be speaking about equivalent but mutually incompatible states of well-being.

DEUTSCH: And in that case there could be an even better peak, which is better than either.

HARRIS: Exactly, and we might never discover it, either because we're just unlucky or we don't have the right minds to discover it.

DEUTSCH: Since we're general-purpose thinking machines, I don't think the latter is possible.

HARRIS: Given enough memory and time—right. That's another issue which need not distract us. In that case, it could be just a contingent fact of the history of the cosmos that *Homo sapiens* will not explore this one peak that could be explored with the right technology. And yet that peak is better, in every rational way we could use the term "better," than where we are currently standing.

DEUTSCH: Yes. But we'll just bypass that one and find an even better one.

HARRIS: Well, yes, the frontiers of well-being could continually recede. We might never arrive at a true peak, or know that we have.

DEUTSCH: Yes. Well, the real fact is that whenever we make a discovery, it creates more problems. And the same is true of morality. We improve, and then we find that the improvement itself creates more problems.

HARRIS: But these problems become more refined. You're trying to decide which brand of solar panels to put on your roof, not how best to enslave your neighbors.

DEUTSCH: Or, we've abolished war and therefore we find self-defense more difficult.

HARRIS: But those seem like local wrinkles, due to the fact that many of us are still barbarians. They'll be smoothed out eventually, provided we keep making progress.

DEUTSCH: Yes, all problems are parochial. But I think the fact that improvements create new problems is a universal fact. A peak will only look like a peak while we're approaching it. When we're on top of it, we'll see lots of problems there.

HARRIS: But you can imagine how ethereal these high-class problems could be.

DEUTSCH: From our perspective, unimaginably so.

HARRIS: Certainly you've been in some state of high creativity and high pleasure and very low physical complication—a state in which, if it could endure for a long while, the kinds of problems you'd notice would be on the order of "Which is more sublimely beautiful? A or B?" As opposed to, say, "I can't get the cockroaches out of my kitchen, and I feel like killing myself."

DEUTSCH: I don't know. I'm agnostic on that one. For example, will there always be existential problems? I don't know. But I don't know why there should be a limit on the size of mistakes we can make.

HARRIS: Well, that is a current concern, to be sure. There seems to be no limit currently.

DEUTSCH: There will always be a way we can improve, but we may not take that path.

HARRIS: However, by your own description, we tend to successfully automate the solutions to problems in a way that doesn't require further work. As you said, we don't have to reinvent clothing. We just buy a new jacket when we need one, and the problem is solved.

DEUTSCH: But, you know, in a few billion years we'll have an existential problem. We'll have to get out of the solar system because the sun is going to become a red giant, and who knows what kinds of moral problems that will present? Presumably not the problem of who gets to leave, because by that time we'll have very powerful machinery. And maybe by that time whole classes of misery simply won't exist anymore, even slightly. But as I said, I don't see why that should be. How can there be a limit on the size of the mistakes we can make? I don't know. May that be our biggest problem!

HARRIS: How to escape this red giant in time without breaking our other commitments?

DEUTSCH: Yes.

HARRIS: I'm afraid I've genuinely lost the thread of our disagreement. One issue seems to be that you're allergic to the concept of there being a foundation to knowledge, moral or otherwise, and you follow Popper in this vein. I basically agree with you in that what most people claim to be a "foundation" clearly isn't. But the claim that reality exceeds our knowledge and remains perpetually open for exploration, whether we know it or not—and that this requires that we continually correct our theories—seems a fairly Popperian foundation. As I said, I think about morality as a navigation problem, constrained by the laws of nature, whatever they turn out to be. We can even dispense with the concept of morality without changing my thesis. We are conscious systems moving in a space of all possible experiences, and we will continually discover that some are better and some are worse, some are more creative, some are less so, and we're not wrong to want to move away from pointless misery.

DEUTSCH: We'll be changing our opinion of what constitutes better and worse, and we'll be doing that by the methods of reason. But this may be an even more fundamental disagreement between us. I think we will do this not predominantly by the methods of science. In *The Moral Landscape* you quote somebody as saying, "There couldn't be a science of the human condition," and you're very scathing about that. You describe that as faith in the intrinsic limits of reason. Again, you use the word "science" in a slightly different way than I do, but I have faith, if you like, in the *non*existence of limits on reason. You can form theories about moral questions. You can improve those by the methods of reason. And *science* is only occasionally relevant to that. I don't think it's fundamentally relevant to it.

HARRIS: My criticism of that quotation—about there being no science of human nature—is synonymous with the faith in reason that I share with you. The boundary between science and the rest of reason is not clear, and we'll continue to surmount it in surprising ways. I use this example somewhere, on the question of whether or not the Shroud of Turin is a relic of the historical Jesus. That's a religious claim. It's a claim about history. It doesn't seem like a claim about science at all. But then someone invents radiocarbon dating, and now it's a claim about chemistry—or physics, depending on who's doing the experiment. This sort of thing continually happens, and it's going to happen more and more, and it's unidirectional. The movement is always toward science and never away. Science keeps capturing ground which it never loses.

DEUTSCH: If we decide to all migrate into the Matrix and stay there, then all questions about what we should do next will not be scientific questions, apart from extending the Matrix or something.

HARRIS: Well, let's plant a flag there. That's a fascinating topic for a future conversation. Obviously, the question about where we're headed technologically isn't going away; it will only become more and more interesting. Thank you for being so generous with your time, David.

Consciousness and the Self

A CONVERSATION WITH ANIL SETH

Anil Seth is a professor of cognitive and computational neuroscience at the University of Sussex and founding codirector of the Sackler Centre for Consciousness Science. The aim of the Sackler Centre is to translate an understanding of the complex brain networks underpinning consciousness into new clinical approaches to psychiatric and neurological disorders.

Seth focuses on the biological basis of consciousness, bringing neuroscience, mathematics, artificial intelligence, psychology, philosophy, and psychiatry together in his laboratory. In our conversation, we discuss how consciousness might emerge in nature, perception as a "controlled hallucination," emotion, the experience of "pure consciousness," consciousness as "integrated information," measures of "brain complexity," psychedelics, different aspects of the self, conscious AI, and many other topics.

HARRIS: I first discovered you after your much-loved 2017 TED Talk entitled "Your Brain Hallucinates Your Conscious Reality."* Before we get started, perhaps you can briefly describe your scientific and intellectual background.

SETH: My intellectual interest has always been in understanding the physical and biological basis of consciousness and what practical implications that might have in neurology and psychiatry. But when I was an undergraduate at Cambridge University in the early 1990s, consciousness was not something you could study scientifically; it was still very much in the domain of philosophy. At that time, I still thought physics was the way to solve every difficult problem in science and philosophy. So I started off studying physics, but then I became diverted toward psychology as offering a more direct route to issues of mind and brain. I ended up graduating with a degree in experimental psychology in 1994.

After that, I moved to Sussex University to do a master's and then a PhD in computer science and AI. This was partly because I felt the need to move beyond the box-and-arrow models of cognition that so dominated psychology and cognitive science in the nineties, toward something with more explanatory power, and the rise of connectionism along with the new methods and tools in AI seemed to provide that. So I stayed at Sussex and did a PhD in the area now called artificial life, where my thesis involved some ecological modeling and computational and conceptual work on how brains, bodies, and environments interact and in doing so coconstruct cognitive processes.

But I'd left consciousness behind a little bit, so when I finished my PhD, in 2000, I went to San Diego to the Neurosciences Institute (NSI) to work with Gerald Edelman, because San Diego was one of the few places you could legitimately study consciousness and work on its neural basis. Edelman was there; Francis Crick was at the Salk Institute, in La Jolla; people were really doing this stuff. So I stayed for about six years, working on consciousness, bringing together the different tra-

---

* https://www.ted.com/talks/anil_seth_how_your_brain_hallucinates_your_conscious
  _reality.

ditions of math, physics, and computer science, as well as the tools of cognitive neuroscience. And for the last ten years or so I've been back at Sussex, where I codirect a lab called the Sackler Centre for Consciousness Science. It's one of a growing number of research centers explicitly dedicated to studying the brain as the biological basis of consciousness.

HARRIS: That's a wonderful pedigree. I never met Edelman. I've read his books, and I'm familiar with his work on consciousness; he had a famously titanic ego, if I'm not mistaken. I don't want you to say anything you're not comfortable with, but everyone who I've ever heard had an encounter with Edelman was amazed at how much space he personally took up in the conversation.

SETH: I've heard that, too, and I think there's some truth to it. What I can say from the other side is that when I worked for him and with him, I found it an inspirational experience, and I felt very lucky to be there. He had a large ego, but he also knew a lot and had contributed to major revolutions in biology and neuroscience. Often he treated the people he worked with very kindly. He didn't go outside of the Neurosciences Institute that much—it was very much his empire—but when you were within it you got a lot of his time.

I remember most days being called into his office for a discussion about this or that subject, or this or that new paper. These were very instructive experiences for me. I know he was quite difficult in interviews and conversations outside the NSI, which is a shame, because his legacy really is pretty extraordinary.

HARRIS: No doubt you and I have many interests in common. Consciousness is really the bull's-eye as far as my interests go, and this is probably true for everyone, if they actually thought about it. It's the most important thing in the universe, because it's the basis of all of our happiness and suffering and everything we value. It's the only space in which anything that matters *can* matter. So the fact that you're studying it and thinking about it as much as you are makes you the perfect person to talk to. How do you define consciousness?

SETH: There's a sort of easy, folk definition, which is that consciousness is the presence of any kind of subjective experience whatsoever. There is a phenomenal world of subjective experience that has the character of being private, that's full of perceptual qualia, or content—colors, shapes, beliefs, emotions, other kinds of feeling states, and this world can go away completely in states of general anesthesia or dreamless sleep. It's very easy to define consciousness that way. To define it more technically will always be a bit of a challenge.

Sometimes there's too much emphasis on having a technical definition of consciousness. The history of science has shown us many times that definitions evolve, along with our scientific understanding of a phenomenon. We don't take the definition and then transcribe it into scientific knowledge in a unidirectional way. So as long as we agree that consciousness picks out a significant phenomenon in nature, which is the presence of subjective experience, then we're on reasonably safe terrain.

HARRIS: All of our definitions of consciousness are circular: we just substitute another word for consciousness in the definition, like "sentience," "awareness," "subjectivity," or "experience." Even a term like "qualia," I think, is parasitic on the undefined concept of consciousness.

SETH: There's a lot of confusion. I'm always surprised by how often people confuse consciousness with self-consciousness. Our conscious experience of selfhood is part of our conscious experiences, but only a subset of those experiences. And then there are arguments about whether there's such a thing as a "phenomenal" consciousness that's different from "access" consciousness—where "phenomenal consciousness" refers to the impression we have of a rich scene before us which might exceed whatever we have cognitive access to, and "access consciousness" refers to the way in which the contents of consciousness can be flexibly deployed for a variety of different functions. Here I am drawing on the work of people such as the philosopher Ned Block, who maintain that this distinction is crucial; others would say, "No, there's no such thing as phenomenal consciousness beyond access consciousness." So yes, there is a certain circularity, but some of the distinctions that have been made are very useful when interpreting experimental results. For instance, when we consider evidence that consciousness involves a widespread "ignition" of brain activity, it's important to know whether we are talking about access consciousness or about phenomenal consciousness (or at least whether the experimenters accept, or do not accept, this distinction). For my money, I should say, the distinction is highly relevant to a science of consciousness.

HARRIS: I want to revisit the point you made about not transcribing a definition of a concept into our science as a way of capturing reality. There are things that we have a folk-psychological sense of, which completely break apart once we start studying them at the level of the brain. Take memory, for instance. We have the intuitive sense that memory is one thing. That is, we have the sense that to remember something is more or less the same operation regardless of what we are remembering—what you ate for dinner last night, remembering your name, remembering who the first president of the United States was, remembering how to swing a tennis racket. We have this one word for the way in which the past can be etched into our minds and brains, but neurologically these are distinct operations. You can disrupt one while the others remain intact.

Consciousness may be something like that, or it may not. I'm more enamored of the so-called hard problem of consciousness than you are, I think. We should talk about that, but before we do, the definition I want to put in play—which I know you're familiar with—is the one that the philosopher Thomas Nagel put forward in his famous essay "What Is It Like to Be a Bat?" which reads in part:

> Conscious experience is a widespread phenomenon. It occurs at many levels of animal life, though we cannot be sure of its presence in the simpler organisms, and it is very difficult to say in general what provides evidence of it. (Some extremists have been prepared to deny it even of mammals other than man.) No doubt it occurs in countless forms totally unimaginable to

us, on other planets in other solar systems throughout the universe. But no matter how the form may vary, the fact that an organism has conscious experience *at all* means, basically, that there is something it is like to *be* that organism. There may be further implications about the form of the experience; there may even (though I doubt it) be implications about the behavior of the organism. But fundamentally an organism has conscious mental states if and only if there is something that it is like to *be* that organism—something it is like *for* the organism.

That definition isn't easy to operationalize, and it's not a technical definition, but there's something sufficiently rudimentary about it that has always worked for me. How do you feel about Nagel's definition as a starting point?

SETH: I like it very much. It's difficult to argue with, as a fundamental expression of what we mean by consciousness. When considering whether consciousness is best thought of as "one thing" or as something that breaks down into separable phenomena, I'm sympathetic to the view that—heuristically, at least—the best way to scientifically study consciousness, and philosophically to think about it, is to recognize that we might be misled about the extent to which consciousness is a unified phenomenon: just as you said for memory, it's possible to see how conscious experiences of the world and of the self can come apart in various ways.

HARRIS: To be clear, I agree with you there: we could be misled about how unified consciousness is. The thing that's irreducible to me is, there's a difference between there being something that it's like to be what one is, and not. There are many different ways in which the lights can be on, and some might surprise us; for instance, it's possible that the lights are on in our brains in more than one spot. But the question is always, "Is there something that it's like to be that bit of information processing, or that bit of matter?" And that's always the cash value of a claim about consciousness.

SETH: Yes, I'd agree with that. It's perfectly reasonable to put the question that way—that for a conscious organism, there's something it's like to be that organism. And the thought is, there will be some physical, biological, or perhaps informational basis to that distinction.

HARRIS: You've written about why we don't need to waste much time on the hard problem. Let's briefly remind people what the hard problem is. David Chalmers and I have spoken about it, and I've spoken about it with others, but perhaps you could introduce us to the hard problem as you see it.

SETH: The hard problem has been—and rightly so—one of the most influential philosophical contributions to the consciousness debate for the last twenty years or so. It encapsulates the fundamental mystery that for some physical systems there is also an inner universe. For some systems, there is the presence of conscious experience, there is something-it-is-like-to-be that system. Whereas for other systems—tables, chairs, probably all current computers—there is nothing-it-is-like-to-be that system. What the hard problem does is push that intuition a bit further, to distinguish it from a set of so-called easy problems. The easy problems, according to Chalmers, are those of figuring out how the brain works in terms of its functions, at every level of detail: how perception works; how we utter certain linguistic phrases; how we move around in the world adaptively; how the brain supports perception, cognition, behavior in all its richness. The hard problem is understanding how and why any solution to the easy problem—any explanation of how the brain does what it does in terms of behavior, perception, and so on—has anything to do with conscious experiences.[*]

The hard problem has its conceptual power over us because it invites us to imagine systems—very often philosophical zombies—that are equivalent in terms of their function and behavior to you or me or a bat, but that instantiate no phenomenal properties at all. The lights are

---

[*] Here is the *locus classicus* for the hard problem: D. J. Chalmers, *The Conscious Mind: In Search of a Fundamental Theory* (New York: Oxford University Press, 1996).

off for the philosophical zombies. And if we can imagine such a system, then it becomes an enormous challenge to answer the question "Well, what could it be about real me, real you, real bat, that also gives rise to these phenomenal properties?" And it's because Chalmers argues that such things as philosophical zombies are conceivable that the hard problem seems to present such an obstacle.

These conceivability arguments, I think, are pretty weak. The more you know about a system—the more we know about the easy problem— the less plausible it becomes to imagine a zombie alternative. Think about being a kid and looking up at the sky and seeing a 747 flying overhead, and somebody asks you to imagine a 747 flying backwards. Well, you can imagine a 747 flying backwards, but the more you learn about aerodynamics, about engineering, the harder it is to do so. You simply can't build a 747 that way. That's my worry about this kind of conceivability argument. I can't imagine in a serious way the existence of a philosophical zombie. I don't think this is a failure of imagination on my part. Rather, it rests on a highly incomplete knowledge of neuroscience. And if I can't imagine a zombie, then the hard problem loses some of its force.

HARRIS: That's interesting. I don't think it loses all of its force, or at least it doesn't for me. For me, the hard problem has never rested on the zombie argument.* So let's just stipulate that philosophical zombies are impossible, or at least what's called nomologically impossible. Let's assume that we live in a universe where, if you built something that can do what I can do, that something would be conscious. For me, the hard problem arises from the fact that no explanation of consciousness promises the same sort of intuitive closure that other scientific explanations do.

Consciousness is not like life, which is an analogy you and many other scientists have drawn as to how we can make an explanatory break-

---

* **SETH:** Following up with Dave Chalmers substantiates this point. His original conception of the hard problem did not reference zombies. It focused on explanatory sufficiency. However, it's still the case that the zombie argument (e.g., in Chalmers, 1996) is a powerful way to motivate the hard problem.

through here. It used to be that people thought life could never be explained in mechanistic terms. The philosophical view called vitalism suggested that we needed some animating spirit, an élan vital, in the wheelworks to make sense of the fact that living systems appear to be so different from dead ones. It was thought very difficult to understand that difference in mechanistic terms, and then, lo and behold, we managed to do just that.

I'm happy to have you defend this analogy, but the difference for me is that everything you want to say about life—with the exception of the *conscious experience of being alive*—can be defined in terms of extrinsic functional relationships among material parts: reproduction, growth, healing, metabolism, homeostasis, and so forth. All of this is physics, chemistry, and biology, and need not be described in any other terms. Even something like vision—the transduction of light energy into electrical and chemical energy in the brain and the mapping of visual space onto a visual cortex—all of this makes sense in mechanistic, physical terms, until you add this business of "Oh, but for some of these processes there's something that it is like to be that process." So with or without zombies, the hard problem remains hard.

SETH: I think it's an open question whether the analogy to life will turn out to be false or not. Scientists and philosophers over the centuries have encountered things that have seemed inexplicable that have turned out to be explicable. So I don't think we should rule out the analogy and say there'll be something really different this time about consciousness.

There's a more heuristic aspect to this. If we run with the life analogy, what that leads us to do is to isolate the phenomenal properties that coconstitute what it is for us to be conscious. We think about conscious selfhood as being distinct from conscious perception of the outside world. We can think about conscious experiences of volition and of agency that are also central to our experience of self. These give us phenomenological explanatory targets that we can then try to account for with particular kinds of mechanisms. It may turn out that after doing this we still find some hard-problem residue. But maybe it won't turn out like that.

We need to retain a focus on phenomenology. And this is another reason why I think the hard-/easy-problem distinction is unhelpful. When addressing the easy problem we are basically instructed to not worry about phenomenology; all we should worry about is function and behavior. So the hard problem, this central mystery of why there is experience rather than no experience, gathers within its remit everything to do with phenomenology.

The alternative approach is something I've characterized as the "real problem." David Chalmers has described a similar approach as the "mapping problem." The Chilean neuroscientist Francisco Varela talked about a similar set of ideas that he called "neurophenomenology." What these approaches share is the following idea: to not try to solve the hard problem, to not try to explain how it's possible that consciousness is part of the universe, but rather to individuate different kinds of phenomenological properties and draw explanatory mapping between neurological, biological, physical mechanisms and these phenomenological properties.

Now, once we've done that, we can begin to explain, not why is there experience at all, but why a certain experience is the way it is and not some other way. And we can predict when certain experiences will have particular phenomenal characters, and so on. Then we'll have achieved a lot more than is currently the case, and along the way we have developed novel kinds of conceptual frameworks.

There's another aspect to how we think about the hard problem, which has to do with the scope of explanation. Why should we ask more of a theory of consciousness than we ask of other kinds of scientific theories? We seem to want more from an explanation of consciousness than we do from explanations in biology or physics. We want it to feel intuitively right. And I wonder why. Just because we're trying to explain something fundamental about ourselves doesn't mean we should apply different standards than those we would apply in other fields of science. It just might be that we won't get a feeling that something is intuitively correct when it is in fact a very good scientific account of the origin and nature of phenomenal properties. An account that allows explanation, prediction, and control. Certainly, scientific explanations are not instantiations. There's no sense in which a good theory of consciousness should be expected to suddenly realize the phenomenal properties it's explaining. I worry that we ask too much of theories of consciousness in these ways.

HARRIS: It's not a matter of asking too much of a theory of consciousness. There are a few areas in science where the accepted explanation is taken as a brute fact or as a mere instrument of predicting the results of future experiments. Quantum mechanics famously falls in this category—and, to this day, it resists being understood in realistic terms. But everything we can say about life, even the strange details of molecular biology—how information in the genome gets out and creates the rest of a human body—still runs through when we look at the details. It can be difficult to visualize, but the more we visualize it, the more we describe it, the closer we get to something that conserves our intuitions.

Consider the flow of water—the fact that in its liquid state, the molecules of water are loosely bound and slide past one another. Well, that seems exactly like what should happen at the microscopic level to explain the gross property of the wetness of water. However, if consciousness just happens to arise from some minimum number of information-processing units knit together in a certain configuration, firing at a certain hertz—and if you change any of those parameters and the lights go out—that, for me, still seems like a mere brute fact, rather than an explanation of consciousness. It may be a correlation that we decide is the crucial one, but I've never heard a description of consciousness of a sort like "integrated information," Giulio Tononi's phrase, that makes the emergence of consciousness any more intelligible than that.

SETH: Sure, I'd be terribly disappointed too, if the answer turned out to be, "Yes, you need 612,000 neurons wired up in a small network," and that's it. That would seem ridiculous and arbitrary and unsatisfying. The hope is that as we progress beyond simply identifying brute correlates of conscious states, toward accounts that provide more satisfying bridges between mechanism and phenomenology—that explain, for instance, why a visual experience has the phenomenal character it does and not some other kind of phenomenal character—the hope is that things won't seem so arbitrary. I believe that following this route will turn out to be empirically productive, to provide a way to actually do science by thinking about how to operationalize phenomenology in various ways, and then to put these operationalizations to the empirical test.

It's difficult to think how, scientifically, to solve the hard problem head-on. However, if we follow the "real problem" route instead, then I agree there might still be a residue of mystery, a kernel of something fundamental left unexplained. But I don't think we can take that as a given, because we can't—I certainly can't—predict what I'd feel as being intuitively or scientifically satisfying, when I don't know what the explanations bridging mechanism and phenomenology are going to look like in ten or twenty years. We've already moved past just saying this area or that area is the seat of consciousness, or that mere synchronous activity between groups of neurons in the so-called gamma band, about forty Hz, as being the mechanism of awareness. These sorts of "explanations" indeed do not explain very much at all. More recently, and I'm sure we'll talk more about this later, frameworks like predictive processing and integrated information have emerged prominently in the intellectual landscape. These frameworks offer much more interesting connections between mechanism and phenomenology. Now as things stand, as we'll discuss, they aren't completely satisfying either, but there's a trajectory here that's beginning to take shape.

HARRIS: Well, let's talk about that trajectory. But before we do, I'm just wondering: At what point do you think consciousness emerges in lower animals? Do you think there's something that it's like to be a fly, say?

SETH: That's a really difficult problem. I have to be agnostic about this. Again, it's striking how views on these things seem to have changed over recent decades. It seems completely unarguable to me that other mammals, all other mammals, have conscious experiences of one sort or another. We share so much in the way of the relevant neuroanatomy and neurophysiology, and we exhibit so many of the same behaviors, that it would be remarkable to claim otherwise.

HARRIS: Actually, it wasn't that long ago that you could still hear people say that consciousness was so dependent on language that they wondered whether human infants were conscious—to say nothing of dogs and anything else not human.

SETH: Yes, that's absolutely right. The idea that consciousness was intimately and constitutively bound up with language or with higher-order executive processing of one sort or another exemplifies the pernicious anthropocentrism that we bring to questions of consciousness, sometimes without realizing it. We think we're superintelligent, we know we're conscious, and we tend to judge everything by that benchmark. And what's the most advanced thing about humans? Well, if you're gifted with language, you're going to say "language." In hindsight it seems to me remarkable that people should make these naive errors, associating consciousness so closely with language. This is not to say that consciousness and language don't have any intimate relation. I think they do. Language shapes a lot of our conscious experiences and has its own distinct phenomenology. But certainly it's a very poor criterion for attributing subjective states to other creatures.

So, mammals for sure are conscious. That's easy to say, given the neurophysiological and behavioral similarities with primates and with humans. But then it gets more complicated. Birds have brain structures for which one can establish analogies, and in some cases homologies, with mammalian brain structures. And in some bird species, especially scrub jays and corvids, one can observe sophisticated behavior suggestive of consciousness. It seems very possible that birds have conscious experiences. I realize that the only basis to make these judgments is in light of what we know about the neural mechanisms underlying consciousness, and the functional behavioral properties of consciousness, as they appear in mammals. It has to be a slow extrapolation from such cases, because we lack the mechanistic answer about the sufficient basis of consciousness, and so we can't look for it directly in another species.

Then we get beyond birds, and way out on a distant phylogenetic branch there is the octopus, which provides an extraordinary example of convergent evolution. They're very smart, they have a lot of neurons (about half a billion), but our common ancestor was about 750 million years ago, probably some simple kind of worm. We have very little in common. They have three hearts, eight appendages that behave semi-autonomously, jet propulsion, skin that tastes. Back in 2009 I was lucky enough to spend a week with them in a lab in Naples, the Stazione Zoologica. You certainly get the impression of another conscious presence, but of a very different kind. This is instructive, because it challenges the assumption that there's only one way of being conscious and that's our way. There's likely many ways of being conscious, and the octopus is an example of a very different mind and likely a conscious mind, too.

Now, when we consider creatures like fish and insects, which are simpler in all sorts of ways than mammals, it's difficult to know where to draw the line—if indeed there is a line to be drawn, if it's not just the gradual shading out of consciousness with no categorical divide, which I think is plausible. Many fish exhibit behaviors that seem suggestive of consciousness. They'll self-administer analgesia when they're given painful stimulation, they'll avoid places associated with painful stimulation, and so on. The precautionary principle comes into play here: the idea that the possibility of conscious suffering is sufficient to establish an ethical imperative to avoid imposing such potentially aversive states on other creatures. We should assume that creatures are conscious unless we have good evidence that they're not.

HARRIS: Let's talk about aspects of consciousness you've identified as distinct. There are at least three. You've spoken about the level of consciousness, the contents of consciousness, and the experience of having a conscious self, which many people conflate with consciousness as a mental property. There's obviously a relationship between these three, but they're not the same. Let's start with this notion of the level of consciousness. How is being conscious nonsynonymous with being awake in the human sense?

SETH: Let me first amplify what you said. In making these distinctions—level, content, and self—I'm not claiming that they pick out completely independent aspects of conscious experience; there are lots of interdependencies. I just think that they are heuristically useful ways to address the issue. By making these distinctions we can do different kinds of experiments, trying to isolate the mechanistic basis of distinct phenomenal properties. Now, when it comes to conscious level, the simplest way to think of it is as a scale, ranging from when the lights are out—when you're brain dead or under general anesthesia, or perhaps in a very deep dreamless state of sleep—passing through diminished levels of consciousness as in drowsiness, all the way to being vividly awake and alert: full conscious experience.

Articulated this way, in most cases the level of consciousness will parallel wakefulness or physiological arousal. But there are exceptions which are sufficient to establish consciousness and wakefulness as distinct properties. When you fall asleep, you lose consciousness in early stages, but you can be conscious when you're asleep. One example of this is called dreaming. You're physiologically asleep, but you're experiencing a vivid inner life. On the other side—and this is where the rubber of consciousness science hits the road of neurology—you have putatively unconsciousness states with high levels of physiological arousal. This condition is called the vegetative state or "unresponsive wakefulness syndrome." The idea is that the body is going through physiological cycles of arousal, from sleep to wakefulness, but there's no consciousness happening at all. The lights simply aren't on.

HARRIS: There are a few other distinctions to make here. For instance, general anesthesia is distinct from deep sleep, as a matter of neurophysiology.

SETH: Certainly. Deep general anesthesia is nothing like sleep. Whenever you go in for an operation and the anesthesiologist tries to make you feel comfortable by saying, "We'll just send you to sleep for a while, and then you'll wake up and it'll all be done," they're lying to you. The state of general anesthesia is different and for good reason: if you were just put into a state of sleep, you'd wake up as soon as the operation started, and that wouldn't be very pleasant. It's surprising how far down you can take people in general anesthesia—almost to a level of isoelectric brain activity, where there's pretty much nothing going on at all—and still bring them back. Deep states of anesthesia have more in common with coma than with sleep. When you fall asleep, you might not be sure what time it is when you wake up, but you'll still have the sense of some time having passed. Coming round from general anesthesia you could have been under five minutes, five hours, or five years.

Many people have had the nonexperience of general anesthesia, and in some weird way I look forward to the next time I get to have it, because it's almost a reassuring experience, at least at the edges. It's complete oblivion.

HARRIS: Except we have this problem of anesthesia awareness, which is everyone's worst nightmare. People have surgery but the anesthesia hasn't taken them deep enough, yet they're immobilized and can't signal that they're aware of what is happening to them.

SETH: I know, but that's a failure of anesthesia, not a characteristic of the anesthetic state. In most serious operations, you're also administered a muscle paralytic so you don't move around while you're being operated on, and that's why it's a particularly nightmarish scenario. But if anesthesia is working properly, it's oblivion all the way. To experience those moments of complete oblivion, or rather the edges of them, is very enlightening.

HARRIS: Here's where the hard problem does emerge, because it's difficult, perhaps impossible, to distinguish between oblivion and a failure of memory. Has consciousness really been interrupted? Take anesthesia and deep sleep. Most people think that with both there is a true hiatus in consciousness. I'm prepared to believe that that's not true of deep sleep. Stage four sleep might have a qualitative character, but we just don't remember what it's like. I'm someone who rarely remembers his dreams, but I'm prepared to believe that I dream vividly every night. And we know, even in the case of general anesthesia, that we give people amnesia drugs so they won't remember whatever they wouldn't want to remember.

Recently, during a procedure that did not require me to go under full anesthesia, I had the experience of what's called twilight sleep. There was a period when I was coming to, about a half hour, that I don't remember. And although my wife and I were having a conversation, it was clear to her that I wouldn't remember a word of it. I was saying how perfectly recovered I was, and how miraculous it was to be back, and she said, "Yes, but you're not going to remember any of this." Apparently I said, "Okay, well, let's test it. Say something now, and we'll see if I remember it." And she said, "This whole conversation is the test, dummy! You're not going to remember any of this." And I have no memory of that conversation.

SETH: You're right, of course; even in stages of deep sleep, people underestimate the presence of conscious experiences. This has been demonstrated by so-called serial awakening experiments, in which you wake somebody up at various times during sleep cycles and ask them straightaway, "What's on your mind?" Quite often people will report very simple sorts of experiences—static images and so on—even when they're not in the REM sleep that is normally associated with dreaming. And I concede that amnesia may contribute to the posthoc impression of what general anesthesia was like. But there's all the difference in the world between the twilight zone of deep sleep and the oblivion of full-on general anesthesia, where it's not just that you don't remember anything, it's a real hiatus of consciousness.

HARRIS: I've had a general anesthetic as well, and there is something uncanny about disappearing and being brought back without a sense of intervening time. Many people can go to sleep and set an intention to wake up at a certain time, and they wake up at that time, often to the minute. It's clear there's some time-keeping function happening in our brain all the while. But there's something about a general anesthetic which seems like the hard drive just got rebooted and who knows how long the computer was off?

SETH: Exactly.

HARRIS: Okay, let's talk about the other two aspects of consciousness. How do you think about the contents of consciousness?

SETH: When we're conscious, we're conscious of something, and this is what most empirical consciousness research focuses on. You take somebody who is conscious, and you can investigate what aspects of their perception are unconscious and not reflected in any phenomenal properties, and what aspects of their perception are reflected or instantiated in a phenomenal property. What's the difference between conscious and unconscious processing, if you like. Another question would be: What's the difference between different modalities of conscious perception?

In laboratory situations, we normally focus on one or two modalities: vision, or touch, for example. But in normal life, outside the lab, our consciousness has an evident multimodal character. There will be sound, sight, experiences of touch—say, if you're sitting down or holding something—and a whole range of self-related experiences of body ownership, including all the signals coming from deep inside the body. The basic idea of conscious content is to study what mechanisms give rise to the particular composition of consciousness at any one time. The reason it's useful to think of conscious content as separate from conscious level is partly that we can appeal to different theoretical and empirical frameworks.

The way I like to think about conscious perception is in terms of prediction, in terms of what's often called the Bayesian brain, or predictive processing. The idea that perception in general works more from the top down, or from the inside out, rather than the bottom up or the outside in. This has a long history in philosophy—back to Kant and long before that too. The straw man here is that perception happens when sensory signals impinge on receptors and progress deeper and deeper into the brain, so that at some point a kind of "ignition" happens—or something happens—and at that point you become conscious of those sensory signals, or of what those sensory signals represent.

That is the wrong way to think about perception. Let's simplify it. The problem is something like the following: The brain is locked inside a bony skull, and let's assume for the sake of this argument that the perception problem is the problem of figuring out what's out there in the world giving rise to sensory signals impinging on our sensory surfaces—eyes and ears, and so on. Now, these sensory signals are noisy and ambiguous. They won't have a one-to-one mapping with things out there in the world, whatever those may be. They don't come labeled for the brain with convenient tags like "this is vision" or "this is hearing." So perception has to involve a process of inference, of "best guessing," in which the brain combines the sensory data with prior expectations or (usually implicit) beliefs about the way the world is, to come up with its best guess about the causes of that sensory data. Within this framework, what we perceive is constituted by those multilevel predictions that try to account for the sensory signals. We perceive what the brain infers caused those signals, not the sensory signals themselves, nor things in the world "in themselves" either. There is no such thing as "direct perception" of the world or of the self.

In this view, there is no place for "raw sensory experience" of any kind. All perceptual experience is an inference of one sort or another. Taking the predictive processing perspective, you can ask all sorts of interesting questions, like "What kinds of predictions? How do predictions or expectations affect what we consciously perceive, consciously report? What kinds of predictions may still go on 'under the hood' and not instantiate any phenomenal properties?"

Predictive processing gives us a set of conceptual and mathematical tools we can use to build bridges between phenomenology and mechanism. In this case the bridges between descriptions of phenomenology and functional properties of consciousness on the one side, and neural circuitry on the other, linked by the computational mechanisms of Bayesian inference. So instead of asking questions like "Is the early visual cortex associated with visual experience?" we might ask questions like "Are Bayesian priors or posteriors associated with conscious phenomenology?" Or "Are prediction errors associated with conscious phenomenology?"

HARRIS: In your TED Talk, you talk about consciousness as a controlled hallucination. The psychologist Chris Frith has called consciousness a fantasy that coincides with reality. Can you say a little more about that and how it relates to the role of top-down prediction in perception?

SETH: They're both nice phrases. It's been difficult to pin down where the phrase "controlled hallucination" came from. I heard it from Chris Frith as well, and I've asked him and others where it originated. We can trace it to a seminar given by Ramesh Jain at UC San Diego sometime in the nineties, but there the trail goes cold.

Anyway, the idea of "controlled hallucination" stands in contrast to a naive realism about perception wherein we assume that what we visually perceive is the way things actually are in the real world. We might call that idea "veridical perception." In hallucinations, as standardly understood, we have perceptual experiences that have no corresponding reference in the real world. The idea of a controlled hallucination, or of a fantasy that coincides with reality, is simply to say that normal perception always involves a balancing act between sensory signals coming from the world and interpretations and predictions about the causes of those sensations. We see what we expect to see in this Bayesian sense; we never just "see" the sensory data, whatever that would mean. For example, it's built into our visual systems that light comes from above, because our visual systems have evolved in a situation where the sun is never below us. This implicit expectation causes us to perceive shadows in a particular way, or, rather, we'll perceive curved surfaces as being curved one way or another under the assumption that light comes from above. We're not aware of having that constraint built deep into our visual system, but it's there.

The idea is that every perception we have is partly constituted by such predictions, these interpretive powers that the brain brings to bear on sensory data. What we call hallucinations are just the result of tipping the balance slightly more toward the brain's own internal predictions. Here's another everyday example of this. When there are lots of white, fluffy clouds, you can sometimes perceive faces in them if you try hard enough. This is called pareidolia: the perception of patterns in noise. Now, that's a kind of hallucination. You're seeing something that other people might not see. In this example it's not accompanied by delusion—you know it's a hallucination—but it does show how our perceptual content is always framed by interpretation.

HARRIS: Another good everyday example is dreams. In dreams, our brain is doing something similar to what it does in the waking state, except the frontal lobes have come offline enough so that there's not the same kind of reality testing going on. And our perception in this case is not being constrained by outer stimuli, it's being generated from within. Would this be an analogous situation, where our top-down prediction mechanisms are roving unconstrained by sensory data?

SETH: Dreams certainly show that you don't need external sensory data to have vivid conscious perception. The phenomenon of dreaming is interestingly different. Dream content is very much less constrained. Naive realism just goes nuts in dreams, doesn't it? People can change identity, locations can change, weird things happen and you don't experience them as being weird.

HARRIS: That's the weirdest part of dreams—that the weirdness generally goes undetected.

SETH: Yes, which is, I think, a great example of how we often overestimate the insight we have about what our conscious experiences are like. We tend to assume we know exactly what's happening in our conscious experience all the time, whether it's weird or not. Dreams show that that's not always the case.

But controlled hallucination is as present in normal nondreaming perception as it is in dreaming. All our perception is constituted by our brain's predictions of the causes of sensory input. Most of the time we'll agree about this perceptual content. If I see a table and claim it's such-and-such a color, you'll probably agree with me, and we don't have to go into the philosophical, inverted-spectra debate here. It's just a case of tending to report the same sorts of things when faced with the same sorts of sensory input. We don't think there's anything particularly constructed about the way we perceive things, because we all generally agree about what we perceive. But when something tips the balance—maybe under certain pharmacological stimulus, maybe in dreams, maybe in certain states of psychosis and mental illness—then one person's predictions about the causes of sensory information may differ from those of other people. And if you're an outlier, then these other people will say, "Ah, now you're hallucinating! You're reporting something that isn't there." My friend the musician and playwright Baba Brinkman—whom I worked with on *The Rap Guide to Consciousness*—put it beautifully: "What we call reality is just when we all agree about our hallucinations."

HARRIS: This leaves open the question of what's happening when we experience something fundamentally new or where our expectations are violated. We're using terms like "predictions" or "expectations," but there's scope for confusion here. Just imagine, for instance, that some malicious zookeeper put a fully grown tiger in your kitchen while you were sleeping. When you come down for your morning coffee, you will see this tiger in the kitchen, even though you have no reasonable expectation to be met by a tiger in the morning. I think it's safe to assume you'll see it even before you've had your cup of coffee. So, given this, what do we mean by expectations at the level of the brain?

SETH: That's an important point. The language of the Bayesian brain and of predictive processing bandies around terms like "prediction," "expectation," "prediction error," "surprise," and so on. It's important to recognize that these terms don't connote psychological surprise, or explicit beliefs, or expectations I might consciously hold. Certainly, if I go downstairs in the morning I'm not consciously expecting to see a tiger; however, if there are sensory inputs that pick out things like edges, my visual system will best interpret them as edges, and if they pick out stripes, it will interpret those as stripes. It's not unexpected to see something with an edge, and it may not be unexpected, at a deeper level of my visual cortex, to see something with stripes. It may not even be unexpected, from my brain's point of view, to see something that looks a bit like a face. These low-level "best guesses" about the causes of sensory input then give rise to high-level predictions about those causes. And ultimately, the "best guess" which reaches conscious experience is that there's some kind of animal there and, indeed, that it's a tiger. I don't think there's a conflict here. We can see new things because new things are built up from simpler elements for which we'll have adequate predictions built up over evolution and over development and over prior experience.

HARRIS: And one thing you pointed out—at least in one of your papers, or maybe in the TED Talk—is that different contents of consciousness have different characteristics, so that visual perception is object-based in a way that internal perception is not. This sensing of an experience—like nausea, say, or even an emotion, like sadness—doesn't have all of the features of perceiving an object in visual space. When you're looking at an object in visual space, there's the sense of location, there's the sense that anything that has a front will also have a back, that if you walked around the object you'd be given different views of it. I'm looking at my computer now, and I've probably never seen my computer from precisely this angle, and if I walked around it, I'd see thousands of different slices of this thing in the movie of my life, yet there's this unitary sense of an object in space with a front and back and sides. None of this applies when we're thinking about our internal experience. That's an interesting distinction, which, again, is an instance in which our terminology for being conscious of things or perceiving things doesn't get at the phenomenology very well.

SETH: Thank you for raising that point; it's something I've thought quite a lot about. I'll start by talking about the phenomenology of objecthood that you beautifully described for vision, and then get into interoception, which refers to perception of the internal state of the body. For most of us most of the time, visual experiences have the character of consisting in a world of objects around us—coffee cups on the table, computers in front of me, and so forth. But that's not always the case. If for instance I'm trying to catch a cricket ball someone's thrown to me, what my perceptual system is geared to do is not so much figure out what's out there, as to catch the cricket ball.

There's a branch of psychology, with roots in James Gibson's "ecological psychology" and William Powers's "perceptual control theory," that inverts our thinking about perception and its interaction with behavior. It's easy and intuitive to think that we perceive the world and then we behave: perception in the service of controlling behavior. But we can also think of it the other way around—of behavior controlling perception, so that when we catch the cricket ball, what we're really doing is maintaining a perceptual variable at a constant value. In this case, it would be the acceleration of the angle of the ball to the horizon. If I keep that as close to zero as possible, I'll catch the cricket ball—or at least it will hit me in the face. Phenomenologically, when engaged in an act like this, I'm not so much perceiving the world as distinct objects arranged in particular ways, I'm perceiving how well my catching the cricket ball is happening. Am I likely to catch it? Is it going well or not? That's a different kind of description of visual phenomenology, and one that is not so apparent in many laboratory experiments when we just ask people to tell us what they see.

So the experience of objecthood—or the lack of such experience—is something that needs to be explained. One way to think of this is that when I perceive an object as a three-dimensional thing occupying a particular location and volume, what that means is that I'm perceiving how that object would behave if I were to interact with it in different ways.

This idea calls on another tradition—well, it's back to Gibson again with his ecological psychology, but now augmented by the "sensorimotor theory" of Alva Noë and Kevin O'Regan—which says that what I perceive is, roughly, how I can interact with an object. I perceive an object as having a back not because I can see the back but because my brain is encoding, somehow, how different actions would reveal the back. And that's a distinctive kind of phenomenology—a phenomenology of objecthood. One thing I've been trying to do, is to cash out that account of the phenomenology of objecthood in the language of predictive processing. And these turn out to be conditional or counterfactual predictions about the sensory consequences of actions. So, in order to perceive something as having objecthood, my brain is encoding how sensory data would change if I were to move around it—if I were to pick it up, and so on. And if we think about the actual brain mechanisms that might underlie this process, they fall out quite naturally from this Bayesian brain perspective, because to engage in predictive perception, brains need something like a generative model.

What does this mean? It means a model of the mapping from things in the world (hidden or latent causes) to sensory data, and the ability to invert that mapping—to infer the most likely causes given some sensory data. That's how you do Bayesian inference in the brain. And if you've got a sufficient generative model, then it can generate "fictive" data samples—it can predict how sensory signals would change, conditional on different kinds of actions. This introduces an extension of predictive processing that's technically called active inference, where we think about reducing prediction errors not only by updating our predictions, but also by acting so as to make predictions come true.

It's possible to make some interesting, empirically tested hypotheses about how our experience of something as an object depends on what the brain learns about ways of interacting with it. We've started to test some of these ideas in the lab, because we can now use virtual reality and augmented reality to generate objects that will be initially unfamiliar, and which behave in weird ways when you try to interact with them. Using these tricks, we can either support or confound these kinds of conditional expectations and then try to understand what the phenomenological consequences of doing so are.

We can also account for situations in which this phenomenology of objecthood seems to be lacking—for instance, in synesthesia, which is an interesting phenomenon in consciousness research. The canonical example of synesthesia is grapheme-color synesthesia: when people with this form of synesthesia look at a black letter or number, they will often have a concurrent color experience. This is well established. What's often not focused on is that pretty much across the board in grapheme-color synesthesia, people don't see the letter as actually being red or actually being green. They still experience the letter as black; they just have an additional experience of color along with it.

But this additional color experience doesn't have the phenomenology of objecthood. It doesn't appear to be part of an object—the inducing grapheme—in the real world. Why not? Well, one possibility is that it doesn't exhibit the same kinds of sensorimotor contingencies that an object that actually has a particular color does. If I'm synesthetic and I'm looking at the letter F, which is actually red, and I change the lighting condition somewhat, and move myself with respect to this red F, its luminance and reflectance properties will change the incoming sensory signals in subtle but significant ways. On sensorimotor theory, perception of these changes underlies the qualitative character of a real color experience. But in my synesthetic experience, if I move with respect to a black F—an F which, because I am synesthetic, happens to generate a concurrent experience of redness—the incoming sensory signals don't change in the same sorts of ways as they would for a really red F. So I don't experience the synesthetic redness as a real property of a black F. This is a promising example of how concepts and mechanisms from predictive processing can start to unravel some pervasive and modality-specific phenomenological properties of consciousness.

HARRIS: It's worth emphasizing the connection between perception and action. It's one thing to talk about it in the context of catching a cricket ball, but when you talk about the evolutionary logic of having developed perceptual capacities in the first place, the link to action becomes even more explicit. We haven't evolved to perceive the world as it is for some abstract epistemological reason. We've evolved to perceive what's biologically useful. And what's biologically useful is always connected—at least when we're talking about the outside world—to actions. If you can't move, if you can't act in any way, there would have been very little reason to evolve a capacity for sight, for instance.

SETH: Absolutely. The sea squirt—a very simple marine creature—swims about during its juvenile phase looking for a place to settle, and once it settles and starts filter feeding, it digests its own brain, because it no longer has any need for perceptual or motor competence. This is often used as an unkind analogy for getting tenure in academia. But you're absolutely right: perception is not about figuring out what's really there. We perceive the world as it's useful for us to do so.

This is particularly important when we think about perception of the internal state of the body, which we mentioned earlier. Brains are not for perceiving the world as it is. They didn't evolve for doing philosophy or complex language, they evolved to guide action. But even more fundamentally, brains evolved to keep themselves and their bodies alive. The most basic cycle of perception and action doesn't involve the outside world or the exterior surfaces of the body at all. It's all about regulating the internal physiology of the body and keeping it within bounds compatible with survival. This gives us a clue about why experiences of mood and emotion, and the basic experiences of selfhood, have a fundamentally nonobject-like character.

Just as we perceive the outside world on the basis of sensory signals met with a top-down flow of perceptual expectations and predictions, the same applies to perceptions of the internal state of the body. The brain has to know what the internal state of the body is like. It doesn't have direct access to it, even though both the brain and body happen to be wrapped within a single layer of skin. As with perception of the outside world, all the brain gets from the inside of the body are noisy, ambiguous electrical signals. Therefore it has to bring to bear predictions and expectations in order to make sense of the barrage of sensory signals coming from inside the body, in just the same way as for vision and all the other "classic" senses. And this is what's collectively called interoception—perception of the body from within. The same computational principles apply. In this view, we can think of emotional conscious experiences, feeling states, in the framework of "interoceptive inference." So emotions become predictions—"best guesses"—about the hidden causes of interoceptive signals, in the same way that experiences of the outside world are constituted by predictions of the causes of sensory signals.

This gives a nice computational and mechanistic gloss to old theories of emotion that originated with William James and Karl Lange—that emotion has to do with perception of physiological change in the body and by the subsequent cognitive "appraisal" of these changes. The predictive-processing view adds to these theories by saying that emotional experience is the joint content of predictions about the causes of interoceptive signals at all levels of abstraction.

The other important aspect of the "interoceptive inference" view is that the purpose of perceiving the body from within has little to do with figuring out what's there. My brain couldn't care less that my internal organs are objects with particular locations within my body. The only thing that's important about my internal physiology is that it works, that it keeps me alive. The brain cares primarily about control and regulation of the body's internal state. So perceptual predictions for the body's interior are of a very different kind: they're instrumental, they're control-oriented, they're not epistemic, they're not to do with "finding out." For me, this is suggestive of why our experiences of being a body have this nonobject-based phenomenological character, compared to our experiences of the outside world. More speculatively, there is the idea that all forms of perception, conscious and unconscious, derive from this fundamental imperative for physiological regulation. If we understand that the original (evolutionary) purpose of predictive perception was to control and regulate the internal state of the body, and that all the other kinds of perceptual prediction are built on that evolutionary imperative, then ultimately the way we perceive the outside world is predicated on these mechanisms that have their primary objective in the regulation of an internal bodily state.

This idea is really important for me, because it gets away from pretheoretical associations of consciousness and perception with cognition, with language, and maybe also with social interaction—all "higher order" properties of cognition. Instead, it grounds consciousness and perception much more strongly in the basic mechanisms of life. It might not just be that life provides a nice analogy with consciousness in terms of hard problems and mysteries, but that there are actually deep obligate connections between mechanisms of life and the way we perceive, consciously and unconsciously, ourselves and the world.

HARRIS: If interoception is purposed toward what is sometimes call allostatic control—that is, the behavioral and endocrine responses that maintain homeostasis—emotions like anger and disgust are essentially parasitic on these processes, and much of the same neural machinery is giving rise to them. What precipitates emotion is most often just a thought, or a memory of something that's happened, but its referent is usually out in the world, very likely in some social circumstance. What's the logic of emotion in terms of this picture of prediction and control in our internal system?

SETH: That's more of a research program than a question that's easy to answer here and now, but the idea would be that emotional content of any sort is ultimately marking out in our conscious experience the allostatic relevance of something in the world—an object or a social situation or a course of action—so that our brain can predict the allostatic consequences and thereby better maintain homeostasis. Our brain needs to be able to predict the allostatic consequences of every reaction or action the body produces, whether it's an internal action of autonomic regulation, an external motor action, a speech act, or a behavioral act. What are the consequences of that for our physiological condition and the maintenance of physiological viability?

Emotional content, in this view, is the way in which those consequences become represented in conscious experience. They can be quite simple; primordial emotions like disgust have to do with a rejection of something you try to put inside your body that shouldn't be there. But there are other, more sophisticated emotions, like regret. Regret is not the same as disappointment. Disappointment is "I did A, I was expecting X, and I got Y," but regret has a counterfactual element: "Oh, I could've done B instead, and then I would've got X." My own personal emotional life involves many experiences of regret and even anticipatory regret, when I regret things I haven't done yet because I assume they'll turn out badly. These sorts of emotional experiences depend on high-level predictions about counterfactual situations—about what other people might think or believe about me. So we can have an ordering of the richness of emotional experience defined by the kind of predictions brought to bear, but they're all ultimately rooted in their relevance for physiological viability.

HARRIS: What do you think about the alleged experience of pure consciousness, consciousness without content—or without obvious content? Is this something you find plausible?

SETH: I think it probably does exist, though I don't know for sure. Unlike you, I haven't been a disciplined meditator. I've tried it, but it's not something you probably gain much from dabbling in. It's conceivable there's a phenomenal state characterized by the absence of specific contents. But I'm skeptical of people's reports of these states, and this gets back to what we talked about earlier—that we tend to overestimate our ability to have insight into what we are conscious of. The possibility does raise an interesting question, which I haven't thought about a lot: What would the computational vehicles of such a state be in terms of predictive perception? Would it be the absence of predictions? Or would it be the prediction that nothing is causing my sensory input at that particular time? I don't know. I'll have to think about that some more.

HARRIS: It's an experience I believe I've had, but I agree with you that we're not subjectively incorrigible; we can be wrong about how things seem to us. We can certainly be wrong about what actually explains the character of our experience, and if we become more sensitive to what an experience is like, we can notice things about it that we weren't first noticing. Obviously, there are conceptual questions here—about whether being able to discriminate more is a matter of finding qualia that were there all along, or whether one is changing the character of one's experience by paying attention in new ways. When you learn how to taste wine, are you having a fundamentally different experience? Or are you noticing things you had not noticed before, but which were fully present? Or are both processes operating simultaneously? I think it's probably both.

SETH: At least to some extent, your experiences are actually changing, because you're developing a different set of predictions. Your new predictions are better able to distinguish initially similar sensory signals, so it's not just that you're noticing different things, your experiences are changing as well.

HARRIS: Regarding the experience of pure consciousness that many meditators believe they've had: people have had it on psychedelics as well. The question is, Are there some contents in what I'm calling pure consciousness that I could have noticed but didn't? The significance of the experience doesn't so much hinge for me on whether or not consciousness is really without any content. It's enough that it lacks the usual gross, cognitive, and perceptual content.

It's quite possible to have an experience wherein you no longer feel your body. There's no sensation, no sense of proprioception, no sense of being located in space. The experience is of consciousness denuded of those usual reference points, and that's what's so interesting and expansive about it. That's why it suddenly seems so unusual to be you in that moment, because all the normal experiences—seeing, hearing, smelling, tasting, touching, and even thinking—have dropped away. This is where, for me, the hard problem comes screaming back into the conversation.

Take Tononi's notion of integrated information: on his account, consciousness is simply a matter of integrated information, and the more information and the more integrated, the more consciousness. But an experience of the sort I'm describing—of consciousness stripped of its usual reference points—is not an experience of diminished consciousness. In fact, the people who have this experience tend to celebrate it as the quintessence of being conscious, as opposed to its loss. Yet the information content seems negligible.

I guess you could say it's integrated, but there are other experiences I could describe where the criterion of integration seems to fall apart and yet consciousness remains. Again, this is one of those definitional problems, but if we're going to call consciousness a matter of integrated information, and we find a case where there's-something-that-it's-like-to-be-you, and yet information and integration are not its hallmarks—that's kind of like defining all ravens as being black and then finding a white one. What do we call it, a white raven or some other bird? Do you have any intuitions on this front?

And just to be clear, I would distinguish the experience of pure consciousness from the loss of self. You can lose your sense of self with all of the normal phenomenology in place. You can be seeing and hearing and tasting and even thinking normally, and yet the sense of self—or at least one sense of self—can drop away completely. I'm talking about a different sort of experience here.

SETH: Thinking about pure consciousness and whether a putative experience of this kind serves as some phenomenological counterexample to integrated-information theory (IIT) gets us to whether we consider IIT to be primarily a theory of conscious level, or of conscious content, or of both together. Perhaps it's best to start by summarizing the claims of IIT, because it's come to occupy an interesting position in the academic landscape of consciousness research. A lot of people talk about it, although in the last couple of meetings of the Association for the Scientific Study of Consciousness[*] there was surprisingly little discussion about it. It starts with phenomenological axioms; it doesn't start by asking, "What's in the brain and how does that go along with consciousness?" It tries to identify axiomatic features of conscious experience, things that should be self-evident, and then derive what the necessary and sufficient mechanisms are, given these axioms. IIT calls these postulates.

In the current version of IIT, there are five axioms. But we can just consider a couple of them, the fundamental ones: information and in-

---

* http://theassc.org/. Interview recorded in early 2018.

tegration. This is what all conscious experiences seem to have in common: information integration. The relevant notion of information here is that every conscious experience is informative for the organism, in the sense of ruling out a vast repertoire of alternative experiences. You're having this experience right now, instead of all the other experiences you could have, so that the current occurrence of that experience is generating an enormous amount of information, because it's ruling out so many alternatives.

HARRIS: I'll flag a few points where this phenomenologically breaks down for me. You say the uniqueness of each conscious experience is highly informative because it rules out so many other conscious experiences, but this doesn't track the experience of meditation, because what one notices there is an underlying sameness to every experience. When I really pay attention, what I notice is the unchanging, qualitative character of consciousness—so the distinctness of each experience isn't what's salient. What's salient is the intrinsic qualities of consciousness in the midst of any experience—its openness, centerlessness, vividness, and so forth.

Imagine that you're in a restaurant that has a full-length mirror across one of its walls. You haven't noticed that it's a mirror, and so you mistakenly perceive the restaurant to be twice as large as it is. However, the moment you discover the mirror, you notice that what you took to be the real world is just a play of light on a wall; all those people over there aren't really people, they're just reflections. One way to describe that shift is almost as a loss of information—nothing's really happening in the glass. And meditation does begin to converge on that kind of experience. The Tibetan Buddhists talk about everything having a single taste when one really pays attention. I don't know if that sounds like gibberish to you, but this is why Tononi's first criterion seems not to map onto what I consider some of the clearest moments of consciousness—again, not a diminished state of consciousness.

SETH: I'm not sure that the state of being aware of an unchanging nature to consciousness is misaligned with Tononi's intuition here. The experience you're having in that meditative state—of becoming aware of the unchanging nature of being conscious—that itself is a specific experience. And the having of that experience is ruling out all the other experiences that you could be having instead. So it's not so much how informative this experience is for you at the psychological level, what's in play here is a much more reductionist interpretation of information. The other way to get at that is to think of it from the "bottom up." Tononi uses an analogy: Why is a photodiode not conscious? Well, for a photodiode the whole world is either dark or light. The photodiode doesn't have an experience of darkness and lightness; it's just on or off, one or zero. Generalizing this: a particular state has the informational content it has by virtue of all the things it isn't, rather than the specific thing it is. We can think about this in terms of color; red is red not because of any intrinsic redness that inheres in a combination of wavelengths but because of all the other combinations of wavelengths that are excluded by that particular combination.

This point actually precedes IIT; it goes back to the "dynamic core" ideas of Tononi and Edelman, which was what first attracted me to San Diego seventeen years ago. Even then, the point was made that an experience of pure darkness—or complete sensory deprivation where there's no sensory input, no perceptual content—has exactly the same informational content as a busy street scene, because it's ruling out the same number of alternatives. It may seem subjectively different, psychologically less informative, but in terms of the number of alternative states that it's ruling out, it's the same. Of course, this idea does get us onto tricky territory, about whether we're talking about a theory of level or a theory of content. But I think it can account for your experiences.

HARRIS: So the total number of states you can possibly experience as a conscious mind defines how much information is encoded in any specific state?

SETH: That's right; that would be the claim. One of the quantities associated with the technical definition of information theory is entropy, which is a measure of the uncertainty associated with a system state. A photodiode can be only in one of two possible states. A single die can be in six possible states. A combination of two dice can be in eleven possible states, with some being more likely than others (for example, seven versus twelve). It's in these technical details about information theory that IIT runs aground, because it's trying—at least on some readings—to address the hard problem. It's because Tononi argues for an identity relationship between consciousness and integrated information. He says, and I paraphrase, "Consciousness simply is integrated information measured the right way." The whole theory becomes empirically untestable, because if we're to make the claim that a system's content and level of consciousness is identical to the amount of integrated information it has, that means that in order to assess this, I need to know not only what state the system is in and what state it was in at previous points in time but I also need to know all the states the system could be in but hasn't been in. I need to know all its possible combinations, its entire repertoire of possible states. And that's just impossible for anything other than really simple, toy systems.

There's a metaphysical claim that goes along with this, too, which is that information has ontological status, that information "exists." This goes back to the theoretical physicist John Wheeler and his concept of "It from Bit." On this view, the fact that a system could occupy a certain state, but hasn't, is still causally contributing to the conscious level and state of the system now. That's a very strong claim, but who knows what the ontological status of information in the universe will turn out to be?

HARRIS: But you also have an added problem of how you bound this possibility. Not only can you not know all the possible states my conscious mind could be in, so as to determine the information density of its current state, but what counts as possible if, or I should say when, it becomes possible to augment my brain? Do we have to incorporate those possibilities into the definition of my consciousness in the current moment?

SETH: I'm guessing here, but probably not. In the theory as I understand it, the repertoire of possible states is with respect to a mechanism as it is at any given time, not how the mechanism might be in the future.

HARRIS: There's a related problem I had with Tononi's earlier work with Edelman. It's their notion that the integration of information must happen over a certain time period, but that period was stipulated more or less axiomatically. Who's to say it couldn't be integrated over five hundred years? Imagine we have a mind supervened by everything that happens on the internet in a five-hundred-year period. Or the more absurd example I gave in one of my books refers to geological processes: Just imagine that the rumblings in the Earth amount to integrated information. Does that mean that plate tectonics is at the basis of some sort of conscious mind? It seems kind of post hoc to stipulate, "No, this has to happen in five hundred milliseconds."

SETH: I'm sympathetic to that. It comes down to one of the other axioms in more recent versions of IIT, which is exclusion: that there's a particular spatial and temporal granularity, which is the spatiotemporal granularity of a system at which integrated information is maximized, and that this is the only one that counts. The axiomatic approach taken by IIT is innovative but a little tricky to motivate since axioms are supposed to be self-evident. I'm not sure to what extent we can conceive of any of the properties of consciousness highlighted as axiomatic within IIT as being truly self-evident. And certainly the axiom of there being a single dominant spatiotemporal granularity I think is potentially the weakest of all that have been put forward so far, axiomatically speaking.

These are the problems you get into when you try going after the hard problem. You come up with these weird, potentially absurd scenarios, which could perhaps be taken as forms of reductio ad absurdum. There are others: you could glom a whole bunch of neurons onto your brain. And let's say they never fire, but they could, in some (unencountered) situation. IIT would predict that your conscious experience has changed because of that—because the repertoire would have also changed. That's a weird, counterintuitive prediction.

I don't want to rule out a theory of consciousness because it makes counterintuitive predictions. Let's take a slightly weaker version of IIT, which is that experiences do indeed seem phenomenologically to exhibit information and integration. We can argue about whether this is less the case for certain kinds of meditative experiences than for other kinds of experiences. But in general, conscious experiences do consist of one particular conscious scene among a large number of possibilities, and they do so in a generally integrated way. These are general phenomenological observations. I hesitate to say they're axiomatic, because I think they probably aren't, but they're certainly general and generalizable. So in a weak version of IIT it's useful to ask what kind of mathematics and mechanisms would operationalize these observations, and can we measure or observe anything like that in the brain?

If you take the weaker view, you don't have to worry about all the things that trip up the strong view of IIT when trying to measure integrated information "from the outside." I could compute a measure of IIT—let's call it Φ (Phi, pronounced "Fy"); that's what Tononi calls it, after all. Now, I can easily write down equations for Phi that depend only on observations of what a system has actually done—what we might call the empirical or stationary distribution of a system. This is work I've done with my colleague Adam Barrett at Sussex; other people have done similar things as well. We've developed approximations of Phi, or versions of Phi, that retain the same core insights of IIT, inasmuch as they capture a balance, or rather the coexistence, of informativeness and integration.

But these approximations are based on a different assumption about what the relevant repertoire of states of the system is. In this case we say, "I don't care about the hard problem, I'm just trying to map this interesting phenomenological insight onto mechanisms. In this case, I just need to measure what states the system has been in, and then I can use these measurements to calculate a version of Phi." I think this is a useful thing to do. Unfortunately, at least so far, it turns out that when we try to do this, the measures don't work very well, likely because of other things the theory involves—like the fact that we have to find the "minimum information partition," which is the way of splitting up a system which maximally differentiates the system as a whole, compared to its parts. That's how, technically, the axiom of integration gets in. We look at part/whole relationships, mereological relationships in terms of information across time.

It's kind of annoying, but also illuminating, that when you develop empirically applicable measures based on these insights, they don't work very well in practice. It's a bit of a warning sign. What you'd want for a theory with legs is that the closer you get to operationalizing it, the more, not less, empirical purchase it should have. This may be one reason why we've seen less IIT stuff out there in the last year or so, because it's just very difficult to get practically interesting results. If you take the hammer of IIT and hit the problem of consciousness with it, it doesn't split apart nicely, at least not yet.

HARRIS: Isn't there an additional wrinkle here, where some version of panpsychism comes sneaking in? If consciousness is really just identical to integrated information at any level, then wouldn't lights come on very early in an entirely piecemeal way? You could imagine thousands or even millions of loci of consciousness at levels far below what we think of as being the level of consciousness in a human brain, and then you could imagine other systems as potentially conscious—all the way down to David Chalmers and his conscious thermostats—depending on how you defined integration and information.

SETH: I agree that the theory as expounded by Tononi—and also more recently by Chalmers, and by Christof Koch as well— invites this interpretation. Indeed, some kind of panpsychist interpretation is unavoidable if you accept that consciousness *is* integrated information, because then you'll find small amounts of integrated information in unexpected places, not just in brains. Even a hydrogen atom, in this story, will exhibit a tiny amount of integrated information, and will be conscious to a correspondingly tiny degree. Having said this, you won't find integrated information consciousness absolutely everywhere, and so you won't find consciousness absolutely everywhere either. This is because not all systems have a nonzero integrated information. You can design systems that have no integrated information. In fact, you can do versions of the zombie experiment here. You imagine all the recurrent dynamics of a biological brain (which will have nonzero Phi and hence be conscious) being unwrapped into a single feed-forward network where information flows in one direction (which will have zero Phi and hence no consciousness).

HARRIS: Well, we almost have such a network. Take the human cerebellum, the little brain at the back of our big brain which actually has four times the number of neurons the rest of the brain has. Few people imagine that there's something that it's like to be the human cerebellum. And yet it has all of the gross features of a brain. But it doesn't have the necessary integration to be a basis of consciousness, or at least so it would seem.

SETH: Yes. These simple gross features of neuroanatomy and neurophysiology, like sheer number of neurons, aren't the relevant ones. Of course the cerebellum differs in many ways from the rest of the cortical and subcortical systems, not just in its lack of association with something like integrated information. But certainly a relevant feature is that the cerebellum seems to be constituted of an enormous number of relatively functionally independent circuits. People often focus on the cerebral cortex while neglecting the cerebellum, but there's a sort of dirty secret in neuroimaging experiments: you often see a cerebellum light up in contrasts of various sorts (where brain activity in one experimental condition is compared with, "contrasted against," brain activity in another). And it's often completely ignored because "Ah, it's not relevant, it's just the cerebellum."

But back to panpsychism. It's an interesting thought experiment—that if you take this identity relation between integrated information and consciousness, you'll start attributing consciousness very broadly. But I don't know what you do with that. I'm always trying to evaluate philosophical positions and theories on whether they lead to a productive set of experiments or not. Panpsychism doesn't really motivate any particular experiment. It just sits there as an interesting metaphysical possibility.

HARRIS: Yes, it doesn't do anything operationally. I wouldn't expect the world would appear different if everything were humming with some kind of rudimentary experience. I wouldn't expect my computer to start talking to me if it were something that it's like to be a computer. I would expect it to be doing exactly what it's doing now, given its constraints. And yet, despite the fact that I wouldn't expect the world to be different, panpsychism still strikes me as highly counterintuitive—which doesn't make a lot of sense. In any case, panpsychism isn't the most obnoxious thing on the menu of counterintuitive things.

Should we segue to another topic? I want to talk about the self and how you differentiate the ways in which we use this term. And I'd like to talk about artificial intelligence. Do you want to say anything more about Tononi's work before we move on?

SETH: Let me say one final thing, which is that there are whole sets of empirical approaches that do seem to shed some light on the mechanistic basis of conscious level and that are associated with the basic principles of IIT. In particular, there's the "perturbational complexity index," which was developed by a team of researchers led by Marcello Massimini at the University of Milan, interested in the clinical application of these ideas. Basically, you use TMS—transcranial magnetic stimulation—to generate a strong and very brief pulse of electromagnetic activity into the cortex, and then you listen to the echo of that pulse with EEG (electroencephalography). Crudely, you bang on the brain with an electrical hammer, and you listen to the echo. It turns out if you quantify the spatiotemporal richness of that echo in specific ways, you get an empirically robust number which stands as a measure of consciousness. This gets us back to our conversation about general anesthesia and distinguishing conscious levels from deep sleep to wakefulness. This is productive, and at Sussex we've been doing the same thing without the stimulation: calculating the complexity—more formally, the "signal diversity" of the EEG without any TMS pulse: the so-called spontaneous EEG. This number, which is closely related to the perturbational complexity index, also nicely tracks changes in conscious level. And, oddly, we found that in the psychedelic state this measure of signal diversity is a little bit *higher* than the normal baseline of wakeful awareness.

HARRIS: Or not so oddly.

SETH: Or not so oddly. Although it's not evidence for—as was written up by a number of people—a "higher state of consciousness." It's more that we found a specific increase in neuronal signal diversity, possibly reflecting an increased repertoire of brain states. All this is just by way of saying that the framework of IIT is motivating a number of interesting empirical developments that do tell us something about the neuronal basis of conscious level and how it interacts with content.

HARRIS: Well, I'll ask the obvious question now: Has anyone done that experiment for the cerebellum?

SETH: You know, I don't think they have. Don't hold me to that, though.

HARRIS: I don't know if there's a problem doing TMS on the cerebellum. I don't recall people doing that, or recording EEGs from it.

SETH: These measurements, even when they have empirical utility, typically only do when you're contrasting different states. It might be interesting to see how the cerebellum behaves differently when the whole organism is awake versus asleep. But I'm not sure what just looking at the activity of the cerebellum per se would tell you.

HARRIS: You also raise a point concerning differentiating the level of consciousness and its contents. I see how IIT can track changes in level of consciousness, but when you're talking about contents, I can certainly imagine—and believe I've experienced—states of consciousness where the contents are a mess and certainly less informative, biologically and behaviorally and perceptually, than is ordinarily the case. And yet they're no less vivid. We can think of certain neurological conditions where there's something that it's like to be the person, but what it's like is just a buzzing confusion that has very little behavioral utility. Does that pose any problem, or am I just sliding among different uses of the term "information"?

SETH: Perhaps. However introspectively informative a state might appear to you, it's probably different from the technical usage of "information" within IIT theory. Within IIT there's a theory of conscious content having to do with shapes in what Tononi would call "qualia space." But the problem is it's even less testable than when taking IIT as a theory of level of consciousness. It becomes detached from empirical data—or at least nonspecific with respect to empirical data, which is why I believe it's more productive to think of conscious content within a theoretical framework that more directly addresses the problem of content. For me, the more productive framework is the Bayesian brain and predictive processing, because you're not contorting a grand theory to account for everything. We can hope everything will coalesce into a single framework in the end. But for now, I prefer to use whatever sheds the most light on these mechanism/phenomenology relations.

HARRIS: Okay, let's move on to the self, which is a category of thinking about consciousness that people find confusing. I want to read a paragraph from one of your articles:

> There is the bodily self, which is the experience of being a body and of having a particular body. There is the perspectival self, which is the experience of perceiving the world from a particular first-person point of view. The volitional self involves experiences of intention and of agency—of urges to do this or that, and of being the causes of things that happen. At higher levels, we encounter narrative and social selves. The narrative self is where the "I" comes in, as the experience of being a continuous and distinctive person over time, built from a rich set of autobiographical memories. And the social self is that aspect of self-experience that is refracted through the perceived minds of others shaped by our unique social milieu.[*]

---

[*] https://aeon.co/essays/the-hard-problem-of-consciousness-is-a-distraction-from-the-real-one.

That's an incredibly useful way of partitioning the different experiences we have when we talk about being a self, and when using terms like the personal pronoun "I." There's some fluidity among these various concepts, but let's try to differentiate them. Another relevant word here is "ego," the loss of which is the goal of meditation—and this is also something that happens to people using psychedelics. But whatever one does, one doesn't lose all the selves you've mentioned, nor would one want to.

Have you ever taken psychedelics? What does the possibility of losing the sense of self mean to you? Is it something you've experienced in flow states, or in any other condition?

SETH: I've always thought of the experience of being a self as not one thing. I agree that when people say they've lost their sense of self, one must ask, "Which aspects of selfhood are you talking about?" In flow states, during sports practice, say, you can lose certain aspects of self—the narrative aspects, perhaps. To answer your question about my use of psychedelics: not frequently, but yes, for the sole purpose of experiencing what manipulations of consciousness derive from those sorts of compounds. And I find it illuminating and interesting, more in the way I experience the external world than in how I experience myself within it.

We don't reflect much on what it is to be "our self." Without reflection, we typically consider that the self is unified. That's just wrong, but it's nonetheless at least superficially consistent with our day-to-day experience, if we're healthy, without psychiatric or neurological illness. The deeper truth is that selfhood is indeed constituted by all these different aspects, which can be manipulated relatively independently, either experimentally or through drugs, and which can be affected by various kinds of brain damage and psychiatric illness.

My experience of self is constructed in the same way as my experience of the outside world. It's put together by virtue of a number of predictions about the causes of (self-related) sensory signals, which are then bound together in an overall and perhaps unitary perception of me-ness. But it's all built on a range of distinct predictive processes happening in parallel.

How far can you strip these levels away and still have some core experience of selfhood left? I think you could probably go pretty far; you can certainly experience selfhood without having a rich social environment. Some people would disagree with that. The psychologist Chris Frith might disagree with that. But it's hard—for me, anyway—to believe that a necessary component of selfhood is that our experiences of ourselves be seen through the eyes of others.

HARRIS: Is the doubt whether one can have a rich experience of self without ever having had a social experience? Or merely without currently having a social experience—living as a hermit, say? In the latter case, the answer is obvious: there's no necessary loss of self just by being physically isolated from other people, provided you grew up in normal circumstances.

SETH: I agree. It's an interesting question: if you grew up in an environment without any social interaction, you might never develop an ability to experience social dimensions of selfhood. Does that mean you'd have no sense of self? Probably not. There are other levels of selfhood that probably don't depend on social contact at all—for example, experiences of volition and agency. These are aspects of selfhood that don't seem to depend in any obvious way on episodic memory or social context. And, of course, these aspects can go away, too. People with akinetic mutism don't display any kind of voluntary action at all. At the other end of the scale, people with schizophrenia or alien hand syndrome experience some of their voluntary actions as happening involuntarily. But again, one can imagine that that's not the core of the self.

Then we have the first-person perspective. Is that the core of the self? Experiencing the world from a particular first-person point of view may be associated with a control of attention. This is getting close to what might be intrinsic to any kind of selfhood. But again, I'm not sure, because we can readily manipulate first-person perspective. For example, people have out-of-body experiences, or autoscopic hallucinations. We can induce things like that in the lab, using virtual reality—so that people experience their subjective viewpoint—their first-person perspective on the world (and the self) as having shifted to some location outside the body. However, people in these experiments still *have* a first-person perspective. It is unclear whether that perspective is something that can be completely got rid of.

But the really basic stuff comes down to experiences of the body itself.

We can experience our body from the outside, as an object in the world: "This is my hand, which is part of my body." We know that perception can be manipulated; classic experiences like the rubber hand illusion* show that it's surprisingly easy to change the brain's perception of what is, and what is not, part of one's body. But all this goes back to what we were talking about earlier: the fundamental phylogenetic justification for having brains in the first place, in terms of the regulation of one's internal state and how this is based on perceiving in a predictive but control-oriented way.

Seen this way, all perception originates—in evolution and in development—from a fundamental "drive to stay alive." Everything we perceive is warped or shaped by this drive. Our perceptual experiences reflect the relevance of hidden causes (sensory signals) for the ongoing survival of the body. For me, this is probably the essence of self, which I don't know can ever be completely gotten rid of. There is always this inchoate sense of being a body, of being a flesh-and-blood organism persisting over time, independent of a first-person perspective, independent of volition, independent of memory.

The only potential counterexamples I can think of are weird pathological cases like Cotard syndrome, where people believe that they're dead, that they no longer exist—which is, of course, a self-contradiction, but nonetheless they believe it. What perceptual experiences lead them

---

* The stroking of a rubber hand synchronously with a subject's real hand as the subject's gaze is focused on the rubber hand leads to the subject's experiencing the rubber hand in some sense as part of his or her body—though the strength of the effect differs substantially across individuals.

to adopt this belief? The few studies that have been done implicate problems with interoceptive regulation and control of the internal state of the body, and that's a clue to what may lie at the bottom of our experience of selfhood.

HARRIS: I've never known what to make of that condition. It's one of those cases where you're not sure a person's words mean what they seem to mean.

SETH: That's true. I've never met anybody in that state, so I'm also wondering, like you, "What do they really mean?" But Cotard patients consistently make those claims, and it suggests that there's some peculiar phenomenology going on.

HARRIS: Well, let's stay with these five terms: bodily, perspectival, volitional, narrative, and social selves. I can connect these dots in a way that may seem odd. There are experiences where the body is rather vividly absent—the experience is one of having completely lost touch with the body—and there are experiences in dreams where there's no sense of having a dream body. And you can definitely have these experiences in meditation when your body has been zeroed out. There's just a vast expanse of disembodied consciousness.

Yet there can be no lesser sense of being a perspectival self. Thomas Metzinger and I spoke about this, and it occurred to me at the time that the most rudimentary feeling of self that drops away in meditation—and here I am merging the perspectival and volitional selves—is the sense that I am the source of attention and volition. In losing that sense of being the subject of experience, one can still distinguish between volitional and nonvolitional actions. But the sense that there's an inner agent guiding attention and volition drops away.

SETH: This again leads to the idea that it's the control of attentional focus—whether internal or external—that's central. Or rather, you can lose the sense of control of attention, but there's still the effect of attention on action.

HARRIS: It's definitely not what schizophrenics report, the feeling of being imposed on from the outside. The hallmark of an action being volitional is that it's associated with intent. But from this point of view it's clear that intentions arise without an agent producing them.

SETH: That's quite a detailed and deep insight into what intentions, if there are any such things, actually are. They don't emerge from some original source of "willed action" at all. They emerge in our conscious experience in the same way that other conscious experiences emerge. Experiences of intentions to do this or that are inferences that relate to hidden causes that arise preferentially from the internal mechanics of the brain and the body, as compared to external causes. This way, you can think about volitional actions without falling foul of the naive assumption that there's some "essence of self" causing volitional actions to happen.

In thinking about the relation between volition, agency, and will, the problem has always been to resist the temptation to think that "experiences of will" cause things to happen. It's more useful to ask, "Well, under what circumstances and constraints do we have experiences of volition and agency?" And you can then think of them as perceptual inferences.

HARRIS: Much of it is retrospective, as well. For instance, I just reached for a bottle of water and took a sip. That's the quintessential volitional action, but I noticed that my experience of it as a volitional action was retrospective, in that I wasn't aware of my intention to reach for the bottle before it produced the behavior. I just noticed that I'd done it, and the behavior seemed in harmony with my intent. It was not something that was imposed on me; it would have felt different if an alien hand had reached for the bottle of water. Probably your predictive model works pretty well here. It's a matter of conforming to some internal model of what's about to happen. The absence of having generated an internal model would be the experience of having this thing imposed on you.

SETH: Right. When I have the most vivid experience of volition and will, it's when I'm facing a difficult decision, or trying to exert a lot of cognitive control in order to *not* do something. Let's take that specific example again: you pick up the bottle of water. There's a whole bunch of relevant sensory information about that act. There's visual information that your hand has moved and picked something up. There's tactile information when you grasp the bottle. There's proprioceptive and kinesthetic information about your joint positions and angles and how they're changing. There's probably some auditory feedback as well when you pick up the bottle. And, of course, there are motor commands themselves. It's plausible to think that one's experience of volition is just the brain's best guess of the hidden causes of all these signals and their correlations. This gets to a key question, which is, Can you have experiences of volition even without motor intentions? At Sussex we're using virtual reality to explore some of these questions. We have virtual-reality hands that you feel a sense of ownership of, and they occasionally make plausibly voluntary actions that you didn't yourself make. And then we can measure whether these actions show the characteristics of voluntary action—are they experienced as voluntary, even though there were no motor intentions at all? One way to do this is to look at intentional binding: a phenomenon where you perceive self-caused events to be closer together in time than events that aren't self-caused. Can there be intentional binding even for nonintended actions?

HARRIS: Do you get something like a rubber-hand illusion for volitional action there?

SETH: Yes, you do. In our initial experiments, we saw an equivalent amount of intentional binding for both intentional and nonintentional movements. That is to say, there is an equivalent "drawing together" of the time between the virtual hand movement and the outcome (a beep), whether or not you moved your real hand or not. We think this is because all the other sources of information—visual, tactile, auditory, and so on—are preserved. So in this case a nonintentional action exhibits a characteristic hallmark of intentional or voluntary action: intentional binding. Having said this, when the virtual hand moves by itself people are not fooled into thinking they actually did move their real hand. They still know they didn't. So the illusion is not complete.

HARRIS: Before we talk about AI, let's talk about the social self for a moment, because that strikes me as quite different from the other selves—in the sense that not only is it dependent on one's interactions with other people but it's also more a matter of the different roles we play in life. You might be a father and a husband and a professor and an employee and a son. So you can be in many different contexts as a self. And very different properties of our minds come online and offline in those situations. You can feel very confident in one context and quite neurotic in another. People can shift in and out of these states, but if you feel like an "I" in one, you'll feel like an "I" in the other. It's the perspectival, volitional, perhaps bodily, and narrative selves that move into those different social contexts and get knocked around by the various parameters. How do you think about the social self?

SETH: Nicely put. I love the idea of "attracting states" for different expressions of social selfhood. It's probably the aspect of selfhood most open to being shaped by one's immediate external context. I will move from one room to another, I'll leave my house and go to work, and I'll inhabit a different social context. But I'll still have the same body and I'll still have the same first-person perspective. So the perceptual predictions that underlie those aspects of self are more stable than the experience of social self. Certain aspects of selfhood can be more malleable than others. I think of it in terms of an aspect of self that can be present or absent to different degrees. People with autism can indeed still read emotional expressions, yet they don't seem to perceive others' mental states in quite the same way as people without autism do.

The other interesting thing that social selfhood gets at is the extent to which we experience our self as unchanging over time. As you said, there's still this "I" that seems continuous in all social contexts. We (implicitly) expect our experiences of the outside world to change as we move around, but we somehow expect our experience of self to be stable. Now, I think there's a sense in which that experience is more stable, and the lower you go toward the regulation of the body's inter-nal state, the more stable it is. But I also suspect that we're perceptu-ally biased, for good evolutionary reasons, to overestimate the degree of self-continuity. I've recently been thinking about this in terms of change blindness. There's an experiment in which the background of a scene slowly changes color, from red to green or red to blue, and if the change is slow enough and you don't know it's going to happen, you don't notice it.

HARRIS: Alternatively, you can suddenly change whatever's in the pic-ture's background—a lawn, for example—or you can move a tree, and people don't notice.

SETH: That's right, but it's the slow change that I find more interest-ing in this context, because you're looking at this scene the whole time, and the question arises: Did your experience change and you just didn't notice? Or did your experience not change, until it was pointed out to you? I tend to favor the first account—that perception of change is not the same thing as change of perception. It's perfectly consistent to have changing perception and not be aware that your perception is changing. And I think this probably applies in spades to how we experience "self." We're strongly biased toward perceiving ourselves as not changing very much; we have this hugely powerful "self-change-blindness." Our ex-perience of self, even probably at some of the lower levels, can change quite a lot, but we won't experience that change.

HARRIS: I think it's actually worse than that. I think the sense of self is blinking in and out of existence all the time, for everybody, whether they learn to meditate or not. But only someone who learns to medi-tate notices it, or can produce that blinking on demand, by paying at-tention to this feeling we're calling "I." Change blindness is a great example. Perhaps a better example, based on its ever-present reality, is a visual saccade. People don't notice that when they're continuously moving their eyes around the visual scene, their vision is being inter-rupted, because the brain has learned, for evolutionary reasons, not to take in information during the eye-traveling phase, otherwise you'd experience the world lurching around whenever you changed your gaze. We're functionally blind in those moments, and they occur all the time. In some sense, we're experiencing saccades of self, moment by moment, and just not coding them as interruptions in the continuity of self. Whether the same thing could be said for consciousness I don't know, but it seems like a possibility.

SETH: I hadn't thought about internal saccades, but yes, you might be right.

HARRIS: Let's touch on the topic of AI. You and I probably have different intuitions about the prospects of building conscious AI. I've heard you sound fairly skeptical on that topic. First, we should distinguish consciousness from intelligence, because obviously they're different.

SETH: That's a good place to start. It's too often assumed that, though they're not the same thing, a sufficiently intelligent system will at some point develop consciousness—that one naturally follows the other. Intelligence, and artificial intelligence, is doing the right thing at the right time—I think it's as simple as that. It's efficient, adaptive action selection. And AI is making great strides at the moment. Consciousness, as we discussed at the beginning, is a question of the instantiation of phenomenal properties: Is there something it is like to be you or me or a machine? Intelligence and consciousness are almost certainly related, but they're not the same thing at all.

HARRIS: Let's just linger on this fundamental point. A lot of people assume that if we build anything with human-level intelligence, no matter how different from a human it might be in its hardware implementation, consciousness will have to come along for the ride. They assume it would be impossible to make something as functionally intelligent as a human being that wouldn't also be conscious. Is it safe to assume that you would believe that, since you're so skeptical of the zombie argument?

SETH: No, actually, because the zombie argument turns on the idea that a zombie would be completely functionally indistinguishable from a human being. And general (human-level) AI doesn't have to be completely functionally indistinguishable from a human being. General AI, that holy grail of artificial intelligence, means not just being able to play Go very well but having the general functional capabilities of a human being. But nowhere in this definition is it assumed that such a system would be completely indistinguishable from a human being. So I don't think this is relevant to the zombie argument. And I also don't think it's a safe assumption that in order to reach that level of general AI, the system would need to be conscious.

I think it's an open question, which comes down to this pretheoretical association of intelligence with consciousness, which in turn traces to our pernicious anthropocentrism: we're intelligent and we're conscious, so we think the two things have to go together. But from another perspective, the most ethically and biologically important conscious experiences have pretty much nothing to do with intelligence; they have to do with physiological integrity, with suffering, with fear, with disgust. And what are the necessary and sufficient components of a system to have those kinds of conscious experiences? I don't think you have to be that smart.

The ethically relevant question here is what animals are capable of suffering. All that intelligence brings to the picture is the ability to suffer in increasingly weird ways. I can suffer from things I haven't even done, through experiencing anticipatory regret. It's unlikely that a bacterium—and probably unlikely that a bee—will experience anticipatory regret. There have been experiments about whether rats can experience regret as distinct from disappointment that are quite fascinating. But the point here is that intelligence is a bad criterion for assessing whether something is conscious, whether it's a nonhuman animal or a robot or the next iteration of AlphaGo.[*]

---

[*] AlphaGo—the first computer program to defeat a current world champion at Go. The system, designed by the company DeepMind, defeated Lee Sedol over five games in 2015. This was considered such a seminal event in the history of AI that it has already been made into a film: https://www.alphagomovie.com/.

HARRIS: I fully agree. For me, the scariest possibility is that we'll build a superhuman AI that's not conscious and it will destroy us because we built it badly. And it would be no comfort at all to know that what remains is more intelligent than we are. The only ethically interesting thing would be if the superhuman AI that remained was actually more important than we are, because of all the unimaginable beauty and profundity that it could experience. If there's a silver lining to being destroyed by our artifacts, it can only be because we will have given birth to something more important than we are, ethically speaking. And the criterion for that would be that it experiences a much wider range of conscious states. It would be important that these conscious machines also be built so that they not suffer terribly.

SETH: That's right. This is exactly where we started: that without consciousness, there's no meaning to anything. We could argue about whether conscious experience in general, for most creatures and most species, is characterized by an oversupply of suffering compared to beauty. In which case maybe ethically it's not a bad thing if we have nonconscious successors. But I still lurch away from that prospect, in the hope that there's a point in the unfolding of future possibilities that allows for conscious experiences that are not overwhelmingly characterized by suffering.

HARRIS: I think it was in your TED Talk that you said something about the necessity of intelligent systems being alive and having bodies for consciousness, and that struck me as counterintuitive. Because I don't imagine you meant that there's something especially important about being made of meat in order to be conscious. You can imagine replacing individual neurons in the human brain with their functional equivalents that aren't made of meat. But we've run into a Ship of Theseus example here, where you replace all the parts but they have all of the same functional characteristics. Has consciousness disappeared because most or all of your brain is now made of silicon? Or imagine that we just change all of your brain's inputs. Your brain itself is unchanged, but we've replaced all the inputs. Everything that terminates in your cortex is now artificial, but functionally equivalent. So now your brain is in a vat. You wouldn't assume that consciousness would be lost under those conditions, would you?

SETH: In the second condition, no. But then we would have to ask, "What if the system had never been alive in the first place?" Since without a developmental trajectory of some sort, the brain's wiring would be very different and perhaps not sufficient to sustain conscious states. With the first scenario, replacing neurons with their functional equivalents, I'm left ambivalent. I'm not sure functionalism is a safe assumption. First, I'm skeptical of that kind of argument. It's the "sorites paradox": it's difficult to generate a reasonable intuition about the cumulative effect of a lot of small changes. It seems perfectly plausible to me that consciousness would fade, and also that we wouldn't notice it fading, because, again, perception of change is different from the change of perception.

HARRIS: But isn't the information-integration argument implicitly functional, provided that all these new neurons have the same inputs and outputs and integrate in the same way with one another? What remains to be conserved?

SETH: Yes. If you just replace each neuron with its functional equivalent, and they're all connected up the same way, then I think IIT would say, "Yes, it will be conscious in the same way." But if you just replicated the whole input-output structure, with a different kind of functional equivalence that had a different causal mechanism, that was a feed-forward network of some enormous depth and complexity, then IIT would say it wasn't conscious.

IIT makes a claim not only about the input-output relations characteristic of functionalism but also about the causal mechanisms that give rise to that functional profile. But it's substrate-independent regarding the implementation of any such mechanism. You don't have to be made out of meat. So that's true for IIT.

Why do I think life is so important? In a way, it's a bit of a challenge to this lazy assumption that consciousness simply has to do with information processing and functionalism. That's just an assumption, and it's got a lot to do with our fondness for technological prowess as a metaphor: computers do smart things, so we're some kind of computer and information processing is what matters. I don't think that's remotely obvious at all.

But it's not just that. The story about life goes back to an idea about what brains are ultimately for: the maintenance of the organism in the state of being alive. And then from being alive and the importance of maintaining that state, you can start to derive mechanistic constraints on perception and on action that then can map to phenomenological experiences of one sort or another, starting with the experience of things like suffering and so on that reflect in more complex ways the challenges of adaptive allostatic regulation.

It seems to me that one is never going to find the right path to instantiating experiences, certainly of self and the core experience of embodied selfhood, unless there is an organismic context that needs to be proactively preserved. And then that might apply more generally to conscious experiences. For example, we can start to understand my visual experience of the outside world as deriving from the fundamental imperative to stay alive that shaped the brain's predictive mechanisms.

HARRIS: But wouldn't it be just a matter of the functional and structural integration of the system at a point in time? For instance, we could copy you perfectly. Let's say we've mastered nanotechnology, and we know exactly how to take all of the carbon and nitrogen and everything else in the human body and assemble it at will. We can make perfect copies of a person just like yourself, down to every receptor and every charge in your brain. But obviously this new thing, this new person, has not grown up as an integrated system in an environment. It was compiled one second ago by little nanobots out of fundamental elements. Wouldn't you expect—if, in fact, it's an exact copy of you—that it would have exactly the experience you're having at this moment and be just as conscious?

SETH: Yes, absolutely I would. I think that's just a statement of materialism.

HARRIS: Exactly.

SETH: If it's the same thing, then yes. Of course, it's then going to diverge and start to inhabit a distinct different experience of selfhood. But yes, the conscious experience associated with a physical system at any point is determined by the state of that system at that time.

HARRIS: So we're talking just about atoms in the right arrangement. That closes the door to any significance we put on something's history—how it has grown up embodied in the world, for instance.

SETH: Well, it still allows that historical experience—the particular phylogenetic and developmental trajectory of an organism is what you might call diachronically necessary for conscious experiences—that in order to get systems that exhibit the structural properties, dynamical properties, that are associated with conscious experiences, one has to go through a trajectory of being alive. I don't think you can close that particular door that quickly.

HARRIS: But if substrate independence is the case, and you could have the appropriately organized system made of other material, or even simulated—it can just be on the hard drive of some supercomputer—then you could imagine, even if you needed some life course of experience in order to tune up all the relevant variables, there could be some version of doing just that, across millions of simulated experiments and simulated worlds, and you would wind up with conscious minds in those contexts. Are you skeptical of that possibility?

SETH: Yes, I'm skeptical of that, because I think there's a lot of clear air between saying the physical state of a system is what matters, and that simulation is sufficient. First, it's not clear to me what "substrate independence" really means. It seems to turn on an overzealous application of the hardware/software distinction—that the mind and consciousness is just a matter of getting the functional relations right and it doesn't matter what hardware or wetware you run it on. But it's unclear whether I can really partition how a biological system like the brain works according to these categories. Where does the wetware stop and the mindware start, given that the dynamics of the brain are continually reshaping the structure and the structure is continually reshaping the dynamics? It becomes a bit difficult to define what the substrate really is. Of course, if you're willing to say, "Well, we're not just capturing input-output relations, we're going to make an exact physical duplicate," then that's fine. That's just a statement about materialism. But I don't find it intuitive to go from making an exact physical replicate, all the way up to simulations, and therefore simulations of lots of possible life histories, and so on. It's really not clear to me that simulation will ever be sufficient to instantiate phenomenal properties.

I think about it in this way: a simulation of a chess-playing person is actually playing chess. It's doing it a different way, but nonetheless a chess computer plays chess. But take a simulation of a hurricane in a meteorological center. It doesn't get wet and windy inside the computer. We don't expect simulation to instantiate certain properties and we do expect it to instantiate other properties. And to just assume that consciousness is the kind of thing that can be instantiated through simulation is to fully take onboard functionalism and metaphors of information processing that are plausible but I don't think should be taken for granted.

HARRIS: What do you think the prospects are that we'll lose sight of these concerns and even forget why they were at all interesting in the first place? What if we build machines that pass the Turing Test, and we find ourselves in the presence of humanoid robots that seem as intelligent and aware as any of us, because we built them to seem that way? In that case, they will seem conscious—whether or not we actually know that they are. I know you're interested in this area, because I read the review you wrote of the film *Ex Machina*, which I also liked a lot. If we're in the presence of a robot of that sort, whether or not we understand how consciousness emerges in the physical universe, we'll think it is conscious because of how it appears to us. And we might stop wondering whether or not it's conscious, just as we don't wonder about that when interacting with other human beings. Do you think we're headed toward that world, especially if building such machines turns out to be easier than understanding consciousness?

SETH: Yes, I think there is a worry there—actually two separate worries. Of course, the Turing Test was never supposed to be a test of consciousness but a test of intelligence, which gets us back to that distinction. And it was also operationalized in a disembodied way, so that a system passes the Turing Test if a human observer can't distinguish between it and a real human on the basis of disembodied exchanges of text messages. So I don't think the Turing Test is a criterion for consciousness.

Ex Machina is a brilliant film. People should really go and see it. It's beautifully made, too. There's a piece of dialogue in there that's so sharp that my friend and colleague Murray Shanahan, who was an adviser for *Ex Machina*, named it the Garland Test, after the writer and director Alex Garland. It's a quote from one of the main characters, Nathan, the creator. He's talking about this robot that certainly behaves as if she's conscious. And Nathan says the challenge is to show you that she's a robot and see if you still feel she has consciousness. The Garland Test shares something with the Turing Test, which is that as much as it's a test of the capabilities of the system, it's also a test of the human. But this time it's about emotional response and not so much about intelligence. Something that film intuits is that emotional and embodied bodily states are probably better criteria for consciousness, or for ascriptions of consciousness, than criteria based on intelligence.

Anyway, let's say we get to the stage where we have these robots running around. There are two important concerns here. One is that we certainly don't want to build machines that have the potential to suffer, and we don't really understand yet what the sufficient conditions for suffering are. But a more immediate and pressing concern might be what interacting with these devices would do to our understanding of what it is to be human. What if our environment becomes populated by these devices that behave as if they're conscious but which we know or assume or believe are not conscious? What will that do to how we treat other biological organisms who might behave in similar ways?

Are we going to widen the circle of concern because we now have systems that look as if they're conscious? Or might we diminish it because we now retreat more into our own individual existence, into what we can be sure about? Might we become more destructively solipsistic? Such a retreat toward the solipsistic self, and the loss of concern for other creatures, might be an unintended consequence of the increasing prevalence of AI.

HARRIS: Take the TV series *Westworld*—which focuses on a theme park where people interact with robots that are indistinguishable from humans. Part of the fun, or so it is imagined, is to take all kinds of ethical liberties that one can't take with other human beings. So guests at the park can rape and kill robots, if they like. What I realized in watching this show is that the idea of such a park is impossible. Westworld would be a theme park for psychopaths; you'd have to be a psychopath to mistreat something that was indistinguishable from a person. And you would view anyone who could mistreat robots in this way as a psychopath too. It's exactly what you describe as the Garland Test.

SETH: That's right. And of course the worry is that instead of this Westworld scenario suddenly being available, what if the path to Westworld is more gradual? You can imagine that you don't have to be a psychopath to start interacting with systems in these sorts of ways. Maybe we'll see that happen in the next ten or twenty years, with the development of sex robots. Maybe there's a more gradual process already underway, in which the existence of these sorts of opportunities turns people into psychopaths eventually.

HARRIS: Yes. This gradual walk toward not taking human suffering seriously anymore is something we experience in context-dependent ways already, and when you think of the global implications it's scary to consider how malleable our experience might be. I'm thinking of a few local cases, like how surgeons and ER doctors need to inure themselves to the constant evidence of other people's suffering, because otherwise they can't get the job done. And every parent knows what it's like to understand that the suffering of one's three-year-old who bursts into tears over a lost toy is not something that needs to concern you as much as an adult bursting into tears over something else, and yet that suffering is no less vivid for the child. You can imagine that kind of immunity to the evident pain of other, seemingly conscious systems, growing over time. Life could seem more and more like a video game where everyone else becomes a prop.

SETH: Just to introduce a note of optimism: in recent history—and of course this could be reversed—most societies seem to be following a different trajectory. We no longer consider the suffering of people of a different race as unimportant ethically. Our circle of ethical concern seems to have widened and now also extends to other animals. This certainly is not something we should take for granted, though, because these trends are so malleable. It takes only one or two generations for us not to understand how our grandparents or their grandparents perceived certain kinds of other people or held certain other belief systems.

HARRIS: Bring into that picture all our virtual interactions with one another, when our encounters are no longer face-to-face but with one another's avatars in increasingly compelling VR landscapes. As our culture gets virtualized and we interact with people online, we may succumb to repertoires of behavior that wouldn't be possible face-to-face—behavior having more and more the character of road rage, where suddenly it becomes possible to behave in a way that's totally maladaptive, and the only reason you can do it is because you're in a metal box with a pane of glass between you and the person you're screaming at. Caution is definitely warranted as we continue to engage with these technologies.

SETH: That's right. These issues don't depend on thinking about what the basis of consciousness itself is. It's equally important to think about how perceptual and emotional contents form, completely independently of the hard problem or AI. Learning that perception is dependent on predictions in a context-dependent and fluid way should alert us to these kinds of dangers, but also to the opportunities they afford.

Yes, we can be in a context where our perceptions, and therefore our actions, are ethically undesirable. On the other hand, there's the equal potential that in the right context we can alter people's perceptions of themselves and the world so that the ethical value of society as a whole is increased.

The Nature of Consciousness

A CONVERSATION WITH THOMAS METZINGER

Thomas Metzinger's research centers on the analytic philosophy of mind, applied ethics, and the philosophy of cognitive science. He is a senior research professor at Johannes Gutenberg University in Germany, where he was previously a professor of theoretical philosophy and director of the research group on neuroethics and neurophilosophy. In addition to being a philosopher of mind, Metzinger is also very interested in the practice of meditation.

Our conversation starts on a political note: the significance of World War Two for the history of ideas, and the connection between Nietzsche and the Holocaust. Metzinger also summarizes the German view of current US politics. Then we plunge into questions of consciousness and the self.

We discuss the role of intuition in science, the ethics of building conscious AI, the self as a hallucination, the paradox of identifying with our thoughts, attention as the foundation of our felt sense of self, and the modern influence of Eastern methods of meditation on Western science.

HARRIS: I've followed you for some time now, Thomas, and am a happy reader of your books and the anthologies you've edited. You've done really fine work in the philosophy of mind, which is an area I've long focused on. So we'll get into questions of consciousness and AI and the self, and all your areas of interest, but first, how do you summarize what you do as a philosopher?

METZINGER: Well, my core competencies are in something called "analytic philosophy of mind"—that's where I come from. I've done that for more than three decades. But one thing that's special about me is that I've done it in close cooperation with neuroscientists, cognitive scientists, and AI people. So my job has been to turn analytic philosophy of mind into a deeper and more productive interdisciplinary effort. I faced a lot of resistance over this; it's been bad for my academic career. But in the last twenty years, people like me have come along in Germany, and now it's a movement. All the good young philosophers have taken up one or another empirical area of study, like dreaming, social cognition, predictive coding.

HARRIS: What form did the academic resistance to your work take?

METZINGER: Oh, different kinds. First, in Germany, philosophy has always meant the history of philosophy. Secondly, something like naturalism has always received bad press. Philosophers thought—at least I learned this as a student—that empirical scientists couldn't contribute anything. Or that the whole idea that empirical evidence could be relevant meant that you hadn't understood what philosophy is in the first place, because it was purely a priori theorizing.

Then there's also this territorial thing—for example, in the debate over free will. This turned very hot and public a little while ago, wherein a prominent neuroscientist insisted there was no such thing as freedom of the will. And it got to the point where a philosopher said, "Listen, this is a philosophical problem, and there will be a philosophical solution." And my neuroscience friends said, "You are beginning to get the point:

it's *not* your problem anymore. We have solved it." And then all the humanities people rose up in protest. So it's also about who's allowed to answer which questions.

But you have to understand the historical situation. During World War Two we either murdered or drove out of the country all the Jewish intelligentsia, so many teacher-disciple relationships were completely cut off. And I'm grateful to the generation of analytic philosophers who came before me for reconnecting German philosophy to the global discussion again—to humankind's philosophical conversation. That was something that had to be reestablished after World War Two, because many Germans still thought the hottest and most recent stuff in philosophy was Heidegger.

HARRIS: Who, needless to say, had more than a superficial connection to the trends that got so many people murdered and exiled. That's a fascinating moment in intellectual history. I'm sure someone in Germany has written about this, but I haven't encountered in English much about the way the war affected what's known in the States as "Continental Philosophy." It's interesting to picture those teacher-student relationships being severed and Germany becoming isolated as a result.

METZINGER: Well, there are deeper dimensions to it. Every German child, at one age or another, learns what happened. I still remember the precise moment when I discovered the atrocities my tribe had committed. I don't know if you want to hear the story.

HARRIS: I would! How old are you, Thomas?

METZINGER: I'm fifty-nine.

HARRIS: And how old were you when you learned about the Holocaust?

METZINGER: I was ten when the little scholar in me was awakening, and I was getting interested in the books on my parents' shelves. I noticed there was one book they put up very high, because they didn't want me to see it. So, of course, the next time they were out, I put a chair on my father's writing desk and reached up there. It was a photo book called *The Yellow Star*. And there I saw bulldozers pushing piles of corpses into mass graves and photo documentation of medical experiments on Jews, with phosphor burning away their flesh, and stuff like that. I vividly remember the feeling: it was like an invisible, ice-cold hand slowly enveloping my heart. That was the moment when my childhood ended.

When I was sixteen, I was still firmly and honestly convinced that I had been born in the worst country in the whole world. There's the aftermath, when you ask your parents, "How much did you know?" And they all say, "We didn't know anything." And then you ask the other schoolchildren in the schoolyard, and they all say, "My parents also say they didn't know anything about this." And then you ask your history teachers, and they tell you, "Don't let yourselves be fooled. Almost everybody knew."

HARRIS: At what point in school do children begin to learn about these things?

METZINGER: I wouldn't know the curriculum. Maybe you're fourteen, fifteen. You get it in history class at that time. And for those of us who studied philosophy, of course, it was different, because we were all trying to find out what in our intellectual tradition had made this possible. Where did this come from? Nietzsche and *On the Genealogy of Morality*? Because we were always a great philosophical nation—German idealism, phenomenology and everything. The urgent question was, "How could this have happened?"

HARRIS: An intellectual and moral autopsy.

METZINGER: Yes.

HARRIS: Did you come up with any answers, or are there any answers that are agreed upon?

METZINGER: Well, there's a centuries-long European tradition of anti-Semitism. Many people don't know that Martin Luther, for instance, was a hate pundit. He was the first to explicitly recommend in his writings that synagogues ought to be burned. And what many people also don't know is that the *Reichskristallnacht*, the "Night of Broken Glass," actually was a birthday present for Luther, occurring on the evening preceding his birthday. It was a gift the Nazis made to the founder of Protestantism, to honor Luther on his anniversary. So over the centuries there was a deep connection between the Christian Church and systematic anti-Semitism. Consider, too, the role of Pope Pius the Twelfth and the Catholics in supporting the Nazis, continuing even after everything was over—take the organization of "ratlines" as an example, helping top-level mass murderers like Adolf Eichmann and Josef Mengele and many others to get to South America. Ratlines were a system of escape routes for Nazis and other fascists fleeing Europe in the aftermath of World War Two. All of this was supported by clergy of the Catholic Church and very likely the Vatican itself. But then, outside of the Christian Church, there was also plain old racism, and even some philosophical contributions.

HARRIS: It's widely believed that Nietzsche was cynically used by his sister and the Nazis, and that they consciously misrepresented his philosophy. I must say, I've never been totally convinced of this, given some of the ranting one encounters in Nietzsche. What's your view of that?

METZINGER: It's a long and complicated story. Of course, he couldn't have been a fascist and a Nazi. Technically I don't regard him as a philosopher, because in my view he didn't have a serious interest in the growth of knowledge. He's more of a brilliant racist writer. But if you read *On the Genealogy of Morality* and you're a young German, what you take away from it is that we are a warrior race. The Jews are smarter than we are. The Jews have come up with something "to poison our blood. They are poisoning our blood with Christian slave morality." And the only thing we can do is remember that we're stronger—not smarter, but stronger—because we are a warrior race. And that was, of course, a preparation. Because imagine you're a young intellectual at that time, and this is presented to you as coming from one of your best philosophers. This was dangerous, and it was not innocent. It was certainly a preparation for what came afterward.

HARRIS: This is a topic I didn't expect to get into, but I just can't leave it. It's not often I get a direct window onto this experience—and not many people have even *had* this experience. Your description of what it was like to be a child, stumbling upon that book, and then talking about this with your parents and with friends who talked about it with their parents, and meeting what sounds like a blanket denial of culpability. And yet the official story from your teachers is that nearly everyone knew a genocide was occurring and the whole culture was complicit on some level.

How do you reconcile those two accounts? Because in terms of Germany's reputation, it's followed your teachers. It seems that Germany has lived in a kind of purgatory of self-criticism since World War Two, in a way that Austria and Japan haven't. In Austria and Japan, you have a more or less official denial of just how morally dark their behavior was. But with Germany, everyone seems to acknowledge that there has been an impressive, and perhaps even sufficient, degree of hand-wringing over the Holocaust and World War Two. But your experience suggests the opposite—that the grown-ups are more or less living in total denial about the past. How do you square those two things?

METZINGER: Well, Sam, the last witnesses are dying right now, and many have finished their lives in denial. They were also psychologically traumatized. For instance, my father had to go to war at seventeen, and he wrote a book about things he couldn't talk about. They saw horrible things as children. He told me that when they saw eight hundred American airplanes fly over the Rhine Valley in broad daylight—they counted them—and come back without their bomb load, it was the first time it dawned on them that they might not be winning this war, like everybody had told them.

I didn't want to go in this direction at all, but this, of course, connects to Trump and your political situation. And I think as a German

I can bring a unique perspective to what you're living through. I am so very grateful for the thousands of beautiful young men America sacrificed to defeat the generation of my grandfather and father. You brought us democracy, the Marshall Plan, and everything. And now seventy years later you are lying on the ground in this very serious situation.

It's bizarre to be a German right now. Everybody says, "Hey, you're the leaders of the civilized world now. Are you aware of that? Do something!"

And one thing I think we can bring to the table is to urge Americans to remember Trump is not going to last very long, and there will be an aftermath. Children will ask their parents questions, "Did you stand your ground?" and "What did you do, Daddy? Where were you in these decisive years?" There will be a deep intergenerational rift in the society, and it will be a major threat to social cohesion that may take decades to get over. Climate change, for example, is going to go on for centuries even in the best possible scenario, and the United States is now what I would call a "climate rogue nation," they're completely isolated from the rest of humankind. And your children and grandchildren will have to deal with that too.

I just want to say one more thing and then we can leave this topic. It is one thing if you guys break down your own country, but Trump is hard to predict. I don't know who he'll pick a fight with in order to distract from his domestic failures, but I'm afraid that he underestimates China when he threatens to incinerate North Korea.

This is a very dangerous situation. I never thought I'd say this, but my hope actually is with the higher ranks of the American military. Some of them seem decent, and our main hope now is that if the day comes when they're given horrific orders they do not follow them.

HARRIS: Obviously, as a German and a scholar of the relevant history, you're in a good position to warn our society what it means to elect somebody who's not disposed to pay attention to constitutional or democratic norms. Germany in particular is aware of how people go to the polls not knowing that they're voting away their freedom. This is an experience other democracies have had but we haven't had in the United States.

There's an assumption that our institutions are strong enough so that when we put a selfish imbecile in charge nothing terrible will happen. But I think it's not a safe assumption.

But let's pivot from politics and get to the nature of the mind. There are questions of intellectual and moral interest that will probably outlive us. They outlived Plato and the Buddha, and they outlived everyone who has tackled them since. So I think they will probably endure. The mystery of consciousness may be one of them. How do you think about consciousness?

METZINGER: Well, I've been at this for thirty years. You may know that I'm one of the people who founded the ASSC—the Association for the Scientific Study of Consciousness—twenty-two years ago. I think the first thing we have to understand is that consciousness is not one problem but a whole bundle of problems, some conceptual, some more empirical. There's sensory discrimination, and there are conceptual issues about what may be conceivable, and so forth. And the consciousness community, in the last two decades, has made breathtaking progress. We're getting somewhere. In my 2009 book *The Ego Tunnel*, I predicted that by 2050 we'll have the global neural correlate of consciousness—we'll isolate that in humans. And that's only a first step. Life isn't a mystery anymore, but 150 years ago many people thought it was. Consciousness will be like that.

HARRIS: So you're not a fan of the framing, due to David Chalmers, of "the hard problem of consciousness"?

METZINGER: No, that's so boring—that's last century. We all respect David, and we know he's very smart and has a very fast mind. There's no debate about that. But conceivability arguments are just very, very weak. If you have an ill-defined, folk-psychological umbrella term like "consciousness," then you can pull off all kinds of scenarios and zombie thought experiments. It helped to clarify some issues in the midnineties. But the consciousness community has moved on.

HARRIS: Well, maybe we should just state it for people who are unfamiliar with it. Basically, the issue is that consciousness—if you define it as the philosopher Thomas Nagel does—is what it's *like* to be what you are. It would seem that a brain of sufficient complexity, at a certain evolutionary point, has a subjective, qualitative perspective on the world. The lights go on. There have been many variants of this formulation, but Nagel wrote a famously influential paper in the early seventies titled "What Is It Like to Be a Bat?" And he said we may never know. A bat experience could be totally unlike our own. But if it is like something to be a bat, and you could switch places with one, you'd be privy to a different domain of experience. And that would be the reality of consciousness in the bat's case. Whether we ever understand it or not, the fact that the lights are on, the fact that there's a perspectival, qualitative character there—that's what we mean by consciousness.

I've always thought that was a good definition. It doesn't answer any of what Chalmers called the easy problems of consciousness—you know, how does the eye and the visual cortex transduce light energy into a visual mapping of the external world? The hard problem, in Chalmers's account, is the fact that it's *like* something to do any of that. It's the difference between unconscious seeing—which our brains and computers both do—and the conscious experience of seeing, which we know that we accomplish somehow. At the moment there's no good reason to think our computers have visual *experience*—or any other experience, for that matter.

And a corollary to this framing is as follows: let's just say we open the back of the Book of Nature and get the right answer about consciousness, and it turns out that you need exactly ten thousand information-processing units of a certain character, which have to be wired in a certain way and firing at a certain hertz. And lo and behold, that's what gives rise to consciousness. If you change any of those parameters, then the lights go out.

Let's say we knew that to be true. It still wouldn't explain the emergence of consciousness in a way that's intuitively graspable. It still would seem like a miracle. And that's not the way most scientific explanations—or, really, any satisfying explanations—work. When I give you an explanation for any higher-level property—say, the fluidity of water, or the brittleness of glass in terms of its microconstituents—that explanation conserves your intuitions about how things function at a lower level so as to appear as they do on a higher level.

And it's the same way, I would argue, even with the example you just gave, of life. You said that 150 years ago—I'd say even as recently as 90 years ago—people felt that we'd never have a satisfactory explanation of what life is, or how the energy of life relates to physical structure, or how heredity could arise from mere mechanism, or how the healing of a wound could be just a matter of chemistry. But with the advent of molecular biology and other fields, we figured all of that out. Vitalism, the old notion that there has to be a kind of spirit in matter, has gone out the window. But that's another analogy that doesn't really get at how mysterious consciousness is, because reproduction, growth, healing from injury, and so on, can all be explained mechanistically, and our intuitions aren't violated.

The issue for me isn't so much about what is true. It's not that I doubt that consciousness could be an emergent property of information processing simply because it's so difficult, or impossible, to conceive how that would work. That's only a statement about the limits of explanation. But it seems to me that whatever you put in the space provided will still sound like the restatement of a miracle. To make a cosmological analogy: it's like the idea that everything, including the laws of nature, emerged out of nothing. Now, that may be true, but I'd argue that it's the statement of a miracle. So my fondness for the hard problem is as a matter of epistemology more than ontology.

METZINGER: Beautiful, beautiful. You've mentioned so many important points that I don't know where to start. So maybe we should just start by saying that the phenomenological properties of sweetness, or redness, or whatever the bat perceives, are determined by the information flow in its brain, determined by the laws of nature that hold in this world. But there are other worlds, where we can imagine that the bat is a zombie, with exactly the same information flow in its brain, right? Some entity that has the same functional features on a certain level of granularity but which instantiates no phenomenal properties.

There could be other universes, logically possible worlds in which our laws of nature do not hold. So the idea that consciousness is determined from the brain in an "upward fashion" may hold only in this world, with this world's laws of nature, but it's not conceptually something that may hold across all possible worlds. That's the mystery you're trying to isolate: that we can always imagine that Sam Harris is a zombie—that he would talk, even about his emotions and his color experiences, but he would not have any inner perspective. That's the mystery.

HARRIS: Well, I'll shift the emphasis slightly here, Thomas, just to make sure everyone understands the distinctions you're making. As you say, we can conceive of a zombie, a being that functions and appears exactly like a human but has no conscious experience. The lights are not on in a zombie. It's just a perfectly humanoid robot that has no subjectivity or qualitative experience.

Now, the fact that we can imagine a zombie does not suggest that such a thing is possible. It just may be that in order to get something that functions like a human being, and seems like a human being from the outside, consciousness will always be necessary. I'm agnostic as to whether or not that is the case.

So I'm not saying that since there *could* be a zombie Sam, therefore there *is* a hard problem of consciousness. I'm saying that whatever I imagine the explanation of consciousness to be, first the lights are off, and then they come on—by virtue of some complexity of information, or integration, or something else. Whatever the answer is, and there have been various answers proffered in recent decades, it still sounds like a brute fact that doesn't actually explain anything. And that, again, is not the way other scientific explanations, even with respect to life, function.

METZINGER: Well, the last point may not be right. But what you're getting at is, What's the value of intuition? Can we demand of a good theory of consciousness that it intuitively seem right? We'd never ask this of a theoretical physicist. If the string theorists propose eleven dimensions, nobody says, "But that is completely counterintuitive. These are only brute facts they're stipulating." Because we trust these people. They know math, they have theories with high predictive power, and they're very smart. We don't demand that their theories seem intuitively right.

HARRIS: I would say we actually do. This is what has been so unsatisfying about quantum mechanics. No one, not even Richard Feynman, can pretend to intuitively understand it. All the physicists can say is that the math works out and it has immense predictive value.

METZINGER: That is enough.

HARRIS: Yes, it *could* be enough, in one sense. I take your point about the limits of intuition, in that our intuitions weren't designed by evolution to enable us to grasp reality as it is. Our intuitions were designed to avoid getting hit over the head by another ape and to mate with his sister. Our intuitions are very crude. But again, we use some of our intuitions, mathematical or otherwise, to leverage ourselves into areas where our common sense and our folk-psychological intuitions are no good.

So I can follow you there, but it still seems that consciousness provides some extra impediments. Consider the possibility that there's nothing magical about having a computer made of meat, and that consciousness is substrate-independent—as intelligence clearly is—and therefore we could, in principle, build conscious, nonbiological computers. How would we move from identifying the neural correlate of consciousness in the human brain to identifying it in a computer running on a completely different architecture?

What I imagine the future of AI will look like is that we'll build computers that pass the Turing Test, imitating human behavior well enough that we cannot tell the difference. And this will probably happen whether or not we've figured out the neural correlate of consciousness in apes like ourselves. So our computers will *seem* conscious to us. But unless we fully understand how consciousness emerges, in a substrate-independent way, we won't know whether they *are* conscious. They might even say they are conscious, and we might lose sight of the fact that we don't truly know whether or not they are.

I think we both agree that whether or not such machines are conscious will be hugely important, ethically speaking. It would be monstrous to create computers that can suffer. So let's bring the substrate-independence issue into this conversation.

METZINGER: But we have to think about intuitions a little bit more. They have a long evolutionary history. If I have an intuition that an explanation is satisfactory, that is *itself* a kind of conscious experience. There's not just a phenomenology of redness, there's also a phenomenology of "I just know this—but I don't know how I know it." And in many cases, intuitive knowledge is fantastic. It condenses knowledge from the world of our ancestors. Just think about social cognition. If you have an intuition that this guy is dangerous, or that she's a good person, this is, in some way, computing. It doesn't generate sentences in your head but intuitions. Your question is, Can we ever be intuitively satisfied about an explanation for consciousness? I think we cannot, because our theory of consciousness will also entail what a self is, and what a first-person perspective is, and that's something we can't grasp intuitively. For a number of years I've argued against trying to create phenomenal states in machines. We should in no way attempt to create conscious machines, or even get close, because we might cause a cascade of suffering. And for just this reason, it's important to have a theory of consciousness.

What would we have if we discovered the neural correlate of consciousness? That was your question. The hardware doesn't matter. We need to know the flow of information, the computation that's being carried out. Then we have to describe this on the right level of conceptual granularity. That is, "What corresponds to my experience of redness?" and "What in that information flow is minimally sufficient for my intuition that we'll never understand consciousness?" and "What is minimally sufficient for my sense of selfhood?" and so forth. And if from our own phenomenology we can map to fine-grained computational descriptions, then we can see whether it's instantiated in a machine or not. The problem, though, is that machines could have forms of suffering or forms of selfhood that we cannot grasp because they're so alien, so different from our biological form of conscious experience or emotion. They might develop emotion and we wouldn't see it—or maybe it was already there and we couldn't discover it.

Just as with the bat. You will never understand what it feels like to be a bat. To hear the echo of your own ultrasonics calls—is that like seeing? I've heard people say it must be a tactile experience for the bat, like feeling a surface. If it has data formats, as I call them—internal data formats that we don't have in our own sensory processing—we will never know how it feels to instantiate those data formats. And that may be the case with your machines as well.

HARRIS: Just on this point of echolocation: contrary to what most people assume, we can echolocate to some degree. If you hold your hand in front of your face and hum and then move your hand back and forth, you'll notice that your humming reveals to you the location of your hand. So you can be a lousy bat whenever you want.

You raised the topic of the self, which is another thing people find inscrutable. The self, of course, relates to consciousness, and yet it's quite different. You've written a lot about the self. I feel there's some significant agreement between the way you and I view it and the way traditions like Buddhism or Advaita Vedanta view it—that the self, as most people conceive of it, is an illusion.

I wouldn't say that *people* are illusions, but most people walk around with a sense that they have a self inside their head—that there's a subject in the head, a thinker of thoughts, an experiencer of experience, an unchanging rider on the horse of consciousness, who gets carried through from one moment to the next and has various adventures but is never fundamentally changed by them. The self is the center of the whole drama. How do you think about the self, and in what sense are people confused about it?

METZINGER: Well, when I looked at the problem of consciousness, I thought that if I was an anti-reductionist, the most pressing problem would be, "What is a first-person perspective, and what would it mean for any information-processing system to have a sense of selfhood and a first-person perspective?" This is a really difficult problem to solve. I have, like you, been guilty of this "illusion" talk in my popular writings. It is conceptual nonsense to say that the self is an illusion, because the term "illusion" supposes a sensory misrepresentation of some existing outside stimulus.

A hallucination is something where there's no stimulus and you nevertheless have a misrepresentation. But the sense of selfhood is only partly a sensory experience. It's grounded in what I call the "interoceptive self-model"—in gut feelings, perceptions of weight, balance, heartbeat, breath, inner sensations in the body, in the emotions, in elementary bioregulation. And yet we have this robust misrepresentation of transtemporal identity. I have always firmly said that no one ever was, or "had," a self, and that we can scientifically explain self-consciousness in a much more parsimonious way, with much simpler structural assumptions.

For me, the point is that in a system that obviously has no immortal soul and no self, we don't find anything like that in the brain. So how does this robust sense of selfhood emerge? Because the idea that we don't have a self is counterintuitive. Imagine people trying to believe that there's no such thing as a self. You cannot believe this. Even if you wanted to believe this, you couldn't. Nobody can.

HARRIS: Well, let me stop you there, because I not only believe it, I experience it. I don't know whether you have any significant experience with meditation or psychedelics. Have you gone down that path to see if you could confirm any of the Buddhist claims here?

METZINGER: I'm a regular practitioner, for almost forty-one years. I've been at many ashrams and monasteries in Asia. And I've gone to many silent Buddhist retreats.

HARRIS: Then when you say that no one can believe that the self is an illusion or that the self doesn't exist, what do you mean? Because many people have an experience of losing their sense of self in meditation—losing the sense that there's a thinker in addition to thoughts, or that there's a seer behind their eyes.

METZINGER: If it's just losing the cognitive self-model, if you just mean this pure experience of effortless mindfulness, "seeing out of emptiness" amounts to selflessness, then I know what you're talking about. But I think there's a much deeper problem. If somebody reports experiencing selflessness and you're this conservative, stubborn, analytic armchair philosopher who cannot imagine consciousness without self-consciousness, you'll say, "This is a performative fallacy of self-contradiction, an infelicity of performance. If you weren't there, why do you have an autobiographical memory of it? If you weren't there, this is not an episode in *your* life. So I don't have to believe your phenomenological reports about this, because they contain a logical contradiction." That's one aspect.

Another aspect is, many philosophers have such a lack of imagination that they always conflate self-consciousness and consciousness. They think this perspective of centeredness is a necessary part of consciousness. But now, if you try to mentally imagine a selfless experience, that's a mental action. That's an act of imagination, and it creates a subtle sense of effort, and that's the selfiness. That act of imagination is where the selfhood sits. I'm sure these experiences exist, and they're probably the most valuable states of consciousness human beings can experience. I also think that psychedelics play a major role in getting many people to take this possibility seriously. The standard route for many is to first experience ego dissolution with a pharmacological stimulus. And then, suddenly, they see the depths and the meaning that is there. But at the same time, they see that this is a little risky and it's not sustainable, and then go about it in another way.

HARRIS: Yeah. That was certainly my route.

METZINGER: You are, I think, not aware of our commonalities. Did you know that both of us have had rough times on that lake in Pokhara?

HARRIS: Really? I wasn't aware of that. I hope yours wasn't as rough as mine.

METZINGER: You're putting me in a difficult situation. You're asking me to admit to illegal activities!

HARRIS: It's just us, Thomas.

METZINGER: I'll just put it like this: either you're a consciousness researcher or you are not. But I think anybody who has a serious and deep interest in these issues will generally try everything—psychedelics as well as sustained meditation practice.

HARRIS: I want to backtrack to something you said earlier. You made a distinction between the cognitive self and other things one might mean by "self." You said that if, when I talked about the dissolution of the sense of self that comes with meditation, I meant the cognitive self, then of course one could experience selflessness—but that it runs quite a bit deeper than that. What did you mean? How are you demarcating the cognitive self from other forms of the self?

METZINGER: Well, I have this theory. It's called the self-model theory of subjectivity. There's my seven-hundred-page unreadable book called *Being No One*.

HARRIS: It's not unreadable. If one is a student of philosophy, it's a wonderful book to read, and I recommend it. It's very thick, but if a person can get through Chalmers, they can survive you.

METZINGER: What it says is that you have no self, but you have a self-model active in your brain, and it's a naturally evolved representational structure that's transparent. "Transparent" means you cannot experience it *as* a representation. Right now, as you're listening to me, you're identifying yourself with the content of your self-model.

What I've been interested in is this phenomenology of identification. How is the attachment created? And over the last thirty years, I've treated this theory as a research program and filled in many different layers of the human self-model. The last four papers I wrote were on mind-wandering and the cognitive self-model. And so I've developed a theory about what it actually means to fall into this illusion of being a mental agent, a thinker of thoughts.

But before that, I worked for many years on embodiment, and I asked a question that's maybe even more important, What is the simplest form of selfhood, of the feeling of self? Say you're sitting in meditation, and you're in an emotionally neutral state, and there's complete quietness in your mind. There's still an elementary sense of selfhood that we call spatial-temporal self-location, which we've tried to manipulate in virtual-reality experiments and done a lot of empirical work on. Even with the completely quiet mind, there is still bodily self-identification, a deep bodily sense of self. And the question is, What forms of meditation, or what hallucinogens, dissolve this more fundamental bodily sense? Of course our thoughts can go away. If that's enough to say the self is dissolved, it's an experience many people can have.

HARRIS: That's a great question. What is the most rudimentary form of self? For me, it's a matter of feeling that one is a locus of attention—or, perhaps, just attention itself. In the Dzogchen tradition of Tibetan Buddhism, they talk about dualistic fixation—subject-object perception. And this, in my experience, can persist even if the feeling of the body disappears. Most people, if they close their eyes, will still feel all the perceptual signs that they have a body. They'll feel the heaviness of their body in space, or they'll feel tingling or pressure or temperature. But in various states of meditation, especially when you're very concentrated, you can lose the feeling of having a body entirely.

METZINGER: Dream research supports that. There's a rare subcategory of bodiless dreams. There are dreams in which you just experience yourself as a point in space. But the interesting thing is the sense of self-stability. And you can control your visual attention in such a dream. I think the simplest form of mental agency, way below symbolic thought, is this experience of, as you said, controlling the focus of attention. In my last four papers, I've written about this. And in meditation, if you take the standard Wendy Hasenkamp model of mindfulness meditation, you alternate between mental action and letting it go. You're mind wandering in phase one. In phase two, there's meta awareness; you suddenly realize, "Oh, boy, I've lost it again," and then you act. Then you control your attention and go back to your breath. But then you have to do two more things. One, you have to let go of the subtle negative feeling of disappointment with yourself, and the other thing you have to relinquish is the sense of effort that was involved in bringing your attention back to the breath.

If you can rest for a while in a nonfragmented state, in an effortless form of mindfulness, you'll have no sense of self. And then you'll be jolted out of it by the next mind-wandering phase. This is the usual cycle for the meditator. The biggest problem in meditation is the meditator, as everybody knows. You're trying to coax or manipulate yourself into something that's rewarding. And that's effortful.

I think you're right. The most subtle form of selfhood on the non-bodily level is what I call "attentional agency"—the experience of agency that's created when you're controlling your attention. And, of course, in meditation that eventually has to go.

HARRIS: It strikes me that identification with *anything*, from the point of view of attention, is fairly paradoxical. How is it that we come to feel identical to a thought? The default experience is to feel identical to an object in consciousness—something that's actually being known from the outside, as an appearance—for, otherwise, you couldn't be aware of it in the first place. First it wasn't there, and now it is—whether it's an image or a phrase or some other mental object.

Imagine that I say something you don't agree with. The voice in your head says, "That's not right," and that bit of language *feels* like you. And yet it's just a transitory appearance in consciousness. How do you think about identification?

METZINGER: Well, it's a horrible source of fragmentation. I don't know if you've noticed this. There is a holistic quality to the wholeness of the moment, and the instant an identification intervenes, there's fragmentation of consciousness—it starts to break apart into different elements. I have a theory about this, called the cognitive-affordance theory. An American neuroscientist, Paul Cisek, has a wonderful idea that what the brain actually does is navigate an affordance landscape. Now, affordance is an old Gibsonian theory from psychology that says, "What you actually perceive is not a chair, but something I can sit on." The psychologist James Gibson said that the "affordances" of the environment are what it *offers* the animal, what it provides or furnishes, either for good or ill. His theory states that the world is perceived not only in terms of object shapes and spatial relationships but also in terms of possibilities for action. Perception drives action, the animal and the environment are complementary and sometimes they form a larger whole. And you don't perceive the glass of water, but something you could reach for. That's the actual content of the perception. A lot of neuroscientific data supports this idea. What I'm now saying is that the mind-wandering network does not entirely overlap with the default network—I call it the DMN-plus network. It sets up an internal affordance landscape. So all those thoughts that arise in meditation are actually protoselves, or protothoughts, calling out to you: "Think me! Pursue me! I am the last of my kind. I will never come again if you don't *think* me." The idea is that prefrontal cortex areas latch onto elements from the default-mode network that continuously compete within you, and then you identify with them. To give you an image: when I'm meditating and one thought after another comes, it's like a long line of children queuing up in front of me. And every child raises their hands to be lifted up, wants to be briefly hugged, or else they won't go away. And what you have to do is notice every single one of these protothoughts and, as it were, briefly pick them up, squeeze them to your chest, and then let them go. If you do this for a while—just observing them in choiceless awareness—they'll wither away.

So there's something like an affordance landscape in the brain, and these spontaneously arising thoughts are affordances for inner action. It's not like the chair or the glass of water, it's a cognitive or affective state that says, "Feel *me* now! Remember *me* now!" and then the next thought comes and says, "Think *me*! Attach to *me*!" There's this internal competition for attention. And if you can interrupt that competition, break your identification with that mode of latching onto thoughts, you can see that what people call conscious thought actually is a subpersonal process. That's quite revolutionary: it is not you, the whole person, that thinks, but only your *brain*. It's like your breath or your heartbeat. It's a local process in the brain, and if you manage to see it without getting entangled in it, a completely new way of being emerges—but I guess you understand all this very well.

HARRIS: Yes. But I've often thought that people lose their sense of self all the time, much more often than we give them credit for. We have a phrase "to lose oneself in one's work." You're concentrating on something, and there's no distance between you and the thing you're paying attention to, and then the time flies. This happens in athletics, and it is more or less synonymous with any peak experience. These are often referred to as "flow" states.

However, even during the ordinary experience of being distracted I feel as if the sense of self is often dimmed to the point of nothingness. It's not as though there's a self there, and meditation destroys it. There *is* no self, so there's nothing to destroy. People often experience this interruption of the self sense without being vividly aware of it. It can happen when they're diverted by anything—whether by a thought or by use of attention. It's only retrospectively, when they come back to themselves, that they feel they have a self that has been carried through each of those moments.

In your work, you draw the analogy to anosognosia, where a person who has suffered an injury to the right hemisphere, leading to hemiplegia on the left side of the body, may be in total denial of her disability. The denial seems to come with injury to the parietal cortex. So you have a person who is completely unaware of that she can't move her left arm, but can be made aware of it for a brief moment. You draw an analogy between anosognosia, this denial of paralysis, to a denial of what it's like to be us in terms of the self-model.

METZINGER: Yes. Could we suffer from something like introspective neglect? Could we have systemic blind spots, in-built blind spots, and so not notice the discontinuities in our sense of selfhood? We all have gaps, hundreds of times a day. I'll never forget a talk I gave to eminent analytic philosophers about mind wandering. And one excellent philosopher said, "What do you mean? I've been listening to your talk for an hour. Are you saying I've not been an epistemic subject the whole time?" And I said, "Oh, yes. You lost focus hundreds of times—briefly, perhaps only for three hundred milliseconds." And I told him about all the empirical data. If you test people, we're lost in thought for 30 percent to 50 percent of our waking hours and we don't realize it. We suffer from introspective neglect. If you count your dream life as well, we're out of control mentally for two thirds of our conscious lifetime. And then this other wonderful American philosopher denied the empirical data and said, "I know what this is. We're intellectual athletes; only normal people suffer from this!" Actually, the opposite is true: they are, as top-notch intellectuals, so immersed in their cognitive activity that they are unaware of it. And the beauty of this new mind-wandering research is that it shows how discontinuous this mental level of selfhood actually is.

I've formulated an empirical hypothesis I call the "self-representational blink." I believe there must be these short "fade to black" moments, similar to what happens in films, in the conscious self-model. If you're sitting at a bus stop, say, and you just watch your thoughts, you'll notice there's a gap between two thoughts. What is it that's aware of the gap between two thoughts? It is not the thinker, it is not the attending self.

HARRIS: It's analogous to what happens in the visual suppression during a saccade. You're moving your eyes from point to point in your visual field. And your brain suppresses data from the visual cortex so that the visual scene isn't continually lurching around with every eye movement. We are functionally blind in those moments. That's analogous, it seems to me, to what you describe about thought. We don't notice the breaks in the chain. Unless we're trained to notice them.

METZINGER: Yes. And isn't it important to train that awareness?

HARRIS: Of course. It's amazing, the lack of understanding we in the West have inherited on this point. We had a brief moment, with people like William James, who thought there was something to be learned by paying attention to the flow of conscious experience from the first-person side. But then, with the dawn of behaviorism, we lost the thread. In the East, there has never been any question that there's something of importance, both psychologically and ethically, to be understood through introspection. Obviously, one also needs to study the brain and behavior to understand the mind—but the idea that one could ignore the first-person point of view entirely was always crazy.

METZINGER: We also have to see that the human self-model is a product of millions of years of evolution. But, as opposed to the chimpanzee self-model, it opened the door to a cultural evolution. The overall process was not in our interest. The self-model we have as human beings is something that brings a lot of conscious suffering into the world. It wasn't optimized to make us happy, it was optimized to make us greedy, to have many children, to continually compete. Mother Nature embedded many nasty inventions in our self-model—for instance, self-esteem, and this sense of self-worth that drives human beings forward and makes them religious and so forth. It's important also to understand the foundations of this process from two perspectives: from an internal, first-person perspective and from the third-person perspective of science. What would have been even better is if we could have a zero-person methodology, and that's the great contribution that Asian cultures and Asian philosophy have made.

HARRIS: It seems to me that the culture has not yet been created that fully embodies the totality of human wisdom. Clearly we need rationality and empiricism—third-person empiricism of the sort that is typical of Western science. And we also need an understanding that third-person methods must be paired with a clearer observation of what the human mind is like from the first-person perspective.

And all this has to be wrapped up in an ethical worldview that prioritizes the right things: What does it mean to live a good life, and what does it mean for seven billion of us to attempt such a project together? We're not there politically, economically, or socially. It has to be an ongoing conversation unimpeded by cultural, geographical, and linguistic boundaries. At this point in history, we have no right to be provincial.

METZINGER: That's very nicely put. But on the other hand, you can meet monks and nuns with fifteen thousand hours of meditation practice, and they say, "Tell us about your consciousness philosophy in the West. We want to know all about it." And then you say, "Well, we don't believe in reincarnation," and then the shutters go down and all that open-mindedness is suddenly gone. There are many Buddhists in the West now who pose as secular Buddhists in a certain sense. But my suspicion is that for many long-term practitioners, there's some delusional core. Because they need something to motivate themselves, to sustain a systematic practice for years. So they're often not liberated from tradition. Many of the spiritual traditions you've mentioned that have developed a practical knowledge of meditation are also traditions that deny mortality.

HARRIS: I once wrote a short article in *Shambhala* magazine titled "Killing the Buddha," and there I argued that, if they want any wisdom from Buddhism to be brought into the current moment, students of Buddhist teaching must get out of the religion business. And that's not a very popular position in Buddhist circles.

Although I would point out that the logic of karma and rebirth is counter to what most people assume. Rebirth isn't viewed as a good thing within Buddhism. So it's not really death denial in the usual sense. If you told a Tibetan lama that we had proved there was no such thing as rebirth and when you're dead, you're dead, it would actually be good news, from a Buddhist point of view, because they conceive the wheel of rebirth as intrinsically unsatisfactory, and the whole point of enlightenment is to get off it.

This connects nicely to the final topic we should touch on. You sent me a wonderful short essay you wrote titled "Benevolent Artificial Antinatalism." You talk about what you call an existence bias we all have, wherein we assume existence to be a good thing. That assumption connects to everything we've talked about here—matters of life and death, artificial intelligence, the prospect of building conscious machines. Give us a summary of your thinking there.

METZINGER: I've been involved a little in the ethics of artificial intelligence. There are constant public debates on this, but they're growing stale. Everybody repeats the same old arguments. But there's a much deeper dimension to it, which we actually haven't noted. Benevolent artificial anti-natalism (a.k.a. the "BAAN-scenario") is a kind of thought experiment. Suppose a full-blown superintelligence comes into existence. It's autonomously self-optimizing. It has an enormous store of factual knowledge and general domain-independent intelligence. It has irrevocably become much more intelligent than human beings, uses all of the internet, and is continuously expanding its database.

Now, we accept this. We are its creators. It's an epistemic authority. But it also follows that it's an authority on moral cognition. We recognize this aspect, too; it's much better to think of ethics in an analytic way. And it's benevolent, in that there's no value-alignment problem; it will never try to dominate us; it doesn't compete with us. The system fully respects our interests and the deep values we gave to it. Fundamentally it altruistically supports us, including political counseling and social engineering.

HARRIS: What you're describing is the absolute best possible case. In building artificial intelligence, if we do everything correctly, this is where we would hope to arrive.

METZINGER: Yes. But the point of the thought experiment is that even this may present a great risk, because this superintelligence knows many things we don't know about ourselves—for instance, about introspective neglect and things like that. It knows many things we don't understand, sees deep patterns in our behavior, abstract features of our brain dynamics, and so forth. It also has a deep knowledge of the cognitive biases that evolution has planted in our cognitive self-model, and it sees why we cannot really think in a rational, evidenced-based manner about ethics. And it also knows that the conscious states of all sentient beings on this planet are much more frequently characterized by suffering and frustration than they'd ever be able to discover themselves. So the superintelligence concludes that we cannot act in our own enlightened best interest.

And it also concludes that instead of striving to maximize happiness, we should instead primarily reduce suffering, because that's much more urgent. And it decides, because of this asymmetry between suffering and joy, that the highest value is to minimize suffering in all sentient creatures. It is ethically superintelligent not only in terms of processing speed but in coming to qualitatively new results. It knows that no entity can suffer from its own nonexistence, so it concludes that nonexistence is in the best interest of all future self-conscious beings on this planet. It knows empirically that we can't realize this fact because we have this existence bias.

I've dubbed it "existence bias" because that may actually be the deepest core of selfhood: the craving for eternally continuing existence. A superintelligence would have no difficulty imagining turning itself off if it came to the rational conclusion that it would be better off not existing anymore. But we're biological antientropic systems that have this horrible craving for existence and this fear of death planted in us. And so we can't see certain important truths about our conscious way of being in this world.

What is this craving for existence? Have you thought about it, Sam?

HARRIS: Not much, frankly. I see it in myself, but it's paradoxical. For instance, when you think about what worries us about death, most people assume that losing experience, having the lights go out, is part of the problem. But, of course, we do that every night when we fall asleep. There are very few of us who clutch the sheets in terror as we drop off to sleep because we don't want to lose the experience of seeing, hearing, smelling, tasting, touching, and thinking. In fact, those nights when you can't lose these things, because you're suffering from insomnia, become a kind of torture. So we're not afraid of being subjectively canceled—

leaving aside the interesting question of whether or not deep sleep is analogous to a total loss of consciousness.

To get a handle on what does worry us, we have to think about everything we'll be missing. We think about the people we love being bereaved and missing us, and we think about the future states of the world that we won't be around to see. But just to follow the logic of your AI superintelligence here, nonexistent people can't suffer, so we won't actually be suffering our own absence—any more than we suffered because we weren't around a thousand years ago. So the existence bias is somewhat paradoxical, and yet I certainly feel it.

In your thought experiment, there's an asymmetry between the ethical significance of suffering and states of well-being. And I would agree that suffering appears to be much worse than well-being seems good. But aren't you open to the possibility that this asymmetry may disappear? Presumably there's some way of creating minds far happier than our own. Perhaps some future generation, more integrated with its machines or which has been genetically engineered, will suffer far less and spend more time in awe at the beauty of the cosmos. There must be some way of improving our circumstances with the help of this very benevolent AI that would make life more reliably worth living. Are you skeptical about that?

METZINGER: For many of the sentient beings on this planet, yes. There's an empirical premise in the thought experiment, which is that the AI discovers that the functional architecture of our brains is so rigid that it cannot be changed. Another possibility is, of course, the "Bodhisattva-AI scenario," that an AI helps us all to become enlightened, but this sounds much too Californian for me. You're a Buddhist. Maybe you've noticed that this craving for existence was named *bhava tanha* in the Second Noble Truth. So existence bias was conceptually isolated in the core of the Buddhist teachings.

But I don't want to avoid your question. I think there are three circles of suffering on this planet. First, there are the 7.3 billion human beings who suffer. Then there are the 60 billion farm animals in factory farming who suffer for human beings. Finally, there is an unknown

number of wild animals suffering. Most wild animals have two preferences. One is to live as long as possible and the second is to procreate.
But more than 90 percent of them get eaten before they can procreate, so that's massive preference frustration. And one could argue that
even if the AI turned all human beings into enlightened vegan Bud-
dhas so they'd not only stop suffering but factory farming would also
stop, there would still be this ocean of suffering around us—the wild
animal suffering.

I think if one goes deep into this, the world is a very problematic
place. And the early Buddhists thought that, too. But I want to add one
more point. The human self-model has something like a rift. We have a
low-level self-model that implements biological imperatives and says,
"You must not die under any circumstances." But, as opposed to every
other sentient being on the planet, we have this brand-new cognitive
self-model that tells us, "Your future horizon will shrink to zero. You will
die." So information gets into our self-model that shouldn't be there, and
it creates a constant internal conflict.

The explicit conscious knowledge of our own mortality has to do
with the evolution of religion. Religions are what I call adaptive delusional systems; they help human beings deny their mortality. I think
also that criticizing jihadi fundamentalists as irrational is a bit superficial, because our more secular Western lifestyle causes an unconscious
fear of death in these and other cultures. When they see how we live, a
deep mechanism in their self-model gets touched unconsciously, and
that's why they're ready to sacrifice themselves.

HARRIS: If one really believes in paradise, as a true jihadist would, then
sacrificing one's life becomes a perfectly rational thing to do. There's not
much inner conflict to overcome. If your denial of death is sufficiently
explicit and persuasive that you believe death isn't real, then what you
deny isn't death but the significance of life. Weighed against eternity,
this life is meaningless. That's what worries me about the consequences
of these religious ideas. What's more, these memes are contagious. It's
possible to acquire religious beliefs of this kind even relatively late in
life, and they change a person's operating instructions totally—making

it completely rational to sacrifice one's life, and in this case, to kill as many infidels and apostates as one can in the process.

METZINGER: At this point in our history, it's one of the deepest problems we have. Some 80 percent of us are still somehow anchored to delusional worldviews that work as a form of mortality denial. And now science and modern philosophy threaten those delusions. Nevertheless, against these contagious models of reality, as you've analyzed it, rational argument doesn't help.

And the big question is, of course, what *will* help? And maybe understanding their suffering and what drives them into identifying with these alternative ontologies would help, but I'm pessimistic that we can achieve this on a global level. And don't you agree that a lot of secular humanism today is a bit superficial? There are people who proudly declare, "I'm an atheist. I don't believe in God. I believe in evolution. I'm not afraid of dying." But it's not enough. There's a certain complacency. I think we need something like a secularized spiritual tradition, or something like that.

HARRIS: Yes. I've been thinking about this for many years. In fact, I stumbled into my identity as an atheist. In my first book, *The End of Faith*, I was very critical of religion, but I never used the word "atheism." It was only after that book was published and Richard Dawkins, Christopher Hitchens, Daniel Dennett, and I began to be treated like a four-headed atheist, that I got inducted into this conversation about atheism per se. But atheism, on my account, is just a way of clearing the space for better conversations. It's not a philosophy, or an ethics, or a worldview, and it certainly doesn't select for people who are especially aware of the things we've been talking about.

Most people who seek spiritual experience—whether through psychedelics or meditation—tend to do it in a context that's riddled with religious confusion. They become Buddhists, or Christian contemplatives, or they just grab concepts from half a dozen traditions they find attractive and jettison the rest—and then they wind up with something like what Deepak Chopra peddles to people. While there might be interesting and valid experiences at the core, the result is philosophically and scientifically indefensible. These people generally become an object of ridicule for atheists—who, if nothing else, are very clear about what they don't want to endorse.

But what we need is a fully rational "spirituality," for lack of a better word. I always put that term in scare quotes. We need an ethical worldview and methodology to substitute for the indefensible doctrines that have come to us courtesy of religion. It has to be embraced in the spirit of science, with logical and empirical rigor. But, as we've discussed, there's more to the story than just understanding the brain and the mind in third-person terms. We have to figure out what we mean by "a life worth living." How good is it possible to feel, personally and collectively, as a human being? How do we build a civilization that maximizes the flourishing of conscious creatures like ourselves?

And it could be that your thought experiment is in fact true, and we're now stumbling toward a future wherein the wisest authority on ethics in the universe will tell us that it's better to pull the plug. That's an interesting scenario. But I suspect that our navigation of the space of possible experience is more open-ended than that. We have to find out how to navigate in a landscape of all possible minds, where it's possible to suffer excruciating and pointless misery for a very long time and it's possible to move as far away from that as we can conceive, into spaces of purely creative, aesthetically beautiful, and intellectually rewarding contact with the cosmos, both within and without. As to whether we can drag the hyenas, and the rats, and the squid along with us to do more than just suffer here, I'm skeptical, but maybe we'll just dump MDMA into the water supply as we leave this planet and set out for the stars.

METZINGER: As you know, it tastes really bad.

The Road to Tyranny

A CONVERSATION WITH TIMOTHY SNYDER

Timothy Snyder is the Richard C. Levin professor of history at Yale University and a permanent fellow at the Institute for Human Sciences in Vienna. Our conversation primarily focuses on his book *On Tyranny: Twenty Lessons from the Twentieth Century*, but we touch on themes he further develops in *The Road to Unfreedom: Russia, Europe, America*.

This was a timely exchange when it took place in 2017, and remains relevant today. Whether or not President Trump is truly an example of Snyder's thesis can be held to one side. Snyder's work applies far more generally to questions of how any society can remain perpetually responsive to popular opinion without succumbing to tyranny.

HARRIS: You have written a beautiful little book, *On Tyranny*. It's short, and it's very timely. It reads as though you wrote it the moment Donald Trump became president. When did you actually start typing?

SNYDER: I'll give you a slightly pompous historian's answer. It's true that I wrote it quickly, but it compresses the history of the twentieth century, which I've spent twenty-five years trying to understand. Along the way, I invested years, very pleasantly, in friendships with people who had lived through communism and fascism and with students from Eastern Europe who lived through the failed promise of democracy, and I tried to learn from them all.

I couldn't have sat down and written this book without all of that previous time weighing down on me. What I tried to do was convert it all into a format that would be immediately useful. So yes, I wrote the twenty lessons in the hours after the 2016 election, and the book itself I wrote over a few days in December. But, in a way, this demonstrates one of the points of the book, which is that we're at a critical moment. We don't have much time, so whatever would make a difference had to appear immediately, at the very beginning.

HARRIS: I don't view this conversation as a substitute for buying the book, no matter how comprehensive our discussion of it. Your writing is so lapidary and aphoristic that your thoughts really deserve to be encountered on the page.

One criticism people might have is that *On Tyranny* exaggerates the danger of a Trump presidency. I'm wondering how you feel the book is aging. Is there anything that has reassured you in recent months? Or are you exactly where you were when you sent the manuscript to your publisher?

SNYDER: I didn't write the book as a direct response to Trump as a person, but rather as an invitation to citizens to be alert and broaden our sense of what can happen. The whole point of the book is that we have to expand our political imagination beyond the unreflective day-to-day sense of the normal. And the danger at the moment is that we just go day by day—so that every day seems normal even if today is worse than yesterday. We're very good at getting used to today.

But it's also striking that much of what I wrote about has indeed happened in the meantime. It was clear in 2016 that we were dealing with a candidate who didn't respect basic American institutions, like democracy or the rule of law—that we were dealing with a man who was not tolerant, to put it mildly, and who had a certain idea about how things should be run which was inconsistent with checks and balances and institutional constraints. Trump's political heroes, after all, are foreign dictators who did away with the rule of law after being elected. When a person of his character finds himself in an institutional situation that constrains him, he'll push against those constraints. He can't really do anything else—that's who he is. But the issue is not really Trump. The issue is us. The relevant question is less about whether those constraints can hold him and more about what we can do to make sure they do. That's what the book is really about.

When I first posted these twenty lessons on Facebook in November 2016, a lot of people, as you say, thought I was going overboard. But with the passage of time that has been replaced by, "How did you see this coming?"

And the simple answer is that history doesn't repeat itself so much as offer you a broad palette of what's possible. The main idea of the book is not to go into the particular things Trump will do but rather to prepare us to act in ways that will make an authoritarian regime change less likely. I've been reassured by lawyers filing briefs in advance, and by the spontaneous protests at airports, and the marches. I've been reassured by the setting up of nongovernmental organizations that didn't exist before. I've been reassured by the civic-mindedness and patriotism of some of our civil servants. I've been reassured by the investigative journalism—for example, at the *Washington Post*.

On the other hand, there are plenty of people who don't see a problem at all. They're doing the normal human thing, normalizing the situation and basically taking whatever they're given from day to day. Americans are extremely provincial. We don't really have a sense of what's possible, because we have been lucky. We overestimate how much we deserve our luck, and we underestimate how easily we could get unlucky. At the moment, we *are* unlucky—which means that at the moment more is demanded of us.

HARRIS: I don't want people to misunderstand the connection between your book and the current moment, because it doesn't read as narrowly focused on Trump. You're talking about how democracies can fail, and how people don't realize they're being pulled by the tide of history in a very unlucky direction, toward the ruination of everything they care about. Even if Trump magically becomes the perfect president, the generic case still holds. And his election proves that our system is vulnerable to a demagogue in ways many of us never anticipated. It's scary to imagine someone much more competent than Trump—and more ideological and nefarious—who can come to power exploiting the very weaknesses in our system that Trump found.

I want to discuss the point you just raised, about how provincial Americans are. You say here in the beginning of the book, "Americans today are no wiser than the Europeans who saw democracy yield to fascism, Nazism, or communism in the twentieth century. Our one advantage is that we might learn from their experience. Now is a good time to do so."

Why are we so blinkered?

SNYDER: Thank you for putting the question so boldly, because it's an important one. If we're going to get out of this mess, we'll have to take note of our weaknesses. We've gotten into the habit of congratulating ourselves on our strengths, and this is a ritual both Democrats and Republicans engage in, in their different ways. One of the weaknesses of Obama's rhetoric, for example, was that we got used to hearing how good we were at certain things.

There are three factors at play here. The first is the long-standing religious tradition of exceptionalism, the notion that Americans escaped from an evil old world into a pure new world, which is, of course, ridiculous on a whole number of fronts. The second is the obvious fact that in many ways we're a world unto ourselves. Our historians of American history rarely venture *beyond* American history, so you can hardly expect the American citizen to do so. And the third factor, and maybe the most relevant, is metaphysical laziness.

After 1989, when the Berlin Wall fell, we decided that history was over, and we disarmed ourselves against the very threats that history warns us of. We adopted various versions of a story whereby human nature would lead to the so-called free market, which would in turn lead to democracy and enlightenment, which would lead to peace, or something like that—all of which is ahistorical nonsense.

All these teleological stories are basically wrong. There's no such thing as a free market, the relationship between capitalism and democracy is not at all straightforward, and history is all about the things people did not anticipate at the time. The future will always be full of surprises, structural forces we don't anticipate, and accidents. The very claim that history is over is itself a historical choice. It's a choice to be ignorant, to forget concepts that once were useful. It's a choice to be vulnerable when threats begin to arise again. That has happened to us. Part of the perfect storm of 2016 is that it happened a full generation after 1989. In a way, it's payback for our having decided that history was over.

HARRIS: You describe both fascism and communism as responses to globalization, and an antipathy toward globalization obviously played an important role in the 2016 election. How is a withdrawal from the world responsible for these antidemocratic tendencies?

SNYDER: The paradigm of globalization, as we've invented it for ourselves in the twenty-first century, assumes that it's something new. This is a good example of how we're trapped in the present and have trouble seeing the past. When you assume something is new, you don't see that it has an arc. You don't see that it has patterns, or where it might be going. Our failure to reckon with the past in that sense is one of the things that historians bang their foreheads against the table about.

The basic fact is that this is the second globalization. There was a similar movement in the late nineteenth and early twentieth centuries. We had a similar expansion of foreign trade, a similar export-driven growth.

And maybe most interestingly, in the late nineteenth century we had much the same worldview as in the late twentieth century. Many Europeans and Americans were sure that this expansion of trade would inevitably lead to an expansion of enlightened consciousness and that universal ideas would inevitably triumph. And yet that globalization ended in, as we all know, the First World War, the Great Depression, and the Second World War.

So we've been down this road before. This is the intellectual history of the late nineteenth and early twentieth centuries. The whole point of remembering this history is to be braced, in the sense of being sobered up, by the realization that globalization can boomerang and that some of the reactions to it can be quite extreme. But it's also bracing in the sense that it reminds us that people lived through this the first time around, and when they survived and came out the other end, some of them were more articulate and perhaps wiser than we are. So we can save a lot of time by drawing upon what they left behind.

But to answer your question: globalization, even if it brings an average improvement measurable by some kind of abstract notion of well-being, like GDP per capita, will also produce local, or fractally local, inequalities and resentments—because globalization also entails the globalization of comparison. It means that people compare themselves to other people in ways they hadn't before and thus will often see themselves as victims. That's clearly happened in the United States in the twenty-first century. Something similar happened in Central Europe in the early twentieth century. And in such an environment, it's easy for clever politicians to rise up and say, "Globalization isn't complicated, it's simple. It's actually a conspiracy. I will put a face on globalization for you."

And what fascism and national socialism did was to put a Jewish face on globalization and declare, "All these problems are not the result of an unhindered process that nobody controls completely but the result of a particular conspiracy by a particular group." That's very powerful politically, because then you can figuratively and literally get your hands on members of that group who are inside your country and thereby imagine you're carrying out some kind of political change.

So, in a minor key, this is happening in the United States in the twenty-first century. You see basically the same reaction to globalization. The problem being presented to us is not that globalization will always be full of challenges, which we need to address. "No, no," says Mr. Trump. The problem is that globalization has a face. It has a Chinese face. It has a Mexican face. It has a Jewish face. And that's a familiar form of politics, because it relieves Mr. Trump, and the government in general, of any obligation to actually address the challenges of globalization and replaces it with a form of politics in which we're supposed to thwart members of these various groups. And while we're doing that, we're forgetting about what the government is failing to do for us—namely, to enable us to prosper.

For instance, the attempt at a Muslim ban isn't really about Muslims, it's about getting us into the habit of seeing Muslims as the source of our problems. Or take VOICE (the Victims of Immigration Crime Engagement), the new denunciation office at Homeland Security, where you're supposed to call up a bureaucrat in Washington if you think you've been the victim of a crime by an undocumented migrant. That's not about the migrants; it's about getting you into the habit of denouncing your neighbors. It's about ushering in a new form of politics.

HARRIS: But when you put it that way—that it's not about undocumented migrants but about establishing a new kind of politics that will encourage people to inform on their neighbors—that seems to attribute some kind of nefarious intent to the current government. In other words, it's not a system working unconsciously in that direction. It sounds like you're alleging that people are consciously harboring undemocratic thoughts—whether fascistic or some other flavor—and intentionally edging us toward tyranny.

SNYDER: Yes, we've had such people in the White House—Steve Bannon, for instance—who are quite consciously ideological and hold to far-right traditions that are antidemocratic. We have a president of the United States who spent 2016 telling us that democracy is basically faked, which is one of the things people say in the first stages of regime change. With regard to denunciation, whether it's the administration or the citizens doing the denouncing, I think people half understand what they're doing. And when they cross that moral threshold, they take the next step. If you've denounced somebody, you get praised for doing it and maybe you get the first crack at their property, or whatever. So a new cycle begins.

So yes, I would say that clearly there are people who have antidemocratic thoughts, absolutely! Part of the point of history is to recognize that democracy isn't automatic and there are plenty of people who don't like it. And that there are processes by which civil servants and citizens get drawn in, with denunciations, for example, and thereafter find themselves in a different moral place, even if in the beginning they didn't fully understand what they were doing.

HARRIS: Okay, on that happy note, I want to get directly into your book and into the lessons. The first lesson is, "Do not obey in advance." And then you summarize it: "Most of the power of authoritarianism is freely given. In times like these, individuals think ahead about what a more repressive government will want, and then offer themselves without being asked. A citizen who adapts in this way is teaching power what it can do." And then you go on to talk about how the Nazis moved into Austria and how the behavior of the Austrians, more or less unbidden, taught the Nazis how far they could go in victimizing Austrian Jews. You suggest that there is something to learn from how readily people acquiesced to this project.

SNYDER: That's lesson number one for many reasons. It's at the core of what historians think we understand about authoritarian regime changes—Nazi Germany in particular. Namely, that at the very beginning, whether it's the takeover in Germany itself or the Anschluss in Austria, authoritarian leaders require consent.

This is an important thought, because when we think of authoritarians, we think of villains and then of supervillains and then of superpowers. You know, we imagine these guys in uniform striding across the stage of history and doing whatever they want. And maybe toward the end something like that is true. But at the beginning it's not. At the beginning, people in fact have more power than they do normally, because they have the power to resist. The problem is that we don't usually realize that. We tend to take new situations as normal and then align ourselves with them. We follow along. We drift. And most of the time that's appropriate, but sometimes it's a disaster. Historians generally agree on this—which is notable, because historians, particularly historians of Nazi Germany, don't always agree, to put it mildly.

The other reason this lesson is at the front of the book is that if you blow it, you can forget about the rest. Fail to learn the first lesson and things that would have seemed abnormal to an earlier version of you will start to seem normal. You'll keep saying, "Tomorrow, tomorrow, tomorrow." And in fact, you'll just be internally adjusting, adjusting, adjusting. Psychologically, you become a different person, but incapable of seeing the difference.

And the final reason it's lesson number one is political. If people don't take advantage of the moment they have in the first weeks, months, and maybe, at the outside, the first year, then the system changes and the costs of resistance become much higher. Right now, the little things we do that will make a difference—like looking people in the eye, subscribing to newspapers, founding a neighborhood organization, running for local office, protesting, having political conversations like the one you and I are having—these things don't require all that much courage, at least for you and me. Later, when these things have become suspect or even illegal, they require much more.

Hitler didn't know that he could absorb Austria in a few days. He took that decision on the fly because of the messages he got from Austrians who could see how power was shifting. Austrian Jews didn't know they were so seriously threatened. They found out because of how people reacted to the arrival of German forces. The actions that a population chooses or doesn't choose to take at the beginning are crucial to authoritarianism. That choice, to act or not, means we have power; it also means we have responsibility. You don't have the option of doing nothing. In America, in the spring of 2017, if you're doing nothing, you're actually doing something. If you're doing nothing, you're helping a regime change come about.

HARRIS: You and I are largely in agreement about how seriously to take these concerns, given what's happening in the White House. But some people will think that everything you just said, when mapped onto the present, sounds like paranoia—because, they'll argue, we're simply not in the situation you've just described. I'd like to avoid what they'll, doubtless, view as a partisan line in this conversation, because everything you're saying applies generically. Even if one is a fan of Trump, one can agree that these dynamics are in play potentially everywhere, all the time, no matter how stable a democracy seems.

So I want to move to lesson number two: "Defend institutions." You write, "Institutions do not protect themselves. They fall one after the other unless each is defended from the beginning." You use Nazi Germany as an example, and then you quote from an editorial I had never seen. I've read a lot about the Holocaust, but I'd never seen an editorial like this, in a newspaper for German Jews. Imagine the *New York Times* running an editorial like this in 1933, on the eve of the decade that would usher in the Final Solution. This is the perspective of German Jews in 1933:

> We do not subscribe to the view that Mr. Hitler and his friends, now finally in possession of the power they have so long desired, will implement the proposals circulating in [Nazi newspapers]; they will not suddenly deprive German Jews of their constitutional rights, nor enclose them in ghettos, nor subject them to the jealous and murderous impulses of the mob. They cannot do this, because a number of critical factors hold powers in check . . . and they clearly do not want to go down that road. When one acts as a European power, the whole atmosphere tends toward ethical reflection upon one's better self and away from revisiting one's earlier oppositional posture.

And then you say, "Such was the view of many reasonable people in 1933, just as it is the view of many reasonable people now. The mistake is to assume that rulers who came to power through institutions cannot change or destroy those very institutions—even when that is exactly what they have announced that they will do."

The phrase "cautionary tale" doesn't really do this justice. It's amazing to put yourself in the position of people living on the brink of the Holocaust, before such an implosion of a cosmopolitan society was conceivable—before one could even dimly imagine that places of business would be marked as Jewish-owned and that then one's property could be seized by one's neighbors in an ecstasy of greed, resentment, and tribal hatred.

Please say more about the defense of institutions and about this myopia that keeps people from seeing that they're swimming in the stream of history.

SNYDER: Let me start with history. I'm glad you cited that editorial, because it gives me a chance to express my appreciation for my colleagues working in the history of Nazi Germany. It's not that I just knew about it, it was published in a very important collection of documents from the Nazi period. And one of my points in writing the book is that as confusing as the present is, the clarity we now have on moments in the past gives us an advantage. If it strikes us as strange that people could do what they did or think what they thought, that's precisely the wake-up call we need, because we'll otherwise fall into the same ruts, and do things that people seventy years on will find strange.

It's interesting that you use the word "paranoia." If someone had told the editorial board of that newspaper, which was a Jewish newspaper, what was coming, they'd have likely had the same reaction—that people were being paranoid. The advantage in looking back at the past is that we can get some distance on our own default reactions.

Since I wrote the book, a few new reasons for taking 1933 seriously have emerged. In the book, I say, "History does not repeat, but it does instruct." I meant that in two senses. One sense is that we can learn from people, both their failures and their insights. The other is that history is instructing people who want the 1930s to come back. Unfortunately, there's more of that going on than one would like to think.

For example, Sean Spicer's odd claim that Hitler "was not using gas on his own people," by which he apparently meant that the handicapped and the German Jews were not actually German people. Or Attorney General Jeff Sessions saying he was "amazed that a judge sitting on an island in the Pacific" could tell the president what to do, forgetting that we entered the Second World War because of that island in the Pacific.

When we have Mr. Bannon saying that the 1930s were an exciting time, when we have Mr. Trump branding our foreign policy and our energy policy "America First," we have before us explicit and deliberate references to the 1930s, coming from the administration itself. Remember that America First was not just a populist but often an isolationist and anti-Semitic movement that was trying to keep us out of the Second World War. You said, "Imagine if the *New York Times* in 1933 published an editorial like this." But they did. They did.

One of the reasons the *Times* is so much on its toes now is, if you look back at how it dealt with both Nazi Germany and the Soviet Union in the 1930s, it did not cover itself with glory. There was a huge amount of explaining and normalizing of both Stalin and Hitler. And the *Times* was not at all the worst. There was a good deal of actual praise of Hitler in the American press. It's very striking. So it's not just that Germans, and German Jews, tended to normalize and ignore the possibilities. Our newspapers did as well, and that's one more reason to be cautious.

So why are institutions important? The answer is that we need a plurality of them, and if we don't recognize that the election of somebody with authoritarian propensities is a threat to those institutions, they will fall. Elections played an important part in Hitler's rise to power. If we look at the rise of authoritarian regimes around today in the twenty-first century, in most cases it involved an election. Elections don't guarantee democracy. Unfortunately, if you elect a tyrant, that tyrant will push against the institutions and try to pick them off one by one. As we know from the playbook of the twentieth century, authoritarianism, whether it's from the far right or the far left, works that way. You can't take power all at once; you have to pick off one thing at a time. Often it's journalism or the high court at the beginning. But the point is that if you don't draw a line around the first institution, there's a tendency for all the dominoes to fall.

HARRIS: You reminded me about that disastrous press conference where Trump's press secretary, Sean Spicer, inadvertently produced a comic masterpiece when he began a riff about "Holocaust centers" and flubbed his answers to direct questions as badly as any beauty pageant contestant ever has. It was brutal.

Here's lesson number three: "Beware the one-party state." Your summary: "The parties that remade states and suppressed rivals were not omnipotent from the start. They exploited a historic moment to make political life impossible for their opponents." Again, that's a phenomenon we can inch toward imperceptibly, I suspect. One party acquires more and more power and disallows more and more of what were once the legitimate political norms of a multiparty system. How are we functioning with respect to that particular criterion now?

SNYDER: This is part of the confluence of circumstances in 2016. It's related to Mr. Trump, but it's also, in a way, distinct. There's a story Americans tell themselves, which is that we've had democracy for two hundred years and therefore we'll continue to have it. Whereas we've really had democracy for only a few decades, since the Civil Rights Act. And in the last half of those few decades, we've been markedly drifting away from democracy, allowing unlimited money into politics, so that, in effect, a couple of people with lots of cash can determine a state's elections even if they do not reside there, which is clearly not democratic.

Gerrymandering, to take the example of Ohio, where I'm from, means that if you vote for one ticket your vote basically counts half of what someone else's vote for the other ticket counts. Then there's the Electoral College, in which a voter from California has much less weight than a voter from, let's say, Wyoming. And that's leaving aside the voter-suppression laws, which are probably going to get worse.

My point is that we were drifting away from democracy already, and Mr. Trump took advantage of that. Obviously, in the simplest sense, he couldn't have won without the Electoral College. But since people are well aware that there's too much money in politics, he could pose as a friendly oligarch. He could say, "Everybody knows the system is corrupt. It's oligarchical. But I'm *your* oligarch and Hillary Clinton is somebody else's oligarch." And this is where allegations of a global conspiracy come in. His message, in effect, was to say, "You know, there are mysterious people behind the curtain who are backing Hillary Clinton, but I stand before you, me myself, Donald Trump. I'm your oligarch."

Of course, that wasn't true. First, it's not clear that Mr. Trump actually has that much money. It's also not true that there were no oligarchs backing him. There were; they just weren't American citizens. But he couldn't have made that pitch without the problem of there being too much money in politics to begin with.

Another issue is the way the game is now structured so that Republicans tend to win, but that creates a problem even for themselves. Thirty-four of the fifty statehouses are Republican, and gerrymandering has become so surgically precise that it doesn't help Republicans in the long run—at least not if they want to remain in a two-party system—because it puts them in a position to win when, as happened this time, they don't have policies that most people would support. It would be fine if people supported their policies; it's just a fact that the majority of American voters don't.

So the Republicans find themselves in a position of undeserved success. And this then becomes a danger for democracy. When you have a party that controls the levers of power and that party cannot democratically legitimize itself, there's a temptation to do things to stay in power by undemocratic means. And this is, again, not about Republicans or about Democrats, it's about human nature. It's about the need for checks and balances, which the Founding Fathers quite rightly foresaw.

So we're edging into a situation I hope we can avoid. And I hope and trust that many decent-minded, patriotic, constitutionally oriented Republicans will also understand this. We're edging toward a moment where if we are not careful we will slip into a one-party state. It's not just unhealthy for Democrats, it's also unhealthy for Republicans, and, above all, it leads to a situation that's very hard to get out of. Everything gets harder when people get used to having power without being demo-cratically legitimized.

HARRIS: You quote a poignant and beautiful line from a David Lodge novel, "You don't know, when you make love for the last time, that you're making love for the last time." And then you say, "Voting is like that." And you go on, "No doubt the Russians who voted in 1990 did not think that this would be the last free and fair election in their country's history, which (thus far) it has been." And a little further down the page, "The Russian oligarchy established after the 1990 elections continues to function and promotes a foreign policy designed to destroy democracy elsewhere." This is a generic human experience—people can behave democratically in a way that destroys democracy. And they do this without having any idea that it is happening.

I'd like to know what you make of the fact that so many of Trump's defenders—of course, there are some Republicans who don't defend him—seem perfectly sanguine about, or oblivious to, Russia's transparent attempt to undermine our democracy. We're talking about the party that won the Cold War, or think they did. If you look back three years, no one on Earth harbored more bias toward Russia and its history of Communist authoritarianism than Republicans. How did we get here?

SNYDER: I'll follow my own advice and start not with America but with the world. One of the elements of our provincialism is that we imagine that things happen here and then roll outward, whether it's politics or economics or political theory or movies or fashion. We imagine that it happens here first and then everyone else gets it and follows along. But that's not nearly as true as we think it is, and in some crucial respects the reverse is happening. The main political ideas and trends now tend to move from the East to the West.

I'm not saying that the Russian system is stable. I don't think it is, but they have maintained a certain equilibrium that lets them institutionalize and stabilize radical economic inequality by way of an efficiently and beautifully produced diet of fake news complemented by a series of manufactured "triumphs abroad." This is the model. We have to be aware that it's out there and that it's attractive to certain kinds of people.

Now, that model cannot generate wealth. But it can stabilize what might appear to be unsustainable inequality of wealth. It can justify inequality by claiming that we're in a constant struggle against evil forces, which for Russia are terrorism and America. Nor can it generate reform, because reform would put the kleptocrats out of power. It can only justify a status quo of extreme inequality.

And since Russia is not alone in the world, what the Russians—or Mr. Putin, who's a very intelligent man in many respects—came to understand is that you have to remove the competition. You have to make the rest of the world more like Russia. If Russia's not going to be more like Europe, make Europe more like Russia. And the way to make Europe more like Russia is to support, with propaganda and money, right-wing populists—and then to do so in the United States as well. This has been going on for some time. To give an example: way back in 2010 when Mr. Trump started talking about "birtherism," Russian propaganda also started talking about birtherism.

So they have a smart idea that is also a disaster for humanity. The idea is to bring everyone else down to Russia's level and to do so partly by supporting the far right but also by spreading the idea that there's no such thing as truth, that everything is relative, and that there are no facts. Because if those convictions take hold, political activity and political opposition become incoherent and impossible.

They've succeeded at this at home and now they're trying to spread it abroad, and they've had some success. One has to recognize their intelligence and one has to be clear about their aims, because we are now in the middle of this. What's happening to us has been very much a result of intelligent Russians acting intelligently, according to what they see as their own interests.

So now to get to your question. When it comes to Republicans and Russia, first of all one has to accept that there are plenty of people who do see Russia as a positive model. It's not just the white supremacist Richard Spencer who talks about Russia as a positive model. There are plenty of evangelical Christians who, perhaps more quietly, regard Russia's stand against a perceived Islamic problem, and Russia's embrace of Orthodoxy as positive. And they approve of Russia's stand on homosexuality. There's been a fair amount of circulation of ideas via Moscow throughout the American heartland.

So there are plenty of people who see Russia quite properly as the leader of a right-wing movement. And this also addresses what you say about the Cold War. You and I might still think about the Cold War when we think of Russia, but the modern American right no longer does. The American right looks at Russia and sees a model of an antiterrorist, religion-loving leadership. That, of course, is complete manufactured hogwash. It's just as bogus as the image of the Soviet Union in the 1930s that buffaloed the American left. In many ways, it's very similar.

In fact Russia is a very poor country, where people are not free, where basically nobody goes to church, and where one of the top figures in the country, Ramzan Kadyrov, is himself a Muslim terrorist. Russia is not what people on the American right think it is, but they've bought into the image—partly as a result of the fact that no one actually travels to Russia and partly as result of Russian propaganda.

We have to accept that in some sense these elements of the American right are correct: if you want a kleptocratic, extremely unequal, authoritarian, nominally though not really Christian regime, then Russia can be seen as a positive model. That makes a certain kind of sense.

Now, if that's not you, but you still think Russian meddling is not an issue, it's probably an information-siloing problem, because if you follow even the Russian press, which is where I started—I wrote about this in early 2016 using open Russian sources, it's clear that the Russian political and media elites sided with Mr. Trump. Not just in the general election but during the primaries. And then there were a whole series of revelations indicating this over the course of 2016.

But there's a siloing of information whereby some people think, "okay, a Russian connection is bad for Trump, so therefore it must have been manufactured by his enemies." And that's a way of thinking which is dangerous and antidemocratic. One test of whether you are a free person is whether you can change your mind. If you haven't changed your mind on a major issue, you have a problem with freedom. As citizens, we all have to confront the facts as they are and welcome an investigation. If there was no collusion, then fine, there was no collusion. If there was collusion, it benefits us all to know about it.

HARRIS: The siloing of information is an enormous problem, which we'll spend the rest of our lives grappling with. But this allegation of siloing cuts both ways. People who discount Russia's influence will simply view what you said as a symptom of your own siloing. You've been taken in by "fake news" in the *Washington Post* and the *New York Times* and whatever your Russian-language sources are, and you've been bamboozled just as you claim other people have been by Breitbart, Fox, and Infowars. It's a stalemate.

Obviously, there's no parity between the two sides. Neither of us will lose sleep tonight wondering whether we're right to generally trust the *Washington Post*, the *New York Times*, and the *Atlantic* over Breitbart, Fox, and Infowars. But siloing makes these particular conversations almost impossible to have.

SNYDER: Yes, and there's something basic I want to say about that. It's one thing to say, "I know fact A and you know fact B." It's another when government officials are promoting suspicion of facts as such, which I'm afraid is where we are now. When Kellyanne Conway talks about "alternative facts" or our president says that journalists are the "enemies of the people," when Bannon says the media are an opposition party, what we have is not one set of facts versus another set of facts. We have people actually instructing Americans to be ignorant in a committed way. That's the language of authoritarianism. And authoritarianism is attractive for that reason, because it's more comfortable to hear the things you want to hear, over and over.

John Maynard Keynes put siloing in its place very nicely: "When the facts change, I change my mind. What do you do, sir?" That's my view, too. My opinions about Russia and Trump could be changed by a preponderance of evidence on the other side. Thus far there is no such evidence. And the evidence we do have points the other way, right down to the fact that the president fulminates against Robert Mueller's investigation—which, to my mind, is basically a confession. It seems to me that this is the basic issue: Are we actually open to facts? Can we actually change our minds?

As it happens, I read Russian and I read Ukrainian and I know a lot of people who are fairly close to these events. I've spent time in those countries. I've watched those things unfold. The name "Paul Manafort" has been familiar to me for a very long time. The whole cast of characters appearing on the news are people I've been reading about for years or even decades. So I think I have some sense of the larger patterns.

HARRIS: Well, I would extend this discussion to the question of why Trump won't release his tax returns. I'm pretty sure I know why. For one thing, he's almost certainly not as wealthy as he claims, and he's probably largely indebted to the Russians. Neither of these things is a crime, but they would be politically inconvenient.

The greater question is, Why would a supporter of Trump not want him to release his tax returns? If you think he's not a con man or a liar, then what's the harm in having him release his tax returns? The burden is on you to explain why you think that would be a bad idea, when every candidate and every president in recent decades has done it.

Let's jump to lesson number ten here, because it's of a piece with what you just said: "Believe in truth. To abandon facts is to abandon freedom. If nothing is true, then no one can criticize power, because there is no basis upon which to do so. If nothing is true, then all is spectacle. The biggest wallet pays for the most blinding lights."

What has been infuriating to me, more than anything else, has been this assault on truth, this eroding of the norms of honest conversation. There should be personal shame associated with failing to acknowledge established facts. There should be reputational costs. No one should listen to you if you're sufficiently out of register with what is well known to true, and you perversely deny the obvious.

We seem to have crossed over into some new place, where the president and his surrogates can go on television and confabulate without consequence. To its credit, the media has become less and less patient with this. And so there have been these delightful moments when journalists have pushed back in ways that Trump supporters no doubt view as media bias and a lack of civility.

But the time for civility has long passed. I'll read a little more of your language here: "You submit to tyranny when you renounce the difference between what you want to hear and what is actually the case. This renunciation of reality can feel natural and pleasant, but the result is your demise as an individual—and thus the collapse of any political system that depends upon individualism."

And then you reference the German-Jewish philologist Victor Klemperer, who talked about how truth dies in four modes: "The first mode is the open hostility to verifiable reality, which takes the form of presenting inventions and lies as if they were facts. The president does this at a high rate and at a fast pace. One attempt during the 2016 campaign to track his utterances found that 78 percent of his factual claims were false. This proportion is so high that it makes the correct assertions seem like unintended oversights on the path toward total fiction. Demeaning the world as it is begins the creation of a fictional counterworld."

SNYDER: The assault on truth is more fundamental to authoritarian regime change than we sometimes realize, and that's because if we do read histories of communism or histories of fascism, the words we're reading are produced by historians, who naturally function in a reasonable, factual mode. So it's hard to recall the original poetry and magic of the ideology. In my book I was careful to cite people who had experienced national socialism, or fascism, or communism, and their recollections of their experience of propaganda, so that we have a sense of how vulnerable people are and how propaganda works.

Propaganda isn't just a kind of meddling with reality. Propaganda basically works by replacing our own apprehension of facts with something else. The fascist says, "It's not what you think, or what you think you know, that is important. The only truth is whether or not you feel subjectively, spiritually, part of a larger national community—and if you do, wonderful! And if you don't, then you're an enemy." And the Communist says, "The only truth is the vision of the beautiful utopian socialist future; therefore what seems to be happening today is not important.

Today is important only insofar as it leads to that future." Therefore it's not only justified but actually required that we lie about things happening today, because lying will help us achieve that future.

The difference in the twenty-first century is that those people trying to bring about authoritarian regime changes don't have the same grandeur of vision. Their attack on truth is entirely negative. It doesn't do anything except to expand the openings for the things that are already going wrong. Nevertheless, it's effective.

What I'm about to describe has happened in Russia, and it's happening in the United States. The first step is what Trump did in 2016. You fill the public sphere with falsehoods and you contradict yourself all the time, not just for political convenience but because you're attacking the notion of truthful discussion.

Then step two: you blame the people who are responsible for factuality. You call journalists "enemies" or "opponents." You talk about how you're going to discipline them, crack down on them, and so on.

And then the third step, if you win, is that nobody knows what truth is anymore. Because nobody trusts the authority of journalists, you end up having a monopoly, or at least the strongest position from which to manufacture the symbols of the day. That's clearly what the White House is up to.

I think this is probably more central and more important than we generally realize, because no one can say where we're going, but we *can* say what democracy requires. Democracy requires the rule of law. The rule of law requires trust, and trust requires that we all think that there are facts out there. If you do away with the belief that there are facts, you've gone straight to the heart of the matter. You've destroyed democracy. That's the cheap and easy way to do it. And that's what the twenty-first-century authoritarians have discovered, and that's the process underway before our eyes.

HARRIS: I'm jumping around with impunity here, because what you just said connects to lesson number nine, which is "Be kind to our language. Avoid pronouncing the phrases everyone else does. Think up your own way of speaking, even if only to convey that thing you think everyone is saying. Make an effort to separate yourself from the internet. Read books." And you say something relevant to the way the press has, inadvertently or not, normalized Trump: "Politicians in our times feed their clichés to television, where even those who wish to disagree repeat them. Television purports to challenge political language by conveying images, but the succession from one frame to another can hinder a sense of resolution. Everything happens fast, but nothing actually happens. Each story on televised news is 'breaking' until it is displaced by the next one. So we are hit by wave upon wave but never see the ocean."

I now realize that this has been bothering me, but I hadn't thought about it in those terms. This connects to something I've said before, which is that if Trump were one tenth as bad, he would seem much worse. The velocity of the lying and the scandals and the conflicts of interest, the fact that there's something new to absorb every few hours, puts the news cycle into a perpetual frenzy. And you don't have time to absorb the significance of "breaking news," because four hours later something new will have happened, and it will be absolutely astonishing—or, at least, it would have been astonishing if our capacity for astonishment hadn't been beaten out of us. This is especially true of television. In order to present their explanation for what's going on, journalists are forced to interact with the people in power, which tends to normalize even the craziest things these people say. Even when journalists seem critical, they're adopting language that distorts our perception of what is politically normal.

SNYDER: Yes. This is one reason I'm so careful with language in the book and why the formulations in the book will seem different from the formulations you hear on television or read in the newspapers. I'm trying hard to conceptualize the present, and I think we can all do that.

I'll put a more optimistic spin on your comments: I agree with your premises, but we're not really trapped by all this. We can decide to watch the TV news for half an hour a day, or a couple of hours a week, rather than getting lost in it. Likewise with the internet. We can schedule to spend half an hour a day reading our newsfeeds rather than just getting drawn in. The truth is, we don't gain anything by watching more. If you want the news, reading a good newspaper for, say, half an hour a day is better than watching television or clicking on the internet for three or four hours a day. That also frees up time for reading and for speaking with other people.

This recalls the 1970s and 1980s and our history as a country that was once, in its public political discussions, against fascism and communism. In part because we read books, we once had all these concepts, constructs, and phrases we could apply to something that struck us. Because when something happens, you can react in one of two ways: you can react in terms of the mental preparation you've made, or you can react according to how people want you to react. And even though this administration is in many ways incompetent, and we sometimes laugh at its messaging, nevertheless they have a way they want us to follow, and many people follow it.

We're not really free unless we can put matters in our own words. And if we can't put them in our own words, we can't talk to other people, because if we speak the words of the internet or the TV news, other people will recognize that, and they are not really in our company, but somewhere else. But if we can find some other way, a specific personal way, to frame our concerns, then we may evoke in the minds of others some associations that go beyond what they're constantly watching. Reading is a precondition of conversation, and conversation is something we very much need politically.

HARRIS: I'll take up one more chapter here, which is lesson number four: "Take responsibility for the face of the world. The symbols of today enable the reality of tomorrow. Notice the swastikas and the other signs of hate. Do not look away, and do not get used to them. Remove them yourself and set an example for others to do so." You start this chapter saying, "Life is political, not because the world cares about how you feel, but because the world reacts to what you do. The minor choices we make are a kind of vote, making it more or less likely that free and fair elections will be held in the future."

And then you go on to talk about something Vaclav Havel wrote in "The Power of the Powerless": "[H]e was explaining the continuity of an oppressive regime in whose goals and ideology few people still believed. He offered a parable of a greengrocer who places a sign reading 'Workers of the world, unite!' in his shop window. It is not that the man actually endorses the content of this quotation from *The Communist Manifesto*. He places the sign in his window so that he can withdraw into daily life without trouble from the authorities. When everyone else follows the same logic, the public sphere is covered with signs of loyalty, and resistance becomes unthinkable."

It's that withdrawal into daily life that interests me. People who would never, at least at this stage, post or utter any sign of loyalty still find it too painful to express any dissent—too risky socially, or just not worth the hassle. What's the point of taking a public stand on these issues?

SNYDER: The fundamental point in lesson number four, and also in a number of the other lessons, like the one about small talk, has to do with everyday power. What Havel is saying is a bit like what we were talking about with lesson number one. It's precisely when we're facing incipient authoritarianism that we have more power than we do at other times, because gestures and words and handshakes count for very much more. They count in terms of our own psychological alignment of ourselves as free people. They count in their affirmation and their encouragement of people who might feel marginalized.

With regard to people who think, "Yes, this is bad but I don't want to take the risk," I'd point out that most Americans don't take very many risks by marching, or by subscribing to a newspaper, or by running for local office, or by giving to a nongovernmental organization. At this particular moment, the risks most of us are running are small compared to what faced others before us, who so generously left us all this wonderful writing. People like Victor Klemperer or Hannah Arendt weren't writing for themselves. They were writing because they knew people, later on, would face similar challenges. We have what they've left us, and all we have to do is use it.

The other thing I would say about risk is that even if I'm completely wrong about Trump, the twenty lessons are good for you anyway. These are daily practices that are good for civil society in general, regardless of your political convictions.

But let's say that I'm right, or basically right. There's some chance that we could lose the kinds of freedoms that many Americans are used to taking for granted. That's the risk—the risk that our children and grandchildren won't know what it's like to be free.

When freedom is gone, people will no longer know what it is, and then you have a real struggle to get it back. I see so much evidence in the United States now that suggests that people are forgetting what freedom is. And that's what I worry about.

What Is Racism?

A CONVERSATION WITH GLENN C. LOURY

Glenn C. Loury is the Merton P. Stoltz professor of the social sciences and professor of economics at Brown University, a fellow of the American Academy
of Arts and Sciences, and a former Guggenheim fellowship recipient, with an
interest in applied microeconomics, game theory, industrial organization, natural resource economics, and the economics of race and inequality. He is a
prominent social critic whose popular work focuses mainly on racial inequality
and social policy.

I first discovered Glenn on his own podcast, where he has been having some
extraordinarily candid and illuminating conversations about race and racism
with the linguist John McWhorter. Loury spends a fair amount of time giving
the counterpoint to his positions—steel-manning rather than straw-manning
the views of his opponents—and this is one reason why conversation with him
can be so productive.

In the exchange that follows, we cover many issues—ranging from police
violence to identity politics—in an attempt to better understand the enduring
problem of racial inequality and what to do about it.

HARRIS: Glenn, it's been bothering me that so much of what I hear about race, racism, and police violence in America doesn't make any sense, and that I've been worried about speaking to these issues in public. But I've since stiffened my spine. As you probably know, I think identity politics is simply poison—unless your identity at this point happens to be *Homo sapiens*.

We are now living in a culture that is addicted to outrage—especially among young people—and it's becoming impossible to have productive conversations on important topics like religion, violence, gender, inequality, etc. And race is obviously one of the most polarizing issues. You've been covering this difficult terrain on your podcast in a way that's really unusual and unusually enlightening. So it's great to finally be speaking with you.

LOURY: I appreciate that. One of my motivations is that in the face of this addiction to outrage—and that's an artful way of putting it—and moral certitude and intolerance of argument, I felt compelled, because I care so much about these questions of race and equality and justice, to keep challenging and raising questions. I don't think I'm deserving of any heroic celebration for doing that; it just seems like the right thing to do.

HARRIS: Before we dive into this topic, perhaps you could say a few words about your background and your areas of intellectual focus. How do you describe what you do in general?

LOURY: I'm a professor of economics at Brown University, and I've been there for ten years. I've also taught economics at a number of other universities: Harvard in the 1980s, Boston University in the 1990s. I was trained at MIT in the 1970s, took a PhD in economics there, and for much of my early career focused on mathematical modeling of various economic processes in the labor market and industrial organizations. Competition, research and development, natural-resource economics, economics of invention and exploration—things of this kind. Game theory. Information economics.

I became a professor at the Kennedy School of Government at Harvard, and while there I got very interested in public policy. I began writing essays and reviews and commentaries on issues of race in the United States particularly. At the time I was a Reagan conservative—quite rare for an African American. I moved away from that political identity and toward the center of the spectrum, and I now think of myself as a centrist Democrat, or maybe a mildly right-of-center Democrat. Though that's not an identity I cling to with any intensity.

HARRIS: Obviously your background in mathematics, statistics, and social science makes you well placed to have this kind of conversation. Race and racism is a topic that attracts a fair amount of logical and moral confusion, which renders people unable to reason with each other. It's not just a problem across racial lines, and it's not just a problem in public. I have white friends with whom I can't have this conversation because they become so emotionally hijacked. From my point of view, they don't realize that almost everything coming out of their mouths makes no moral or logical or historical or psychological sense. This worries me, because I view the maintenance of civilization and moral progress as a series of successful conversations. In fact, it seems to me that we perpetually confront a choice between conversation and violence. So when I see conversations reliably fail, I start to get worried.

As a final preliminary point, I should acknowledge a couple of things that should be obvious. The first is that the history of racism in the United States has been horrific. No sane person could dispute that. And there's no doubt that racism remains a problem in our society—just how big a problem is something I want us to discuss. Third, I can admit to my privileged position here: I have reaped many advantages from being white. Finally, I have no idea what it's like to grow up as a black man in our society. I get that I don't get it, and if there's any way in which my not getting it seems relevant to the issues we'll touch, I hope you'll point that out to me. But my goal in this conversation is to produce an accurate picture of race and racism in our country, as well as of police violence as it occurs now, so that we can think about how to move forward.

I wanted to erect that bulwark against calumny at the outset, because

I expect we'll say some things that will lend themselves to selective quotation, and the bad-faith attacks will not be far behind.

LOURY: I think your caveat is well taken and, I'd say, that it speaks well of you, but it's a pity that it's necessary for you to make that kind of elaborate, preemptive move. It reflects how closed and tortured the environment is in which we're having this conversation. I mean, I'm black, all right? I grew up on the South Side of Chicago from a working-class background in the 1950s and 1960s. I've had many a run-in with American racism all across the board, and I descend from people who were slaves in the United States.

On the other hand, the Emancipation Proclamation is a century and a half in the past. Jim Crow segregation is a distant memory. Barack Hussein Obama is about to step down, having served two terms, comfortably winning election to the highest office in the land. The police commissioners in many of the cities in which police and black community relations are most troubled are themselves African American, as are many of the administrative officials running the governments of those cities. We are fifty years past the advent of affirmative action. The idea that white privilege is such a stain on the country that an otherwise rational and intelligent person who happens to be white needs to give an elaborate preamble to a conversation about race relations in this country—that someone like yourself needs to apologize in advance for having an opinion—that's awful, that's poisonous.

HARRIS: Needless to say, I agree with you. But, unfortunately, I think it's still necessary, because, again, even my private conversations suggest that this topic is so radioactive that it's difficult for people to hear what's being said, much less appreciate the nuances and implications. Let's start with a deceptively simple question: What is racism?

LOURY: All right. This isn't necessarily a scientific response, this is a more off-the-cuff response. I would say it is a contempt for or devaluation of the humanity of another by virtue of their presumed racial identity. Racism is the suspension of the rational faculty and a perception of unfitness for intimate relations, a presumption about intelligence, an imputation of bad character—this kind of thing—vis-à-vis another person or group of people because of what one understands their racial identity to be.

HARRIS: Okay, so given that definition, which I agree with, who is the evil genius who first convinced the world that being able to honestly say, "Some of my best friends are black" is not an adequate defense against the charge of racism toward black people? If the path toward some color-blind utopia doesn't entail having best friends, or even a spouse, from a different race, if that doesn't represent an adequate surmounting of the problem of racism, what does? I'm speaking personally; we can leave aside institutional or structural racism for the moment.

LOURY: It's interesting that you brought up the phrase "some of my best friends are . . ." because I wrote an article more than twenty years ago called "Self-Censorship in Public Discourse: A Theory of Political Correctness." It was published in the journal *Rationality and Society*, and in it I develop an account of political correctness. I could go into it in greater detail should you be interested, but I can say this much about political correctness: it is a moral-signaling equilibrium whereby people who don't want to be thought of as on the wrong side of history suppress an honest expression of what they believe about some controversial issue because people known to be on the wrong side of history are prominently saying the same thing. For example, back when the fight for black independence in South Africa was going on, if a person trying to help South African blacks thought that boycotting South African businesses was not a good policy and constructive engagement with those businesses was a better policy, that person might be unwilling to say so in public because other people criticizing sanctions were supporting apartheid. Once a dodge of that kind comes into existence, it's robust and difficult to dispel.

With declarations like "I'm not really racist. Some of my best friends are black"—the sincerity of such declarations is called into question, because who's going to say such a thing except somebody who wants to avoid being sanctioned? Talk is cheap. Anybody can say it. There was a time in American cultural and social history—maybe the 1940s, '50s, maybe even into the '60s—when a person could say sincerely, "Some of my best friends are gay, but I'm against gay marriage," or "Some of my best friends are black, but I think affirmative action is a very poor policy," and it would have had some kind of weight. But the politically correct convention of value signaling—in which correct positions on sensitive issues like affirmative action or homosexual marriage are ways of signaling moral virtue—implies that the cover that one might have gotten from making these declarations no longer applies.

What did Shakespeare say? "Methinks the lady doth protest too much." The guy who says, "Some of my best friends are . . ." doth protest too much. That guy is seeking an exemption from the moral judgment of others for having what he knows the others know would be unacceptable positions, so he's donning some kind of fig leaf here. But we see it for what it is, a fig leaf, and we don't take it seriously.

HARRIS: Given your definition of racism, I think we have to distinguish between the mere harboring of certain biases and a belief that those biases are good or shouldn't be corrected for. Racism can't be just a matter of harboring biases; it can't be merely that you fail to be neutral on the implicit association test, because if that's the standard, almost no one would escape hanging. Even many black people would be convicted of racism against blacks in that case.

LOURY: The Harvard social psychologist Mahzarin Banaji, who was one of the founders of the implicit-bias literature, would agree with that. I don't think she'd claim an equivalency between implicit bias, as measured by one of her tests, and racism. Or in the case of gender differences, implicit bias about women's roles in society—which can be detected in almost every population of people who take these tests—and misogyny. She'd want to draw a distinction between those two.

Many African Americans will also score positive on these tests in terms of implicit bias about race. That doesn't make them racist; it just means that their cognitive processes implicitly incorporate certain presumptions or stereotypes about racial roles or racial behaviors that are a part of our culture and are shared across racial lines.

HARRIS: I should briefly describe the implicit-association test, or IAT, so that people know what we're talking about. Mahzarin Banaji has used it probably for twenty years. And we should also note that its validity has recently been called into question. The purpose of the test is to expose beliefs and biases that people are unaware that they hold, so can't report, or because the beliefs are socially undesirable wish not to report. It's been shown that, for instance, many white people will be faster at associating negative concepts with black faces than positive ones and show the opposite bias for white faces. And this is interpreted as meaning that they harbor a preference for white people over black people.

It's easy to see why people would view this as either a source or a consequence of racism. And you can do this kind of test with other things: You can do it with cats and dogs, or flowers and insects—you can do it with anything, really. But let's stipulate that most people will show an in-group bias on the IAT, and we can even go further and admit that this underlying psychology has something to do with racism. Again, this has always been a controversial claim, but let's remove the controversy, for the sake of argument. Let's say it's the cause, or the consequence, or both. Even in that case, racism as a social problem to be condemned and eradicated would be something else. Showing white bias on the IAT doesn't make you a racist; racism is the *endorsement* of norms that support that bias. It's a person's understanding that he's biased and his further claim that he's happy to be that way. A real racist believes that society shouldn't correct for such biases, because white people really are better than black people. He wants society to be unfair, based on the color of a person's skin, because he thinks skin color is a good way to determine a human being's moral worth.

There's no question that such people exist, but they must be a tiny minority in our society at this point. The rest of us—people of goodwill and moral enlightenment who may or may not be biased to one or another degree—clearly support laws and policies that seek to cancel that kind of racism, along with the pernicious effects of our underlying biases. As you say, we've elected our first black president, who's finishing his second term. This isn't tokenism. The people who voted for Obama with enthusiasm, whatever an IAT would have shown about them, are people who have nullified their personal bigotry in the form in which any real racist worthy of the name would champion it.

LOURY: I think that's true, although I know that many people would object to that conclusion. You've more or less cleverly defined racism out of the picture, because there wouldn't be many racists left if we had such a strict definition. So I'm challenging myself right now to think where the problem might be.

Let me just make an observation. Suppose someone observes that the homicide rate is high in certain quarters of our society that can be distinguished by race. Chicago, for instance, where so many people have been killed in past years: A disproportionate number of both victims and apparent perpetrators are black. The homicide rate for whites, victims and perpetrators, is much lower, and therefore there seems to be something going on in terms of black proclivity to resort to violence in settling disputes, or something like that. Suppose someone says that. Suppose someone says, "No wonder the police are so afraid when they encounter African Americans on the street. Have you taken a look at the crime statistics?" Or somebody says, "Yes, blacks may be more likely than whites to be shot by the police in terms of the rate per number in the population. But blacks are also overrepresented among violent criminals. Who can be surprised that they're overrepresented among those who are shot by police officers?"

In both cases, these are statements that in some way or another could be consistent with a person who might have certain kinds of implicit biases but who wouldn't endorse the norm that those biases are justified, or not a problem, or not indicative of a malady that needs to be addressed. They would still nevertheless be thought to be racist.

Someone who says, "The Asians are all over the sciences and the engineering departments in our best universities, and the blacks are as scarce as hens' teeth" is simply making an observation about the facts.

That would be thought by many people to be racism, and yet it couldn't be so classified, given the definition we've just been developing.

HARRIS: But hence my definition. Because I'd argue that while it's possible for racists—*real* racists—to make precisely those observations, those observations themselves are, to my ear, merely factual. I'm going to make observations of that sort with respect to crime in a minute. If that's the signature of racism—merely reporting statistics—then we can't even talk about the problem.

LOURY: Well, yes. Again, I can imagine how a critic might push back—something like, "Look, talking about this problem is not something that's going on in the abstract or on the moon. It's embedded within a structure whose legitimacy is up for debate." You call that merely a recitation of facts, without attempting to place those facts within a context, or with a deeper understanding of what history and contemporary social structure have wrought in terms of racial hierarchy, in terms of white supremacy. The comfort that we take in enunciating those facts, in terms of the political consequences of so many people enunciating those facts, it abets, reproduces, reifies, legitimates, etches in more firmly the hierarchical structures of racial domination. So the words "racist" or "racism" are entirely appropriate, no? Maybe your formulation doesn't identify a kind of classical antipathy on the basis of race, because we're no longer living in 1955, but the race-based disparities and inequalities of wealth, power, privilege, opportunity, and comfort in this society are very, very great.

So it's what the Harvard sociologist Larry Bobo calls "laissez-faire racism." In public opinion surveys, if you ask people things like, "Would you be willing to see your daughter or son married to someone of the opposite race?"—a black person, if the subject is white—they'll say yes at high rates. If you ask them, "Do you think blacks are inferior?" they'll say no at high rates. The old, classical racism would dictate the opposite response. But if you say, "Are white people disadvantaged by affirmative action?" and they say "Well, yes, because my kid didn't get into Harvard and some black kid with a lower score got in," that's laissez-faire racism. Well, Harvard accepts only one in fifteen applicants, and a lot of people got in who aren't black and who had lower scores than their son, but they focused on the black kid. They think they're not racist because they're willing to see their son or daughter married to someone who's black. They're willing to stay in the same neighborhood if a black neighbor moves next door. But they interpret their son's rejection at Harvard as a consequence of racial affirmative action. Maybe I'm trying to make the definition of racism more elastic than makes sense, but I think some of the proponents of a more capacious definition would say, of your definition, that in the 1950s it was fine. In the year 2016, though, we need to have a more subtle and expansive understanding of how this American disease is currently functioning.

HARRIS: Let's make the definition as capacious as possible. I want you to define what's often called structural or institutional racism. It seems to me that people can participate in a structure that is de facto racist, perpetuating unfair treatment of people on the basis of race, and yet the people operating within this structure may not, in fact, be racist. Let's say everyone passes Banaji's test. Nobody is harboring any bias, yet their structures and institutions could still be deeply unfair.

LOURY: I want to say at the outset that I am not a big fan of the current fad for invoking "structural racism" as a meaningful category of social analysis. I don't quite know what people are talking about beyond observing that blacks come out on the short end of the stick by many measures of social achievement or status. Let me give incarceration as a case in point. Blacks are 12 percent or so of the American population and 40 percent or so of the people who are behind bars.

Now, that's a complicated big social phenomenon, and you could do an elaborate social-scientific investigation of what the sources of that disparity are. But simply put, the weight of the state, the violence of the state, where the police come and drag you away in handcuffs and lock you up, where you're guarded and surveilled, where you're pursued by agents of the state, stigmatized, civically excommunicated, held in contempt, and treated badly differs by race. A large disparity exists in treatments of that kind based on race.

That is ipso facto an indication of structural racism: the state creates police forces, they build these cages, they corral people into them—and this impacts the black community. In some cities, the proportion of young black men who are incarcerated or have a criminal record is a third, or more like 40 percent of the total population. It becomes a normal way of life. Young women visit the prison to try to find mates and pen pals. Kids have ex-cons as role models, with their tattoos and their buffed-up bodies, going in and out of prison. It becomes normative in these communities. We have a school-to-prison pipeline, because the discipline of youngsters in schools seems somehow connected to their subsequent development into criminals. We have a prison-industrial complex—because, indeed, there's money to be made in the provision of the services associated with incarceration, and it's being made by private corporations and so on. I think many people would say this is a prime example of structural racism. The structures of law enforcement come down like a ton of bricks on people who, because of our history of racism, are at the margins of society.

And, by the way, if the same forces had been coming down with the same degree of severity on white people, the structure would be able to reform itself. Questions would arise. "Three strikes and you're out" would look very different if most of the people suffering under that kind of punitive regime were white. But because they're black and brown, we can write them off. We don't question ourselves. Business as usual seems acceptable when the people who are bearing the cost of it are black. I'm not sure I'm answering your question.

HARRIS: You are.

LOURY: This is one of the reasons the term "structural racism" is so compelling to many people. But I, as a social scientist, find the evocation of that kind of one-size-fits-all narrative—structural racism—inadequate to account for what's actually going on. It's not as if a bunch of white people meeting somewhere decided to make the laws in order to repress blacks. And it's not as if the outcomes people are concerned about—here, the disparities in the incidence of incarceration—are independent of the free choices being made by black people at risk of finding themselves in prison. They made a decision to participate in criminal activities that they clearly knew to be illicit and perhaps carried the consequences that they're now suffering, didn't they?

Sometimes the decisions they make have enormous negative consequences for other black people. Do we want to inquire into what's going on in the homes and communities of the people who are the subjects of this disparity? Or must we assume that any such disadvantages that are causally associated with their involvement in lawbreaking, any deficits in black community organization, family structures, parental attentiveness, and so forth, are nevertheless the consequence of white racism? Must we assume that black people wouldn't be acting that way if it weren't for white racism? If there were greater opportunity, if the schools were better funded, if it hadn't been for slavery, that the black family wouldn't have . . . so forth and so on.

If that's what you mean by "structural racism"—which is to say, every racial disparity is by definition a consequence of racism, either because it reflects contempt for the value of black life and neglect of the development of black people, or because the choices black people themselves make they only make because of the despair, the neglect, the lack of opportunity, and so on, that they've experienced—then it seems to me that's a kind of tautology. It says, "Any racial disparity is, by definition, a reflection of structural racism."

That's a tautology that, as a social scientist, I don't want to embrace. And as an African American, I'm profoundly skeptical of it, because at some level it denies the possibility of African American agency. It suggests that everything of a negative character, every example of inequality, of disparity, is a consequence of this history. How is it that blacks are unable to make something of our own lives, notwithstanding whatever the history may have been? Are there not variations and differentiations within the black population that one could identify and extol the virtue of—certain patterns of behavior and reactions to environmental conditions that seem effective and more life-affirming, more successful, than others?

I don't like structural racism because it's imprecise, because it's a kind of dead end. It leaves African Americans dependent on a kind of dispensation, to be bestowed by powerful whites—who are moral agents, who do have the ability to choose, or reject, various ways of life, including responding affirmatively to our demands for redress of our subordination. Blacks are merely historical chips. We're mere cogs, driven by the fact of slavery, by the fact of Jim Crow segregation, and so on, and ultimately not responsible for our own and our children's lives.

HARRIS: It's a very complex picture. And even if it's true—even if you could, as a matter of history and causality, draw a straight line from slavery and Jim Crow to the state of inequality and social dysfunction in the black community—that's not to say that today the ambient level of white racism is the ongoing cause of these problems. If you really can trace that line—that two-hundred-year-old line to the present—where does that leave you? It seems to leave you with something like Ta-Nehisi Coates's picture of reality, where what we should be talking about now is reparations for slavery. I don't know what I think about that as a remedy, but I know what I think about Coates's style of talking about this issue, and the fact that I'm talking to you and not to him suggests where I think the more profitable, civil, and rational conversation will be had.

At one point, someone recommended that I have this discussion with Coates, and honestly I feel that the conversation would have been a disaster. His way of speaking about these issues strikes me—to put this in starkly invidious terms, from which he would want to defend himself—as not intellectually honest. There's a kind of pandering to white guilt and black anger that never stops—where one can't just talk about facts in a civil way. And given the intemperance of his writing, I find Coates's status as a secular saint on the left to be symptomatic of how far we are from having a rational conversation on these topics. More than anything, Coates strikes me as a pornographer of race, and person who mistakes his own psychological problems for the state of the world.

LOURY: We can talk more about Coates if it suits you. And I'm happy to not do so. But I want to mention Thomas Chatterton Williams. He's an African American, maybe ten years younger than Coates, which puts him in his early thirties. He lives in Paris, he's a trained philosopher, graduated from Georgetown University, and I'm not sure where he did his graduate study, but I think he did some graduate study in philosophy as well.

He has an essay in the *London Review of Books*, an absolutely brilliant, if controversial, engagement with Ta-Nehisi Coates's *Between the World and Me*. Coates's book, which is an open letter to his son—advises, in effect, that America is so thoroughly contemptuous of your value as a human being that you must not ever, ever relax. You must not trust these people or turn your back on them. They will rip you to shreds. There's nothing more American than taking a guy like you, hanging you from a lamppost, and tearing your limbs off one by one. Don't believe in the American Dream. We are up against an implacable force. That force erases your humanity. It's always been so, and it will always be so. This is a paraphrase of the posture Coates takes in *Between the World and Me*; I think it's an accurate paraphrase.

Williams uses it as a point of departure to say that for black people there's no place to go from here. This is an absolutely bleak landscape—and it's disempowering. It just surrenders agency. Such a posture is a soul killer, an essential surrender of one's humanity. Williams thinks it's untrue of the actual sociohistorical circumstances in the United States. American history, he thinks, is rather more complicated than that.

By the way, Williams submitted that essay to *The New Yorker*, I happen to know on good authority, and it sat on an editor's desk for many months and was eventually killed. Williams ended up taking it to the *London Review of Books* because it couldn't get published in the United States. The liberal cognoscenti, America's ruling class of cultural mandarins, will not tolerate that kind of argument from an African American, contra the stance that Ta-Nehisi Coates is taking.

So that's one thing I wanted to mention. The other, and I'll be brief, is Mitch Landrieu, former mayor of the city of New Orleans. At the

Ideas Festival at Aspen a couple of years ago, Landrieu and Coates were paired on a panel where they were discussing race and inequality in America. Coates was taking the posture we know he would take, and Landrieu was armed with what he called "The Books of the Dead"— literally the casebooks from his Police Department in New Orleans which recorded the details of as yet unresolved homicide cases in that city. There were hundreds of them. And 90 percent or more of the victims in these cases were black people, and Landrieu was trying to say, in response to Coates's arguments about the implacability of American racism and the erasure of black humanity and the devaluation of the black body, that black people are killing themselves in very large numbers. He's not a Sean Hannity conservative wagging his finger about black-on-black crime: This is Mitch Landrieu, a centrist Democrat, mayor of New Orleans, a scion of a political family of some prominence, Democrats in Louisiana. And confronting Ta-Nehisi Coates in a debate about race and inequality in America, Landrieu tried to gently call to the attention of the audience the observation that much of the threat to the integrity of black bodies and black life is coming from other black people, offering as evidence his so-called Books of the Dead.

Coates's response to Landrieu was to dismiss him with the back of his hand—this, by the way, is written up in *New York* magazine, where you'll find a very long essay about Ta-Nehisi Coates that reports on this. Coates's response to Landrieu was, in effect: "There ain't nothing wrong with black people that ending white supremacy wouldn't fix. What do you expect people to do? They're rats in a barrel, you've got the lid on the barrel. You open the lid and peek down in there and you find that they're at each other's throats. Well, what would you expect to happen? It's the friggin' barrel, man. You gonna blame the rats?"

Okay, that's my metaphor and not what Ta-Nehisi Coates might have used. But it captures this idea that the mayhem—the despicable devaluation of life reflected in people riding up and down streets in automobiles firing heavy weapons more or less aimlessly out the window at their gang rivals and killing innocent bystanders along the way —that kind of contempt for human life shown by black people toward other black people is not relevant to assessing what it is that actually imperils black life, because those behaviors are the consequence of a system and a history of oppression.

Now, you can say this. You can say this with eloquence and style, you can say this with anger, you can say this with economy of words and clever turns of phrase, as Ta-Nehisi Coates does. But that doesn't make it a valid moral argument. It seems to me, and I've said this before, that Coates was holding a pair of queens and looking at an ace face up, and he was bluffing. In other words, he was daring Mitch Landrieu to come back at him and say, *What an absurdity. You're telling me that people drive up and down the street firing guns out of windows and killing their brethren because we didn't hand reparations for slavery over to you yet? Because somebody who was mayor of this city ten years ago happened to be a racist? Because a member of the Police Department is affiliated with the Ku Klux Klan? You're telling me that that explains, or somehow excuses or cancels, the moral judgment I would make in any other community in which I saw this happening? You're telling me that the history of slavery and Jim Crow, now essentially in the past, is responsible for this daily experience of African Americans? You're beneath contempt to talk in that way. You're the one who has no real respect for the value of black life—you live in a bubble. Why don't you get out of it and walk the streets of some of these places where people are dying?*

Then Coates could flash out, *Well, I was raised in Baltimore, and I've seen enough gang activity, and I know what's going on inside and out, and I've been there,* and so on. And Landrieu could say, *The body count continues to mount while your blather titillates the cultural elite in Washington and New York City and gives guilty white people an excuse not to feel so guilty. While you blather on, we're burying the dead.*

Landrieu might have responded to him like that. He might have said, *Get the heck out of here with that nonsense that attempts to intellectualize what anyone with common sense can see is a disaster. You're blaming white people for black people living like barbarians?*

HARRIS: You've convinced me we need a public debate between you and Coates, on prime-time television.

Let's talk about the mayhem. Here's the basic picture as I understand it: America is one of the most violent societies in the developed world, but this is almost entirely due to the level of crime and violence in the black community—even if you include all the mass shootings by crazy white guys. Violent crime in America is overwhelmingly a problem of black men killing other black men.

What I've learned in preparation for this conversation is that this has been a problem more or less since the end of slavery. I'm embarrassed not to have had a complete picture of the history before now. On your podcast you recommended Jill Leovy's *Ghettoside*, which I also now recommend. I learned that this disparity in violence didn't start with the crack epidemic of the 1980s, which is more or less what I assumed and what I think many people believe. You can read nineteenth-century newspaper editorials that give the predictable racist topspin to this status quo, saying more or less, "This is God's form of population control. Let the black man kill himself out of existence. That works for us."

Again, I'm not saying that white racism or structural racism don't play some role here, but the fact is that black men have been killing other black men in overwhelming numbers. Violent crime in America peaked in 1993 and has fallen since, but there has been a recent uptick in major cities. Some say this uptick is due to police fearing they'll be caught on cell phone cameras abusing suspects, so they don't make as many arrests, and as a result the violence has increased. This has been called the "Ferguson effect." Do you think the Ferguson effect is real, or is the jury still out on that?

LOURY: I think the jury is still out. I don't think enough time has gone by with enough data for there to be a persuasive empirical argument. You have accounts of people active in law enforcement in cities around the country saying that, yes, morale is low, or because everybody's got a mobile-phone recording device now the cops are afraid to do their jobs. You have that kind of anecdotal evidence. Heather Mac Donald, whose book *The War on Cops* has just come out, is a leading proponent of the Ferguson effect. The criminologist Richard Rosenfeld at the University of Missouri–St. Louis says that at first he thought the Ferguson effect was an exaggeration, but now, with the uptick in violent crime in some major cities, he's not so sure. Rosenfeld is a relatively objective observer, so I'll go with him and say it's not yet clear one way or the other.

HARRIS: Many of the following numbers I have are plucked from *Ghettoside*. At its peak in 1993, the homicide rate for black male victims in their early twenties in Los Angeles was 368 per 100,000 per year. That is probably 200 times higher than most cities in Western Europe, and don't even think of comparing it to a place like Japan. This rate of death by homicide was similar to the mortality rate of US soldiers deployed to Iraq at the height of the war. The crime rate has fallen since, but it hasn't fallen as much in the black community. The facts at the moment, as I understand them, are that black men make up 6 percent of the US population and 40 percent of those who get murdered. And they die, in the vast majority of cases, at the hands of other black men, who commit more than 50 percent of the murders in the country. Do I have my facts straight up to this point?

LOURY: I don't have a book open in front of me to give exact numbers, but as far as I know, those numbers are accurate. Certainly they're in the ballpark. I've seen the same kind of statistics.

HARRIS: I'll put one other fact in play here: policing in the black community, far too often by white cops, has been extraordinarily bad. As you know, there have been some very visible instances of cops who've used inappropriate force in arresting or defending themselves from black suspects, and the result is that the black community believes itself to be unfairly profiled for crime, and that it therefore suffers an inordinate number of lethal encounters with cops. We'll talk about whether that perception is true, but there's no question that a movement like Black Lives Matter follows from the perception that these things are true, and that white racism, whether implicit or explicit, is the underlying cause.

As you mentioned earlier, many people believe that the criminal justice system disproportionately targets and incarcerates young black men. That seems to be true when we're talking about petty crimes or drug offenses. The War on Drugs has been a disaster. But murders in the black community generally go unsolved, and the main reason is that witnesses refuse to testify. Some of that reluctance is understandable: witnesses are afraid of getting killed. But that is a problem that can't be pinned just on police misconduct or white racism.

So you have murderers walking around unpunished. The state monopoly on violence doesn't exist in these neighborhoods and people either refuse to testify or they take the law into their own hands, and it perpetuates the cycle of violence. So the black community is suffering from too much application of law and order on petty crimes and nonviolent drug offenses—which I think no one should be punished for—and too little law and order for crimes that really matter. If the Ferguson effect is real, it would be a terrible irony, because the solution to violence in the black community can't be less law enforcement; it must be better law enforcement.

LOURY: In *Ghettoside*, Jill Leovy has done a great service with her granular, on-the-ground, detailed account of what homicide detectives are up against in South Central Los Angeles. And you're right: One of the things they're up against is the difficulty of persuading people to cooperate with the police, let alone testify in court against someone alleged to have committed a murder. Leovy wants to underscore the horrible consequences that follow from the fact that it's possible to kill more or less with impunity. If people don't want to testify, it's unlikely that anybody will ever be brought to account. You can see how this becomes a self-reinforcing dynamic. The idea that you can kill with impunity makes it possible to intimidate witnesses.

One thing sympathizers of Black Lives Matter and others would insist I say here—and I don't mind saying it—is that the unwillingness of witnesses to cooperate with the police partly reflects their distrust of the police, which is a consequence of historical police practices in these communities. If the police have been bad actors—maybe only a few, but they get away with it—if they're unsympathetic, if they don't know the community, don't live there, if they treat black people with contempt, if they're too quick to resort to violence in their encounters with black people, and in the extreme, if they're prepared to use unjustifiable lethal force against black people, who can blame the community for not wanting to have anything to do with the police? So in a way this cycle of violence can indeed be traced to racism. Alienation between black communities and the police is a consequence of racism having infected the police in days gone by.

I should also say that it's no surprise that most of the murders of blacks have been perpetrated by blacks because it's the kind of crime in which often the victim and the perpetrator are connected in some way. They may be part of the same social network, or they're in the same general neighborhood. Given the segregated patterns of residence and social affiliation in our society, we can't be surprised that most of the blacks who are killed are killed by other blacks. It's also true that most of the murdered whites are killed by other whites. People do make this argument, but I don't think it's an adequate explanation of the problem you've described, because it doesn't account for the two-orders-of-magnitude difference in the murder rates. It still makes sense to talk about black people killing black people—not as a matter of emphasizing the race of the persons who are killed as much as emphasizing the qualitatively distinct character of the killing.

Finally, I want to say something that my colleague and friend Rajiv Sethi, an economist at Barnard, would insist I say—and it's a point worth making—that sometimes epidemics of killing have their own logic. Suppose I have a dispute. Suppose I step on this fellow's newly shined shoe? He's sitting on the bus with his foot slightly out, and I walk past and I step on the shoe. He looks up at me and expects an apology, and I sneer at him and keep walking. Everybody sees it, and laughter breaks out somewhere in the bus: "Aw, man, he dissed you. He stepped on your shoe. You gonna let him do that?" So now we have a beef, right? He says to me, "You m-f, you dissed me like that? You step on my shoe and don't apologize? I'm gonna friggin' kill you." And then he gets off the bus. Now, how do I know whether or not, tonight or tomorrow, I'll be sitting on my porch and that fella will drive by with his homeboys, and they'll start blasting out the car window, and I or somebody I love will be dead? It's not like I can go to the cops and say, "This man threatened my life" and expect that anything effective will happen. So I might want to take preemptive action. I might want to make sure that I'm the one doing the shooting and he's the one doing the dying.

So we have a situation where the fact that there's no dispute-resolution mechanism I can rely on, one that will protect me and my family and my household, leads me to want to take matters into my own hands.

Alice Goffman is a young sociologist whose book *On the Run* is an account of guys in Philadelphia who are on the lam and being sought by the police. And she lives among them and gets to know them very well and writes an ethnographic study of what life is like in this quarter of our society, among people who are being sought by the law. She gets to know these guys very well, and one of their number is killed in a gang dispute that leads to gunplay. And the surviving friends decide to take matters into their own hands and get revenge, because otherwise nothing will happen to the murderer. Given that there are so many unresolved homicide cases in America's big cities, they know the chances that justice will be done are slim, and they decide that they can't let it stand. She actually records this in her book: She's in the vehicle with the surviving buddies, riding around looking for the assailant. In fact, she's driving. And this became a notorious thing, because, after all, she's a scholar, an academic, a professor of sociology at the University of Wisconsin. What would the institutional review board that's supposed to supervise research involving human subjects have to say about this?

However, they don't find the assailant, so she doesn't actually become an accomplice to murder. But the anecdote underscores the fact that people may feel the need to take matters into their own hands, tit for tat, because they can't rely on civil authority to resolve these things in a satisfactory way. Both the strategic-preemption element and the kind of Wild West thing—"There is no law except the law I make, and I'm going to settle this in my own way"—will tend to elevate this kind of violence within racially classed, geographically defined areas, like inner-city neighborhoods. They might account for some of the elevated homicide rates, although given the numbers—6 percent of the population, 50 percent of the murders. All of it? I'm dubious. Other things must be going on.

HARRIS: Well, to stick with your anecdote for a second, other things *have* to be going on, because nobody, certainly not the cops, can preemptively resolve a problem like that, even when it crops up in the most effete and privileged circles in white society. If I'm walking through a Starbucks and I step on someone's shoe, and this person gets pissed, the situation doesn't escalate, because I'll almost certainly apologize. And if I'm so distracted that I don't apologize and he says something, one hopes my culturally acquired conflict-resolution skills will kick in to a degree that will mollify him, and I won't be left with the sense that this person is now planning to kill me. But at no point in that process do I get to appeal to the cops, or even to the barista in the Starbucks, to resolve the matter. And if it does escalate, if it comes to the point where this guy is actually committed to killing me, I'm in the same situation as that fellow in the 'hood. I do receive death threats, in fact, and I know what it's like to talk to the FBI or to the cops to try to resolve those situations. There's very little they can do preemptively. This isn't *Minority Report*, where we can arrest people for "precrime." The level of threat has to be extraordinarily high before anyone from the state will take action preemptively.

So we're talking about cultural memes, attitudes, and norms that are allowing for the regular eruption of lethal violence in the black community. And we're often talking about the behavior of teenagers.

LOURY: Let me say this to you, Sam, just very quickly. Your Starbucks analogy is interesting in the sense that it underscores your privilege in the following way—

HARRIS: I was deliberately underscoring my privilege. In fact, I was trying to think of something fancier than Starbucks but came up short.

LOURY: What I mean is this: You say "cultural memes." I think we ought to unpack that a little. You, as an affluent white person at a Starbucks, have no investment in your public persona as a tough guy. The advantages of your cultural and socioeconomic location are such that you lose nothing from offering an apology—or by, as you say, deploying your "conflict-resolution skills." Well, yeah, partly they're skills, but also partly they're the advantage of being nestled comfortably within a complex of social interactions in which a reputation for toughness is of no particular value.

On the other hand, if you were someone like Ta-Nehisi Coates, growing up in inner-city Baltimore twenty-five years ago, it would absolutely be a burden on you to be thought of as a pussy, as a wuss, as weak, as somebody who backs down, as someone who doesn't have the courage to fight. The cultivation of the opposite of that persona or reputation is an automatic reflex in that kind of environment. You can't be seen to back down. People living in inner-city Baltimore simply don't have that luxury.

It's not as if they don't know it's not in their cultural toolkit to rely on more civil means of conflict resolution, lowering the temperature and so forth. It's that the bitter fruit of their isolation, their lack of opportunity, and all the damage that's been done, is partly that they have to carry themselves with a certain swagger. They have to evince a hair-trigger sensibility and a willingness to go to the ultimate level if it comes to that.

That's just a way of being in the world, cultivated of necessity in that environment. You can call it "culture" if you want, but if you fail to see that it's a product of history and the social oppression of African Americans in these ghettos, you'll be doing a grave disservice to the people who live there.

HARRIS: I agree. And I could easily imagine suddenly finding myself in more or less the same condition if I were sent to a maximum-security prison. Despite my best intentions and everything I know about how people should behave so as to maximize their mutual well-being, I'd have no choice—given the way incentives are aligned there—but to behave just as you've described. I've written about this before. It seems that the only rational choice for a person sent to a maximum-security prison, even if he doesn't have a racist bone in his body, is to become immediately affiliated with the gang of his appropriate skin color so as to be as safe as possible in the perpetual race war that goes on in those prisons. So I do understand that there are certain contexts—such as the inner city, among gang members—that promote many of the incentives one notices in a prison.

Let's pivot to the issue of police violence. I want to bring up the recent study by the Harvard economist Roland Fryer, which got a lot of press. Let's review a few facts first: Something like 4 percent of black homicide victims are killed by cops. So around 96 percent are *not* killed by cops. Virtually all of those are killed by black men—there aren't a lot of white men killing black men. And, as you pointed out, not a lot of black men are killing white men either, though more homicides run in that direction. The fact is that most violence is intraracial. Incidentally, around 12 percent of whites and Hispanics who die by homicide are killed by cops—so at least by one measure, this is several times the rate at which blacks are killed by cops.

As we get into this data, we should admit that statistics are a bit of a Rorschach test. It's possible to read even valid statistics in misleading ways or in ways guided by bias. Needless to say, we'll do our best not to do that, but here are just a few more facts as I understand them: Around twelve hundred people are killed each year in the US by cops, more or less. Around 50 percent of these fatalities are white, and about 25 percent are black.

LOURY: Right.

HARRIS: Now, that's double what you'd expect from the demographics, because about 12 percent to 13 percent of the population is black but they commit 50 percent of all violent crime, at least. In some cities it's as much as two thirds of all violent crime. So my question is, Given how much violent crime black men are committing—again, mostly against other black men—and given how much attention from the police they will naturally attract because of this, and *should* attract in the hopes of keeping black communities safe, what percentage of fatal encounters with cops would make sense? I mean, honestly, I'm surprised. Even if I'd never heard of the Fryer study, which we'll talk about, and was just considering the percent of all violent crime committed, I'd be surprised that only 25 percent of police-involved fatalities are black—that strikes me as surprisingly low.

LOURY: I cannot respond to your question—what percent should we expect, given the aggregate statistics?—since those statistics are inadequate to assess the individual encounters between black people and police that lead to shootings.

Let me explain that. Here's an analogy: Let's suppose that a survey finds that on average women make seventy cents for every dollar that men make in the labor market. I just made that number up, but something like it is undoubtedly true. And someone says to me, "Given the fact that women have the bulk of the child-rearing responsibilities, often take time off from work to attend to those responsibilities, are disproportionately electing to pursue careers in caregiving or teaching or similar activities, which pay less than, say, construction work or engineering—given that men and women are different in so many ways, exactly what proportion of their earnings on the dollar would you expect? If you think seventy cents is too low, should it be eighty-five? Certainly it shouldn't be a dollar, given the fact that women are leaving the labor force to take on the child-rearing responsibilities" and so on. Let's say someone says something like that.

Now, I don't know how to answer that question when the moral issue is, Are women being treated fairly in the workplace? Are they getting paid the same as men for the same work? That's a question about what happens to an individual woman when she encounters an employer, and these aggregate averages don't answer that question.

HARRIS: Understood. Given the background facts you describe, I'd expect that women would work less, but I'd still expect them to get paid the same for doing the same job. I'm not saying there wouldn't be economic consequences for working less: they might not advance up the hierarchy as far as men, in the aggregate. But two vice presidents, man and woman, in the same company, doing the same work, should be paid the same, and I think that's clear.

The issue here, is that if there's much more crime being perpetrated by black men, the call to the cops usually runs:

> "Somebody's just been shot."
>
> "Can you describe the shooter?"
>
> "Yeah, he was a black guy."

When the cops show up, they're going to be looking for, and encountering, more black men than white men. Given that any encounter with a cop can escalate to the point of lethal violence, whether reasonably or by dint of police incompetence, you'd expect the rate of blacks killed by cops to be higher than their demographic representation of 12 percent would suggest.

LOURY: We're on the same page here. Yes, we would expect the rate to be higher. The question is, How much higher? That was the question you asked me. Likewise, as you say, fairness would dictate that if it were the same job, the man and the woman should be paid the same rate. But the question is, How would I know, from aggregate statistics, whether or not I was comparing like with like? I need individualized data. I need data at the level of the encounters between police and citizens to assess whether or not the circumstances in which blacks and the police encounter each other, and the subsequent rate of killing, are similar.

HARRIS: That seems like a perfect segue to talk about the Fryer study.

LOURY: It is. What I regard as a virtue of that study is the fact that such conclusions as are drawn there—subject to certain qualifications we might want to note—are based on individualized data of encounters between officers and citizens, not on a comparison of aggregate rates across large collectivities, where you don't really know whether you're comparing like with like.

HARRIS: Roland Fryer was a student of yours, is that correct?

LOURY: And that's an important qualifier. I like Roland Fryer very much. I was his mentor when he was in graduate school, and he and I have written some papers together. We're good friends and close colleagues. I'm proud of him. He's now one of the leading young—"young" meaning under forty—applied economists working today.

HARRIS: So you're probably better qualified to summarize the findings of his study, as well as its flaws. Some people, and one of them is Rajiv Sethi, whom you've mentioned, have pointed out specific limitations. Perhaps you can discuss the Fryer findings and the limitations as you see them. Also, Fryer's data aren't representative of the whole nation; he looked at specific cities.

LOURY: It's an ongoing project and I expect we'll see more of it as time goes on. The study in question, which was reported on in a front-page piece in the *New York Times* just after it was released, is now a working paper at the National Bureau of Economic Research. Anyone can find it online. It's based on data from the city of Houston. Fryer's ongoing project has data from other cities as well, but the main findings of the study are based on data from Houston. Fryer is trying to control for the specific aspects of the encounter between a police officer and a citizen—things like, What part of town did it occur in? What time of day? Was the suspect armed? Did the police arrive on the scene because of a report of illegal activity? Was the suspect resisting, or in some other way attempting to avoid being processed by a police officer? Were innocent third parties endangered by the behavior of the suspect?

All these details of the encounter are known to Fryer, and he attempts to control for them in an effort to ascertain whether the likelihood that the police officer discharges his weapon is greater when the suspect is black, other things being equal. Now, this last—other things being equal, ceteris paribus—is critical. The way he proceeds is, he's got two populations of people in citizen/police encounters in the city of Houston, and this is based on data made available by the Houston Police Department to his research team.

One population is arrestees. For everyone arrested by Houston police, a detailed report has to be filed by the police officer, and Fryer has access to these reports. The police officers write up what happened leading to the arrest, the justification for the arrest, and so on. So Fryer knows, for example, whether or not the officer discharged a weapon in the process.

Separately, he has the population of people who were shot by police officers. And the population of people arrested but not shot by police officers. The fact that they were arrested means there was an encounter in which such a shooting might have occurred but didn't. So he's got this zero/one variable: it's one if a shooting occurred, and zero if it didn't occur. Of course, in the vast majority of arrests, a shooting didn't occur. We use this so-called logistic regression analysis to estimate the probability that a shooting would occur in the context of an arrest as a function of the features of the arrest, the features I described: where, when, and under what conditions did the policeman encounter the citizen, and also whether or not the citizen is black.

And what Fryer is finding is that the likelihood of a police officer shooting in this arrestee population—once you control for every aspect that Fryer can observe about the encounter—is no greater if the citizen is black than if the citizen is white. Indeed, it's slightly greater if the citizen is white.

On that basis, he concludes that the likelihood of deadly force being used by a police officer against a citizen is not greater if that citizen is black, once you control for the features of the encounter between the police officer and the citizen. But he also finds that the likelihood that the police will use nonlethal force in their encounter—putting cuffs on someone, using a baton or a Taser, forcing them to lie down on the street while they're being interrogated, what Fryer speaks of generically as the laying on of hands—is greater if you're black. There's about a 25 percent greater chance that some kind of force, short of shooting, will be used against the suspect if he's black than if he's white—other things being equal—and about a 28 percent lower probability that the suspect will be shot if he's black.

So that's the broad outline of his findings. Race *is* implicated. Blackness is a factor in the police use of force, short of deadly force. But it's not implicated as a factor, and indeed the number goes the other way, in police shooting a suspect. This is in Houston.

Now, here are some of the concerns that Rajiv Sethi and others have raised about this finding: the only way we know about it is because the police department was willing to let this research team look at their data in depth. Some police departments do that, some don't. Not only is this finding limited to Houston and we don't know if it applies to New Orleans or Dallas or Los Angeles, but also we should be suspicious because the fact that Houston would let you see the data could indicate that Houston knows the data are largely exculpatory and the police department whose data would not be exculpatory won't let you see the data.

You can't draw any valid conclusion about policing, as such, from these data. That's one major line of critique. Fryer is aware of this, but he can only analyze the data he has. It's an ongoing project. He has been in contact with other cities. I know he's been very active in Camden, New Jersey. New York City has turned over all its stop-and-frisk data to him over a period of years, which he's also in the process of analyzing. And by the way, the preliminary analysis of the New York City stop-and-frisk data confirms his finding that police are more likely to use force, short of deadly force, against suspects if the suspects are black. The other criticism, though, is that because he relies on arrest data for the universe of people who might be shot by the police, he has implicitly assumed that the processes leading to an arrest work in the same way regardless of the race of the suspect. In order to draw any valid conclusion about whether or not the police are more or less likely to shoot at somebody who's black, he has to assume, for example, that the pool of black arrestees is comparable, in its degree of threat posed to police officers, to the pool of white arrestees. But suppose, says Rajiv and others, that the police are menacing relatively innocent black people and arresting them. Sandra Bland gets arrested in Texas for talking back to a police officer when she's stopped for not signaling a lane change, and she's taken into custody. But a white person in the same circumstance perhaps wouldn't have been taken into custody. Suppose something like that is true, so that the black population of arrestees disproportionately consists of people who are relatively less threatening than the white population.

Rajiv points out that there are differences by race in some of the other characteristics of the arrestee population. The blacks who were arrested were less likely to be armed than the whites, for example. There are relatively more women among blacks in the arrested population than there are among whites in the arrested population, and things of this kind. So suppose the police are discriminatory in how they decide about arresting people and are quicker to arrest blacks who are less threatening, than whites.

Finding that the rate at which blacks are shot is comparable to the rate at which whites are shot is not proof of no discrimination but rather of the fact that they're being discriminated against because the arrested blacks were less threatening. We should expect a much lower rate of shooting, not a comparable rate of shooting.

So if Fryer is wrong about the implicit assumption that the police don't discriminate in the processes leading to an arrest, then he's also wrong in the conclusion from his data that the likelihood of being shot by a police officer is roughly the same or maybe even a little bit lower if you're black. It's based on assumptions that aren't verified in the data—an assumption in this case that the police are not biased in the process of arrest.

HARRIS: That's fascinating, and it's hugely important research to continue. I would add that at least one other study I know of—I just saw the coverage of it in the *Washington Post*—lends some support to Fryer. It wasn't a real-world data study, it was a simulator study, where they put cops in a shooting simulator and watched their choices about whom they shot. In that case, they were actually slower to shoot black suspects than white ones.

Again, if valid, who knows if this is a recent phenomenon, resulting from all the attention that's been brought to this problem? But in any case, data are out there. I think there are other data that add another wrinkle here, where black officers are more likely to shoot unarmed black suspects than white officers are—which works against the narrative of racist policing.

LOURY: You said this earlier, and I think it deserves to be underscored. The energy, the animus, the angst, the sense of outrage behind the Black Lives Matter movement—"Just stop killing us. We want you to stop killing us"—is premised on a claim that we know that people are being shot. You say, "What should the number be, given the disproportion of blacks and crime?" I say, "That's a hard question to answer without individualized data, which we don't have enough of," and so on. But behind the movement lies the presumption that race is factoring causally in police officers' decision to use deadly force in their encounters with black citizens.

In effect, the counterfactual that's being entertained is "If this person had been white, they wouldn't have been killed." To take a graphic example: Tamir Rice—that's the twelve-year-old in Cleveland, in a park, playing with a toy gun that the police presumably mistook for a real gun, and they killed him. The sense people have is, had he been a twelve-year-old white boy in exactly the same circumstance, he wouldn't have been killed. Now, as a social scientist, I recognize that question. I recognize it because of the difficulty of being able to give a valid statistical answer to it, because no one will ever live in the parallel universe in which the suspects in these particular instances were, as an experiment, sometimes black, sometimes white, and we'd see what the police do.

Nobody lives in that parallel universe, and the problem of drawing a valid statistical inference about a question like that, when we have imperfect data and live in a nonexperimental world, is a huge problem. That's spoken as a social scientist. We don't have good data to draw statistical conclusions, but we do have the videotape evidence, and we do have cell phone recordings of other incidences.

You pointed out correctly that around twelve hundred people are killed by the police in this country every year. Twelve hundred. We have a dozen videos. We have twelve hundred people killed, and we have a dozen videos. Let's make it fifty. Let's suppose we have fifty videos. So what we've got are crumbs. We've got anecdotes, we've got sensation-alized cases. Perhaps they're cherry-picked, perhaps they're not repre-sentative, perhaps the most egregious cases are the only ones that come to our attention. Should, on the strength of those videos, we have a na-tional narrative leading to a movement, leading to large demonstrations in dozens of cities across the country, leading in some instances to vio-lent, retaliatory actions?

I'm not blaming the violence on the movement. I'm just saying it hap-pens in the context in which this kind of discussion is ongoing, driven by anecdotes and untethered from any rigorous and systematic inves-tigation of available evidence that attempts at least to be comprehen-sive—to deal with the whole and not the cherry-picked cases. As a social scientist, I'd say no, we should not; as an observer of culture and politics, I would say that it's very hard to keep the narrative in a box.

Once it gets out of the box, once it becomes compelling to people to start making analogies to slavery, and American cities in the 1930s, '40s, and '50s, and they start saying, "This is a part of an old American story"—once we turn Ta-Nehisi Coates loose on a dozen cases, all of them buttressed by tape recordings and such, the narrative takes on a life of its own. And this is a grave concern to me—that serious political consequences can flow from circumstances that aren't well understood.

HARRIS: I worry about this as well. I'm not aware of everything occur-ring under the banner of Black Lives Matter, and it could be that rational and impeccable people are advocating in the stream of this movement. But I've seen it filtered through the left-wing media, which is largely, if not entirely, sympathetic to it. And most of what I've heard—in particu-lar about these videos and about the cases where we don't have videos but that have been well described, like the Michael Brown shooting—has struck me as dangerously and offensively irrational. And I'm wor-ried that the excesses of the Black Lives Matter movement could set race relations in this country back a generation.

Here's the core issue for me: these cases run the full gamut—of police malfeasance and culpability on the one end to completely predictable and even rational uses of force on the other, and everything in between.

On the one end, you have cops who are obviously guilty of murder, whether stemming from racism or some other derangement—and I'd put the Walter Scott and Laquan McDonald shootings there. Those cops clearly should never have been given a gun and a badge, and they belong in prison. And if I'm not mistaken, the cops involved in those shootings are being prosecuted for murder, so the system appears to be working in those cases.[*]

But at the other extreme, we find legitimate uses of force that would have happened ninety-nine times out of a hundred in the presence of any sane cop, and race surely had nothing to do with it. I'd put the Michael Brown case, from what I know of it, fairly close to that end of the continuum. We don't have a video of what happened, but the facts as reported suggest that he attacked a police officer and tried to get his gun. If you're trying to get a cop's gun, it's only rational for him to believe you intend to kill him with it. Whatever the color of your skin, you'll be shot. And if you aren't shot, it's either because you got lucky, because the cop had amazing hand-to-hand skills, and he decided to spare your life, or because there were enough cops on hand to physically overpower you without requiring the use of lethal force.

In the rest of these cases, you see almost every variety of incompetence, bad luck, poor training, and just basic human chaos, and I'd put all these recent incidents, like Philando Castile and Alton Sterling and, frankly, even Eric Garner somewhere in the middle. Those three cases are totally unlike the extremes, but they're importantly different from one another, too. One thing to point out is that in some of these videos, the video record itself can be profoundly misleading. Some start after the shooting occurred—you simply don't know what precipitated it—and some that show the shooting don't show you what the cops themselves saw. So you can't really judge whether or not it was rational for them to think their lives were in danger. The range of these cases,

---

* The murder trial of the police officer who killed Walter Scott ended in mistrial. The officer later pled guilty to civil rights offenses; in sentencing him to twenty years in prison, a federal judge found that he had committed second-degree murder. The police officer who killed Laquan McDonald was convicted of second-degree murder and was sentenced to just under seven years in prison.

ethically and as a matter of police procedure, is impossible to exaggerate.

And then you throw the Trayvon Martin case into the mix, where the guy who shot him wasn't a cop and arguably wasn't even white—and you realize that the rules of rational conversation have completely broken down. All of these cases are spoken about in the same breath as intolerable examples of murderous racism on the part of the police. So my problem—and again, this doesn't subsume everything Black Lives Matter does—is that this seems to be the moral core of the movement, as far as I can tell. And these claims are not only inaccurate and unfair, they seem truly dangerous.

LOURY: Okay, that's a lot, and I need to respond. First, Black Lives Matter is not one thing. It's an aggregation of a fairly large number of loosely connected initiatives and movements, so it's going to be a little ragged around the edges. And you said you're sure that some decent, upstanding, sensible people are involved. I don't know the movement as well as I might, but from what I know, that's certainly true.

I perhaps should make a confession. In the January 2015 *Boston Review*—that's a literary and political magazine—I have a piece on the Ferguson matter, Michael Brown and Officer Darren Wilson, in which I say Michael Brown is no Rosa Parks and no Emmett Till, either. What I meant by "no Rosa Parks" is that Rosa Parks was a woman who refused to give up her seat on a bus in Alabama and in effect started the civil rights movement, with the subsequent protest in Montgomery, Alabama, and the bus boycott, and so on. She is thought of in some circles as the mother of the civil rights movement. When I wrote Michael Brown is no Rosa Parks, I only meant to say, "Please don't use this case as the template on which to build a national movement for racial justice." And the reason I said that was precisely because I thought Brown was culpable in what happened, as best we know. Two separate investigations came to the same conclusion. The local authorities and the federal government both concluded that the officer had acted reasonably under the circumstances.

And Michael Brown wasn't Emmett Till, either. Emmett Till was the victim of a lynching in the 1950s in the South, and his became a celebrated case of racist violence against black people because his body was displayed for public viewing in a casket, even though it was partly decomposed, because he had been murdered and then thrown in the Tallahatchie River. It was a horrible thing to behold. So I'm saying that Michael Brown, as best we understand the facts, tried to assault a police officer, tried to take his weapon, and placed the police officer in fear for his life.

I got tremendous negative reaction to that article, and I bring it up in order to put my finger on a phenomenon. You say these cases are all different. Of course they're different. You say that it's dangerous and disconcerting that people would aggregate such cases into a generic indictment and then mount a movement on the basis of it. I agree with that. On the other hand, if we stepped back, as social analysts, and tried to understand the dynamics of the phenomenon, we'd recognize that there's a kind of logic to it. A movement will have its own momentum from the appropriation of these varied cases and the eliding of important differences between them, and the suppression of specific factual information—for example, like the fact that George Zimmerman, who shot Trayvon Martin in Florida, was not white. He was of Latino background, and he was acquitted by a jury of his peers after they concluded that he had acted in defense of his life.

People will say, "Well, he should never have been following Trayvon Martin in the first place." I'm prepared to credit that. But that doesn't change the fact that these inconvenient details in these various cases will be suppressed in the interest of affirming a narrative. The case is made to fit the narrative, not the facts. The narrative has a momentum and a kind of "integrity"—I use the word in inverted commas—of its own. People are looking for evidence of racism. They don't trust the proceedings of duly authorized tribunals that attempt to assess the facts. "We all know," they assert, "don't we, that the police lie. Why should I believe the outcome of any particular grand jury?"

The guy who applied the chokehold in the Eric Garner case wasn't indicted. No one's going to ask, "Well, why was Eric Garner resisting arrest in the first place?" If he'd complied, the encounter would have

ended in a mundane manner. Perhaps the cop shouldn't have been using the chokehold, but he certainly didn't attempt to kill anybody. The
narrative has such a power of its own that those features are going to be
suppressed, and indeed anybody who raises them—even a black person like myself—will be suspect. "Don't you know that by dwelling on
that kind of detail you're undercutting our effort to get justice for our
people?"

HARRIS: I've seen a lot of these videos, and I've trained with police officers, so I can see this from the other side. One overwhelming fact that
comes through is that people, whether black or white, don't understand
how to behave around cops so as to keep themselves safe. You mentioned resisting arrest. People simply have to stop resisting arrest. And
they have to understand how the force continuum looks from a cop's
point of view.

This is a bit of a public service announcement—something I want
our listeners to take away that will keep them safer, and I think it's
something that Black Lives Matter should be teaching explicitly: if you
put your hands on a cop—if start wrestling with a cop, or grabbing him,
or pushing him, or striking him—you're likely to get shot, whatever the
color of your skin.

When you're with a cop, there is always a gun out in the open. And
any physical struggle has to be perceived by him as a fight for the gun.
A cop doesn't know what you're going to do if you overpower him, so
he has to assume the worst. Most cops are not all that confident in their
ability to physically control a person without shooting him—for good
reason, because they're not well trained for that, and they're continually confronting people who are bigger, or younger, or more athletic,
or more aggressive than they are. Cops aren't superheroes. They're ordinary people with surprisingly little training, and once things turn
physical they can't afford to give a person who just assaulted a police
officer the benefit of the doubt.

This is something that people are confused about. If they see a video
of somebody trying to punch a cop in the face and the person's unarmed, they think the cop should just punch back, and any use of deadly

force would be disproportionate and, therefore, unwarranted. But that's not how violence works. It's not the cop's job to be the best bare-knuckled boxer on Earth so he doesn't have to use his gun. He can't risk getting repeatedly hit in the face and knocked out, because there's always a gun in play. This is the cop's perception of the world, and it's a justifiable one given the dynamics of human violence.

In your podcast with Rajiv Sethi there was a part where I felt you guys were talking past one another. He was right to insist that you should be able to be rude to a cop in our society without being physically punished for it, much less killed. And he was right to think that it's a measure of a civilized society that cops don't start beating you just because you've been disrespectful. But you were right to insist that people shouldn't be rude to cops because it's unwise. You should be respectful to a cop, because you don't want things to escalate. And, again, Rajiv is right in saying that it's the cop's job to have a thick skin and be totally professional in his dealings with the public. But do you really want to risk your life by testing the emotional maturity of the guy with a gun? No, you do not.

In my view, you have to deal with a cop as if he were a lethal robot who could malfunction at any time. And what I see in these videos are people who have no idea what the implications are of grabbing a cop, pushing a cop, of doing whatever they're doing to resist arrest.

Think about it this way, again this is a public service announcement: it's never up to you whether or not you should be arrested. Does it matter that *you* know you didn't do anything wrong? No. And how could that fact be effectively communicated by your not following police commands? Unless you called the cop yourself, you never know what situation you're in. If I'm walking down the street, I don't know if the cop who approaches me didn't get a call that some guy who looks like Ben Stiller just committed an armed robbery. I know I didn't do anything, but I don't know what's in the cop's head. The time to find out what's going on—the time to complain about racist cops, the time to yell at them and go ballistic—is *after* cooperating, at the police station, in the presence of a lawyer. But to not comply in the heat of the moment, when the guy with the gun is issuing commands—this raises your risk astronomically, and it's something that most people, it seems, just do not intuitively understand.

LOURY: That was a long statement, Sam, and worth every minute. I couldn't agree more. With respect to my colloquy with my friend Rajiv Sethi, you're right: I do think we were talking past one another. I was making your point, which is that it's unwise not to comply with a police officer when you're in a situation in which he might arrest you or detain you. He may be doing so unfairly, but you should not try to resolve that dispute by resisting him. You should do that in another context. But I was also making the point that, as a citizen, one has an obligation to avoid conflict with a police officer, notwithstanding the fact that the police officer may have made a mistake. That civility or interaction with the duly constituted institutions of authority in this society, which are there on your behalf, is a duty of citizenship. You may not agree with that, but I was making that claim. That's leading me to what I really want to say, which is that people for whom the institutions of police and authority have lost legitimacy are not going to be compelled by the observation that one has a duty to comply.

They may be persuaded by the observation that it's unwise not to comply, but there will be resentment, maybe intense resentment. I'm thinking of some of these cases I mentioned in my conversation with Rajiv: Sandra Bland, the woman who was found dead in her jail cell—evidently of suicide, although that's disputed—who gets into an altercation with a police officer who pulls her over for a minor traffic violation. She blows smoke in the police officer's face, and he tells her to put the cigarette out, and she doesn't comply. He loses his cool. Maybe he shouldn't have lost his cool. Maybe he should have been more temperate in the circumstance. But she's provoking him. She ends up being arrested.

Henry Louis Gates Jr.—another celebrated case. This is the Harvard professor arrested on his doorstep for breaking into his own house; he gets into an altercation with a police officer who's been called to the scene thinking a burglary might be in progress and the officer asks Gates to produce ID. He doesn't respond politely. Instead he berates the police officer for singling him out for attention because he's black. He ends up in handcuffs and being taken to the police station. The president of the United States even has to weigh in on the case.

But these are cases where I'd say that contempt for the institutions of authority and thinking of police as not necessarily being friendly to you simply because you are black, thinking they're profiling you, thinking they've singled you out for attention, leads to the disrespect or refusal to honor the law-enforcement officer. And that can, of course, backfire on people.

Rajiv's response to me was to suggest that I wanted black people to be passive and servile in their interactions with police officers. He was saying, "Why should a person have to lower themselves to the position of being passive and servile simply because the other person is wearing a uniform?" Of course, I didn't counsel passivity, I counseled civility. But the perception that even an act of civility is a kind of passivity is more likely to arise in the mind of somebody who resents the very fact of the police presence in the first place, and thinks "the police" have it in for their kind: "You're asking me to be civil? I want to show my contempt, as a reaction to what I believe to be the contempt that the officer has toward me."

That's not a justification, but it may be, at least in part, an explanation for why so many black people don't follow your very sage advice.

The Biology of Good and Evil

A CONVERSATION WITH ROBERT SAPOLSKY

Robert Sapolsky is a neuroendocrinologist and a primatologist. He is a professor of biology and neurology at Stanford University and the recipient of a MacArthur Foundation "genius" grant. He is a gifted communicator of science as well as a top-flight scientist.

I remember taking a class at Stanford where Sapolsky appeared as a guest lecturer. This was one of the moments that nudged me toward doing my PhD in neuroscience rather than philosophy.

During our conversation, we explore a wide range of topics, including his work with baboons, the opposition between reason and emotion, the evolution of the brain, justice and vengeance, brain-machine interface, and religious belief. We also discuss the illusion of free will, along with the ethical and legal benefits of dispensing with it.

HARRIS: I don't think we've ever met, but I recall that when I was at Stanford, I took a course with John Gabrieli on the neuroanatomy of memory, and you came in as a guest lecturer. You gave this very cool interdisciplinary talk, because you're both a neurobiologist and a primatologist. So I just wanted you to know that you stood in front of a class of undergraduates for the better part of an hour, and you inspired me to go further in the direction I did, studying the brain. So thank you for that.

SAPOLSKY: Well, thanks. That's good to hear.

HARRIS: Your book *Behave* is a monumental tour of the brain and behavior, and you do a fantastic job of providing scientific detail in a way that's not at all boring. This is not easy to do, and that's why, when I bring up the relevant neuroscience in my books, I get in and out as quickly as possible because it makes for brutal reading. It's not so much that the concepts are hard, but once you get into the details and start naming parts, it becomes this thicket of neuroanatomical terms and people lose the plot. But you've struck a wonderful balance here.

SAPOLSKY: Thanks. I've had to survive neuroanatomy classes, so I know exactly how awful all the multisyllabic names can be.

HARRIS: Before we get into your book, let's talk about your background and the way you've married neuroendocrinology and primatology, which is a fairly unique combination. I can't imagine you meet too many people at conferences with the same bio. How has primatology informed your study of the brain?

SAPOLSKY: Well, the common theme in my work has been to understand the effects of stress on health, and particularly the effects of stress on the brain. What I've spent many decades doing is oscillating between being a lab scientist—growing neurons in petri dishes and mucking around with genes—and then spending thirty-two summers at a national park in East Africa studying baboons. These are the animals I return to each year—animals I can dart, anesthetize, and when they're unconscious do a whole bunch of the basic clinical tests you do on a human.

These two occupations have always complemented each other, in that you observe something interesting about the brain based on your petri dish neurons or your lab rats, and that's great, but the question of course is whether this tells us anything about the real world. And then you see something interesting behaviorally about these wild primates and you say, "Jeez, I wonder if it's this part of the brain," or "What's going on in there?" And thus you go back to the lab and your cultured neurons.

HARRIS: I'm picturing you darting these baboons and getting nervous. Do you do it yourself? Do you actually fire the gun?

SAPOLSKY: It's a blowgun. It takes surprisingly little practice. Fortunately, baboons have very large rear ends, which is what you aim for. And, you know, I'm your clichéd nice liberal. So being able to sneak around the bush with a blowgun and shoot at wild baboons is a blast. And you're doing conservation work the whole time.

HARRIS: Do the baboons recognize you enough to realize what you're doing? Enough to hold a grudge against you for darting them?

SAPOLSKY: Not if things go well. Ninety percent of the time out there, you're collecting behavioral data—just hanging with the baboons from dawn till dusk, and there's a whole science of doing that in a quantitative, objective way. I'm not darting them every day.

But one thing that makes it difficult is that you have to dart some guy when no one else is around, nobody's looking, and he's turned the other way. You dart him, and he responds as if he's been stung by a bee or has sat on a thorn. He jumps up, scratches his rear for a second, sits back down, and then three minutes later he's unconscious.

HARRIS: So you get one alone, and when he's unconscious you can approach him and no one else from the troop notices what you're doing?

SAPOLSKY: That's when it all goes smoothly. When it doesn't, he decides to pick up in those three minutes before going under and walk over and sit down right in the middle of a gazillion other baboons, or get into a fight with one, and those are the times it doesn't go so well.

HARRIS: What are you doing to the reputations of these baboons that start a fight with one of their rivals and then promptly faint in front of the whole troop from your anesthesia?

SAPOLSKY: Well, it's got to cause all sorts of interesting belief systems in these animals which I can't quite access.

HARRIS: That's very funny. Are there disanalogies between baboons and humans that are of interest here? They're farther from us than chimps. Are there ways in which chimps are similar to humans and baboons aren't—and if so, why the choice to study baboons?

SAPOLSKY: Chimps would be better insofar as they share 98 percent of our genome, and they're far closer in terms of social structure and cognitive and emotional capacities—all of that. Nonetheless, baboons still count as close relatives—I think we share 96 percent of our DNA with them. And for many reasons, baboons are perfect for what I do. They live out in the open, in these big open grasslands, so you can spot them twelve hours a day, and you can see them well enough to dart them. They don't live up in trees. They're not endangered. They're big, and they've got lots of blood you can take for your tests.

But probably most of all, given that I study stress, baboons are useful for doing that. None of us are stressed because we're riddled with diphtheria or some horrible chronic illness. None of us are stressed because we're chased by saber-toothed tigers every day. Instead, we're Westernized humans, which is to say we're under chronic psychosocial stress. And it turns out that baboons are perfect for studying stress. The

Serengeti, where they live, is a perfect ecosystem. They live in large troops of fifty to a hundred animals, so predators don't hassle them much, and they only have to work about three hours a day for their calories. What that means is, they have nine hours of free time every day to devote to making some other baboon miserable. All they do is generate social stress for each other. They're perfect models for Westernized humans.

HARRIS: So let's get into your book, which is this wonderful tour of the brain and morally salient behavior. You and I approach these questions from a similar angle, and we agree about many things. I'm sure we'll talk about free will at one point, because you're one of the few people in science who've made more or less the same noises on the topic that I have. We've broken the same taboo here. That will be fun to talk about.

But to start with where you're coming from: you have a kind of unity-of-knowledge approach, and you look at the various levels of scientific explanation from neurophysiological and genetic to psychological and cultural. So explain how you traverse those levels.

SAPOLSKY: Sure. When a behavior occurs, we behavioral biologists ask, "Why did that behavior just happen?" And it turns out that that's like asking a whole bunch of questions. Part of what we're asking is, "What occurred in the brain of that individual one second ago?" But we're also asking, "What were the sensory cues in the environment a minute ago that triggered those neurons?" And we're also asking, "What did that person's hormone levels this morning have to do with making him more or less sensitive to those sensory cues that then triggered those neurons?"

And then you're off and running to neuroplasticity—over the course of months, back to childhood, and back to the fetal environment (which turns out to be wildly influential in adult behavior). And then you're back to genes. If you're still asking, "Why did that behavior occur?" you're also asking, "What sort of culture was this person raised in?" Which often winds up meaning, "What were this person's ancestors doing a couple of hundred years ago, and what were the ecological influences on that?" And finally, you're asking something about the millions of years of evolutionary pressures.

So it's not just the case that it's important to look at these things at multiple levels. Ultimately they merge into the same. If you're talking about the brain, you're talking about the childhood experiences when the brain was assembled. If you're talking about genes, you're implicitly talking about their evolution. All of these are a confluence of influences on behavior that are all interconnected.

HARRIS: We'll get back to that picture when we talk about free will because there's a lot of confusion about degrees of freedom for the mind when we're talking about the neurophysiology of human behavior or how culture influences brain development. The punch line here, obviously, is that once one grants that the brain is the final common pathway of all these influences, when we're talking about human thought and intention and behavior, then one has to grant that what the brain is doing is the proximate cause of what the person is doing. And either one signs on to the laws of physics here or one doesn't. We'll get back to that.

But there's a common misunderstanding regarding the relationship between reason and emotion, across the board—in particular with respect to human behavior and the answering of moral questions. There's this idea that in forming a worldview you can be emotionally motivated or you can be motivated by emotion-free rationality. Let's perform a little psychosurgery on that idea. How do you think about reason and emotion?

SAPOLSKY: Well, it's the inevitable "Coke versus Pepsi" dichotomy as to which is more important, which influences the other more in terms of our actions. And of course it turns out that, as with most dichotomies of behavior, it's a false one. They're utterly intertwined, and intertwined on a neurobiological level. For example, if you *think* of something terrifying that happened to you long ago, emotional parts of your brain activate and you secrete stress hormones. Or if you have an aroused emotion—you're in an agitated, frightened state—and suddenly you think and reason in a way that's imprudent and ridiculous. We often make terrible decisions when we're aroused. The two parts are equally intertwined.

We assume that as creatures with big cortexes, reason is at the core of most of our decision making. And an awful lot of work has shown that far more often than we'd like to think, we make our decisions based on implicit emotional, automatic reflexes. We make them within milliseconds. Parts of the brain that are marinated in emotion and hormones are activating long, long before the more cortical rational parts activate. And often what we believe is rational thinking is, instead, our cognitive selves playing catch-up, trying to rationalize the notion that our emotional instincts are perfectly logical and make wonderful sense.

We can manipulate the emotional, the automatic, the implicit, the subterranean aspects of our brains unawares, and it changes our decisions, and then we come up with highfalutin explanations—that I did what I just did because of some philosopher I read freshman year. No, actually it's because of this manipulation that just occurred.

HARRIS: And there are two sides to this. That's one side, which is deflationary of cognition and reason: you think reason is driving your cognition, or your belief formation, but when you look closely you find that it's being driven from below, by emotion. But the flip side is that in order to make even the most coolly calculated reasoning effective, it needs to be integrated with other parts of the brain—in this case, the ventral medial prefrontal cortex. You need a felt sense of the consequences of being right or wrong. This connects to the work of Antonio Damasio and others with people who have neurological damage there. These people may know the correct strategy to employ, say, in a gambling task. They may understand the probabilities, but they can't make that understanding effective, because it's not coded appropriately.

SAPOLSKY: And this is a tremendous rebuke to those who say, "If only we could be purely rational creatures. If only we could get rid of all that affective muck from underneath. Why, we'd all be Mr. Spock, and it would be a wondrous world." The ventral medial prefrontal cortex is basically the means by which the emotional parts of the brain talk to the most rational ones. When it's damaged, people make decisions that we view as appalling, beyond the pale, cold-blooded, detached.

For example, you take a normal person and give them a philosophy problem: "Would you kill one stranger to save the life of five?" And they say "Yes" or they say "No." And then you ask them, "Would you kill your parent, a loved one, to save the life of five?" And in half a second they say, "No, of course not, it's my mother," or my child, or whatever. But somebody with damage to this part of the brain will give the same answer to both questions. It doesn't register; they don't process relatedness in the same way. And every primate on Earth would look at that and say there is something desperately wrong with this person's brain.

HARRIS: On this issue of emotion and rationality: I've been thinking about doubt, which is one of the foundations of our rationality. If you say something that I find implausible—whether logically, factually, or semantically—my error-detection mechanism will get tripped. You've uttered a sentence, and I don't buy it. That feeling of doubt, in my view, is an emotion. All the fMRI studies I've done on belief showed that disbelief—doubting the veracity of a proposition—was associated with activity in the anterior insular cortex. I've begun to think of doubt as an emotion on the continuum of disgust—as a kind of propositional or cognitive rejection state. Frankly, when I hear our president speak, I find I'm viscerally in touch with doubt as a form of disgust. A confident charlatan can precipitate—in me, at least—a fairly strong emotion of disgust.

SAPOLSKY: Well, my insular cortex is with you on that one. I thoroughly agree. Obviously, there are some domains where doubt is a purely rational process. You add up two and two, and somehow it comes out to five. That's a fairly pure cognitive state—saying, "I doubt that." But most of the doubts we have in our social world are steeped in emotion—emotion, disgust perhaps, directed toward the person who's sowing that doubt, directed at people who will believe that and act in some destructive way, and so on.

HARRIS: Just to clarify: If I put you in a scanner and gave you propositions just like *two plus two equals five, you're six feet, five inches tall, you're* *a woman with blond hair, George Washington was never president of the United States*—statements you recognize as untrue but which aren't emotionally laden—I would predict, on the basis of now three neuro-imaging studies, that those would be associated with insular activity in your brain. And that the same statements put accurately—statements you'd accept, like *George Washington was the first president of the United States*—wouldn't.

SAPOLSKY: I agree, because this is very much context-dependent. If I were sitting there on my own and adding up two and two and I got five, I'd have a half second's worth of pure rationality, and then I'd say, "That's it, I'm an idiot. Everybody will know I can't even add two plus two." So in the brain imager, you're right, it wouldn't be a purely cognitive experience. It would be, "What are these guys up to? Do I trust them? Do I feel safe here? Do they think I'm an idiot? What do they think of me? Did I say something foolish before?" and so forth—off and running with the emotional aspects.

One of the best ways to look at this is conformity studies, where people go along with something that is patently untrue. A certain percentage of them are just being affable and agree with the group (and, later, when alone will go back to their original, accurate stance), but a certain percentage actually change their minds, will insist afterward on the group's answer, will explain how they came to be wrong initially. In the former group, the ones who go along to get along, you see activation of brain regions associated with anxiety, disgust—like the amygdala and insula cortex. And in the latter, in addition to activation of those regions, you can actually see activation of the visual cortex. It's like the rest of the brain is trying to convince the visual cortex to conform with the crowd—"Hey, remember? You saw something different from what you're saying," or "Remember? You saw what all of them are saying." Totally different from the affable conformers, except for that commonality of activation of the insular cortex and amygdala. It's anxiety. Doubt provokes anxiety. Certainty is a comforting thing, whereas doubt, even about the seemingly most cerebral and soulless of issues, readily taps into all this anxiety running underneath.

HARRIS: This is a constraint of evolution. We weren't built to acquire new cognitive abilities de novo. The only materials used for modern human cognition are these ancient structures that have to be commandeered to new purposes. Everything we do is built on the back of these apeish structures. Here we're talking about the insular cortex, which receives the inputs from the viscera. You find rotting food disgusting—that's the tale told by the insula. And the only way to build a mind that can find abstract ideas unacceptable is to repurpose, or extend the purpose, of those brain areas.

SAPOLSKY: Absolutely. It's a fascinating domain—the fact that the insular cortex, which tells you if you're eating something rotten, also mediates moral disgust in us. That a part of the brain that does temperature sensing for you is also activated when you perceive that somebody has a warm or a cold personality. That the parts of your brain involved in pain detection in a literal sense also activate when you're feeling empathic about somebody else's pain.

As often pointed out, evolution is not an inventor, it's a tinkerer; it makes do with what's already there. When did humans come up with the concept of moral outrage and moral disgust? Maybe in the last twenty thousand years, fifty thousand years, whatever. When did we come up with the concept of people having warm or cold personalities? A lot later than that. So our brain is winging it in a lot of ways.

HARRIS: The role of the brain in producing these purely human-level distinctions—and, therefore, giving rise to civilization—is largely a story of what the frontal cortex is doing. I think you say at one point in your book that this region of the brain is what makes us do the hard thing when the hard thing is the right thing to do. Let's talk about the role of the frontal cortex in the development of our species.

SAPOLSKY: That's exactly a summary of what it does. To get more jargony: it does impulse control, emotional regulation, long-term planning, gratification postponements, executive function. It's the part of the brain that attempts to tell you, "You know, this seems like a good idea right now, but trust me, you'll regret it. Don't do it." It's the most recently evolved part of our brains. Our frontal cortex is proportionately bigger and more complex than that of any other primate. And, most interesting, it's the last part of the brain to get fully wired up.

The frontal cortex is not fully online until people are, on average, about a quarter century old. It's boggling, but it also tells you a lot about why adolescents act in adolescent ways; it's because the frontal cortex isn't very powerful yet. And that has an interesting implication, which is that if the frontal cortex is the last part of the brain to fully mature, by definition it's the part least constrained by genes and most shaped by experience.

So the frontal cortex is your moral barometer, if that's the right metaphor. It's the Calvinist voice whispering in your head. So, for example, the frontal cortex plays a central role if you're tempted to lie about something; and if you manage to avoid that temptation, your frontal cortex had something to do with it. But at the same time, if you *do* decide to lie, your frontal cortex helps you to do so: "Okay, control my voice, don't make eye contact, don't let my face do something funny." That's a frontal task too. This is a very human, very complicated part of our brains.

HARRIS: Following the implications of its being so late to develop: this is why it matters what culture you're in, what early life experiences you have, and what ethical norms you adopt. None of these factors are floating around in the ether; they're getting etched into the brains of all concerned. And this is largely happening in the frontal cortex.

SAPOLSKY: And that's exactly why it can't mature until you're twenty-five years old. It's not that it's a more complex construction project than wiring up the rest of your brain is. You need the first twenty-five years to learn your situational ethics and your culture-specific beliefs and that sort of thing, and those are subtle, often unstated, often exactly the opposite of what people tell you.

Think about it: every culture on Earth bans some types of killing and allows others, and they're all different in that respect. Every culture on Earth supports some types of lying and bans others. In our culture, it's okay to lie to Grandma—to say, "Ooh, I *don't* have that toy! This is wonderful! Thank you, thank you!" when you've got the same toy in your closet. And it's okay for us to lie if somebody asks, "Are you harboring undocumented refugees in your attic?" You say, "No, of course not, officer." Other kinds of lies, we ban. Every culture has prohibitions about sexual behaviors—some types are wondrous and others are blasphemous. That's a lot of subtle stuff to have to master, learning your culture's particular rules, hypocrisies, rationalizations, unprovable myths for which you'd die—all these culture-specific versions of what counts as doing the right thing. That takes time.

HARRIS: Although I'm doing my part to not spare Grandma the brutal truth about that toy.

SAPOLSKY: I know. Your book *Lying* certainly makes the most convincing argument I've seen for the case that lying isn't okay in any domain.

HARRIS: Although I think there might be a misunderstanding there. I think I saw in a footnote or an endnote that you said I'm against lying in *all* conceivable circumstances, which is not the case. If there are Nazis at the door, and you've got Anne Frank in the attic, then I view lying the way most people do—as a necessary act of self-defense or the defense of others. I consider lying to be on a continuum of violence, where it's generally the least violent thing you can do to someone who's no longer behaving rationally.

SAPOLSKY: Sorry for that misrepresentation. Nobody was supposed to read the footnotes.

HARRIS: Just as long as you know that Anne Frank would be safe in my attic.

SAPOLSKY: Oh, good.

HARRIS: Are there primates that show an analogous delay in maturation in the frontal cortex, or is that a uniquely human characteristic?

SAPOLSKY: It's primate-wide. It's even rodent-wide. But with other primates, and certainly with rodents, it's not as dramatic, it's not as delayed, and their brains aren't faced with as complex a task as ours.

HARRIS: There are other interesting details of neuroanatomy here. There are "von Economo neurons," which are unique to primates and cetaceans and elephants, I believe. And they preferentially appear in the insula and anterior cingulate. They relate to social cognition and self-awareness. What's happening with those neurons?

SAPOLSKY: They're cool. When you study human brains, one of the first things you realize is that we're not humans because we've invented a totally novel type of neurotransmitter or a completely new brand of neuron. It's just that we've got more of them and they're more complexly wired. But then, people found this one neuron type that did seem to be unique to humans—these von Economos, which are almost entirely found in the anterior cingulate and insular cortex, the area having to do with empathy and moral disgust and all that interesting stuff.

But, as you say, then people looked further, and these neurons turned up in other species, all the usual suspects when you're looking for the most complex social worlds—other primates, cetaceans, elephants. The best guess is that they play a role in some very complex aspects of sociality. Are they mirror neurons? Don't get me started on the ways in which they aren't, despite the hype; that's a whole separate round. But one of the most interesting things is that these von Economo neurons are the first neurons to die in an obscure neurological disease called frontal temporal dementia—a disease that predominantly damages the frontal cortex.

What that tells you is that these are really expensive, vulnerable neurons to operate, if they're the first ones to keel over. The other interesting thing is what that disease looks like: disinhibited, socially inappropriate behavior. Often it's initially viewed as a psychiatric disorder until you realize that this is a massive neurological carpet bombing of the front part of your brain. Whatever these neurons are doing, they're very, very specialized for the most complex social things we fancy species do.

HARRIS: Well, the last stop on our Cook's tour of the brain, or at least the Cook's tour of the frontal cortex, is the dorsolateral prefrontal cortex, which is associated with much of what we consider to be higher rationality, or executive control. Activity here can dampen activity in emotional parts of the brain, like the limbic system—in the amygdala, in particular—reducing negative affect. It can do this by becoming active in a relevant way. If you cognitively reappraise what an experience means—for instance, you think someone's being rude to you, but then you decide that maybe he's just nervous—that prefrontal activity dampens your initial negative emotional response to what you perceived as rudeness. But what's also interesting is that any use of your dorsolateral prefrontal cortex can dampen negative arousal. If you're feeling negative emotion and you turn your attention to something else—you start doing math problems, or anything that requires an alternate form of cognition—that can have a similar dampening effect.

Does this ever become relevant to you in your life, behaviorally? Is there anything you do differently in your daily experience, given how much time you spend thinking about what's going on under the hood?

SAPOLSKY: For better or worse, yes. The same thing has infested my wife, who's a neuropsychologist by training. I remember a day when our then-four-year-old son had just done something rotten to his two-year-old sister, and we swooped in with, "You're not a bad person, but you did a bad thing." And "Why did you do that?" And at some point one of us said, "Why are we being so hard on him? He has, like, three frontal neurons." And the other said, "Well, how else is he going to develop a good frontal cortex?" So we actually think that way in my house, which is pretty appalling.

Where I have the most trouble applying my worldview as a mechanistic, reductive, determinist sort of guy—I write about this in my book—is in the realm of free will, of course. Much like you, I don't believe there is a shred of free will. I believe that what we call free will is the biology that hasn't been discovered yet. But what I find hugely daunting is how you're supposed to live your life thinking that way. At some critical juncture of social interaction, I'll act as if I absolutely believe there's free will. I hear about somebody who's done something jerky and I wish horrible things on him, instead of thinking, "Oh, but remember what happened to him as a second-trimester fetus." Like most people, I hit a wall with that one. It's a whole lot easier to operate with the notion of agency. Which we must resist.

HARRIS: It's obvious to us, but perhaps not to some people, that coming to a different conclusion about free will has consequences. I would argue that the consequences are generally good.

So let's step back and remind people of the problem here, because many people don't see it. As you know, my friend and colleague Dan Dennett doesn't agree with our take on free will. And many scientists don't want to make the noises we're beginning to make here. I've touched on this topic repeatedly on the podcast, so maybe you should make the case about why the common notion of free will is incoherent, scientifically. You might pull from your book the great description of what you call "car free will."

SAPOLSKY: Okay. One angle I take in trying to persuade people there's no free will is to list the sheer number of factors influencing our behavior. You do something aggressive, and you're asked why you did it, and you come up with a rational explanation that's dripping with a sense of agency. But here are some of the things that influenced how likely you were to do that behavior. If you were sitting in a room with smelly garbage, it made you more likely to behave that way. If your testosterone levels have been elevated for the past day, that also makes it more likely. If you were traumatized five months ago and neurons in your amygdala grew new connections, also more likely. If, as a third-trimester fetus, you were exposed to elevated levels of stress hormones from your mother's circulation, that also made it more likely. If your ancestors were nomadic pastoralists wandering grasslands or deserts with their herds and came up with a culture of honor, and you were raised in that, you're more likely to have done that as well.

Wait a second—ecosystems five hundred years ago have an influence on current behavior? Yes. It turns out that our cultures are greatly shaped by that, and it greatly shapes how our brains develop. There's a lot more going on under the hood—a whole lot more subterranean influences—than one would think.

And when you manipulate one of those variables by, say, placing somebody in a room that smells of rotten garbage, your average person becomes more socially conservative on the questionnaire. And you'll say, "That's interesting. Last month, when you filled this out (in a room that smelled like petunias), you had this or that attitude, and now you've put it differently. Why?" And they'll say, "Well, something that happened in Middle Peoria last month has utterly changed my views." No, it was a sensory influence sensitizing your insular neurons. So you can manipulate people on a biologically unappreciated level and change their behavior.

But for me, the most salient way of getting at the free-will issue is to look historically at the stuff we understand now, if we're reasonably educated, reflective, thoughtful people. We know now that epileptic seizures are neurological disorders, and not the result of having slept with Satan. We know that certain types of learning disabilities aren't because children are lazy and unmotivated. It turns out that these arise from cortical malformations. We know that sometimes when somebody is completely inappropriate in their behavior, it's because they've got a neurochemical disorder called schizophrenia.

Most of us have got to the point where free will has been subtracted from that equation. If somebody has treatment-resistant epilepsy and has occasional seizures, they can't drive a car. But you don't feel that they're being punished when their driver's license is inactivated; you say, "It's not them, it's their disease." There's a biological explanation that sidesteps notions of agency or free will.

All you have to do is look at how much we've learned in the last century, in the last fifty years, in the last ten years, in the last five years.

We'd never heard of von Economo neurons some twenty years ago. And either you conclude, "That's it—after tonight at midnight we'll never get a new scientific fact again." Or you conclude that the march of science is going to continue exactly as before and so will the number of instances in which we say, "Oh, it's not him, it's this weird quirk in his brain."

And when it comes to the issue of inappropriate behavior or criminal activity, when somebody does something violent, it should be seen as a biological phenomenon. That's not to say you don't do anything about it, or you forgive everything. "Forgive" is an irrelevant word. If a car's brakes are faulty, you don't let it out on the streets, because it's going to kill somebody. You fix the brakes if you can, and if you can't, you put the car in the garage for good. But no one would say that the car has a rotten soul or deserves incarceration in the garage—it's just a mechanical problem. And if people say, "Wow, that's dehumanizing—to view us as just biological machines with mechanical problems," well, that's a hell of a lot better than demonizing us as having bad souls.

HARRIS: The case of Charles Whitman, the Texas Tower shooter, really brings home the point. Many people have written about Whitman in this context, as I've done, and you do in the book. Upon his death, his brain was autopsied, and they found a large tumor in his hypothalamus that was pressing on his amygdala. A tumor there can drive this murderous symptomology, and when it's discovered, this understanding of a purely neuroanatomical, causal influence becomes exculpatory. We don't view Whitman as one of the most evil people in human history. We view him as a victim of biology.

My argument has been for years now that a brain tumor is just a coarse-grained example of causality. And if we could have a perfect account of what's happening at every synapse in the average psychopath's brain, causing him to be a psychopath and not Gandhi, that understanding, too, would be as exculpatory as Whitman's brain tumor. We would view psychopaths as unlucky. However they got that way—whether it was the influence of culture, or of the parents they didn't pick, or of genes that mutated—we'd view them as victims of circumstance. We'd warehouse them in prison if we had no cure. But if we had a cure for psychopathy, it would be perverse to withhold it in a spirit of retribution. It would be like withholding neurosurgery from someone with a brain tumor that was making him violent. It would make no moral sense.

So you and I are on the same page with respect to understanding, and rejecting, the retributive impulse to punish people who commit acts of violence. But as you said initially, it's never a question of letting dangerous people roam the streets. Obviously we're in favor of locking up dangerous people, but without any illusions that free will has been motivating their destructive behavior.

You and I differ, though, as to whether we feel that we can live from this point of view. I'm like you in that I'm often taken in by the illusion of agency. Often, my emotional response to bad actions in the world makes sense only if I'm viewing people as real agents, as the authors of their actions. And there's a gray area here that I haven't thought a lot about but which I think can bridge this gulf between our belief about the origins of human behavior and the social and moral responses we have to bad actors.

Given what we've just said, we know that every person is essentially a force of nature. And in this corner of the universe, the laws of physics are playing out perfectly. Whether the universe is purely deterministic or there's an added factor of randomness doesn't matter; that still gives us no basis to believe in free will. Every person is a puppet who didn't pick his own strings, and the strings reach back to the Big Bang.

But people often do modify their behavior because of what we say or do. That process can be fraught with frustration, of course. But these influences are real. You're doing something I want to discourage, and I know that you, as another primate, are susceptible to being influenced by disincentives—or punishments, in the extreme case. And it becomes totally rational to invoke all the usual means of influencing another person's behavior without attributing free will to whomever you're trying to influence.

SAPOLSKY: I agree. Whether in Eric Kandel's classic work with *Aplysia* (a sea slug) and all the way up to us, nervous systems can be conditioned by positive and negative reinforcement. We understand that down to the molecular level. Yes, nervous systems can be changed by inputs. They abundantly are, and the inputs sometimes take the form of what we might call punishment, when it may be necessary to change somebody's behavior. If a child gets a "time out" for doing something rotten to another kid, the penalty is going to affect his frontal cortical neurons and strengthen the synapses that tell him not to do that next time. It's a mechanistic thing—and nonetheless it's punitive. What we need to do is use punishment instrumentally, when we know it will accomplish something within a biological framework. But don't stand there and preach while you're doing it, and don't take pleasure from a sense of justice being served.

HARRIS: The wrinkle here is that the pleasure of justice, and even a lust for vengeance, runs so deep in us. The free-will illusion is so compelling that people argue (or at least feel) that the criminal justice system should acknowledge it in some way. Justice isn't satisfying if we medicalize human evil—saying, basically, that every criminal is not guilty by reason of insanity, and we'll either cure them or warehouse those we can't cure, without any moralizing about it. How do you think about the moral improvement of our species in light of the fact that so many people find retribution, and even vengeance, morally compelling, and in some cases psychologically necessary?

SAPOLSKY: This is obviously very powerful, challenging stuff. Neurobiologically, justice is pleasurable. It activates mesolimbic dopamine systems. It feels good. It has an evolutionary logic to it: Third-party punishment (carried out by an objective bystander, rather than by the person who has been wronged) is costly. It costs to have a police department, it costs to have judges, it costs to give dental insurance to prison guards. So there has to have evolved a certain pleasure, a certain reward, in having done the right punitive thing.

But take the historical perspective. There was a time when society's worst people would have been set upon by a mob and beaten to death. And at some point, governmental authorities said, "Yes, yes, we know that's pleasurable, but from now on you have to turn the person over to us so that we can beat them to death, and you can watch." And people had to adjust to that. And then at some later point they'd say, "Yes, but now we're going to do something more humane. We're going to hang people. You can come and see it and bring your picnic baskets. We're going to have a public hanging. But you'll have to get your pleasures in some other way than watching the person being slowly beaten to death." And people adjust to that, and then you don't have crowds at executions anymore. Then we have people designing machines that do lethal injections.

At every step of the way, what essentially has been said is, "Yes, yes, there's a certain visceral sense of pleasurable vengeance in having it done this way. But we're not doing that anymore, and you're going to have to get used to it." And people have gotten used to it at each one of those steps. People will have to get used to the idea that a damaging act by a human is like a bear attack or a hurricane. We already think that way when it's clear the damaging act was unintentional, purely acciden-tal, and the perpetrator is crippled with remorse. We simply will have to expand that recognition further. At each one of those steps, there's a cultural shift as to what punishments we don't impose anymore, and it's just going to keep happening. Yet at any point where the line is cur-rently drawn, it still seems inconceivable: "My God, if somebody did that to my loved one and they then got to spend the rest of their life en-joying three meals a day, that would just consume me."

HARRIS: I fully agree. I think I heard you on a *Radiolab* episode discuss-ing a case where the person had epilepsy and had a surgical treatment for it that resulted in Klüver-Bucy syndrome. The consequence was that although he'd been normal up until that moment, he suddenly got into child pornography and was then prosecuted on child-porn charges. The judge split the difference in sentencing between the fully draco-nian penalty you'd give to the ordinary consumer of child pornography and letting him off as somebody who had a neurological disorder. The sentence was something like eight years in prison—which is not at all trivial. The man himself, and even his wife, along with the producers of the segment, all seem to have judged this to be more or less the right thing, as if the wisdom of Solomon had been achieved here. You were absolutely horrified. Do you remember that case?

SAPOLSKY: Yes, I was horrified. He had the classic Klüver-Bucy syndrome, which was first described I believe in the 1930s, when that part of the brain was damaged in monkeys and you'd see inappropriate sexual behavior afterward—hypersexuality. You'd see hyperphagia—the animals ate compulsively. You'd see inappropriate aggression.

So this guy was surgically damaged in that part of the brain, in an attempt to control his seizures, and he began obsessively eating afterward, along with all sorts of other unusual behaviors. And he got this strange, utterly abnormal hypersexuality focused on child pornography.

Okay, so it's due to his brain damage. But the crux of the issue was that he spent his nights filling up his computer with this stuff, hour after hour, and yet he never once downloaded child pornography on his work computer. "Aha!" concluded the judge, "Yes, the brain damage has something to do with why this person suddenly started manifesting this bizarre unprecedented criminal behavior. But the fact that he could nonetheless suppress that behavior at work shows that there's still some free will there. And given that there's evidence of free will, let's split the difference, and he'll get half the jail time the prosecutors recommended."

There was this notion that if at eight o'clock at night you couldn't keep yourself from bad behavior but at eight o'clock in the morning you could, that was evidence of free will. Whereas it was just evidence that the biology works differently under different circumstances. People with a mild case of Tourette's syndrome—where you get compulsive tics, compulsive scatology, cursing, all sorts of inappropriate gestures—can suppress it. They suppress it during work, throughout the day, and by five p.m. when they step outside they have an explosion of tics and such. Does that mean it's less of a neurological disorder than if somebody manifested Tourette's all throughout the day? No, it just tells you something about how much of their frontal cortex could regulate some of their involuntary sounds.

Or take somebody with moderate dementia. In the morning, they can tell you their name and what century it is, and at the end of the day you get what's called Sundowning Syndrome and their cognition is vastly worse; they have no idea who they are or where they are. Does that mean that some of the time they're choosing not to remember their name and at other times they're perfectly able to? No, it has to do with brain metabolism, the energetics of the brain. Your brain is more tired at the end of the day, and a damaged brain has even more stuff going wrong at that point.

HARRIS: It seems that there's a paradox here. What we're talking about are gradations of responsibility, where you'd expect someone to have a degree of internal freedom to do otherwise. Even people like ourselves who don't believe in free will acknowledge the difference between voluntary and involuntary behavior, and there's a spectrum of competence in regulating behavior of all kinds. You can expect only so much of a three-year-old or someone with Alzheimer's. But when you get to the most competent, the most potentially responsible people—those who should be able to fully own the consequences of their behavior, what I find is that we arrive at a moral mirage.

Take the most scrupulous, saintly person. If that person starts downloading child pornography, or lying to everyone, well, this person should seem the most culpable, right? If anyone should have been able to do otherwise, it's this guy. He's been impeccable his entire life. But since he's been a saint up until now, something has clearly gone wrong with him. He's the victim of some anomaly, because this is not who he was yesterday. So culpability seems to dissipate as we increase a person's prior competence, and I'm not quite sure how to think about that.

SAPOLSKY: That reflects a certain cultural mind-set that I and a lot of rational people in our world share as well, which would be, "Wow, is he sick? Is there something wrong with him? It's not him, it's the disease"— that sort of statement. And your assessment also has elements of a cultural view that accepts the possibility of human foibles: "Hey, we all make mistakes; we're all human"—the sort of mind-set that accepts the occasional shortcomings of people. On the other hand, plenty of cultures will say, "Who cares what he used to do? He should be instantly drawn and quartered."

Part of our view is we've got a certain brand of Christianized belief that happens to like redemption a lot—to see someone who's fallen come clean, admit to it, and climb back up again, like the endless soap opera of various televangelists who turn out to have feet of God-knows-what, and then confess and they're forgiven. That's a cycle that's culturally appealing to us.

HARRIS: We've been talking about bad people here—or unlucky people, if you drill down on the biological details—but I think most of human evil is the result of bad ideas more than bad people. There aren't that many people who consciously do evil. This is a point that goes all the way back to Plato. There are many people, however, who are doing what they imagine to be good. They have a righteous commitment to some cause, and yet they're creating an immense amount of needless misery as a consequence.

There's an endless number of examples of this, but one of the most vivid in recent memory comes from something called the "Auschwitz album." I believe it's now in the Holocaust museum in DC. It was found sometime in the last decade, and it took people a while to figure out what these photos were, because they were photos of happy people sunning themselves on a porch, eating blueberries by the bowlful, and laughing—just men and women in the prime of life, in these black-and-white photographs, just having a grand old time. Some of them, curiously enough, were wearing SS uniforms.

And then based on some sleuthing, it was discovered that these were actually the guards and staff at Auschwitz on their days off, in a chalet that was situated practically under the plume of smoke coming out of the Auschwitz crematoria. These are the people who were gassing and cremating men, women, and children, working slave laborers to death, and so forth, on a daily basis. And so, when you see these photos, it's almost impossible to understand how such a scene of such basic normalcy was possible. I think it's safe to say that not all of them were psychopaths. In fact, I would bet that almost none of them are. It's un-canny: these people are experiencing a range of conscious states we're all familiar with; they're having a fantastic time, eating blueberries in the sun, playing music, teasing one another. They're fully enjoying their social lives. And then they go gas and obliterate more people the next day.

I suspect that it's because their belief system has segmented their world into a moral in-group and out-group so decisively that they're un-conflicted about what they're doing. To them, the people they're killing are scarcely human. I think you share my concern about bad ideas being the malware that can get even psychologically normal people, biologi-cally normal people, to do the unthinkable. How do you view this, in the context of your research?

SAPOLSKY: That's utterly haunting. And I agree, it's at the heart of a huge percentage of our human miseries. As you say, it's a rare person who will simply say, "It's okay to do the following horrible, violent things." The vast majority of people will say, "It's not okay, but here's why I'm an exception. Here's why it's different for me. Here's why my special pains put me in a different category." Or they'll say, "It's terrible to do violent, horrible things to innocent people," and then they'll sim-ply differ as to who counts as innocent. I think that's where much of our misery comes from—our having a lot of shared values that nonethe-less are always a bit context-dependent, and the contexts are personally convenient contexts in a lot of cases.

HARRIS: Let's talk about the future. Just imagine we have a completed science of the mind and we can intervene more directly into brain func-tion in ways that don't require neurosurgery, or that the interventions become so compelling and so safe once you do the surgery that more and more of us opt for neurosurgery. You can add superintelligent AI to fill in the gaps here. What this opens is the possibility of altering our neurophysiology in such a way that our intuitions about right and wrong can be modified. So it's not only a change in how we track what we agree is good; we might actually modify our beliefs and intuitions about what is good. You might cease to find something objectionable that you currently find objectionable, or vice versa. And then the question is, What sort of moral hardware and software should we have or want to have, given that everything about us is now on the table to be revised—and revised by something more than a good education or good relationships or a change of culture? What is reasonable to hope for here? Do you think the ultimate hope for humanity lies in our finding more direct ways to alter our biology?

SAPOLSKY: For one thing, right off the bat, most listeners might view this as way far off. It's a lot closer than a lot of us think. Stunningly, interesting studies use this technique—it's called transcranial magnetic stimulation—where you noninvasively change the activity of small clusters of cortical neurons in people. You change people's moral decisions— you change people's level of generosity in economic games, and then you stop pressing the button and they go back to where they were before. It's mechanistic, and a harbinger of the sorts of things we'll be facing more and more down the line.

I think what we'll do is just continue accepting the various means of manipulation. Few people think of their morning cup of coffee as a sort of neurochemical cognitive enhancement. We've accepted it by now; we don't think of that as an external factor that changes levels of attention and focus, and where you can even identify which parts of the brain and which molecules are dancing in a particular way. People with a history of chronic depression who are finally medicated with something that works—when they're a week into their first experience with Prozac, if they've lucked out on that one, and they're transformed— also often experience the existential crisis of, "Wait a second. Am I a different person now? Or am I finally the person I was meant to be all along?" But once they come to terms with the fact that nonetheless they feel better than they have in years, the existential crisis dissipates and they think, "Thank God for these meds, and I'm going to keep taking them."

I think we'll have more and more of that along the way, as we devise interventions that make us more empathic, more responsive, that increase our sense of who counts as "us"—things of that sort. We'll have the immediate crisis of, "Wait, does this count as good if it's not volitional?" None of it is volitional. Is altruism not as altruistic as we think, if there are hidden benefits? I think what will mostly happen is that we'll recognize that this sort of intervention is very helpful and we'll just run with it. I certainly hope that's the direction things will go.

HARRIS: As a final topic, I want to touch on your view of religion and its relationship to science. You have a very different backstory than I do. You grew up in an Orthodox family surrounded by religious people, and if I'm not mistaken, you were intensely religious until you were around thirteen years old. Do you remember the first chink in the edifice?

SAPOLSKY: Yup. I had a crisis of trying to make sense of theistic determinism. The Exodus story. Moses goes to Pharaoh and says, "Let my people go." And Pharaoh says, "No way." And Moses brings a plague upon Egypt. And Pharaoh says, "Okay, I give up. You can all go." And then, at least in the version I was raised with, "God hardened Pharaoh's heart" and made him say, "I changed my mind, nobody's going anywhere." So now, in comes the second plague, and Pharaoh says, "I give up." And God intervenes again, and at the end we're asked not only to judge Pharaoh but, while we're at it, kill all the firstborns and the horses and whatever poor schmucks have been forced to be in the army running those chariots across the Red Sea. And justice has been served.

But wait a second—God interfered. But then God judged them, and that's very confusing. And when I was thirteen, it became crystal clear. I remember one night waking up at two in the morning and thinking, "None of that makes sense. None of it's for real. It's nonsense." And I've been incapable of a shred of spirituality or religiosity since then.

HARRIS: Did you communicate your doubts directly to your parents at that point, or did you keep them secret? What was the unraveling like for you?

SAPOLSKY: I was a very meek, mild, inexpressive, passive-aggressive kid. So my father, who was the driving force on the religiosity, went to his grave never knowing that I no longer believed.

HARRIS: How old were you when he died?

SAPOLSKY: An adult.

HARRIS: Interesting. Now, when you say you've been incapable of any spiritual intuition since, did you have a psychedelic phase in your life? Have you ever perturbed your consciousness in ways that would give you a glimpse of what people are talking about when they say they've had a spiritual experience?

SAPOLSKY: No. And people are always intensely puzzled by this.

HARRIS: You've got the facial hair that suggests that you may have dropped acid a couple of times.

SAPOLSKY: Yeah, I've got that. I've got a ponytail. I wear Birkenstocks. I live in the Haight in San Francisco. My credentials are in place. Not only have I never taken an illicit drug in my life, I've never taken a sip of alcohol either. I'm actually pretty regimented and driven, underneath this neo-hippie exterior. I'll see the Northern Californian stereotype of people saying, "Well, I don't subscribe to any organized religion but I'm a very spiritual person and I think of nature as personified." And I know that I'd love to be able to believe that and take comfort from that. But I'm an utterly hard-nosed materialist and incapable of anything else.

HARRIS: You must have made a firm decision at some point not to try any of these substances, even alcohol. When did that happen, and what informed it?

SAPOLSKY: Oh, a little bit of being biologically trained and knowing that's not a great thing for one's nervous system. But this was a decision early on, in high school, amid everybody else doing lots of recreational drugs.

HARRIS: Although isn't the research on that somewhat equivocal now? Isn't there some research that suggests that alcohol has a protective effect against dementia? And in particular about alcohol and mortality, at least some studies seem to show a reduction in mortality. I don't know which of those studies to trust, and it's been a long time since I've looked at any. I'm sure some of them have been funded by, say, Anheuser-Busch. But my understanding is that there's at least some data that moderate alcohol use is correlated with the decline of mortality across the board. And there's some potential neuroprotective effect in moderation.

SAPOLSKY: Grudgingly, I'm forced to say that there seems to be some evidence for it. But my guess is half a dozen push-ups a day are equivalent, in their protective effects. Like you, I haven't followed that literature closely. But it does seem a little bit valid.

HARRIS: So you decided at some point that not using any drugs was the healthiest thing you could do. Is there more to it than that? Was there any kind of holdover from your religious upbringing? I've charted a different course here, and I'm probably the worse for wear because of it. I certainly haven't tried everything, but I've tried many things. For me, it would have required some belief that moving from zero to one on any of these substances was something I had good reason not to do and never to reconsider.

SAPOLSKY: Well, to be more honest about this than I usually am, the basic reason was that since early adolescence I've had some pretty severe problems with major depression. And what I learned from all sorts of wise professionals was that my neurochemistry was screwed up enough so that I didn't want to mess with it further.

HARRIS: Have you found a way to mitigate the depression, pharmacologically or otherwise? Is it under control, or is it a continuous struggle?

SAPOLSKY: It's manageable, thanks to all the circumstances that have made me one of the luckier members of our unequal world, by access to a lot of very good professional help, including pharmacological. And there's probably no subject on which I soapbox about the biological roots of behavior more readily. Depression is a biochemical disorder: a *gemisch* of various contributing factors—screwy genes, this or that unideal fetal environment, just the right kinds of significant stressors when you're growing that produce a brain prone toward feeling helpless, and so on. It's as biochemical a disorder as diabetes. And it's hard for people to accept that. It's far easier to decide, "Hey, I have a lot of gumption and backbone. I should be able to overcome this. Come on, pull yourself together."

HARRIS: For any people in our audience who are dealing with this or have a family member dealing with it, do you have any advice? Any other memes you think they should get out of their heads? Any resources you think they should seek out?

SAPOLSKY: Okay, going into preacher mode here, besides noting that a lot of medications are abused, overprescribed, used for the wrong reasons, used as a crutch, blah blah, et cetera, an untreated major depression is one of the most life-threatening diseases out there. So don't think of being mired in a depression as failing at some stupid test of character or tenacity. You don't sit somebody down who has diabetes and say, "Oh, come on, what's with this insulin stuff? Stop babying yourself." Whether it's you or a loved one dealing with the likes of major depression, realize that it's a biological disorder, just like any other.

HARRIS: There have been some great books on depression. William Styron's book *Darkness Visible* is a window onto this experience. And Andrew Solomon's *The Noonday Demon*. Are there any books you recommend here?

SAPOLSKY: In fact, those are two of my favorites in that regard. I'd couple that with reading some of the websites of places like the National

Institute of Mental Health, which make it clear that this is a disease, this is biology, this is not a problem with willpower.

HARRIS: Here's a final question, a Big Picture question. If you could come back in a thousand years, assuming our descendants survive, what do you think you'd see? Will we be recognizably human? How deep will we have gone into genetic engineering, or into integrating ourselves with machines? What will we become, and what is reasonable to hope for?

SAPOLSKY: I suspect we'll be technologically unrecognizable to our present selves, much as our present selves would be technologically un-recognizable to our ancient selves. You take a human from twenty thousand years ago and you look at the fact that now people with sufficiently bad eyesight who'd get eaten by a predator in two seconds are walking around just fine because of the technology of eyeglasses. And our teeth don't fall out, and we can get our hips replaced. We're technologically transformed now. But we're still recognizably human.

The Map of Misunderstanding

A CONVERSATION WITH DANIEL KAHNEMAN

I think it's uncontroversial to say that Daniel Kahneman has been the most influential living psychologist for many years now. He is an emeritus professor of psychology at Princeton University, and also an emeritus professor of public affairs at Princeton's Woodrow Wilson School of Public and International Affairs. He received the Nobel Prize in economics for the work he did on decision making under uncertainty, with Amos Tversky.

This conversation took place in front of a live audience at the Beacon Theatre in New York. We covered a lot of ground that evening, discussing the replication crisis in science, the difference between conscious and unconscious cognitive processes, failures of intuition, the power of framing, moral illusions, the "remembering self" versus the "experiencing self," the utility of worrying, and many other topics. Needless to say, it was a great honor to share the stage with Kahneman and to help bring his many insights to a wide audience.

HARRIS: It's often said, and rarely true, that a guest needs no introduction—but in your case it is virtually true. By way of introduction, I want to ask: How do you think about your body of work? How do you summarize the intellectual problems you've tried to get your hands around?

KAHNEMAN: You know, it's been just a series of problems that occurred that I worked on. There was no big program. When you look back, you see patterns and you see ideas that had been with you for a long time. But there was really no plan. You follow ideas, you follow things that you take a fancy to. That's the story of my intellectual life. It's just one thing after another.

HARRIS: Judging from the outside, it seems to me that you have told us much of what we now think we know about cognitive bias and cognitive illusion. And really, the picture is of human ignorance having a kind of structure. It's not just that we get things wrong, we get things reliably wrong. And because of that, whole groups who market to society are going to get things wrong because the errors don't cancel themselves out and the bias becomes systematic. And that, obviously, has implications that touch more or less everything we care about.

I want to track through your work, as presented in your book *Thinking, Fast and Slow*, to try to tease out what should be significant for all of us at this moment, because human unreason, unfortunately, becomes more and more relevant, and we don't get over these problems. I'd like to begin by asking you about a problem that's very close to home now. It is what's called the "replication crisis" or "reproducibility crisis" in psychology. It seems that when you go back to even some of the most celebrated studies in psychology, their reproducibility is on the order of 50 percent, 60 percent in the best case. There was one study done that took twenty-one papers from *Nature* and *Science*, which are the most highly regarded journals, and reproduced only thirteen of them. So let's talk about the problem we face in even doing science in the first place.

KAHNEMAN: The key problem and the reason that this happens is that research is expensive. It's expensive personally, and it's expensive in terms of money, and so you want it to succeed. When you're a researcher, you know what you want to find, and that creates biases that you are not fully aware of. There is a concept that's known as P-hacking—people very honestly delude themselves about what they find. And there are several tricks of the trade that people know about. You are going to do an experiment, so instead of having one dependent variable where you predict the outcome, you take two dependent variables. If one of them doesn't work, you stay with the one that does.

HARRIS: You've got a spare.

KAHNEMAN: If you do that a few times, it's almost guaranteed that your research will not be replicable. It was first discovered to be an issue in the field of medicine (and it's more important in medicine than it is in psychology; somebody once said that most published research in medicine is false). A fair amount of published psychological research is false, too.

HARRIS: Yes, and even some of the most celebrated results in psychology, like priming and the "marshmallow test."

KAHNEMAN: I think the evidence is strong that the more amazing priming results are not robust, but the rejection of the "marshmallow test" results is still debatable. Results get celebrated, in part, because they are surprising. And the rule is: the more surprising the result, the less likely it is to be true. So that's how celebrated results get to be nonreplicable.

HARRIS: The scariest thing I heard was that someone did a study on trying to replicate unpublished studies and found that they replicated better than published studies. Did you hear about this?

KAHNEMAN: I don't think that's replicable.

HARRIS: Let's hope not!
    Okay, let's talk about System 1 and System 2. This is the division that

gives us a somewhat dispiriting picture of human rationality. What are these two systems?

KAHNEMAN: Before starting with anything else, there are clearly two ways that ideas come to mind. If I say two plus two, then an idea comes to your mind. You haven't asked for it, you're completely passive, and something happens in your memory. If I ask you to multiply twenty-four by seventeen, you have to work to get that idea. So it's that dichotomy between the effortless and the effortful. And that is phenomenologically obvious—you start from there. How you describe it, and whether you choose to describe it in terms of systems, as I did, or in other terms—that's a theoretical choice. In my view, theory is less important than the basic observation that there are two ways for ideas to come to mind. And then you have to describe it in a way that will be useful. What I mean by that is you have to describe the phenomena in a way that will help researchers have good ideas about facts and experiments to run. System 1 and System 2—it's not my dichotomy, and many people object to the terminology, but I chose it quite deliberately.

HARRIS: What are the liabilities? In your book, you try to guard against various misunderstandings of this picture.

KAHNEMAN: Yes. There is a rule that you're taught fairly early in psychology, which is never to invoke what's called "homunculi," which are little people in your head whose behavior explain your behavior or explain the behavior of people. That's a no-no. And System 1 and System 2 are really homunculi. So, I knew what I was doing when I picked those. But the reason I did was that System 1 and System 2 are agents. They have personalities. And it turns out that the mind is very good at forming pictures and images of agents that have intentions and propensities and traits, and they're active, and it's just easy to get your mind around that. That's why I picked the terminology, which many people find objectionable because they're really not agents in the head. But I believe it's a very useful way to think about it.

HARRIS: Is there an analogy to be drawn between a classical, psychological —even Freudian—picture of the conscious and the unconscious minds? How do you think about consciousness, and everything that precedes it, in light of modern psychology?

KAHNEMAN: It's clearly related—one characteristic that System 1 activities have (and these are the automatic ones) is that you're completely unconscious of the process that produces them. You get the results—you get "four" when you hear "two plus two." In System 2 activities, you're often conscious of the process. You know what you're doing when you're calculating; you know what you're doing when you're searching for something in memory. So clearly, consciousness and System 2 tend to go together. It's not perfect, and who knows what consciousness is, anyway? But they tend to go together, and System 1 is much more likely to be unconscious and automatic.

HARRIS: Neither system is a perfect guide for tracking reality, but System 1 is very effective in many cases. Otherwise it wouldn't have evolved the way it has. How do you think about the utility of intuition?

KAHNEMAN: Our representation of the world—most of what we know about the world—is in System 1. We're going along in life, producing expectations, and being surprised or not surprised by what happens. All of this is automatic—we're not aware of it. So most of our thinking is System 1 thinking. And intuition is defined as knowing—or rather, *thinking* that you know something—without knowing why you know it. And it's fairly clear . . . This is a digression, but there is a psychologist by the name of Gary Klein who really doesn't like anything that I do. And . . .

HARRIS: How does your System 1 feel about that?

KAHNEMAN [laughing]: I like Gary a lot, but he believes in intuition, and is a great believer in expert intuition. He has beautiful data showing beautiful observations of expert intuition. I invited him to try and figure out our differences, because obviously I'm a skeptic. So where is intuition marvelous and where is it flawed? We worked for six years before we came up with something, and we published an article called "A Failure to Disagree," because, in fact, there is a fairly clear boundary about when you can trust your intuitions and when you can't. And I think that's summarized in three conditions. The first one is the world has to be regular enough. First of all, intuition is recognition, and Herbert Simon said that. You have an intuition—it's like a child's recognizing what a dog is; it's immediate.

Now, in order to recognize patterns in reality, which is what true intuitions are, the world has to be regular enough so that there are regularities to be picked up. Then you have to have enough exposure to those regularities to have a chance to learn them. And third, it turns out that intuition depends critically on the time between when you're making a guess and a judgment, and when you get feedback about it. The feedback has to be rapid. And if those three conditions are satisfied, then eventually people develop intuition.

Chess is a prime example where all three conditions are satisfied. After countless hours of play, a chess player will have intuitions. All the ideas, all the moves that come to his or her mind are going to be strong moves. That's intuition.

HARRIS: Some intuitions are more innate than others, or we're so adapted to learning certain things that no one remembers learning them—recognizing a human face, for example. But much of what you're calling intuition was at one point learned, so intuition is trainable. There are experts in various domains, chess being a very clear one, who develop what we consider to be expert intuitions. And yet much of the story of the blind spots in our rationality is a story of the failure of expert intuition. So how do you think about the limits of trainability?

KAHNEMAN: What happens is that when those conditions are not satisfied, people have intuitions, too. That is, they have ideas that come to their mind with high confidence, and they think they're right.

HARRIS: I've met these people.

KAHNEMAN: Yeah, we've met them, and we see them in the mirror. . . . So it turns out you can have intuitions for bad reasons. All it takes is a thought that comes to your mind automatically and with high confidence, and you'll think that it's an intuition, and you'll trust it. But the correlation between confidence and accuracy is not high. That's one of the saddest things about the human condition—you can be very confident in ideas and the correlation. You shouldn't trust your confidence.

HARRIS: That's a depressing but fascinating fact. Given what you know, or think you know, about how confidence and truth regularly come apart, how much of this understanding bleeds back into your life and changes your epistemic attitude? How is Danny Kahneman different, given what he knows about the limits of human rationality?

KAHNEMAN: Not at all.

HARRIS: Not at all? Well, then things are even worse than I thought.

KAHNEMAN: In terms of my intuitions being better than they were? No. And furthermore, I have to confess, I'm very overconfident. So even *that* I haven't learned. It's hard to get rid of those things.

HARRIS: So do you just go through life issuing a long string of apologies? Because *you* should know better. If anyone should know better, it's you.

KAHNEMAN: But I don't really feel guilty about it.

HARRIS: I suppose that's good—but what do I know? How hopeful are you that we can improve? And how hopeful are you that we can design systems of conversation and incentives that can make some future generation find us more or less unrecognizable in our capacity for stupidity and self-deception?

KAHNEMAN: I should say that I'm not an optimist in general, but I'm certainly not an optimist about those questions. I've been studying this

phenomenon for more than fifty years, and I don't think that my intuitions have significantly improved. I can catch myself sometimes, and
that's important. I can recognize a situation as one in which I'm likely
to be making a mistake. And this is the way that people protect themselves against visual illusions. You can see the illusion, and then there is
no way you can*not* see it. But you can recognize that this is likely to be
an illusion, so you don't trust your eyes, and you take out a ruler. Something similar happens with cognitive illusions. Sometimes you know
that your confident thought is unlikely to be true. That's quite a rare occurrence. I don't think that I've become in any significant way smarter
because of studying areas of cognition.

HARRIS: But what you must thirst for on some level is that this understanding of ourselves can be made useful, or more useful than it is. Because the consequences can be absolutely dire, right? One could argue
that our decision making is the most important thing on Earth, certainly with respect to human well-being. Everything from how we ne-
gotiate nuclear treaties on down—this is all just human conversation,
human intuition, errors of judgment, pretensions of knowledge, and
sometimes we get it right. But the margin between right and wrong is
extraordinarily consequential.

If I told you that over the course of the next thirty years, we made
astonishing progress on this front so that we will look like bumbling, me-
dieval characters compared to our grandchildren, how did we get there?

KAHNEMAN: You don't get there. It's the same as if you asked me, Will
our perceptual system be very different in sixty years? I don't think so.

HARRIS: Let's take one of these biases that you have found. Consider the
power of framing, for example. We know that if you frame a problem in
terms of loss, and you reframe the same problem in terms of gain, you
will elicit a very different set of preferences from people, because they
are so averse to loss.

Let's say you're a surgeon, and you're recommending, or at least offering a surgery to your patient, and you've taken a Hippocratic oath to

do no harm. And you know, because you've read Danny Kahneman's book, that if you frame the possible outcomes in terms of mortality rates versus survival rates, you are going to be turning several dials in your patient's head, one way or the other. Can you conceive of us ever agreeing that there's a *right* way to present these data, ethically speaking? Is there a correct framing? Or are we just going to keep rolling the dice?

KAHNEMAN: First of all, the patient is going to be completely unaware of the fact that there is an alternative frame. That's why it works. It works because you see one thing, and you accept the formulation as it is given. So that's why framing works. Now, whether there is a true or not true answer leads me to the canonical problem, which my late colleague Amos Tversky invented. In one formulation there is a disease that's going to cause six hundred deaths unless something is done, and you have your choice between saving four hundred people or two-thirds probability of saving six hundred. Or alternatively, other people get the other framing: you have a choice between killing two hundred people for sure and a one-third probability that six hundred people will die. Is there a correct answer? Is there a correct frame? The interesting thing is that depending on which frame you present to people, they make very different choices.

But now let's say you confront them with the fact that they've been inconsistent. Some people will deny it, but you can convince them this is really the same problem. You know, if you save four hundred, then two hundred will die. And then they're dumbfounded. We have clear intuitions about what to do with gains and clear intuitions about what to do with losses. And when you remove that language, we have no idea what to do.

HARRIS: Has the third condition been compared to the first two? What do people do when you give them both framings, and dumbfound them?

KAHNEMAN: This is not something that we've done formally. But I can tell you that I'm dumbfounded. That is, I have absolutely no idea. I have the same intuitions as everybody else. You know, when it's in the gains, I want to save lives, and when it's in the losses, I don't want people to die.

But that's where the intuitions are. When you are talking to me about six hundred more people staying alive with a probability two thirds, or when you're talking about numbers of people living, I have absolutely no intuitions about that. So that is quite common with ethical problems—they're frame-dependent. And when you strip the frames away, people are left without the relevant moral intuition.

HARRIS: These effects become incredibly consequential when thinking about human suffering. Your colleague Paul Slovic has done these brilliant experiments showing that if you ask people to support a charity—you talk about a famine in Africa, for example, and you show them one little girl framed by a heartbreaking narrative about how much she's suffering—you get the maximum charitable response. But then you go to another group, and you show that same little girl and tell her heartbreaking story, but you give her a brother, and the altruistic response diminishes. If you go to another group, and you give them the little girl and her brother, and then you say that in addition to the suffering of these two blameless kids, there are five hundred thousand other children suffering along with them, then the response goes to the floor. So it's precisely the opposite of what we rationally understand about the need. But System 2 should be normative, right? The bigger the problem, the more concerned and charitable we should be.

To take this case, there is a way to correct for this moral illusion at the level of tax codes, foreign aid, and which problems we target once we know that we are emotionally gamed by salient personal stories and perversely bored by statistics. In fact, there is another piece of work that you did, which shows that people are so innumerate, with respect to the magnitude of problems, that they will pay the same amount whether they're saving two thousand lives, twenty thousand lives, or two hundred thousand lives.

KAHNEMAN: Yes. Because basically you're saving one life. You have an image, you have stories, and this is what System 1 works on. And this is what emotions are about. They're about stories, they're not about numbers. It's always about stories. And what happens when you have five hundred thousand? You have lost the story. A story, to be vivid, has to be about an individual case. And when you dilute it by adding cases, you dilute the emotion. Now, what you're describing, in terms of the moral response to this, is no longer an emotional response. This is cognitive morality, this is not emotional morality. You have disconnected from the emotion. You know that it's better to save five hundred thousand than five thousand, even if you don't feel better about saving five hundred thousand. So this is passing on to System 2, this is passing on to the cognitive system, the responsibility for action.

HARRIS: And you don't think that handoff can be made in a durable way?

KAHNEMAN: I think it has to be made by policymakers. And we hire policymakers to think about numbers and to think about them in those ways. But if you want to convince people, you need to convince them by telling them stories about individuals, because numbers just don't catch the imagination of people.

HARRIS: One thing we know from split-brain studies is that the left, linguistic hemisphere tends to confabulate. It continually produces discursive stories that ring true to it. And in the case of actual neurological confabulation, there's no reality testing going on. It seems to me that many of us are often in a similar mode: there's a very little reality testing going on, and it's all too easy to just take one's own word for things most of the time.

KAHNEMAN: Yes, I think this is the normal state. The normal state is that we're telling ourselves stories. We're telling ourselves stories to explain why we believe in things.

HARRIS: And, more often than not, we do this retrospectively, in a way that bears no relationship to the System 1, bottom-up reasons why we feel this way.

KAHNEMAN: Absolutely. For me, the example that was formative is what happened with post-hypnotic suggestions. So you put somebody under hypnosis and you tell them, when I clap my hands, you will feel very warm, and you'll open a window. And you clap your hands, and they get up and open a window. They know why they opened the window, and it has nothing to do with the suggestion. It comes with the story. They felt really warm and uncomfortable and they needed air, and they opened the window. Actually, in this case, you know the cause. The cause was that you clapped your hands.

HARRIS: Is that going to replicate?

KAHNEMAN: That one replicates. I'm pretty sure. . . . Anyway, I hope so.

HARRIS: Do you have a favorite cognitive error, or bias?

KAHNEMAN: Well, it's not the simplest to explain. But my favorite one has to do with extreme predictions—when you have very weak evidence, and on the basis of very weak evidence, you draw extreme conclusions. Technically, it's called "nonregressive prediction."

HARRIS: Where do you see it in the wild?

KAHNEMAN: You see it all over the place, but one obvious situation is in job interviews. You interview someone, and you have a very clear idea of how they will perform. And even when you are told that your ideas are worthless because, in fact, you cannot predict performance (or can predict it only very poorly), it doesn't affect your judgment. Next time you interview a person, you have the same confidence. It's something I discovered very early in my career. I was an officer in the Israeli Army, as a draftee, and I was interviewing candidates for officer training. And I discovered that I had that uncanny power to know who would be a good officer and who wouldn't. And I really could tell while I was interviewing people. I knew their character. You get that sense of confident knowledge. Then the statistics showed that we couldn't predict anything. And yet the confidence remained. It's very strange.

HARRIS: Well, there must be a solution for that. Following from this work, you must recommend that we either not do interviews, or heavily discount them, right?

KAHNEMAN: Yes, that's absolutely true. Because if you run an interview, you will trust it too much. So there have been studies in which you have a lot of information about your candidates, and if you add an interview, it makes your predictions about them worse—especially if the interviewer is the one who makes the final decision. When you interview, the interview itself is so much more vivid than all the other information you have, and you put way too much weight on it.

HARRIS: Is this also a story about the power of face-to-face interaction?

KAHNEMAN: It's face-to-face interaction, it's immediate . . . anything that you experience is very different from being told about it. And you know, as a scientist, one of the remarkable things that I know is how much more I trust my results than anybody else's.

HARRIS: Right.

KAHNEMAN: And that's true of everybody I know. We trust our own results. Why? No reason.

HARRIS: All right, let's talk about regret. What is the power of regret in our lives?

KAHNEMAN: Well, I think regret is an interesting emotion, and it's a special case of an emotion that has to do with counterfactual thinking. That is, regret is not about something that happened, it's about something that could have happened but didn't. And I don't know about regret itself, the *anticipation* of regret plays an important role in lots of decisions. That is, there is a decision, and you tell yourself, well, if I don't do this, and it happens, then how will I feel? That expectation of regret is very powerful. And it's well known in financial decisions and in a lot of other decisions.

HARRIS: And it's connected to loss aversion as well, right?

KAHNEMAN: It's a form of loss, and it's quite vivid. You're able to anticipate how you will feel if something happens, and that becomes very salient.

HARRIS: Does the asymmetry with respect to how we view losses and gains make some psychological or biological sense? At some point in your work I believe you talk about an evolutionary rationale for it, because suffering is worse than pleasure is good, essentially, and because there's a survival advantage for those who are making greater efforts to avoid suffering. It also seems that if you put in the balance of possibility, the worst possible misery on one side and the greatest possible pleasure on the other, they don't cancel each other out. If, for instance, I told you we could have a night of ordinary conversation, or we could experience the worst possible misery followed by the greatest possible pleasure—

KAHNEMAN: Then let's have our conversation.

HARRIS: Yes. We'd take the cheeseburger and a Diet Coke. So it seems that the prospect of suffering in this universe overwhelms the prospect of happiness. I know you put a lot of thought into the power of sequencing—I can imagine that feeling the misery first and the pleasure second would be better than the reverse.

KAHNEMAN: Much.

HARRIS: But it's not going to be enough to make it seem like a good choice, I suspect. How do you think of this asymmetry between pleasure and pain?

KAHNEMAN: Well, the basic asymmetry is between threats and opportunities, and threats are more immediate. It's not true everywhere; there are situations where opportunities are very rare and will be salient. In general, threats are immediate and have to be dealt with. So the priority of threats over opportunities must be built in, by and large, evolutionarily.

HARRIS: Do you think we could extract any ethical norm from this asymmetry? For instance, might it be true to say that it is more important to alleviate suffering than to provide pleasure if we had some way to calibrate the magnitude of each?

KAHNEMAN: Dick Thaler, Jack Knetsch, and I did a study a long time ago about intuitions about fairness, and it's absolutely clear that asymmetry rules intuitions about fairness. That is, there is a very powerful rule of fairness, that people identify with, not to cause losses. You have to have a very good reason to inflict a loss on someone. The injunction to share your gains is much weaker. So that asymmetry—what we call the rights that people have, and quite frequently the negative rights that people have—is the right not to have losses inflicted on you. So there are powerful moral intuitions that go in that direction.

Regarding your second question about well-being: you know, in recent decades, there has been a tremendous emphasis on happiness, and the search for happiness, and the responsibility of governments to make citizens happy, and so on. And one of my doubts about this line of work, and this line of thinking, is that I think preventing misery is a much better and more important objective than promoting happiness. So I have my doubts about the happiness movement, on those grounds.

HARRIS: Given what you've said, it's hard to ever be sure that we've found solid ground here. Regarding the intuition that you just cited—that people have a very strong reaction to imposed losses that they don't have to unshared gains (in other words, if you do something that robs me of something I thought I had, I'm going to feel much worse than I would just knowing you didn't share some abundance that I never had in the first place)—it seems that we could just be a conversation or two away from standing somewhere that makes that default asymmetry appear ridiculous—in a way that is analogous to the Asian disease problem, right? There's a framing effect that we may have an evolutionary rationale, but given some opportunity to be happy in this world, it could seem totally counterproductive. Of course, I say this while being firmly anchored to this intuition. My losses seem to count much more than my gains.

KAHNEMAN: Yes, in philosophical debates about morality and well-being, there are two ways of thinking about it. When you're thinking of final states, and what everybody will have, there's a powerful intuition that you want people more or less to be equal, or at least not to be too different. But there is another way of thinking about it, which is: Given the state of society, how much redistribution do you want to impose? And there is an asymmetry because you are taking from some people and giving it to others. We have powerful moral intuitions of two kinds, and they're not internally consistent, and loss aversion has a great deal to do with that.

HARRIS: Given that there are many things we want and don't want, and we want and don't want them strongly, and we are all moving both individually and collectively into an uncertain future, where there are threats and opportunities, and we're all trying to find our way, how do you think about our capacity to worry? Is there an advantage to worrying? And if there were a way not worry, would that be an optimal strategy? I think the Dalai Lama most recently articulated this, but the sentiment predates him: either there's something we can do about a problem, or there isn't. If there's something we can do about it, well then, we should simply do that thing. If we can't do anything about it, well then, why worry? We're just going to suffer twice in that case. How do you think about worry, given your work here?

KAHNEMAN: Well, I don't think my work leads to any particular conclusions about this. The Dalai Lama is obviously right—why worry? On the other hand, I would like to see people worry a fair amount about the future—and even if they don't know right now whether or not they'll be able to do anything about it.

HARRIS: Right. Maybe worrying is the only way to get enough energy into the system to actually be motivated to do something.

KAHNEMAN: Yes. When you're thinking of climate change, for example, one of the problems is that you can't make people worry about something that is so abstract and distant. If you make people worry enough, things could change. But scientists are incapable of making the public worry sufficiently about climate change.

HARRIS: To steal a technique that you just recommended, if you could make a personal story out of it, that would sell the problem much more effectively. But climate change is a very difficult thing to personalize in that way.

KAHNEMAN: It's very difficult to personalize, and it's not immediate. It's the problem that we are least well equipped to deal with, because it's remote, it's abstract, and it's not a clear and present danger. Now, an asteroid coming to Earth? That would mobilize people. Climate change is a much more difficult problem to deal with. And worry is part of that story.

HARRIS: It's interesting that an asteroid would be different, even if you put it far in the future. An Earth-crossing asteroid in seventy-five years would still invite some counsel of uncertainty. People would say, "We can't be certain that something isn't going to happen in the next seventy-five years that will divert this asteroid." Others would say, "Surely we're going to come up with some technology that would be prohibitively costly for us to invent now, that will divert this thing. Perhaps twenty years from now it will be trivially easy for us to invent. So why waste the money now?" But the problem would crystallized in a way that climate change simply isn't.

KAHNEMAN: The difference is there is a story about the asteroid. You have an image of what happens if it hits . . .

HARRIS: Climate change, ironically.

KAHNEMAN [laughing]: . . . and it's much clearer.

HARRIS: So, increasingly, we are becoming students of the power of framing. It seems, therefore, that we should be able to come up with a list of those problems, which we have every reason to believe are significant, but which we know are very unlikely to produce a sufficient emotional response in us. We know, in advance, that we won't be motivated by what we rationally understand in these areas, and then we should have the cognitive discipline to deliberately focus on these problems. If we did that, we'd be left with the political problem of convincing others to adopt this attitude.

KAHNEMAN: You used a tricky word there, and the word is "we." Who is "we"? You are talking about a group of people, possibly political leaders, who are making a decision on behalf of the population, that in a sense they treat like children who do not understand the problem. It's quite difficult in a democracy.

HARRIS: Surely you can't be talking about our current political leaders.

KAHNEMAN: No, I'm not. But I find it difficult to see how democracies can effectively deal with a problem like climate change. If I had to guess, I would say that China is more likely to come up with effective solutions than the West because they're authoritarian.

HARRIS: So is that an argument for a benevolent dictatorship of some kind to get us out of this mess?

KAHNEMAN: If you ask if it's an argument, yes, it's an argument. Whether it's a winning argument, I wouldn't want to commit myself to that.

HARRIS: It sounded good when I said it. It felt true. It's hard to escape the feeling that we continually have to pull ourselves up by our bootstraps here. Our perception of truth and validity and consistency— where we've got System 1 humming along, delivering into consciousness the results of its machinations—and then we trade in the linguistic representations of these processes. I say something to you, and you have a System 1 response, and we keep sailing along on a river of words.

But it seems to me that we have conquered ground here, and we really want to be able to plant flags in certain places so that we never lose sight of them again. We know our intuitions are going to be wrong— reliably so—and we've understood these errors clearly enough that we shouldn't lose that ground again. We can enshrine our better judgment and use that as an anchor point.

KAHNEMAN: Well, the issue is who is going to do it—again, who is "we"? I think that we're in danger of overestimating the power of System 1 in this conversation. There is System 2, people do think reasonably, they make long-term decisions, they are not slaves of their passions. People are quite capable of long-term thinking, and of investing in the future, and of sacrificing things in the present. Those capabilities exist. And I think that's one suggestion that was implicit in what you said. You said we should make a list, and there I think I agree. There should be a list. When we think about a societal problem, we should be asking ourselves: How can it be framed? Somebody had the responsibility in those cases of choosing a framing. It's going to be framed one way or the other, and so, given the idea that there is no avoiding framing, that you can choose the better frame, well that's the central idea of behavioral economics and "nudging." You should choose the frame that leads to the better decision and the better outcome.

HARRIS: Right. And aligning incentives is part of that. You want to create systems whereby people can behave better and better, with less and less effort, right? And you don't want systems where you have to be a saint to do something reasonable.

KAHNEMAN: Absolutely. You know, the basic psychological rule is if you want people to behave in a particular way, make it easy for them. And that is very different from the incentives you mentioned earlier.

HARRIS: How do you tease those apart?

KAHNEMAN: Well, around the end of World War Two, the social psychologist Kurt Lewin developed ideas about how you can change behavior, and he distinguished two central ways of changing behavior: You can apply pressure in the direction that you want people to go, or you can ask a very different question—why aren't they going there by themselves? What is preventing them from doing what you think they should do? And then remove the obstacles. Make it easier for people. It's perhaps the best psychological idea I know. This distinction between applying pressure, and making things easier, removing obstacles. Incentives, threats, arguments—all three of those are pressure.

HARRIS: Does pressure include things that people want? Carrots as well as sticks? Or you're just talking about sticks?

KAHNEMAN: The idea that I draw from Kurt Lewin is that I would lump arguments, threats, and promises together, and pit them against thinking about what you could do to make it easier for people to move in the direction you want them to move.

HARRIS: Do you have a real-world example of this? Is opting in versus opting out an example here? If you go to the DMV, you have to opt in to being an organ donor, for example, but if you have to opt out you get much more enrollment.

KAHNEMAN: Yes, that's a very good example. Whatever is easier. When you make it easy to do the right thing, people are much more likely to do it, and they'll do it effortlessly and without conflict. The interesting thing about increasing pressure, which means threats, promises, and arguments, is that you create conflict. If you remove the obstacles, you remove the conflict. You make things easier, you reduce stress, and at the same time you achieve behavior change. This idea is very nonintuitive. The intuitive response that people have when they want other people to do something is to look in the arsenal of "What pressure can I apply?"

HARRIS: I'm afraid you've just described my entire career as a writer and podcaster.

Okay, there's another distinction you make that is incredibly useful and troubling for those of us who want to be happy in this life: it's the distinction between the "remembering self" and the "experiencing self." Perhaps you can make this distinction for us, and then let's talk about how you think about living a good life in the context of these two selves.

KAHNEMAN: I'll start with some experiments that we ran because that's the easiest way of explaining it. We have two conditions: In one condition, people are going to put their hand in cold water, at fourteen degrees Celsius, which is unpleasant but tolerable, and they're going to keep it there for sixty seconds. The other condition is ninety seconds, and instead of telling you to take your hand out, and giving you a warm towel, I have you keep your hand in there and I don't tell you anything. And I'll raise the temperature from fourteen degrees Celsius to fifteen degrees Celsius, which is still unpleasant, but less unpleasant. You give people both of these experiences, one to the right hand, one to the left hand, and then you ask them which they'd rather have again if they're going to have to have one of these two unpleasant experiences again. And people choose the longer one.

Now, if you think in terms of the overall amount of pain, it's absolutely clear that the longer episode includes all the pain of the shorter one, and then some. And yet people prefer it. Now, why? What's happening here? In one way, when we think about pain, we're thinking about it as something that happens in a moment, and we integrate over time—over sixty seconds or over ninety seconds. And it's clear that there is more pain in the ninety-second example.

The other way of looking at it is how you'll remember the episode. And when you remember the two episodes, it turns out that the ninety-second example is remembered as better because it ended better. And so memory follows different rules from experience. We ran a bunch of experiments of that kind and demonstrated that people do not order experiences in their memory in the same way that they should be ordered by what they actually went through.

Now, it turns out you can extrapolate this to well-being. Because you could look at well-being in two different ways, and people have been doing these experiments. You can get a measure of well-being over time, say, by sampling. It's now frequently done with phones, that you beep people a few times a day and you ask them a question.

HARRIS: Yes, this is "experience sampling."

KAHNEMAN: Yes, experience sampling. And then you can integrate and get an average measure of happiness, for example. Alternatively, that's the common thing. You get people in a survey and you ask them, "How happy are you?" or "How satisfied are you with your life?" Now, that question is a retrospective question. It's a remembering question. So I tried to formulate that in terms of two selves. There is the self that is living your life, and it's having all those experiences in real time. That's the experiencing self. Then there is the self that comes to life when you ask someone what they think about their life, how happy they are, if their vacation went well—all of those retrospective questions—and this is the remembering self.

Now, the interesting thing, in terms of the human condition, is that the one that's doing the living is the experiencing self, but the one that's making the decisions is the *remembering* self. Because memories are all we get to keep, and when we are faced with a question about what to do, we probe our memories and find out which experience left the better memory—and that's what we'll choose.

So that leads to two conceptions of well-being. One is based on experience or the reality of experience, and the other is the construction that people have—that story that people construct about their life, and that they evaluate when you ask them a question. Now, for several years I was convinced that this question had a right answer, and that the right answer was that the experiencing self is reality, and the remembering self is just a construction. I believed that if you want to make people happy, you should improve their experiences. Eventually I gave up on that. That's one of the occasions where I was just forced to give up on an idea that I had cherished. I gave up because this is clearly not what people want to do. People actually want good memories. They want to be satisfied with their life. They're not thinking of the future in terms of experiences, they're thinking of the future in terms of anticipated memories. And you can't have a theory of well-being that doesn't correspond to what people want. You know, you can be authoritarian, but there is a limit.

HARRIS: Okay, well, the authoritarian in me is now rising up in defense of your former self against your current self. I feel very strongly that the remembering self really is just the experiencing self in one of its modes. We're having an experience right now, and if you ask me in five minutes, "How was that last hour?" I will say something based on dredging my episodic memory. But if you were sampling my experience throughout this conversation, this encounter with my remembering self is just more of the conversation. And it's getting categorized, in this case, as a different self.

I don't doubt that the remembering self has the power you say it does, because when I'm asked to decide something, I will only have reference to my memories. But there's a place to stand outside of a person's psychological timeline where you could say they are right or wrong about what it was like to be them.

Take the case of two vacations: I give you one vacation where your experience is being sampled by an omniscient AI, and at every point along the way, you are having a fantastic time. But toward the end, there's some glitch that causes you to view the previous week negatively, and you think, "I'm never going to go to Hawaii again if they're going to treat me like that at the airport" and that's what you log as your memory of the whole vacation. Alternately, you could have a vacation that is scarcely endurable all the way through, but some bright light shines on you in the last moment, and you remember, "That was actually kind of good. I mean, it was awful, but in a good way. I'd go back there." Viewed from outside, you're essentially someone with brain damage who just doesn't remember his life very clearly.

KAHNEMAN: I actually had the experience that you described. I gave a talk on that topic, and somebody got up during the Q&A, and told a story to the audience. The story was, "The other week, I was listening to a glorious symphony [that was certainly the period when people would listen to records still] and just as it was going to end, there was that horrible screech, and it ruined the whole experience." I said, "It didn't ruin the experience. You'd had the experience—you had twenty minutes of glorious music. It ruined the memory of the experience." People cannot draw that distinction. For him, it ruined the experience because the memory is what he got to keep.

Now, if I had to choose for my children or grandchildren, what would I wish for them? Certainly when they are small I want them to be happy and to experience happiness. When I think of them as adults, is it absolutely clear that I want them to be happy? Or do I really want them to be satisfied with their lives? It's not so clear. It's not obvious.

HARRIS: So that's not incompatible with what I'm saying. I want you to be as happy as you can be, but in such a way that your life will feel as meaningful as it can feel when I ask you about it. When I say, "Danny, how's it going over there? Are you satisfied with your life?" I want your answer to track a very happy life. But it's totally possible that in order to get the best memories for whenever you have to evaluate your life, to get the best story that you will be most satisfied with, there needs to be some frustration, and frustrations overcome, and embarrassments, and embarrassments corrected for in this "experiencing timeline." You shouldn't just be taking heroin and lying on the couch for seventy-five years.

KAHNEMAN: Well, if we could have both a happy life and good memories, that would be wonderful. But it turns out in the research on well-being that it's not the same thing. The conditions that make you happy in your life, and the conditions that make you satisfied with your life, are different. What determines how happy you are is largely social. It's spending a lot of time with people you love—and it's actually friends more than children.

But the conditions that lead people to be satisfied with their life are much more conventional. They're about success. So, for example, money doesn't make you happy in the emotional sense, although poverty makes you unhappy. But money really doesn't buy you much happiness. That said, money does buy life satisfaction. The more they have, and the more they earn, the more people are satisfied. What makes people satisfied is conventional success.

HARRIS: Let's linger on that diabolical point. Because this is the takeaway message from an important paper you wrote. Poverty makes you miserable. So, up until $75,000, I think it is, we see steady gains in both happiness and life satisfaction. After $75,000 there are no gains in happiness, and the two trend lines break apart. The depressing punch line is that the sense of meaning, the sense that your life is going well—the joys of the remembering self—keeps going up in a linear fashion until you become Jeff Bezos.

KAHNEMAN: Yes, that's the essential result, and it illustrates the tension between seeking happiness and seeking satisfaction. There are many trade-offs in life that this touches on. Take a long commute, for example. Quite often, there are economic reasons for a long commute. But a long commute is time that you spend alone—it's not time that you spend with people you love. That's a very important trade-off in terms of happiness.

HARRIS: I want to extract one piece of wisdom from the experiment you described earlier, and it relates to the notion of a "peak-end rule." What you remember is the peak stimulus during any epoch of experience, and how it ended. If the peak was very bad, and the end was bad, then no matter how good it seemed, it was awful. And the opposite holds as well.

If you have a grandchild who needs a medical procedure, and there's a choice between doing the unpleasant procedure for the requisite eighteen minutes and it's over, or doing the unpleasant procedure and then lingering for the extra four minutes because you know that—based on solid data that has now been replicated—those extra four minutes of needless suffering at a lower level will lead to a better memory, what does the compassionate grandfather do?

KAHNEMAN: So yes, we ran that experiment about twenty years ago, with a colonoscopy as the procedure, and at the time it was an unpleasant experience. Now, there's no experience because they put you to sleep. The issue at the time was compliance with the need to have another one. And there, the memory is really important, so that if you're going to remember it as a very bad experience, you won't want to have it again, even if you need it. So there was a real medical reason to go with the memory and not with the experience. Now, I don't know about trauma and memory, and whether you can alleviate trauma by adding a better ending to an experience, or an improved ending.

HARRIS: You would suspect that you could, right?

KAHNEMAN: I suspect you could, but I have no data.

HARRIS: Though you are not an optimist, you have some very optimistic thoughts about the utility of gossip. So what's your take on gossip?

KAHNEMAN: Well, I presented it optimistically in my book as an attempt to educate people about gossip. I said, you know, it's pretty hopeless for people to decide to be smarter, but it's easier, I hope, to teach people how to criticize others. It's just easier and more pleasant than modifying yourself. If you improve the quality of gossip, the quality of behavior would improve. Gossip is something that we anticipate, and negative gossip is something we try to avoid, and if we anticipated intelligent gossip, we might behave more intelligently.

HARRIS: This is perfectly designed for social media.

KAHNEMAN: You would have to teach it. The point is: What is the quality of criticism on social media? And if you could improve the quality, then many of the objections would vanish. When the quality is poor you can have disastrous consequences.

HARRIS: What about envy? We've all had this experience of having a friend for whom something good has happened, and what we feel in the face of our friend's joy is some perverse diminishment of our own happiness in the presence of someone we ostensibly love. But love consists in actually wanting this person to be happy, right? So you're left with that tension. Do you see your emotional life that way? Do you have those same judgments about envy being incompatible with love?

KAHNEMAN: Envy is a net loss. What's the benefit of envy?

HARRIS: But how does it relate to love?

KAHNEMAN: It clearly diminishes love. It's incompatible, and you feel it's incompatible. If there were one emotion you could get rid of, envy would be a strong candidate.

HARRIS: Danny, I know there's a lot that people want to ask you, and so I want to turn this into a proper conversation now. We'll shift into Q&A with our audience.

AUDIENCE MEMBER: If we accept Sam's thesis in the moral landscape that science can answer questions of human morality, would it also be possible if science could answer questions engaging artistic pursuits? Could we determine with any degree of certainty whether or not Picasso was a great painter, or Leo Tolstoy was a great novelist?

HARRIS: Our aesthetic intuitions generally converge; otherwise we would experience very little agreement about what's beautiful, what makes sense, or what's inspiring. Obviously there's a diversity of opinion, and there are fads which don't stand the test of time. But some things provoke massive convergence. For example, we can make claims about Shakespeare that virtually everyone will agree on. Not everyone reads him with pleasure—he's somewhat inaccessible—but no one can dispute that he was a master of metaphor. Half the metaphors and clichés we have bouncing around our brains came from Shakespeare, and that's not an accident. So there's a structure here that, presumably, a more mature science of the mind could understand. I think finding something beautiful or meaningful is analogous to finding something logical.

As you know, my view of the moral landscape is that it's possible to have incompatible peaks. We're generally talking about the human peak for minds like ours, but there could be a peak over there where minds are constituted very differently, and where intuitions of beauty will be quite different. Still, that doesn't mean that anything goes, because there will still be a difference between being on a peak and being on some lower spot on the landscape.

AUDIENCE MEMBER: You talked about how our confidence in our intuitions and their accuracy can be uncoupled. In the context of the resurgence of research on psychedelic drugs and their medical potential, there are noetic experiences that people have in psychedelic states. I'm wondering if you guys think that this is the same mechanism at work, but just cranked up to eleven? Might the medical benefits of these drugs come from these "revealed truths"? Are they, therefore, a bit more "accurate" even though it might be the same intuition at work that might be uncoupled from reality?

HARRIS: Have you ever dropped acid, Danny?

KAHNEMAN: Actually, no.

HARRIS: Have you ever taken any psychedelic? We're just among friends here.

KAHNEMAN: No, I haven't, and I regret it, actually.

HARRIS: The night is young, Danny.

KAHNEMAN: Thank you for the offer.

HARRIS: Have your experiencing self call my remembering self, and we'll sort it out. . . .

So the issue here strikes me as genuinely difficult, and I think we can resolve it in certain cases, but there will be edge cases where we can't. It's precisely the issue that came up earlier in the conversation, which is that feelings of certainty of meaning can be uncoupled from every rational part of our cognitive machinery. You can have pathological certainty, and pathological intuitions about the meaningfulness of things.

The case is very clear for certainty: a person can make epistemic claims about the way the world is that bear no relationship to the way the world actually is. However, when the feeling of meaning becomes uncoupled from any rational story you can tell about the world, it's a different phenomenon and a different problem.

You can take a psychedelic like LSD, or you can meditate in silence for months, and discover that the feeling of profundity, of sublimity, of awe can be accessed in association with any arbitrary object. You can have the beatific vision pointing your gaze at anything. Ultimately this sense of awe is a matter of attention, not what is attended to. Of course, this state of mind seems warranted when someone takes you to the biggest telescope on earth and points it at Andromeda—and you understand something about how many planets might be there, two point two million light-years away. It's an intellectually justified feeling in that context, because there's nothing irrational about being overcome by the magnitude of the cosmos. But on acid, if you're just staring at your shoelaces and having the same experience—people will worry that you've lost your mind. And, granted, being captured by your shoelaces is pathological if you have to get things done in the world. Certainly, if you're going to write a grant proposal, and get Danny to be your PI on it, it can't be about your shoelaces.

But the truth is, the experience of the experiencing self can be made better and better, and deeper and deeper by any discipline of attention that manages to locate the intrinsic "suchness" that is available in any moment of consciousness. There is something intellectually seditious about the project of experimenting with things like meditation and psychedelics. Ironically, Danny and I first met at a summer research intensive that was organized for the purposes of studying meditation scientifically. It was a research intensive that I helped organize with Richie Davidson when I was in graduate school—and Richie has done some of the best neuroimaging work on meditation. Danny, I don't even remember how you found yourself there. Was it based on a prior interest in meditation?

KAHNEMAN: I was hoping to learn meditation, actually.

HARRIS: There is a version of meditation that can begin to look like heroin without the needle—where your states of well-being become uncoupled from any good reason why you should feel that good. It's nice to be able to access those states—but obviously you don't want to feel that way while your kids are wandering in traffic. I think we generally want our sense of how good life is to be linked to the way life really is. And we could one day find ourselves in situations that will push our intuitions around a lot on this front. If we ever spend much more of our time in virtual reality, without apparent cost, and it becomes more and more pleasurable—we'll find ourselves either in some kind of Aldous Huxley–like dystopia, where we've stumbled into some pleasant oblivion, or we we'll be navigating the states of possible minds intelligently, creatively, and without unacceptable costs. It matters that we get this right, and there are certainly ways we might get it wrong. But it's somewhat paradoxical.

KAHNEMAN: What do you have against shoelaces, Sam?

HARRIS [laughing]: Exactly.

KAHNEMAN: I'm sort of serious. I mean, where does the "warrant" come from?

HARRIS: Well, it's a great question. Anything rewards sufficient attention. And—

KAHNEMAN: Including shoelaces.

HARRIS: Including shoelaces. But you have, arguably, a less glamorous story to tell if you just spent the day looking at your shoelaces, and all you can say is that it was one of the best days of your life. So on some level, it comes back to having friends. If you're living in a moral solitude—say you're the last conscious being alive—well then, point your attention any place that feels good. But we have to collaborate with one another. I have to be able to say something that makes sense to you, and vice versa, and we have to decide what to do tomorrow with limited resources. The common projects we undertake are based, to a large degree, on our forming a common understanding of what's going on in the world and what really matters. Just being blissed out by an arbitrary use of attention doesn't have a lot of cash value in that space. What it does have, or what versions of it have, is an ability to regulate a person's negative emotions so that he or she becomes wise to the ways negative and even positive emotions distort cognition and even our ethics. We can become more intelligent stewards of our certainties and priorities.

Meditation is extraordinarily useful—and that's why I created the Waking Up course. I'm just acknowledging that there are apparent deviation points, intellectually and ethically, where it can become fairly masturbatory. You have found a way to imagine yourself into a state of happiness that doesn't do the world a lot of good, and it doesn't make you capable of much, apart from being oblivious to the world's cares, including your own. That would be the criticism of it, from the outside at least.

AUDIENCE MEMBER: Thank you for creating a renaissance of intellectualism within the insane sphere of social media. In the beginning of your conversation, you questioned the rigor of academia within the political sphere. Daniel, you said that authoritarianism could solve some problems. Sam, would you agree?

HARRIS: The obvious problem with authoritarianism is that the kind of person who would seize authority, or be given it, seems likely to be bad. So we're generally right to want to invoke the wisdom of the crowd, insofar as it can ever produce anything like wisdom.

KAHNEMAN: In this day and age, when you're thinking of what democracy can produce—

HARRIS: It's so hard to be very idealistic down either path. But you have a single point of failure with an authoritarian system. If it's just one person who can decide to do everything or not, then if that person becomes deranged, or came into office already deranged, you have an enormous problem. We want to place many smaller bets, it seems to me. Are you familiar with the philosopher Nick Bostrom?

KAHNEMAN: Yes.

HARRIS: He is a very unusual thinker, who focuses on questions of existential risk, and I recently read his paper titled "The Vulnerable World Hypothesis." He asks us to imagine that we have an urn in front of us—he calls it "the urn of invention"—and it is filled with colored balls. We have been reaching into this urn, rather compulsively, lo these many millennia, pulling out either white or gray balls. The white balls are inventions—pieces of technology, memes, cultural norms, institutions that have no real downside—they just make our lives better. The gray balls are inventions that have benefits and costs. Splitting the atom can produce energy, but it can produce radioactive waste and nuclear warheads. Goods and harms come from these inventions.

What Bostrom asks us to consider is that there's a black ball, or perhaps many black balls, somewhere in the urn of invention, and we just haven't pulled one out yet. A black ball is a technology which is synonymous with the end of civilization. Bostrom goes into great detail about what sort of thing this might be, and what we would need to do to stabilize civilization in the face of this possibility. And so the first thing you're asked to acknowledge is that it seems rather plausible that there is a black ball or two in the urn of invention. There are things we could discover, which we can't undiscover, that could spell our doom—because it would thereafter become too easy for one deranged person to destroy the lives of millions or billions of other people.

One example is what he calls the "easy nukes" case. Imagine if it were just a fact of nature that splitting the atom was much easier to do, and it turns out it only took putting two pieces of glass and a magnet together and running some electric current through them—and then you'd have an atom bomb. Now, if it were that easy to make an atom bomb, one in a million people would make one more or less every day of the week, and we would eventually see every major city vaporized. There seems little doubt that if it had been that easy to make an atom bomb, we'd all be dead already.

The punch line of this essay is that the only scenario whereby we can actually deal with this risk and respond to it, should we have the time to realize that we have pulled a black ball from the urn, is to have what Bostrom calls a state of "turnkey totalitarianism" and hypertechnological surveillance, obviously enabled by some AI that we have yet to invent. He's imagining us surveilling one another at all times in as benign a way as possible—with the data anonymized in all the ways we would want it to be. But basically we would need a system where we could intrude on a person's behavior very, very quickly, and there would be an AI watching what you're doing with your hands every moment of the day in a world that has pulled the black ball. It sounds crazy, but if it becomes trivially easy for anyone to weaponize the flu of 1918 because all the data is out, and everyone has an appliance in their home that can do it, and we can't uninvent this thing, then we will need to know what you're doing with your hands.

So, strangely, the net result of this essay was to suddenly make me open-minded about the ethics of something which, if described in the absence of having considered the urn of invention and some of these examples, sounds like pure, dystopian horror. How could turnkey totalitarianism ever be desirable? It becomes at least potentially desirable if you grant that it may, in fact, be the only stable state for civilization, in light of what we're currently doing—which is just reaching into the urn and pulling things out as fast as we can, without giving any thought as to where it's all leading. Anyway, that was a very long answer to a question you almost asked.

AUDIENCE MEMBER: One of the constructs you've been wrestling with is this idea of social redemption. For those people who have transgressed publicly, what can we do to allow them back into the fold? We have a social psychology person here, so I think of the fundamental attribution error, and what we can do to challenge that distortion and allow for people to reenter society after they transgressed. Not psychopathically deviant people like Bill Cosby or Harvey Weinstein, but people that made more minor transgressions.

HARRIS: I'm going to add a little bit to that question and deliver it to Danny. So, since you're not on social media, you may be unaware of just how acute this need is, but what we need is some new norm around what constitutes an acceptable apology. What does it mean to say you're sorry in a credible way, and how does one redeem oneself after one has said or done something unethical? How do you think about the physics of redemption?

KAHNEMAN: I think it's pretty clear that what's happening at the moment around the MeToo movement is that transgressions of very different magnitudes are treated alike. There is a sense that we do not discriminate sufficiently between things that were done in the distant past and more recent things, severe and less severe. You know, you had a senator driven from political life for what looks like a pretty trivial transgression. So clearly something has gone wrong. There ought to be more discrimination by severity, and I don't know what the mechanism is that has produced this flattening of response, that every transgression is maximal.

HARRIS: But what is the path out of the swamp? What should be an adequate apology? What are the dynamics of actual redemption? It's not a matter of getting away with it, it's not that I can say something that mollifies the other person and they forget about me. What does it mean to actually deliver a sincere apology that *should* be accepted?

KAHNEMAN: The situation that we have now is that no apology is accepted. Apologies are not even required. I mean, they would be rejected. That's the problem that I see. What people want to see is genuine contrition. That is what an apology is supposed to convey—that somebody is genuinely sorry that it happened. When things are normal, apologies can be accepted, provided the transgression was not too severe, and the apology is obviously sincere, and so on. When you're in a situation as we are now, I think apologies are almost irrelevant.

HARRIS: It's interesting that you said, "when things are normal." Because when things are in extremis, we also get to a point where apologies must be accepted—because it's the last stop on the way to the abyss. You take a case like Rwanda, where neighbors have been hacking each other to death with machetes. The only way to reboot from that condition is to have something like a truth and reconciliation commission, where the perpetrators confess and apologize for the horrific things they've done, and everyone else seems to acknowledge that the only way to break the cycle of murder is to accept these apologies.

KAHNEMAN: What you're describing here is something that happens between communities. It's not individuals. For communities, it's the *only* possible solution.

HARRIS: Right.

KAHNEMAN: Otherwise they cannot live together. So if they're going to live together, you must have that type of action. And it's been negotiated successfully—Rwanda is certainly a relatively successful example. The dynamics are completely different when it comes to apologies at the individual level.

HARRIS: A final question for you, Danny. You seem fairly skeptical about the prospects of our ever getting much better at cognition. Do you feel the same skepticism about human well-being? What's the best human future you can imagine?

KAHNEMAN: Well, to the extent that you can change the social matrix in which we live (and there are possibilities to train people or teach people how to live with each other) then I think there is some room for optimism. The optimism is limited simply by the fact of human nature. Human nature is not going to change, and a lot of the stuff that we've been talking about is simply manifestations of human nature (including the complexities of well-being, and the remembering self and the experiencing self). There's not going to be a solution to that. You know, that disconnect is just built in because our memories and our experiences don't match, and because our memories are all we keep. So there are aspects of the human condition and of human nature that are not going to change, and they constrain what we can hope for.

HARRIS: Well, I'm going to disprove your thesis by remembering how much pleasure I took in this opportunity to speak with you, Danny. Thank you for taking the time. It's been a real honor to share this stage with you.

Will We Destroy the Future?

A CONVERSATION WITH NICK BOSTROM

Nick Bostrom is a Swedish-born philosopher with a background in theoretical physics, computational neuroscience, logic, artificial intelligence, and many other interesting topics. Officially he is a professor of philosophy at Oxford University, where he leads the Future of Humanity Institute.

In this conversation we explore Bostrom's views on existential risk by focusing on three of his papers. We begin with what he calls the vulnerable world hypothesis, which leads to a discussion of the history of nuclear deterrence and a possible need for "turnkey totalitarianism." We also talk about moral illusions and whether we're living in a computer simulation—Bostrom is the father of what is now widely referred to as the "simulation argument." We also analyze the famous doomsday argument, a philosophical thought experiment that has convinced many people that we might be living close to the end of human history. This conversation encourages reflection on our place in the world and what the future may hold for all of us.

HARRIS: Nick, you are one of the most provocative thinkers I know. How do you summarize your work as a philosopher?

BOSTROM: That's always been a challenge for me. Broadly speaking, I'm interested in humanity's big-picture questions and figuring out which direction is up and which is down. That is, out of all the things you can be pushing on or pulling on in the world, which ones would actually tend to make things better? And then various subquestions that come out of that ultimate quest.

HARRIS: A concern about existential risk unifies much of your work. How do you think about existential risk and why is it difficult for many people to take it seriously?

BOSTROM: I introduced the concept in a paper I wrote back in the early 2000s—the concept being that of a risk either to the survival of Earth-originating intelligent life or a risk that could permanently and drastically reduce our potential for creating desirable future developments. In other words, a risk that could permanently destroy the future.

HARRIS: You have a talent for coming up with phrases that are arresting: "permanently destroy the future." I worry that there may be more people working in my local McDonald's than are thinking about the prospect that we may permanently destroy the future. But it's difficult to communicate the importance of this topic, even to people who claim to be worried about things like climate change. Why is existential risk still such an esoteric concern?

BOSTROM: Well, it's become less so over the last few years. The rationalist community, the effective altruism community, and various academic centers are focusing on existential risk now. So I think your comparison to a McDonald's restaurant is no longer true.

HARRIS: So several McDonald's—

BOSTROM: I don't know that the default expectation should be that questions receive attention in proportion to their importance—I think that's unfortunately a poor descriptive model of how academia works. So one can ask: Why has it changed?

HARRIS: On one level, you're asking people to care about the unborn, and at time horizon that is beyond their lives and even the lives of their children—which seems harder than asking them to care about geographically distant strangers who are currently alive. And we already know that we're bad at the latter. Is that a major variable here?

BOSTROM: Sure. It's an extreme case of a public good. Generally, in a simple model of the market economy, public goods tend to be undersupplied, because their creators capture only a small fraction of the benefits. Global public goods are often seen as the extreme of this—if all of humanity benefits from some activity or is harmed by some activity, as in the case of global warming or something like that, the incentives driving the individual producer are generally dissociated from the activity's overall consequences, and he is likely to proceed regardless of those consequences. But with existential risk, it is even more extreme—because it's a transgenerational good, in the sense that all future generations are also affected by our decisions. And they are not in a position to influence. They can't, in any obvious way, reward us if we do things that are good for them.

So if one thinks of human beings as selfish, one would expect the good of existential risk reduction to be undersupplied. You could imagine, if people could go back in time, that future generations would be willing to spend huge amounts of money to compensate us for our efforts to reduce x risk. But since that transaction is not possible, such efforts are undersupplied. That could be one explanation.

HARRIS: It's also a framing problem in many cases. There's a certain set of facts, say human suffering in some distant country that you have no connection to. If this information is introduced one way, you find that you just don't care. Introduced another way, however, and the reality of the suffering and the analogy to your own life or the lives of your children may be more salient. We know that we are susceptible to moral illusions here. People care more about the fate of one little girl, whose terrible circumstances are communicated in the form of a personalized story, and less about the fate of that same little girl plus her brother. And people care less still if we tell them about the little girl, her brother, and five hundred thousand other children who are also suffering the same misery. As we scale the problem, people care less. This is clearly a bug, not a feature.

BOSTROM: Yeah. So, my original paper about existential risk made the point that from a certain type of ethical theory, it looks like existential risk reduction is a very important goal. If you have a broadly aggregative consequentialist philosophy, say you're a utilitarian, and you work the numbers out (the number of possible future generations, the number of individuals in each of those that can live happy lives, and you multiply that together) and if it looks like there is even a modest probability that we will eventually achieve this astronomically large value, you get a very large expected value. Even a very slight modulation of this quantity will then produce a higher expected value of an action than any direct consequences from the action on the here and now. You might conclude, for example, that reducing existential risk by one thousandth of one percentage point would be worth more than eliminating world hunger or curing cancer. Now, that says nothing about the question of whether this kind of utilitarian perspective is correct or is agreeable to us, but it seems to be an implication of a certain kind of moral theory.

HARRIS: I'm definitely a consequentialist of a certain kind. So we don't need to argue that point. But one thing that's interesting here is that there seems to be a clear asymmetry between how we value suffering and its mitigation, and how we value the prevention of happiness. Suffering is worse than happiness is good. If you told most people, "Here are two scenarios for how you can spend the rest of your day: you can spend it as you were planning to, living within the normal bounds of human experience, or I can give you one hour of the worst possible misery followed by another hour of the deepest possible happiness. Would you like to sample the two extremes on the phenomenological continuum?" I think most people would balk at this because we have a sense that possible suffering is, on some level, much more extreme than any pleasure or happiness could be. So we look at the prospect of curing cancer, and mitigating all the attendant suffering, as being more important ethically than simply not allowing the door to close on all future states of creativity, insight, and beauty.

BOSTROM: I think one might want to decompose different ways in which that intuition could be produced. One might be that for us humans, as we are currently constituted, it's a lot easier to create pain than to create a corresponding degree of pleasure. Evolution may have made our valleys deeper than our peaks are high—we may have more frequently encountered situations where our reproductive fitness suffered catastrophic damage in a short period of time than situations where we could gain a similar amount of fitness in an equally short interval. But of course, when we're considering these possible grand futures, we'll want to factor that out, since we'd have the ability to reengineer, say, human hedonic systems—or the hedonic systems of whatever inhabitants will exist in this future—so that we'll have a much larger capacity for the upside. And then it's not clear that there would be an asymmetry here.

Now, you might think that even if there is in some sense equal amounts of pleasure and pain—admittedly it's a little unclear what the metric is here—there would nevertheless be some more basically ethical reason for placing a higher priority on removing the negative. A lot of people feel, in an economic context, that inequality is intrinsically bad and that helping the worse off is more important than promoting the welfare of the already better off. Maybe that could also be a source of some of those intuitions.

HARRIS: Actually, there's one other variable here: there is no identifiable victim or beneficiary when we close the door to the far future. If you ask someone, "What would be wrong with the prospect of everyone

dying painlessly in their sleep tonight, and there are no future generations?" There's no one to be bereaved by that outcome. There's no one
suffering the pain of the loss. And most of the losses are hypothetical.
So people are unable to locate the moral injury.

BOSTROM: Yes, that is a distinction within utilitarian frameworks, between total utilitarians, who think you basically count up all the good
and subtract all the bad, and utilitarians who take a so-called person
affecting perspective, where the goal is to benefit people, but bringing
new people into existence doesn't count. Now, I would say that some
kinds of existential catastrophe would have a continuing population
that would be experiencing the bad, if, say, the world got locked into
some totalitarian, really dystopian regime. Maybe they would be living for a long time, but their lives would not be very good. In some scenarios of existential catastrophe, there are still inhabitants.

HARRIS: I think it's clear that destroying the future could be pretty unpleasant for people who are forced to come along for the ride.

BOSTROM: Now, I wouldn't describe myself as a utilitarian. I'm just pointing out the consequences. There are various views about how we should
reason about ethics, and there might also be other things to care about
aside from ethics.

Rather than directly trying to answer the difficult question of what
we have most reason to do all things considered, we might break it into
parts and ask, "Given this particular ethical theory, what should we do?
Given this other value, or these other goals that we might have, what
should we do?" Then, at the end of the day, we somehow add all of that
up. Insofar as we are trying to reason through our ethical obligations,
we should acknowledge our normative uncertainty—that is, that we
could be mistaken about which moral framework is correct. I've proposed what I call the moral parliament model that I think we should
use when trying to make moral decisions. It's a kind of metaphor, where
you factor in different ethical theories in proportion to the probability

you give them, and you allow them to make beneficial moral trades so that a more probable moral theory sometimes gives way to a less probable theory on issues that are especially important to the latter and where the former doesn't care that much. It's like the moral theories got to send delegates to an imaginary idealized parliament that then negotiates and votes on what you should do. More probable theories get more representatives. You can also add nonmoral considerations to the mix; for example, some of your delegates might be representatives of your "self-interest" party.

When I'm out and about in the world, I usually have to make the case for utilitarianism, or at least that you should consider that perspective. People are scope-insensitive, you should look at the numbers—if this thing affects a million people and this other thing only affects a hundred people, that difference matters hugely, and so on. And yet when I'm back here at headquarters, I'm usually the one who has to advocate *against* the utilitarian perspective because so many of my friends are such dyed-in-the-wool total utilitarian doctrinaires, and in particular they're so narrowly focused on x-risk mitigation. The only constant is that I'm always the odd one out. Sigh!

HARRIS: I would love to get into a conversation with you about meta-ethics sometime because I think your views about the limits of consequentialism would be fascinating to explore. But I have so much I want to talk to you about with respect to x risk and a few of your papers that we'll have to table that for another time. In fact, we won't have much time to cover your book *Superintelligence*, but I want to say that it was extremely influential for many of us in arguing the case for the potential dangers of artificial general intelligence. I've had several conversations on my podcast that have been deeply informed by your view—with Stuart Russell, Eliezer Yudkowsky, and others. Every time I speak about AI, I consider what I say to be fairly derivative of your book. So my audience will be familiar with your views on AI, even if they're not familiar with you.

I want to discuss a few of your papers. The first is "The Vulnerable

World Hypothesis." The second is "Are You Living in a Computer Simulation?" And the third is "Where Are They?" (which is your analysis of the Fermi problem, asking where is the rest of the intelligent life in the galaxy). Let's start with "The Vulnerable World Hypothesis." What do you mean by that phrase?

BOSTROM: Well, the hypothesis, roughly speaking, is that there is some level of technological development at which the world gets destroyed by default. So what does it mean to get destroyed by default? I define something I call the *semianarchic default condition* in which there is a wide range of actors with a wide range of different humanly recognizable motives. But then, more importantly, two conditions hold. One is that there is no reliable way of resolving global coordination problems. The other is that we don't have an extremely reliable way of preventing individuals from committing acts that are strongly disapproved of by a great majority of people.

Maybe it's better to come at it through a metaphor. You can think of the history of technological discovery as the process of pulling balls out of a giant urn—the urn of creativity. We reach in and we get an idea out, and then we reach in and get another idea out. Throughout history we've extracted a great many of these balls, and the net effect of this has been hugely beneficial, I'd say. This is why, in large parts of the world, we now sit in our air-conditioned offices and struggle not to eat too much, rather than struggling to get enough to eat. But what if there's a black ball in the urn—some possible technology that destroys any civilization that discovers it?

HARRIS: Just to add a little color and context here, you refer to this in your paper as "the urn of inventions," and we have been, as you say, pulling balls out as quickly as we can get our hands on them. And on some level, the scientific ethos is really just a matter of pulling balls out as fast as you can and making sure that everybody knows about them. Thus far we have pulled out only white and gray balls. The white balls are the technologies, memes, norms, social institutions, etc., that have only good consequences. The gray ones are the discoveries and inventions that have mixed consequences—they can be used for good or for ill. Nuclear energy is a prototypical case: we can power our cities with it, but we can also produce fantastic amounts of dangerous pollution that is difficult to deal with—and in the worst case, we can annihilate ourselves with the weapons we build.

BOSTROM: Yes, most technologies are to some degree double-edged, but the positives seem predominant. Some technologies may be mainly negative—nerve gas or other such tools. But what we haven't done so far is extract the black ball, right? One that is so harmful that by default it destroys the civilization that discovers it. What if there is such a black ball in the urn, though? We can ask how likely that is to be the case, and we can also look at what our current strategy is with respect to this possibility. It seems to me that, currently, our strategy is simply to hope that there is no such ball in the urn. We keep extracting balls as fast as we can—we've become quite good at that. But we have no ability to put balls back into the urn. We cannot uninvent our inventions.

So the first part of my paper tries to identify the ways in which the world could be vulnerable, the types of black ball technology that we might invent.

The first and most obvious way the world can be vulnerable is if there is some technology that empowers individuals to cause sufficiently large amounts of destruction. We can illustrate this by means of a historical counterfactual. In the last century, we discovered how to split the atom and release some of the energy contained in the nucleus. It turned out that this is quite difficult to do. You need special materials—plutonium or highly enriched uranium. So only states can produce this stuff. But what if it had turned out that there was an easier way to release the energy of the atom? What if you could have made a nuclear bomb by baking sand in a microwave oven or something like that? Then that might well have been the end of human civilization. So we were lucky. Of course, now we know that it is physically impossible to create an atomic detonation by baking sand in the microwave. But before we actually did the relevant nuclear physics, how could we have possibly known how it would turn out?

HARRIS: I want to conserve everyone's intuitions as we go on this harrowing ride together, because the conclusion of this paper is fairly startling when you discuss what the likely remedies are. So why is it that civilization couldn't survive the prospect of what you call "easy nukes"? Why is it just a foregone conclusion that this would mean the end of cities and perhaps the end of most things we recognize?

BOSTROM: I think "foregone conclusion" is a little too strong. It depends on the parameters we plug in. The intuition is that in a large enough population, there will always be a few people who, for whatever reason, would like to kill a million people or more if they could, whether they are just crazy, or evil, or they have some weird ideological doctrine, or they're trying to extort or threaten other individuals. Human beings are very diverse. Within a large enough set of people, you'll find practically any desire you can specify. So if each of those destructively inclined people could cause a sufficient amount of destruction, then everything would get destroyed.

Now, if one imagines this actually playing out in history, then whether *all* of civilization would get destroyed or some horrible catastrophe short of that would happen instead would depend on various things. What kind of nuclear weapon would it be? A small Hiroshima-type device or a thermonuclear bomb? How easy would it be to build and use? Could literally anybody put it together in five minutes, or would it take an engineer working for half a year?

Depending on what values you pick for these and other variables, you might get scenarios ranging from "very bad" to "existential catastrophe." But the point is to illustrate that historically we have been lucky in that the destructive capabilities we've discovered have been hard to wield.

It's possible that some future highly destructive capability could be easy to wield—say, through developments in biotechnology. It may become easy to create lethal viruses, or other types of weapons that don't require great amounts of energy or rare materials. Then you might even have a case for existential catastrophe. One nuclear weapon can destroy only one city, but viruses can potentially spread across the planet.

HARRIS: Right. We're in an environment now where we talk with some degree of flippancy about the prospect of every household one day having something like a desktop printer that can print DNA sequences. Everyone will print their own bespoke genetic medicine at home. Under those conditions, the 1918 flu could be sent to you like a PDF, and printed on demand. It really would be within the power of one nihilistic or ideological person to destroy the lives of millions or even billions.

BOSTROM: It could be sent to you, or you could just download it yourself from the internet. The full genomes of a number of virulent organisms are in the public domain and available to download.

I would rather see a future in which DNA synthesis was a service provided by only a few places in the world, which could if necessary exert some control, rather than one in which every lab has its own little machine. This is an example of type one vulnerability, where the problem arises from individuals becoming too empowered in their ability to create large amounts of harm.

Now, there are other ways in which the world could be vulnerable which are slightly more subtle but worth bearing in mind. These have to do with technological developments that change the incentives faced by different actors.

We can return to the history of nuclear energy to illustrate this idea. And actually, this case could be the closest we've come to a black ball, with thermonuclear weapons and the Cold War arms race and seventy thousand nuclear warheads on hair-trigger alert. With the recent opening of some of the archives from this period, we can see that the world came quite close to the brink on several occasions. This was a slightly black-ballish technology and we just had enough luck to get through. But you could imagine how it could have been worse. You can imagine scenarios that would have created stronger incentives for a first strike, so you would have had crisis instability. If it had been easier, say, in the first strike to take out all an adversary's nuclear weapons, then in a crisis it might not have taken a lot to encourage one side to strike first for fear that the other side might be about to do that to you.

HARRIS: Yes, in the aftermath of the Cuban Missile Crisis, the people who were closest to the action felt that the odds of a nuclear exchange had been something like the results of a coin toss—something like 30 percent to 50 percent. And what you're envisioning is a situation of a safe first strike, wherein there's no reasonable fear that you'll fail to annihilate your enemy, provided you strike first. That would be a far less stable situation than the one we've been in. And it is easy to forget that the status quo of "mutually assured destruction" was actually a step *toward* stability. Before the Soviets had their own nuclear arsenal, there was a greater concern that we would be tempted to use ours, because nuclear deterrence didn't yet exist.

BOSTROM: Yes, mutually assured destruction brought some degree of stability. Although of course at the expense of the possible outcome's being even worse—that is, both sides being destroyed rather than just one side. If it had been possible to wipe out the enemy's nuclear warheads within a wider radius, or if nuclear submarines were more easily detectable so that you could be more confident that you could target the other side's entire nuclear capability, that could have resulted in a more unstable arms race, one that would be more likely to end in the weapons being used. You can also consider other ways in which future arms races could be worse than the one during the Cold War. For example, if the arms are easier to conceal than nuclear weapons, it could be harder to enforce arms reduction treaties.

So we keep reaching into the urn and just hope that we don't pull out a technology that gives powerful actors the wrong set of incentives. That is one major type of vulnerability.

And then there is the third and last of the major types of vulnerability. Here, too, the problem is the incentives that the black ball creates, except it's not that there is a small number of very powerful actors who face incentives to cause vast destruction—but instead a large number of weak actors are each incentivized to take some action that may be quite negligible on an individual level but added up become very destructive. Here maybe the best illustration is global warming, where a lot of individuals face incentives—the convenience of using fossil fuels to drive cars, for example—that individually contribute trivially to climate change, but if billions of people are doing it the sum total is substantial. Here you can again counterfactually imagine that the situation could be a lot worse than it is. The climate sensitivity could have been much greater. Let's say the same amount of emissions that we've generated to date produced not three degrees of warming over a hundred-year timescale but fifteen degrees instead. Or what if alternative energy sources were much more expensive than they are, so we were even more strongly incentivized to continue using fossil fuels?

Here again we reach into the urn, hoping there won't be some discovery that just happens to create incentives for a lot of individuals to take actions that benefit each individually but have these slight negative externalities that cumulatively doom our civilization.

HARRIS: Let's take a moment to linger over "bad incentives" because this is a meme that virtually everyone has in their head. This is something that I continually worry about, but it's worth defining because it's a surprisingly deep problem. Bad incentives arguably produce most of our problems at this point, because they create the conditions under which normal people with normal motivations reliably do bad or dangerous things. It's the *reliable* part that is so destructive. Bad incentives can select for behavior that no one would accept if done for the explicit purpose of producing such predictable, negative effects.

BOSTROM: It doesn't have to be the case that anybody takes pleasure in the bad outcome. I could drive my car downtown, and it won't make any noticeable difference in CO_2 levels, and I get to where I want to go more quickly. There's an externality, right?

HARRIS: In the case of global warming, many of us will be around, or at least our children will be around, to suffer the consequences, and we could be motivated by that understanding. Still, we so steeply discount the prospect of future suffering that it provides very little motivation.

BOSTROM: Yes. There can be a temporal externality, but even if you were time-neutral in your preference function, you would still only suffer, say, one eight-billionth of the consequences. The other parts of the harm would be incurred by the other eight billion people on the planet, right? Whereas you gain 100 percent of the benefit of driving your car to the city center.

So it looks today like the fossil fuel technologies that are producing global warming do not quite amount to a black ball. But again, we might easily imagine that the dynamics of the climate could have been worse, or the economic characteristics of alternative technologies could have been worse. And then that could have been a black ball.

The main purpose of the paper is not to show that there is a black ball in the urn, or that the vulnerable world hypothesis is true. Instead, it looks at different ways in which it *could* be true and then considers what would follow from that. And then each person can make their own judgment about the probability that the vulnerable world hypothesis is true. We don't know for sure, but to me it seems fairly plausible the world is vulnerable at some level of technological development.

HARRIS: There's the added point that you've referenced, which I want to spell out: we continually find ourselves in a position of *just getting lucky*, and we seem disposed to rely merely on the prospect of getting lucky in the future. We're not acting as though there might be a black ball in the urn. We just keep reaching in, grabbing one, and seeing what it does for us.

BOSTROM: That's it. And we keep hoping for the best. This is very much the ethos across academia and in the sciences—like Harvard's motto of *Veritas*, truth. And the implicit assumption there, I guess, is that truth is good, more truth is better, finding out and disseminating truth and explaining truth is always and everywhere good, and doing that should be encouraged as much as possible. That's actually a nonobvious assumption if you think about it. It might be that the net effect of universally promoting scientific advances and being more open to free investigation has, over the last few hundred years, been vastly beneficial on balance. But just how strong is this evidence for the claim that it will continue to be beneficial into the indefinite future? Not that strong. Certainly it doesn't seem like strong evidence against the claim that there could be exceptions to the general benefit of maximal unrestricted discovery—specific technologies or specific ideas where the harms would outweigh the benefits sufficiently to count as a black ball.

HARRIS: It's worth remembering how cavalier we can be in rolling these particular dice. You reference the Trinity and Castle Bravo tests in the paper and then you come up with a counterfactual you call Castle Bravissimo. Would you like to run through that for a moment?

BOSTROM: Sure. The Trinity test was the first detonation of a nuclear device. And before the scientists of the Manhattan Project did this test, there was some concern. What if the extreme temperature generated in a nuclear explosion could cause a runaway chain reaction and ignite the Earth's atmosphere? They took it seriously. Robert Oppenheimer, the Manhattan Project's scientific director, went to his superior, General Leslie Groves, and he assigned several physicists to do calculations on the problem. They looked into it and concluded that it wouldn't cause a chain reaction in the atmosphere, although they urged that more research be done on the question. So they went ahead with the Trinity test and it turned out they were right.

Research and development of nuclear weapons continued, and a few years later they were working toward the fusion bomb. The first test of an early lithium-based version of the fusion bomb was called the Castle Bravo test, and calculations had shown that it would deliver a yield of about six megatons. But it turned out that an important reaction pathway had been overlooked, and the actual yield was almost three times larger. Neighboring inhabited islands were irradiated by radioactive fallout. A Japanese fishing boat was irradiated too, and one Japanese sailor died as a result, causing an international incident—the Japanese were understandably quite sensitive at this time about being exposed to nuclear weapons. Most of the instruments that were designed to measure the effects of this explosion were actually destroyed by the blast.

It was a huge debacle, all because those involved had overlooked an important pathway when they calculated the yield—they had assumed that the lithium-7 isotope would be inert whereas in fact it contributed to the reaction. Now, the point I make in the paper is that it was a good thing that the calculation they got wrong was the one about the yield in Castle Bravo and not the calculation about whether the Trinity test would ignite the entire atmosphere. Put simply, there's a limit to how confident we can be in our calculations and modeling assumptions when we experiment with new phenomena or put them together in novel ways.

HARRIS: Right. So, let's talk about the remedies here because this is where your paper becomes startling. You list four remedies, and the first two are essentially nonstarters. The first is to restrict technological development. We can talk about whether that's at all plausible, but it seems to not be. The second is to ensure that there are no bad people. And if there are bad people, we have to modify their preferences durably enough so that we can be safe in the presence of these destructive technologies indefinitely, should we pull a black ball. The third is what you call "extreme policing," and the fourth is effective global governance.

As I said, the first two seem to be nonstarters. I don't know if you want to spend any time on them, but some combination of the second two, at a minimum, leads to something that you describe as a "high-tech panopticon" which requires, in the happiest possible case, that we have the ability to initiate what you call "turnkey totalitarianism"—which would require a level of surveillance that, though we all now have tracking devices in our pockets that we make phone calls on, few of us can imagine living under. Let's talk about what you see as a remedy given the assumption that there is a black ball in the urn of invention and we might one day pull it out.

BOSTROM: If the vulnerable world hypothesis is true, then logically it looks as though there are four possible ways of trying to fix the situation. The first two—restricting technological development or ensuring that there are no bad actors—seem rather unpromising. That leaves us with the last two: extremely effective preventive policing and adequate global governance.

The preventive policing remedy is primarily designed to deal with type one vulnerabilities, in which a great many individuals can each gain the capability to cause massive amounts of destruction. It looks like the only way such a world could be stable is if you could continuously, in real time, monitor what everybody was doing and reliably intervene if somebody started to do something dangerous. Exactly what that would require depends on the action you want to prevent, but to have a general ability would seem to require extreme surveillance combined with rapid intervention.

Of course, such a system would bring its own set of risks and downsides. At this point there is no policy prescription. I just note that if we're unlucky, the world could contain a vulnerability and it could be such that the only way to stabilize the world in those circumstances would be extreme, continuous, ubiquitous surveillance combined with a rapid intervention capability.

HARRIS: You spend the better part of a page, I think, on what extreme surveillance could look like, and you paint a fairly rosy picture of some of the possibilities here—it's not, as we might image, just a page ripped out of Aldous Huxley. What is the best case scenario for extreme surveillance?

BOSTROM: Well, I don't know about the best-case scenario. I am glad you find it rosy. Let's say everybody's fitted with a "freedom tag," which would be some wearable surveillance collar that always records everything they do. It has a microphone and multidirectional video cameras and continuously transmits the data feed to the cloud for automated analysis, and anything with indications of suspicious behavior gets immediately routed to a human "freedom officer" for further analysis. I suspect a lot of people would find this rather dystopian.

HARRIS: It's definitely dystopian, but it can be combined with layers of anonymity and protection along with possible advantages. For example, if you're being surveilled in this manner, your risk of dying of cardiac arrest goes way down, because someone will respond to your medical emergencies as well.

To jump to the punch line here: I found the net effect of reading this essay pretty uncanny, because if you'd asked me before reading it how I would view the prospect of extreme surveillance and turnkey totalitarianism, I would have said that this is synonymous with everything I don't want to happen. But once you've led us down this path of acknowledging that the vulnerable world hypothesis is probably true and that the only condition under which civilization could be stable probably requires this level of surveillance, it flips everything around and begins to make it seem like any movement toward totalitarian surveillance has a significant silver lining. Again, this is on the assumption that this is the only condition under which civilization can survive indefinitely.

BOSTROM: Right. I do think that's a fairly substantial argument for moving toward a more transparent society. Maybe this is tangential, but I can imagine some other reasons for favoring surveillance: it would make it easier to keep track of people's past behavior, so that the scoundrels and cheaters would be found out and the good people might more readily rise to the top. If miscreants knew that any attempt to cheat and harm others would be discovered, maybe a lot of them would stop doing it. You could imagine social dynamics shifting into a more desirable equilibrium. But we don't know that it would—maybe it could instead shift into some less desirable equilibrium where there is a kind of inescapable orthodoxy.

Social science does not have the kind of predictive power to say what would happen if you start changing some of the fundamental parameters of social interaction—say, if you had the perfect lie detector, or if you could monitor what everybody was doing all the time and analyze that data. I don't think we can predict very accurately what would happen. We know that past technological changes have had big effects on political systems. For example, writing helped the creation of states, as you could record who had paid their taxes and so forth. Gunpowder helped end the feudal era, the printing press inaugurated a period of religious wars that lasted a century, and so on.

HARRIS: How do you view the variable of global governance?

BOSTROM: That's the fourth possible remedy. In some scenarios, micro-surveillance wouldn't really help. Maybe each state could surveil its own citizens perfectly, but that wouldn't necessarily have helped the Soviet Union and the United States avoid the Cold War. You would have needed some dependable mechanism whereby great powers could avoid harmful conflicts. That could take the form of some sufficiently strong democratic world government, or it could take the form of one side being strong enough that it could lay down the law if it really needed to, like a global hegemon. A world with many top-level players is a world in which there continuously exists the possibility that they will find themselves trapped in some kind of conflict—an arms race, a game of chicken—where even though it may be plain to all that it will lead to catastrophe, they are incapable of unilaterally climbing out of it.

HARRIS: Right. So if you could wave a magic wand and implement some changes, what would you want to see happen at the level of governance, institutions, laws, and so on?

BOSTROM: Well, in terms of actual policy, I think I would start on a much smaller scale, focusing on more specific issues. So, for example, with regard to DNA synthesis, maybe one could try to establish an international regulatory framework. Maybe one could institute licensing requirements for DIY biohacking, as some countries such as Germany have already done. Maybe more rigorous background checks of individuals working in biotech labs. As capabilities expand, maybe some subset of people working with particularly dangerous technologies would be put under more continuous surveillance.

Placing credence on the vulnerable world hypothesis will likely also shift one's views more in favor of surveillance and global governance. But of course there are many other strong considerations that we'd need to take into account, both for and against. Independent of the vulnerable world hypothesis, it would seem desirable if we could develop more robust institutions for global cooperation. The history of mankind is pockmarked with the scars of wars and conflict, right? For thousands of years, we've been devoting a significant fraction of our energies and resources to killing one another. If we could escape that, that would seem to be a fairly robust and good thing. Now, *how* we move closer to that goal is then a complicated question, one where people's political biases would probably largely shape what they think is the best path. But the goal is quite easily recognized: a more peaceful and loving world, and maybe one where that cooperative attitude was entrenched in some institutional framework.

HARRIS: Yes, and if the goal of having a peaceful and loving world sounds too effete, we can just consider the other side, which is the status quo with respect to conflict and tribalism. In the presence of more and more powerful weapons, that seems like a bad recipe for survival.

BOSTROM: Yes. The badness of conflicts and the badness of wars is to a significant degree I think parameterized by the technologies available at that particular time. And so there is a risk that it gets worse if we invent new technologies. Even if it doesn't get worse, I think wars over the last hundred years have been sufficiently bad that it would be well worth trying to prevent more from occurring.

We seem to have a short memory. Consider the efforts toward strengthening global governance after World War One. People said, "Wow, that was horrible. We couldn't possibly have guessed how bad a war could be; but now we know. We definitely must make sure that never happens again!" Then a few years later we couldn't really be bothered— some very halfhearted efforts, no follow-through. *Bam!* World War Two. So, okay, the League of Nations wasn't enough, so after World War Two we're going to have the United Nations, and we're going to make sure to have peace and prosperity, this time for sure. But of course the big powers have vetoes, precisely the countries that most need to be restrained. So we have the very dangerous Cold War, with all the proxy conflicts and the world teetering at the brink on several occasions. Miraculously it ends peacefully. We draw a sigh of relief and say that finally history is over and we'll pledge never to do that again.

And now that promise is all but forgotten. I'm sure if there were another world war or great power conflict, and we survived it, we would slap our foreheads and say, "Ah, now I remember—war is bad, and we were supposed to have done things to make it impossible and then we got sidetracked," and there would be a huge surge of enthusiasm for solving global anarchy. Memories fade.

HARRIS: I want to pivot to your next paper, "Are You Living in a Computer Simulation?," which focuses on a very different consideration but has the same ethical concern at its core, which is existential risk or the prospects of our own survival. Perhaps you can explain the argument. Why even entertain the prospect that we're in a simulation?

BOSTROM: The simulation argument is a probabilistic argument that purports to impose a constraint on what you can coherently believe about the future and your place in the universe. It tries to show that at least one of three propositions is true. The first is that there is a universal pattern where virtually all civilizations at our current stage of technological development go extinct before reaching technological maturity. The second alternative is that there is a very strong convergence among all technologically mature civilizations in that they all lose interest in creating what I call "ancestor simulations." These would be computer simulations of people—such as their historical predecessors—detailed enough that the simulated creatures would be conscious. And the third alternative is that we are almost certainly living in a computer simulation.

The gist of the argument can be understood without looking at formulas. Let's suppose the first proposition is false, so that some nontrivial fraction of civilizations at our stage eventually do reach technological maturity. Furthermore, let's suppose that the second proposition is also false. So some nontrivial fraction of those technologically mature civilizations use some nontrivial fraction of their resources for the purpose of creating ancestor simulations. You can then show that the number of people with our kinds of experiences that would be living inside these ancestor simulations would be vastly greater than the number of people with our kinds of experiences that would be living unmediated, original histories. The vast majority of people with your kind of experiences will be simulated rather than nonsimulated. And conditional on that, I claim, you should think you are almost certainly one of the simulated ones. Therefore, if you reject the first two propositions, you have to accept the third. Therefore, you cannot coherently reject all three. Therefore, the disjunct is true. That's the structure of the argument.

HARRIS: Let me reprise part of that and add this other piece, which is relevant because what you're saying is that if we live on for billions of years—if our descendants, in whatever form they exist, continue to thrive for a very long time—we will almost certainly build simulations of our ancestors. And these simulated ancestors will vastly outnumber the actual ancestors. Therefore, we're more likely to be a simulation than in the real world. And this added point connects to all that we've been talking about: if we're not living in a simulation, then a distant, posthuman future seems unlikely.

BOSTROM: Well, unless it's one where the second proposition holds true—one where there is a universal convergence toward losing interest in creating simulations.

HARRIS: Right. There's an assumption that some posthuman beings would build simulated worlds and therefore that simulated beings would far outnumber real ones.

BOSTROM: Yes, there is an empirical premise that comes in. Maybe we should expand on that a little bit. It is the idea that a mature civilization, using only a tiny fraction of its resources, could produce astronomical numbers of ancestor simulations. This premise comes from a comparison between an estimate of the computing power that the mature civilization could master—say, by converting planets into structures optimized for computing—and estimates of how much computing power would be needed to simulate one human brain and therefore to simulate all human brains that will have existed.

Obviously we don't know the exact values of these quantities. But we have a lower bound on the amount of computing power that a mature civilization would have. And we can estimate very roughly the amount of computing power it would take to simulate human history, human experiences. And we find that these two quantities differ by a vast number of orders of magnitude, such that using 1 percent of the compute power of a single planetary-sized computer, even just for one second, would enable you to create thousands and thousands of runs of all of human history. Even if our estimates are slightly off, it's still a very robust conclusion that if some nontrivial fraction of mature civilizations use some nontrivial fraction of their resources for this purpose, then the simulated people would vastly outnumber the nonsimulated ones.

HARRIS: So it's a probabilistic argument that makes a few assumptions. But, granting those assumptions, there's a straightforward assessment of the probabilities. However, the use of probability here seems fishy to many people, and you point out in the paper that it seems akin to the doomsday argument.

I was first introduced to the doomsday argument in John Leslie's book *The End of the World*, which was published about twenty years ago. I think he published it first in a paper, which you reference in your own, and it originally came, I think, from the astrophysicist Brandon Carter. Let's summarize the doomsday argument, and perhaps you can articulate why you think the flaws that people believe they've detected in it don't apply to the simulation argument.

BOSTROM: The doomsday argument is an interesting piece of reasoning. It became popularized in the midnineties or so. The general reaction to it was that there had to be something wrong with this argument—such a strong conclusion just can't follow from such weak premises. But then when people tried to say *what* was wrong, they all came up with different answers, and a lot of them didn't work.

Here is the argument. Again we can resort to urns to help illustrate the reasoning. This time, though, imagine that the balls in the urn are numbered, so we have an urn containing, say, ten balls, numbered one through ten. We have another urn also filled with balls, but this one has a million balls in it, numbered one, two, three, four, up to a million.

Now let's suppose that one of these two urns is chosen at random and put in front of you, and you have to guess how many balls it contains. Is it the ten-ball urn? The probability of a correct guess is fifty-fifty, right? Two urns, 50 percent chance that this is the ten-ball urn.

Now suppose you reach into the urn and extract one ball. You look at the number and it's ball number seven. At this point you have new information. It's vastly more likely that you'd get such a low-numbered ball if there were only ten balls in the urn than if there were a million. You update and say, "Well, this is almost certainly the ten-ball urn." Bayes's theorem tells you how to do that. Okay, so far this is just uncontroversial, standard, elementary probability theory.

Now, the doomsday argument says that this is analogous to our actual situation with respect to possible futures. Instead of these two urns with different numbers of balls, you now have two different hypotheses about how long the human species will last. Maybe one says that we'll go extinct after the total number of humans who have ever lived reaches two hundred billion. Maybe another hypothesis says that there will be two hundred trillion humans before we go extinct. Corresponding to the observation of pulling out ball number seven, you have the observation that your birth rank, your place in the sequence of all humans so far born, is roughly a hundred billion. That's more or less how many people have come before you.

Similar to the case with the urns, you now have some prior probability of how likely the world is to end soon—that is, when only two hundred billion humans will have existed—or later, when there will have been two hundred trillion.

Then, when you reflect on the relatively low number of your birth rank, you are supposed to update in favor of the doom-soon hypothesis, just like you updated in favor of the ten-ball urn hypothesis after pulling out ball number seven. The reasoning here is that it's much more likely that you'd be number one hundred billion if the human total is two hundred billion people than if it's two hundred trillion. It means you're just somewhere in the middle, a perfectly normal birth rank. But it would be weird to be number one hundred billion if the human species were going to contain hundreds of trillions of people.

That's the basic idea. There's a bit more to it—some argumentation in favor of the idea that you should assign probabilities more or less as though you were a randomly selected sample for the set of all people that will ever have lived. It looks like you have to make an assumption roughly like that—I call it the self-sampling assumption—if you're going to make sense of various philosophical thought experiments and various applications in cosmology and other scientific areas, where you need to be able to take into account indexical, self-locating information. I developed a mathematical theory for how to do this in my doctoral dissertation and later on in my book *Anthropic Bias.*

HARRIS: This is where many people's intuitions pull up short, because our discovery that we exist now, at this point in human history, is not the same thing as our having been randomly selected from a larger population of possible people. This is the place where people tend to get off the ride—it seems that you can't really say that if humanity will exist far into the future, I'd be unlikely to find myself alive right now. I'm alive right now, whether or not doomsday will come in one hundred years or one billion years. I exist under both conditions.

BOSTROM: Yes, ultimately this doomsday argument is very problematic, and I don't particularly want to endorse it. But for the sake of our conversation, let me step into the role of an advocate.

Let's consider a slightly different thought experiment where there are a hundred rooms and one person in each room. The rooms are the same inside, but on the outside, 90 percent of the rooms are painted black and 10 percent are painted white. You find yourself in one of these rooms, and you have to guess whether you are in a black-painted room or a white-painted room. You think, *Well, 90 percent of us are in black-painted rooms, so I give 90 percent probability that I'm in a black-painted room.* In fact, you can run betting arguments suggesting that this is the correct odds for people to assign.

Then you can consider a variation of this: instead of the rooms co-existing in space, they pop into existence, one after another, in time. So imagine an empty world, with just one room. On the first day, somebody is born into that room and disappears at the end of the day. Another person is born into that room on day two. And so forth. Say that on 90 percent of the days, the room is black on the outside, and on 10 percent of the days, it's white on the outside. You find yourself having been born into this world. You're in the room. You will exist for one day. You know that one hundred people, say, will have inhabited the room by the time the world ends. You can't see which color your room is because it's painted on the outside. You have to guess.

Again, it seems you should go with the odds corresponding to the fraction of people in one or the other color of room. Arguments based on optimal betting odds seem to support this. So you get closer to the doomsday argument experiment because here, too, you have people coming into existence at different points in time.

The key remaining difference, I think, is that in the thought experiment I just described, the total number of people is fixed. There will be one hundred people in total. In the case of the doomsday argument, the total number is uncertain. There will either be a small number of people, two hundred billion, or a much larger number, two hundred trillion. That's an important difference in the two situations. It might well be where you want to jump off the ride.

HARRIS: So how do you view the simulation argument as being stronger than the doomsday argument?

BOSTROM: I view it as being stronger in a few ways, but particularly because it doesn't have this feature of involving reasoning about hypotheses with different numbers of people in the key step. That place where this anthropic style of reasoning enters the simulation argument is only in one particular place. You get to the step where you say that, conditional on the first two propositions being false, there are many more simulated people than nonsimulated people. So far no weird anthropic reasoning. But then you go on from that and you say: conditional on this being the case, you are almost certainly one of the simulated people in the majority rather than one of the rare exceptional nonsimulated people in the minority.

This step requires anthropic reasoning. But it doesn't require applying anthropic reasoning to hypotheses stipulating different numbers of people. On both the hypotheses you are considering at this stage, there is a number of X simulated people, and a much smaller number of Y nonsimulated people; on both hypotheses the total number of people is X+Y. The only question is whether you belong to X or to Y. This seems more similar to one of the earlier thought experiments that I described— where the total number of people is fixed—than to the doomsday argument, where the total number of people depends on which hypothesis is true.

I'm not sure this is understandable, much less convincing, in this laconic form. But I think this marks a deep difference between these two applications of anthropic reasoning, and it makes the application in the case of the simulation argument a lot less problematic.

HARRIS: Do you take your own argument seriously? If I gave you an opportunity to wager money on the prospect that we are living in a simulation right now, would you place a very large bet that we are?

BOSTROM: I take it seriously, yes. I'd make a distinction, by the way, between the simulation argument and the simulation hypothesis. So the simulation *argument* is that one of these three propositions that I described is true. In itself, it's agnostic as to which one or how you should allocate probability among them. The simulation *hypothesis* is specifically the claim that the third proposition is true—that we are in a simulation. The simulation argument seems sound, so I take that seriously. I also take the simulation hypothesis seriously. I tend to punt on the question of exactly what probability I assign to it.

HARRIS: But is it some middling probability? Is it like a coin toss, or would you put it much higher or lower than chance?

BOSTROM: Let's just say a "noninsignificant probability," for the purposes of our conversation.

HARRIS: Is that because you actually don't feel you know what level of credence you give it, or you don't want to be on record saying "I would bet half my net worth because I'm fairly confident?"

BOSTROM: A mixture of the two. A precise probability is also the kind of thing that would be quoted a lot, and maybe taken out of context. People might infer more than I meant to imply, and so forth. So I've been a bit coy about that, traditionally.

HARRIS: Well, I won't press you—at least not in this part of the simulation.

In the time remaining, let's discuss this third paper, "Where Are They?," which deals with the prospect that advanced extraterrestrial life should be populating the galaxy, if it's out there at all. Perhaps this question, "Where is everyone?" was asked earlier, but Enrico Fermi is credited as the author of it.

The conclusion of this paper is another arresting one. I think you start by saying that if we find multicellular life (and certainly anything more complicated than that) on Mars or elsewhere in the cosmos, that will be very bad news for us, because it would suggest that we are doomed. You arrive at this by considering the implications of an idea that Robin Hanson calls "the great filter." Perhaps you can summarize this argument. If the *New York Times* publishes an article tomorrow that we have found strange bacteria in our Martian soil samples, why might this be the death knell of the species?

BOSTROM: Well, maybe not the death knell, but it would suggest an update toward it being more likely that our own prospects are limited.

The background here is Fermi's observation that we have seen no sign of any extraterrestrial life, let alone any space-colonizing extraterrestrial life. Yet we know that there are a lot of planets out there, including ones that look like they should be habitable; and billions of billions of them are close enough that a technologically mature civilization could have had ample time by now to reach Earth or to make its presence known. Thus we infer that between the formation of a suitable planet and the stage of development where an extraterrestrial civilization spreads through the universe (in ways that would be perceptible to us) there must be one or more highly improbable steps, a "great filter."

Now we can distinguish two possibilities: either this great filter, this great improbability, lies behind us in our evolutionary past, and we've been lucky and made it through; or this great filter lies in our future, and at some point between where we are now and the point where we're spreading through the galaxy and beyond, it will put a stop to us. It could also be that there is a filter both behind us and ahead of us; but if there is a filter behind us then there's no particular reason to think there's one ahead of us, so in that case we may have pretty good prospects of becoming a space-colonizing supercivilization.

And indeed, there are many plausible steps in our past where some enormous improbability might have been involved: great filter candidates. Maybe getting from a lifeless planet to one even having simple replicators is just wildly improbable—maybe you need gazillions of planets rattling around for billions of years before, by chance, a large number of molecules bump into one another in just the right way to create a simple replicator—that's a candidate. Or the enormously improbable step could have come later, in the transition from prokaryotic to eukaryotic life, which took more than one and a half billion years here on Earth. Maybe that step was radically improbable, and maybe that's what accounts for our failure to sight any extraterrestrials.

But now suppose we read in the *New York Times* that we have discovered independently evolved life on Mars, even some fairly primitive life—maybe some extinct algae or something. That would immediately eliminate a number of places where the great filter could be. If within our own solar system, moderately complex life had evolved independently *twice*, then that would be strong evidence that the great filter is not located anywhere in that segment of the evolutionary trajectory. Suppose you got to, say, squirrel-like life twice in our solar system. That suggests that many, many exoplanets, all through the universe, harbor squirrel-like life at some point in their existence. That also narrows the interval on the evolutionary trajectory where the great filter could be located if it's in our past—and, therefore, shifts the probability over to hypotheses that suggest that the great filter is ahead of us. That would be bad news for our future prospects.

HARRIS: Right. We've spent a lot of time talking about one possible filter: a black ball pulled from the urn of invention—which, in this case, all technological civilizations, for some reason, would find.

BOSTROM: Yes, some kind of technologically mandated destructive scenario is one candidate. It would have to have certain specific characteristics to work as a great filter, though. It wouldn't suffice that it eradicates many civilizations before they spread throughout space, or even 90 percent of them. It would have to almost without exception destroy every civilization that reaches that stage. If the great filter is a technology, it would have to be a technology that any civilization almost inevitably discovers before it starts to colonize its galaxy, and it would have to be a technology that almost inevitably destroys you, even if you had your act together as a civilization.

Think of all the possible weird ways that civilizations could be structured. On one planet, maybe a global religion with a strange set of dogmas has taken over. On another, the environmentalists have had great success. A third has splintered into ten thousand warring factions. On a fourth, they have used genetic engineering to make themselves wise and benevolent before proceeding, with great caution, to develop space-colonizing technology. To have a great technological filter, you would need some technological discovery that would afflict all of these different civilizational trajectories equally.

HARRIS: I think that we should mention something here about the expectation of seeing intelligent life out in the galaxy: this results from the vast amount of time the galaxy has existed and the relatively short time it would take a highly technological civilization to colonize the galaxy.

Generously, this would take something like twenty million years. This sounds like a long time, but in the context of galactic time, on the assumption that complex, intelligent life is common, we would expect to see a galaxy teeming with self-replicating machines that have spread more or less everywhere.

BOSTROM: Yes, our planet is not unusually early in terms of its formation date. Many other Earth-like planets got started a couple of billion years earlier than ours did, and there will be others that will start to form out of their sun's gas cloud billions of years in the future. We're a pretty average planet in that respect. There are many other possible germination points for life which have had billions of years' head start on us. If evolution on those planets had a significant chance of producing space-colonizing life, then they would have had ample time to colonize not just their own galaxy but indeed other galaxies as well, even if they could travel at just 1 percent of the speed of light. And we have reason to think a mature civilization could travel a lot faster than that.

HARRIS: Again, it's a fascinating way to arrive as some estimation of our own prospects for survival. We're talking about extraterrestrial life and the way in which its absence, or apparent absence, or presence (if found), changes our probability calculus with respect to our own long-term survival.

BOSTROM: Yes, there are a number of these puzzle pieces. In fact, we've talked about a few of them. So there's this great filter/Fermi paradox. There's the simulation argument—another important puzzle piece. The doomsday argument, if it is sound, would be a key puzzle piece. (And if the argument is unsound, the reason *why* it's unsound might itself give us further clues.)

Some people have the opinion that the far future is completely unknowable and you can just make up any story you like. But I actually think there are a number of constraints about what we can coherently believe, and it's hard to find even one way of picturing the world that meets all of these constraints. But despite various clues, here we are—still at the fairly fundamental level, in the dark. I think we are still oblivious to at least one or more likely *crucial considerations*—ones that, if we came to understand them, would radically change our picture of the world and our place within it, and our overall scheme of priorities.

HARRIS: In the remaining minutes, let's touch briefly on superintelligence and the prospect of developing artificial general intelligence. I went to the first conference in Puerto Rico, where I met you and many others who had been thinking about this problem for a while. The problem is, if we continue to make progress in developing AI, we will one day find ourselves in the presence of intelligent machines that are more intelligent than we are. In the extreme case, they will become the agents of their own improvement, and then this process could get away from us in what has been referred to as an "intelligence explosion." Perhaps more than anyone, you have spelled out how the space of all possible general intelligences must surely be bigger than the space of intelligences that are aligned with our interests. And nonalignment could well prove fatal.

I've been talking about this over the last couple years with people who imagine that they're very close to the data, but who are profoundly skeptical that this problem is worth thinking about at all. The line "worrying about artificial general intelligence is like worrying about overpopulation on Mars" summarizes the level of dismissal one often encounters here.

Have we made any progress in getting this concern taken seriously? In my experience—really without exception—the dismissal relies on obviously bad analogies and pseudoarguments. The quality of reasoning that one meets is fairly astonishing, especially coming from very smart people.

BOSTROM: I think it's changed a lot even compared to a few short years ago. There is now a subfield of AI safety researchers working on this in a number of places. So some of the dismissive attitudes that greeted these efforts, say, five years ago, have faded away. I think this is due to a combination of efforts, including yours. On the one hand, there was the initial work to explain why AI alignment is an important problem and to develop some of the basic concepts that allow us to think about it. On the other hand, there were specific efforts to develop concrete research projects—and there are now a number of technical lines of research and some very smart people working on them. That also helped legitimize the field. And third, on the prehensile tail, I think the brisk progress we've seen in AI in general has also been a stimulus—the pace of advance in machine learning is now such that it seems less crazy to think ahead about the challenges of machine superintelligence.

So these three factors have combined to make AI safety research more mainstream. You could still make the case that it's far from where it should be—it's still a niche occupation and a niche concern. What fraction of our resources on this planet are we spending on preparing for the advent of superintelligence? I don't know. In general, I think our prioritization scheme as a species doesn't necessarily reflect the objective importance of the various things we could be doing.

HARRIS: That summarizes most of our problems right there. Nick, it's been fascinating to speak with you, and there's much more to talk about. I hope we do round two soon, so we can get into metaethics and any further progress we make or don't make on the AI front. Please come back one of these days.

BOSTROM: Indeed. Thanks again—that was fun.

Complexity and Stupidity

A CONVERSATION WITH DAVID KRAKAUER

David Krakauer is president and William H. Miller professor of complex systems at the Santa Fe Institute. His research explores the evolution of genetic, neural, linguistic, social, and cultural mechanisms that support intelligence. Krakauer is a mathematical biologist, with a PhD in evolutionary theory from Oxford, but running the Santa Fe Institute puts him at the crossroads of many different areas of inquiry.

In this conversation we discuss several concepts that are foundational to science, such as information, complexity, computation, and intelligence, and then explore their implications for the future of civilization.

HARRIS: David, you gave a fascinating lecture in 2016 that I want to talk about. I'm interested in the importance of culture, especially the artifacts we create to support human intelligence—and in resisting our slide into stupidity, which was the focus of your talk. But before we get there, let's set the stage a bit. Tell us about your scientific interests and background.

KRAKAUER: My scientific interests are, essentially, grappling with the evolution of intelligence and stupidity on Earth. It's quite common for people to talk about intelligence. It's less common for people to talk about stupidity, even though, arguably, it's more prevalent.

My background is in mathematical evolutionary theory, and I work on information and computation in nature. That includes the nature we've created—such as technology—as well as where it came from, what it's doing today, and where it's going.

HARRIS: Now you're running the Santa Fe Institute. Its existence is predicated on the porousness of the boundaries between disciplines—or even their nonexistence. Describe the institute for people who aren't familiar with it.

KRAKAUER: The Santa Fe Institute is in Santa Fe, New Mexico, as the name would suggest. It was founded in the mid-1980s by a group of physicists for the most part, and they brought in others who were interested in trying to do for the complex world what mathematical physics does so successfully for the simple world.

I should explain that. The simple world would be, say, the solar system, or inorganic chemistry, or black holes—worlds that are not easy to understand, but whose fundamental properties you can encapsulate by writing down a system of equations.

The complex world, which basically means networked adaptive systems, could be a brain—a network of neurons. It could be a society. It could even be the internet. In those networked adaptive systems—those complex systems—the kinds of formalisms we've created historically to deal with simple systems have failed. That's why we don't have

Maxwell's equations for the brain, right? So the question is, Are there general principles that span the economy, brains, the internet, and so on? And if so, what is the most natural way of articulating those principles mathematically and computationally?

HARRIS: And the institute is truly interdisciplinary. You have economists and mathematicians and biologists and physicists all throwing in their two cents on the same problems.

KRAKAUER: Absolutely. You know, we've been working on the archaeology of the Southwest using computational and physical models, and we've produced a well-known series of theories for why, for example, some of the native civilizations of the American Southwest, the origin of ancient cities, declined. These scenarios are based on computational and energetic theories and close collaborations between archaeologists and, say, physicists. I don't like to call this "interdisciplinary," because that's in some sense genuflecting in the direction of an approach people take seriously. What happens when you ignore all of that and say, "Let's use the skills we've acquired in the disciplines, but let's leave them at the door and just be intelligent about complex problems"?

HARRIS: Let's define a few of the terms we'll need to make headway here. The first is the concept of information. There are many senses in which we use this term, and not all of them are commensurable. It seems to me there's a root concept, however, that potentially unites fields like genetics, brain science, computer science, and even physics. How do you think about information?

KRAKAUER: It's sometimes what I call the "m-cubed mayhem." That is, "m raised to the power of three" mayhem. The mayhem comes from not understanding the difference between mathematics (the first m); mathematical models (the second m); and metaphors, the third. And there are terms—scientific terms, mathematical terms—that have a colloquial meaning and often get us into deep water: energy, fitness, utility, capacity, information, computation. We all use them in our daily lives, probably very effectively, but they also have a technical meaning. And often arguments flare up because one person is using a term mathematically and another person metaphorically and they don't realize they're doing this.

I don't mean to say that there is only a mathematical definition of "information," but it's worth bearing in mind that when I talk about it, that's what I mean. It has a beautiful, scientific, storied history, starting with, essentially, the birth of the field of statistical mechanics. This was Ludwig Boltzmann trying to understand the arrow of time in the physical world—the origin of irreversibility. You know, why is it that you can crack an egg but the reverse almost never happens?

In the 1870s, Boltzmann created a theory called the h theorem, where he had in mind lots of little billiard balls bumping into each other in a chaotic manner. You start with a fairly ordered billiard table, but at the end, through repeated collisions, the balls are distributed randomly all over the table. Boltzmann thought that maybe the underlying molecular structure of matter was like lots of little billiard balls, and that the reason we observe certain phenomena in nature as irreversible is because of molecular chaos.

That proposition was formalized between 1902 and 1904 by the American physicist Josiah Willard Gibbs. In the 1940s these ideas were picked up by an engineer at Bell Labs, Claude Shannon. He saw a connection between physics and irreversibility—between an arrow of time and information. It was a deep insight. He said, "Look, here is what information is. Let's say I want to navigate from one part of the city to another, from A to B. In a car, I could just drive around randomly. It would take an awful long time to get there, but I might eventually get there. Alternatively, I could give you a map or driving directions, and you'd get there very efficiently. The difference between the time taken to get there randomly and the time taken to get there with directions is a measure of information." Shannon mathematized that concept. He formalized that, and he called it information.

This is the opposite of what Boltzmann and Gibbs were talking about. It's a system. Instead of going from the ordered into the disordered state, it's going from a state of being random—because you don't know where to go—to becoming ordered. Shannon realized that information is in fact the negative of thermodynamic entropy, and it was a beautiful connection that he made between what we now think of as the science of information and what was the science of statistical physics.

HARRIS: Let's bring this into the domain of biology. I've been hearing with increasing frequency the idea that biological systems, and even brains, don't process information, and that drawing an analogy between the brain and a computer is no more valid than equating it to a system of hydraulic pumps, or a wheelworks powered by springs and gears, or a telegraph. As you know, these were all old analogies to the most current technology of the time.

No one, to my knowledge, thinks that the brain is a computer in exactly the way our current computers are. We are not talking about Von Neumann architecture in our heads. But the idea that the brain doesn't process information at all, and that claiming it does is like claiming that it's a mechanism of gears and springs, strikes me as fairly delusional. However, I keep meeting people who argue that any notion of neural computation is just a bad analogy like the others, and some of them have careers in science. So I was hoping we could talk a bit about the ways in which biological systems—in particular, brains—encode and transmit information.

KRAKAUER: This takes me back to my *m*-cubed mayhem, because it's a good example of not knowing the difference between a mathematical model and a metaphor. You talk about springs and levers and these are physical artifacts, right? And then there are mathematical *models* of springs and levers, which are actually used in understanding string theory.

So let's talk a bit about the computer and the brain. The analogy spans elegantly that spectrum from mathematics to mathematical models to metaphors. The first real theory of computing we have is due to the mathematician Alan Turing in the 1930s. Many people know him from the movie *The Imitation Game* and for his extraordinary work on Enigma and decoding German submarine codes in the Second World War. But what he's most famous for in *our* world is answering a really deep mathematical question posed by the German mathematician David Hilbert in 1928. Hilbert said, "Could I give a machine a mathematical proposition and it would tell me in a reasonable amount of time whether it was true or false?" That is, could we in some sense automate mathematics? And in 1936, Turing, in answering that question, invented a mathematical model we now know as the Turing machine. Turing did something remarkable. He said, "You can't answer that question. There are certain mathematical statements that are fundamentally 'uncomputable.'" It was a profound breakthrough in mathematics when he said there are certain things in the world that we can never know through computation.

Years later, Turing realized that in solving a mathematical problem, he had actually invented a mathematical model: the Turing machine. And he realized that it wasn't just a model for solving math problems, it was *the* model of problem-solving itself. And the model of problem-solving itself is what we mean by computation.

Then, in the late 1950s, John Von Neumann wrote a famous book, *The Computer and the Brain*. So what Alan Turing did in his paper on intelligent machinery has given us the mathematical machinery for understanding the brain itself. At that point the intelligent machine becomes a metaphor. Von Neumann realized it was a metaphor, but he thought it was a very powerful one.

So that's the history. Now, back to the present. As you point out, there is a tendency to be epistemologically narcissistic. We tend to take whatever current model we're using and project that onto the natural world as the best-fitting template for how the natural world operates. The value of what Turing and Von Neumann did was to give us a framework for starting to understand how a problem-solving machine could operate. We hadn't really had, in our mind's eye, an understanding of how that could work, and they gave us a model of how it could work.

For many reasons, the model is highly imperfect. Computers are not robust. If I stick a pencil into your CPU, your machine will stop working. But I can sever the two hemispheres of your brain and you can still function. You're very efficient. Your brain consumes about 20 percent of the energy of your body; that is, it's consuming about twenty watts. That's 20 percent of a lightbulb. Your laptop consumes about that much, and yet it has only a tiny fraction of your brain's power. And your neurons are highly connected, densely wired, whereas that's not true of computer circuits, which are only locally wired. Most important, the brain is constantly rewiring and adapting based on inputs, and your computer is not. So we know the ways in which these two are not the same. But the analogy is useful as an approach to defining how the brain might operate.

That's the "computer" term. Now let's take the "information" term. We've already determined what information is mathematically: it's the reduction of uncertainty. Think about your visual system. When you open your eyes in the morning and you don't know what's out there in the world, electromagnetic energy, transduced by photoreceptors in your retina and then transmitted through the visual cortex, allows you to know something about the world that you didn't know before. It's like going from the billiard balls all over the table to the billiard balls in a particular configuration. Formally speaking, you've reduced the uncertainty about the world. You've increased information, and it turns out you can measure that mathematically.

The extent to which that measurement is useful is apparent in neuroprosthetics. The information theory of the brain allows us to build cochlear implants. It allows us to control robotic limbs with our brains. So it's not a metaphor. It's a deep mathematical principle—one that allows us to understand how brains operate and how to reengineer them.

Now, that's information. If information processing is synonymous in your vocabulary with computing in the Turing sense, then you and I just agreed that that isn't right. But if information processing is what you do with Shannon information, for example—to transduce electromagnetic impulses into electrical firing patterns in the brain—then it's absolutely applicable, as is how you store it and how you combine information sources.

When I see an orange, it's orange in color, and it's also a sphere. I have tactile mechanical impulses, and I have visual electromagnetic impulses. In my brain, they're combined into a coherent representation of an object in the world. The coherent representation is in the form of an informational language spiking. This insight has allowed us to engineer biologically mimetic architectures, and it's made a huge difference in the lives of many individuals born with severe disabilities.

HARRIS: I'm also thinking of things like genes that can be on or off. There's a digital component going all the way down into the genome—and the genome itself is a kind of memory. It's a memory for structure and physiology, and even for certain behaviors, that have proved adaptive. It's a physical template for producing those features in future organisms.

KRAKAUER: That's exactly right. That's the great power of mathematical concepts. Again, we have to be clear in making distinctions between the metaphor of memory and the mathematical model of memory. The beautiful thing—that's why mathematics is so extraordinarily powerful—is that once we move to the mathematical model of memory, you can demonstrate that there are memories stored in genes, there are memories stored in the brain, and they bear an extraordinary family resemblance, through the resemblance in the mathematical equations. Where we run into trouble is if we don't move to mathematics but remain in the world of metaphor. There, of course, everyone has a slightly different matrix of associations, and you can never fully resolve the ambiguities.

HARRIS: Let's talk about something that's perilously close to metaphor: The cause-and-effect relationships that, in this case, reliably link inputs and outputs. People opposed to the computer/brain analogy talk about the nervous system being changed by experience; they just don't want to talk about the resulting changes in terms of "memory" or "information storage" or "encoding" or anything else that suggests an analogy to a computer. But physical change in a physical structure can produce reliable changes in its capacities going forward. Whether we want to call that memory or learning, physically that's what we're talking about.

KRAKAUER: Absolutely. That's the point. Opposition to the computer analogy comes from a legitimate fear of anthropomorphism, and what we do in these more exact sciences is try to pin down our definitions so as to eliminate some of the ambiguities. They never go away entirely, because they're the most convenient terms we have to explain the regularities we observe.

HARRIS: And yet we don't *have* to use terms like "hydraulic pumps" or "four humors." We can grant that there have been bad analogies in the past and that the details were not conserved going forward.

KRAKAUER: If you're talking about your cardiac system or your urogenital system, it's entirely appropriate to use Harvey's model, which was the pump, right? The ones that worked have stuck, and time will tell whether use of the informational concept will be an anachronism or will have enduring value.

HARRIS: So now we've dealt with information. What is complexity?

KRAKAUER: That's a wonderful example of a term we use in daily life that also has a mathematical meaning. The simplest way to think about complexity is as follows: imagine you have a very regular object, like a cube. You could express it just by describing its linear dimensions, and that would tell you what a cube is. And imagine you want to explain something at the other end of the spectrum, like a gas in a room. You could articulate that very reliably by just giving the mean velocities of the particles in air. So these two extremes—the very regular, a cube, to the very random, a gas—permit of a description that's very short.

Over the phone, I could reliably describe to you a regular object or a very random object. But now let's imagine you asked me to describe a mouse. And I said, "Well, it's a sort of weird tubular thing, and it's got hairs at one end, it's got this long appendage at the other," and so on. It would take an awfully long time to describe. Complexity is proportional to the length of the description. It turns out that, mathematically, complex phenomena live somewhere between the regular and the random. Their hallmark is that their mathematical descriptions are long, and that's what has made complex science so hard.

Einstein could write down a beautiful equation like $e=mc^2$ that captures the equivalence between energy and mass, and has all these beautiful implications for special relativity, in less than a line. But how would you write down an equation for a mouse, which seems like a much more boring thing than energy and matter? You can't. So that's an intuitive way of thinking about a complex phenomenon: How long does the description have to be to reliably capture much of what you consider interesting about it?

One point to make immediately is that descriptions of physical phenomena started off long too. Before Kepler revolutionized our understanding of celestial mechanics, we had armillary spheres with all those epicycles and deferents explaining—incorrectly—the circular motion of a celestial mass. It took a while for us to realize that there was a compact, elegant way of describing that motion. And that could be true for many complex phenomena. But for many others, I don't think that will be the case.

So complexity applies to networked adaptive systems. Complexity itself, as a mathematical concept, tries to capture how hard it is to describe a phenomenon. And as phenomena get more complex, these descriptions get longer and longer. I like to say that complexity theory is extensive (grows in system size) whereas complicated science is intensive (invariant in system size). This implies that we can write down Newton's equations of motion and describe the whole classical universe with them. By adding more mass—for example, stars—we do not need to add more equations. But in order to describe life at this level of resolution we would need a theory that requires more equations as we add more unique forms of species.

HARRIS: You said something about randomness there that caught my ear. My understanding is that randomness generally can't be expressed simply. If I gave you a truly random string of digits, unless you're talking about some method by which to produce it algorithmically—the decimal expansion of pi, for instance—if it's a truly random series of digits, that would not be compressible, correct?

KRAKAUER: That's right. That's an important distinction. I can describe the process of generating heads and tails by describing the dynamics of the coin, and that's very short. But if I'm trying to describe the sequence I observe, it would be incompressible and the description would be as long as the sequence described. You can describe the underlying causal process that generates the pattern, not the pattern itself. And that's a very important distinction.

HARRIS: Let's talk about intelligence. What is it, and how is it related to complexity?

KRAKAUER: Intelligence is, as I like to say, one of the topics about which we have been most stupid. All our definitions of intelligence are based on measurements that can be applied only to humans—and by and large, humans that speak English or what have you. An IQ test is not interesting if you're trying to calculate the intelligence of an octopus (which I would like to know). I think we need to understand where intelligence comes from, and having a definition that only applies to one species doesn't help us. We've talked about entropy and computation, and they'll be the keys to understanding intelligence.

Let's go back to randomness. The example I like to give is that of a Rubik's Cube, because it's a beautiful little mental model, a metaphor. If I gave you a cube and asked you to solve it, and you just randomly manipulated it, you'd have to be immortal to solve it, since it has on the order of ten quintillion solutions. It would take a lifetime of several universes to do so. That's random performance.

Stupid performance is if you took just one face of the cube and manipulated that one face and rotated it forever. As everyone knows, if you did that you'd never solve the Rubik's Cube. It would be an infinite process that would never be resolved. That, by my definition, is stupid. It's significantly worse than chance.

Now let's take someone who's learned how to manipulate a cube and is familiar with various rules that allow you, from any initial configuration, to solve the cube in twenty moves or less. That is intelligent behavior, significantly better than chance. This sounds a little coun-terintuitive, perhaps, until you realize that's how we use the word "intelligent" in our daily lives. If I sat down with an extraordinary math-ematician and said, "I can't solve that equation," and he said, "Well, no, it's easy. Here's what you do," I'd look at what he did and say, "Oh, yes, it *is* easy. You made it look easy." That's what we mean when we say some-one is smart. They make things look easy.

If, on the other hand, I sat down with someone who was incapable of solving the equation and just kept, for whatever reason, dividing by two, I would say, "What on Earth are you doing? What a stupid thing to do. You'll never solve the problem that way." So that's what we mean by intelligence. It's what we do that ensures that the problem is efficiently solved. Stupidity is a set of rules that guarantees the problem will take longer than chance to be solved, or will never be solved, and yet is nev-ertheless employed with alacrity and enthusiasm.

HARRIS: Now we're getting closer to the substance of that lecture you gave. In particular, I'm interested in the distinction you drew be-tween biology and culture, and how culture might be a machine for increasing our intelligence. You also warned that culture threatens to make each of us personally *less* intelligent—perhaps to a dangerous degree.

KRAKAUER: This is a lengthy narrative. I'll try to compress it. Most of us are brainwashed to believe that we're born with a certain innate intelli-gence, and although we learn things to solve problems, our intelligence goes basically unchanged. You hear this all the time in conversations: "She's really smart. It's just that she never worked very hard and so didn't learn much." Or, "That person is not very smart, but he learned a great deal, and it makes him look smart." That sort of thing. I think that's rubbish. There's a very real sense in which education and learning make you smarter. So that's my premise.

HARRIS: Let's pause there for a second. You wouldn't dispute, though, that there are differences in what psychologists have come to call "g," or "general intelligence," and that this is not necessarily predicated upon acquiring new information?

KRAKAUER: I *would* dispute that.

HARRIS: So you think the concept of IQ is useless not just for an octopus but for people?

KRAKAUER: More or less, and I should explain why. Let's take a canonical example, the young Mozart. People say, "Well, look. This is a kid who at the age of *seven* had absolute pitch, and in his teens you could play him a symphony that he could recollect note for note and reproduce on a score." What we now understand, of course, is that his father was a tyrant who drilled him and his sister from an extraordinarily young age in acquiring perfect pitch and in the subtleties of musical notation. Consequently he was able to acquire characteristics as a child that we normally wouldn't acquire until later on in life, if at all, because most of us haven't been drilled.

More and more studies indicate that if you subject individuals to practice regimes, they can acquire skills that seem almost extraordinary. Let's take "g"—and IQ in general. We now know that what it mostly measures is working memory, and many working-memory tasks are correlated; they live in this low-dimensional space we call "g." One of the classic studies in the research on memory looks at the number of numbers you can hold in your head. I recite a series of numbers, and I ask you to remember them, and ten minutes later I ask you to repeat them. You aren't allowed to write them down, so what you do is replay them in your mind. People could do ten, maybe they could do eleven, and this was considered to be some upper limit on our short-term memory for numbers. And yet, in a series of experiments using ingenious means of encoding numbers, subjects could remember up to three hundred numbers in sequence. These were individuals, by the way, who at no point in their lives ever showed any particularly extraordinary memory capacity. So the evidence is on the side of plasticity or adaptability, which might be a better word, not innate aptitude.

And to the extent that IQ fundamentally measures working memory, we now know how to start increasing it. That's an important point. I don't deny that there are innate variations. I am not six-foot-five. I'm not even six-foot, so I will with high probability never be a professional basketball player. So there are functions in the world that are responsive to variation that look somewhat inflexible. But in the world of the brain—given that it's not a computer and the wiring diagram is not fixed in the factory but adapts to inputs—there is much more hope, and in fact evidence, that the variation is much greater than we thought.

I want to stress that it is not that IQ does not exist, or that it does not show intriguing heritability, or that it fails to capture some essential properties of brain or mind. There is no doubt that we are measuring something real, and more to the point, correlations among functions that depend on deep shared machinery. However, at the level of neural and cognitive resolution that I operate, and given my interest in evolution, it is too-coarse-grained. IQ is, after all, a phenomenological statistic.

IQ has always seemed to me rather like the monetary value of an object. Among the most expensive paintings ever sold are a Da Vinci portrait, a de Kooning abstract, and a Cézanne gambling scene. They have very little in common other than the price assigned to them by the free market. The price does not tell us anything about the content, the style, the history, the paints, the subjects, or the patrons. It does tell us about where they are most likely to be found and the social status of their creators at the time of purchase. And there is no disputing the utility of price—it governs the distribution of material resources through trade networks.

In a similar fashion, IQ tells us little to nothing about neural coding, feature selectivity, or functional modularity, for example. That is why very few neuroscientists ever mention the concept. But there are "markets" where IQ could be deemed valuable, perhaps in improving education or measuring trauma and so on, domains where low-resolution metrics can provide utility—assuming that they are not abused—a fact that dominates the history of this concept.

HARRIS: If plasticity and trainability ride atop innate variation, there will be differences in aptitude with and without training.

KRAKAUER: That's right. I think the open question for us is, How much of that innate Lego material—if you like—is universal? How many of those pieces were preassembled into little castles and cars that could then be built upon? How that takes place, and why some people arrive on the stage with an advantage, is actually not known. All I'm reporting is that the current data suggest that presumed innate constraints on intelligent functions are perhaps less real than we have previously thought. As I said, this does not mean that IQ is not stable. It simply means that it does not prevent training from achieving effects at odds with its predictions.

HARRIS: Which puts the onus on culture—and to an even greater degree than most people would expect. So let's discuss the machinery outside the human brain that may be, in a material sense, augmenting its intelligence.

KRAKAUER: Okay. We've basically understood what intelligence is, what stupidity is, and we understand that we're flexible to an extraordinary degree. Maybe not infinitely so, but the inputs then become much more important than we once thought. Now let's turn to intelligent—or what sometimes gets called cognitive—artifacts. Here's an example. Your mathematical ability is not something you were born with. You did not invent numbers, you did not invent geometry or topology or calculus or number theory—or anything else, for that matter. They were all given to you, if you chose to study mathematics in school. And what those things allow you to do is solve problems that others cannot.

Numbers are in some sense the lowest-hanging fruit in our mathematical education. So let's look at numbers. There are many number systems in the world. There are ancient Sumerian cuneiform numbers, about four thousand years old. There are ancient Egyptian numbers. And here is a good example of stupidity in culture: western Europe, for fifteen hundred years, used Roman numerals—from about the second century BC well into the fifteenth century AD. Roman numbers are good at measuring magnitude, the number of objects, but terrible for performing calculations. What's X + V? What's XII multiplied by IV? It just doesn't work, and yet for fifteen hundred years the human brain opted to deliberate over arithmetic operations using Roman numerals that don't work. The consequence was that for much of their history Europeans could not divide and multiply. It's extraordinary, because it's unbelievably stupid when you realize that in India and Arabia, they had a number system. It started in India and then moved to Arabia. It was available by the end of the fourth century AD, and that is the system we use today, which can effortlessly multiply and divide numbers.

That's a beautiful example of the interface between culture and our own reasoning. It's so intriguing because, once I've taught you a number system, like the Hindu-Arabic number system, a base-ten number system, you don't need the world anymore. You don't need paper anymore to write it down. You can do these operations in your mind's eye, and that's what makes them so fascinating. I call objects like that—which were invented over the course of centuries by many, many minds—*complementary cognitive artifacts*. Their unique characteristic is that not only do they augment your ability to reason in the form, for example, of multiplying and dividing, but when I take them away from you, you have in your mind a trace of their attributes that you can deploy. That's probably what's new in thinking about the evolution of cultural intelligence.

For a long time, psychologists, cognitive scientists, and archaeologists have understood that there are objects in the world that allow us to do things we couldn't do otherwise—a fork, a scythe, a wheel. But there is a special kind of object in the world that not only does what the fork and the scythe and the wheel do, but also changes the wiring of your brain so that you can build in your mind a virtual fork or a virtual scythe or a virtual wheel. That, I would claim, is a unique characteristic of human evolution.

HARRIS: Wouldn't you put language itself into this category?

KRAKAUER: Absolutely. The reason I separate them is that many people erroneously assumed, up until quite recently, that mathematical reasoning depended on linguistic reasoning and was, in fact, just a special form of it. This position has been very popular among practicing mathematicians, starting with Galileo, who wrote that "It is written in mathematical language, and its characters are triangles, circles and other geometric figures, without which it is impossible to humanly understand a word; without these one is wandering in a dark labyrinth." And extending into our modern epoch where the algebraic geometer Yuri Manin writes, "The basis of all human culture is language, and mathematics is a special kind of linguistic activity." These sound rather pithy and aphoristic but I am with Einstein in considering them insufficient.

We now know that both humans and nonhuman primates are capable of representing number equally well. In fact, when humans perform mathematics, they're using not the linguistic parts of their brain but the parts that represent number, which we share with nonhuman primates.

HARRIS: What else would you put on this list of complementary cognitive artifacts?

KRAKAUER: The other example I'm enamored of is the abacus. The abacus is a device for doing arithmetic in the world with our hands and eyes. But expert abacus users no longer have to use the physical abacus. They actually create a virtual abacus in the visual cortex. And that's particularly interesting, because a novice abacus user like me thinks about the operations of an abacus either verbally or in terms of our frontal cortex. But as you get better and better, the place in the brain where the abacus is represented shifts from language-like areas to visual, spatial areas. This is a beautiful example of an object in the world restructuring the brain to perform a task efficiently—in other words, by my definition, intelligently.

Maps are another fine example of a complementary cognitive artifact. Let's imagine we don't know how to get around a city. Over the course of centuries or decades, many people contribute to the drawing of an accurate map. But if you sit down and pore over it, you can memorize the whole thing. And you now have in your mind's eye what it took thousands of people many years to construct. You've changed the internal wiring of your brain, in a very real sense, to encode spatial relations that you could never have directly experienced. And then there are some mechanical instruments: as you become more and more familiar with an armillary sphere or an astrolabe or a sextant or a quadrant, you have to use it less and less. You build a kind of simulation in your brain of the physical object, and at some point you can dispense with the object altogether.

HARRIS: The other shoe finally drops. Tell us about the downside of all this cultural creativity.

KRAKAUER: There is another kind of cognitive artifact. Consider a mechanical calculator or a digital calculator on your computer. The presence of the device augments your intelligence. So you and your phone together are really smart, right? But if you take that device away, you're no better than you were before, and you are probably worse, because you may have forgotten how to do long division, because you're now dependent on your phone to do it for you.

Now, I'm not making a normative recommendation here. I'm not saying we should take people's phones away and force them to do long division. I'm simply pointing out the difference between artifacts. What I call *competitive cognitive artifacts* don't so much amplify human representational ability as replace it.

Another example is machine learning. We have an example in AlphaGo, a deep-learning neural network being trained to beat an extraordinary, ninth-dan Go player. That machine is basically opaque, even to its designers, and it *replaces* our ability to reason about the game, it doesn't augment it.

Another example is the automobile. This is one of my favorites, because automobiles clearly allow us to move very quickly over the surface of the Earth, and we are utterly dependent on them, especially in the Southwest. But if you took my car away, I would be no better than I was before and probably worse, because I would be physically unfit to travel under my own power, because of how accustomed I'd been to sitting in the car. Moreover, it's a dangerous artifact, because it kills so many people. So the car is a beautiful example of a competitive artifact that we have accepted because its utility value is so high, even though it compromises our ability to function without it.

I think the world can be divided into these two kinds of cultural objects. And the question, of course, is, Can we depend on these objects always being around? In the case of competitive cognitive artifacts, if we cannot, then we should worry, right? Because when they're taken away, we'll probably be worse off than we were before.

HARRIS: The car is an interesting example, because it's about to become even more competitive, once autonomous vehicles become widely available. You can easily envision a time when self-driving cars will be the norm, because they'll be so much safer than ape-driven cars, and yet that will almost certainly usher in a time when people's driving skills will have deteriorated almost to the point of nonexistence. We won't be able to take over the controls in any competent way once we've lived in the presence of this technology for a generation.

KRAKAUER: That's right, and it's interesting, because the driverless car does several things at once. It eliminates the legs and it eliminates our mapmaking ability. So it assaults two capacities at once. This is where I've been somewhat frustrated by all the AI doom and gloom, because the argument playing out in tech circles is, Will we create a machine that will turn around and say, "You expend too much energy. You have a disrespect for the environment. I'm going to turn you into a battery"? It's the Matrix nightmare. Whereas the real discussion we should be having is about what to do with competitive cognitive artifacts, which are *already* altering our brains in arguably negative ways. When I have a discussion with somebody about this topic, as a rule the only answer they have—and it's totally reasonable—is that these things aren't going away.

But something else hasn't been mentioned here, and this has to do with the complex system of the brain and the domino-like effect and interconnectedness of representation systems. For example, it's been known for a long time that if you become competent at the abacus, you're not just competent at arithmetic. That competency has interesting indirect effects on linguistic competence and geometric reasoning. It doesn't have a firewall around it such that its functional advantages are confined to arithmetic. In fact, I think that's true of all interesting complementary cognitive artifacts.

If I give you a fork or chopsticks or a knife, you're better able to manipulate and eat your food, but you also develop dexterity, and that dexterity can be generalized to new instances. For me, the main concern is not only that the world will go south and we'll no longer have highways and cars. I also worry about the indirect, diffusive effect of eliminating a complementary cognitive artifact like a map on other characteristics we have. Your familiarity with mapmaking and topographical, topological, geometric reasoning is generally valuable in your life, not just in navigating across the city. So taking away a map doesn't just make you worse at getting from one door to another, it makes you worse in other ways. This is where the debate needs to be.

HARRIS: I'm not very close to this research, but I know that many learning experts believe that cursive writing is important to learn even though we're living in an increasingly typewritten world—which will soon be replaced by a speech-recognition world—because cursive writing is intimately connected with the acquisition of literacy. The pace at which one writes cursively seems to be important. And the physical linking of letters is related to learning to read well.

KRAKAUER: Einstein and Frank Lloyd Wright, early in their youth, both liked playing with wooden building blocks and would construct worlds out of them—like people do today with Minecraft. And both of them claimed—Wright in the case of architecture and Einstein in the case of the geometry of the universe—that the intuitions they built up playing with these blocks were instrumental in their later lives. I would claim the same is true for maps. If you know how to navigate through a physical space, like a Euclidean space or a curved space on the Earth's surface, that allows you to think about different kinds of spaces—relationship spaces, idea spaces. The notion of a path from one idea to another, as a metaphor, actually has an immediate and natural implementation in terms of a path in real space. You can see immediately how these aptitudes are of broader value.

HARRIS: You just said a moment ago that you weren't making any normative claims, but the norms come flooding in once you begin talking about the possible changes in our cognition, and perhaps even in our ethics, as we begin altering the cultural landscape with competitive as opposed to complementary technology. So let's talk about the kind of normative claims one might want to make here.

Most of us want to maximize our ability to get what we want out of life. And if we were convinced that some technology was diminishing our ability to do this, or producing a spectrum of negative effects we hadn't considered, once this came to our attention we might want to make a change. There are also collective norms: some societies are capable of a certain kind of creativity or cooperation while others are not. Some societies are in a perpetual state of self-sabotage or civil war. How do you think about individual and collective norms in this context?

KRAKAUER: It's tricky. I do agree that there are, in some domains, better ways of being. I'll give you an example from writing code for computers. Imagine that we still had to write with punch cards—there would be no word processor. The idea of taking a typewriter and connecting it to a computer was an extraordinary invention. Well, let's go a little further. Let's imagine that you could only interact with the computer using machine code or binary. There would be no software as we understand it today, because the projects would always be modest in scale. The evolution of computer languages that allowed us to efficiently write code for machines was extraordinary and is responsible for the world we live in today, including DeepMind and AlphaGo, and so on.

So there are "better" ways of interacting with the world; having a sharp edge is better than not having a sharp edge. But where things get tricky normatively is when you start talking about refined cultural artifacts and objects. I know that an interest of yours is different ways of reasoning: religious, scientific, mathematical, poetical, and so on. Is there a sense in which a certain culture has discovered a more efficient way of interacting with physical and cultural reality? I think we know domains where the answer is yes. Having mathematics is better than not having it. There are certain things that we can do—like navigate and send things to the moon—when we have it.

Not many people think this way about the interaction between brain plasticity and the cultural accumulation of cognitive artifacts—especially in relation to collective intelligence and collective stupidity. Collective stupidity consists of rule systems you've accumulated in the brain, systems that you thought you didn't need, and you didn't, but other people think you do—systems that oblige you to interact with the world in a worse way than you did before. That happens a lot, as we both know.

So this is a brave new frontier. In fact, one project at the Santa Fe Institute is called the Law of the Legal Operating System of Society. Constitutions are a good example of a memory system that encodes historical contingencies and our responses to them that resulted in positive outcomes. We currently have five hundred ninety legal operating systems—constitutions from around the world. We can ask, When do they work? When do they fail? What were their cultural implications? Which ones are more likely to lead to despotism? Which are less likely? These questions need to be addressed.

HARRIS: I wonder if there's a relationship between complexity and intellectual honesty. One difference between religious dogmatism and scientific curiosity is the boundedness of the worldview that results and one's consequent tolerance of ambiguity and complexity. For a dogmatist, the final answers are already given. Reality can't be more complex than what's spelled out in his favorite book. But for a scientist, or for any truly curious person, the investigation of reality is open-ended. Who knows what we will learn in the future, and who knows how it may supersede our current understanding?

When I think about the differences between cultures, I often notice the specific details that more or less tell you everything you need to know about the fundamental differences in question. I'm a father of two daughters. And when I think about the life I want them to have, and I compare this to the general attitude toward women and girls in traditional Muslim cultures—groups like the Taliban and the Islamic State being the ultimate instances—that difference signifies so many other ways in which our worldviews are irreconcilable.

Take the most excruciating case: honor killing. A girl gets raped, or refuses to marry some old man her father picked for her, or simply wants to get an education—and she is then murdered by a male family member because she is believed to have "dishonored" the family. I'm not referring to the actions of a lone psychopath. I'm talking about someone who is psychologically normal but who was raised in a culture that reinforces behavior that only an actual psychopath could support in a culture. We like our own. This single difference, the treatment of women and girls, tells us almost everything we need to know about the difference between two cultures—intellectually and ethically. We know a lot about what a society is *not* going to accomplish if it keeps half its population illiterate and living in cloth bags.

KRAKAUER: The cultures you describe are intriguing instances of the persistence of rule systems whose outcomes we would unhesitatingly describe as stupid—certainly in relation to the treatment of human beings. That is for me a genuine scientific problem. I know, as you do, that many people in those societies are deeply unhappy. These rule systems are imposed upon them. So why are they so persistent? By the way, in Western society, let's be clear, women didn't have the vote until the early twentieth century. But we realized the error of our ways. And racist ideologies persist in this country, with devastating consequences for many people.

Moreover, such rule systems leave an imprint on your reasoning in a very tangible form. If you encode a cultural form that is hateful or intolerant, it leaves, just like the abacus, an imprint on how you reason, on how you think about the world. We might ask, What distinguishes a scientist from someone who has an orthodoxy? I guess it's enshrined in Richard Feynman's definition of a scientist as someone who has a fundamental distrust of experts. My feeling is that we should address these things with a pedagogical schema that allows people to live with uncertainty—and makes them happy about it, rather than unhappy about it. Reassurance should come in the form of possibility, not the lack of it. That's a deeper issue, and I think it's where our education of students is failing. Because it's targeting symptoms, whereas what you're talking about is how we come to terms with the fact that there is no divine purpose, only a plurality of human purposes. Our solar system is a dense bit of matter in an otherwise sparse universe. Our planet abounds with life among planets that are lifeless. Do you delight in the fact of our good fortune, or are you horrified by it? That sort of question is what inclines people toward either science or orthodoxies. Science is inspired by that sentiment encoded in the haiku by Basho: "One insect asleep on a leaf can save your life."

HARRIS: How do you view the future of civilization in light of our basic uncertainty, as well as this schismatic, cultural response to uncertainty itself? Obviously there's the chance that we'll destroy ourselves or that our global civilization will fail. But it's also possible that we'll engineer everything that's wrong with us out of existence and eventually export an unimaginably advanced culture to the rest of the galaxy. Most people seem to feel we're passing through some kind of bottleneck now and that this century is more crucial than most. Do you feel that way?

KRAKAUER: I do, and I don't. There are clearly characteristics of the twentieth century that historically, with respect to our own species, were unprecedented. Population growth happened in the past few decades, right? Computer technology, as we understand it, happened in the past few decades. Medicine that works according to scientific principles, as opposed to trial and error, is very new. Hygiene and an understanding of the implications of biological evolution in terms of the ethical treatment of each other and of nonhuman animals is new, and so on. So it was an incredible century in many ways. But in other ways it wasn't all that incredible. You could argue that the first time we committed our internal representation of the world to cuneiform lettering on clay tablets was a greater event in human history, with greater implications moving forward. There are times in history when extraordinary things have happened. It's hard to apportion differential weight to them.

HARRIS: You certainly can defend the claim that writing was the breakthrough that enabled most of the others that we deem important. But what you don't have with the birth of writing is a technology that gives a single state, or even a single individual, the power to destroy the species.

KRAKAUER: A lot of these arguments are quantitative, not qualitative, right? Gunpowder was extraordinarily important. Machine guns as opposed to the cavalry, as we saw in the devastation of the First World War. Do we ignore past revolutionary transitions in human warfare because they don't involve atomic or biological weaponry? Still, it's true that extraordinary things are happening. Not least, I think, the possibility in our lifetimes of the demise of the nation-state.

The kinds of social networks that are the prequels to territories and ultimately nations are different now, and the possibility of a true reconfiguration of terrestrial social systems is really intriguing. For many people who live on Facebook or in computer games, that has effectively already happened. It hasn't happened in the tax system or in terms of electoral responsibilities. But it's happened in terms of how some people live. With respect to pessimism versus optimism, I believe in intelligence, and I believe in reason, and I believe in civilized discourse. I'm frightened by unconditional optimism and unconditional pessimism. And the extremes of politically correct and politically incorrect are both equally apparent, right? The middle ground has always seemed lukewarm and uninspiring—but that's exactly the bath I want to sit in. And somehow if we are aware of the distinctions—complementary, competitive—and the effects they have on our biological ability to reason, then we should be able to think about our devices as a community of civilized people, and make decisions.

One of my great fears has been what I see as a systematic erosion of human free will. And not "free will" as in "Is it possible in a deterministic universe?" but the moral implications of free will. Free will is only as good as its empirical execution. That is, when you get a chance to exercise it. Having free will doesn't matter if you can't exercise it. So if the Islamic State came to power, your free will wouldn't matter, because they would deny you the ability to exercise it. But we are voluntarily choosing not to exercise it.

A few examples: "Netflix, what movie should I watch?" "Well, David, you watched these movies, so you should watch this one." "Amazon, what book should I read?" "Well, people just like you read books just like this." What this is doing, if you think about it geometrically, is contracting the volume of my free choice—under the economic pretense, in some sense, of assisting me to choose. True, I could say no. But it gets harder and harder. Suppose I wrote an app, let's call it a voter app. What you'd do is enter into this app your economic circumstances, where you live, your history of interest in politics, and it would tell you, better than you ever could, whom you should vote for. And let's imagine the equivalent medical app—a sort of Apple Watch version four. It would measure everything about your body that could be measured, and it would say, when you go to a restaurant, "No, you shouldn't be eating an aubergine tonight. It's time for a chicken sandwich." Over the next decade, more and more decisions will be outsourced in this competitive form, such that what remains will be a tiny particle of freedom.

HARRIS: I must say, I don't see those examples so much in terms of freedom. It's funny that you bring up free will, because I spend a lot of time arguing that it's an incoherent idea. Obviously there are differences between voluntary and involuntary actions, and not a lot changes when you get rid of the notion of free will. But a few things do change. Free will aside, I don't see those examples as a diminution in our freedom. There's certainly a siloing effect here. We're creating machinery that curates the available choices so as to reliably give us choices that we prefer. Is that so bad?

KRAKAUER: Let me give you another example. I'm a Western male; you're a Western male. You're probably wearing trousers and a shirt. The sartorial options available to you are extraordinarily small in comparison with world culture. And historically, how we have chosen to adorn ourselves in Persia or the Roman Empire, or China, has been diverse and fascinating. Yet now, as Western men, we all look like clones. I would claim you're not exercising your judgment, you're being told how to dress. And when you get to exercise your judgment, it's a very low-dimensional space, in terms of texture and color, that the manufacturers of clothing, purely for economic efficiency, have decided to give you. That's what I'm thinking about. You could do your own version of modern civil disobedience and say "No." But it's very hard for people.

What I'm concerned about is not inevitable, it's not deterministic. But unless we choose to assert our individuality and our constructive differences, we will, inevitably, become a clone species—not only in terms of the way we look and dress, but in the way we reason. You asked me about my dystopian singularity—that's it. The optimistic future is the one where we say, "Enough. No more conformity, no more overcuration of what you think I should do and think." There could be a radical accession of diversity, a radical individuality that we somehow reconcile with a constructive communitarian drive. I don't think we've done that very well historically. How can we be as different as we can be but still be congenial with one another? That is a positive future for me, but I think that's the path of great labor.

HARRIS: I certainly take your point on dress. It never occurs to me to even want to wear a kilt or something other than pants and a shirt. In fact, I've embraced these limitations further than most people: I've decided to not even think about what I'm going to wear, so I basically have a uniform. I'm the canary in the coal mine, sartorially speaking. As for the Netflix or Amazon cases: twenty years ago, you'd walk into a video store or a bookstore and just wander the aisles—we can leave film reviews and book reviews aside, because that's another curation process—and you'd find specific titles or artwork alluring. Things would jump out at you, but it was largely a matter of happenstance. And there wasn't much available information that could promote any one among the thousands or tens of thousands of candidates for watching or reading.

Now, based on your reading or film-watching history, based on what millions of people very much like you have rated as enjoyable, you're getting specific recommendations. I do see a danger here, in getting ghettoized intellectually and ethically. This is happening online for most people who choose to follow others on social media whom they already agree with. We get channelized, and the channel walls are getting higher and higher. But it doesn't strike me as a problem generically.

KRAKAUER: Let me be clear: I'm not a Pollyanna about the past. I'm saying something slightly different, which is that the tools we now possess should be according us unprecedented freedoms, not returning us to the ghettos of the past. So I'm with you. I'm not saying the past is great. I'm simply saying that if you develop a technology that could give you incredible freedom, why not use it to do that? What's intriguing about the history of technologies is that every new one that offers some increment of possibility comes with the greater possibility of its own negation. The bookstore example is a good one. We were limited by our access to good bookstores. Amazon is a godsend with respect to access to books when you live in remote parts of the world. But what comes with it is this all-seeing eye that wants to impose, out of largely economic considerations, constraints on what you do. And it's our job to maintain the freedom of the technology. That's all I'm saying. Let's fight the instinct of the technology to treat us as a nuisance in a machine-learning algorithm that wants to be able to predict us perfectly, and let's surprise it constantly.

HARRIS: Taking a wider view now: How do you think about the prospects of there being advanced intelligence elsewhere in the universe? Do you have an opinion about the Fermi paradox—as in, "Where is everybody?"

KRAKAUER: We could talk about that at great length. Statistically, it's a real problem, because any well-informed statistical model has to have multiple independent instances for you to make an inference. The problem in our case is that there's only one. So you can't reason about this question statistically. But you can reason about it in terms of physical law and evolutionary dynamics. Physical law, to the extent we can measure it, is the same everywhere in the universe. And to the extent that biological mechanisms are emerging from physical law, there's nothing particularly special about Earth. By that kind of reasoning, based on mechanics, I think we have every reason to expect that intelligent life exists elsewhere. But you can't reason from the statistics, and that often leads to fruitless discussion. Regardless, though, of whether or not there is intelligent life in the universe beyond our own planet, we have an intellectual obligation to populate it. That's where I stand on the matter. If I have any kind of quasi-mythical belief system, it's something to do with expanding the sphere of reason and sympathy into the world and beyond. If we could take the best of what we've done and send it out into the universe, that would be an extraordinary thing.

HARRIS: That statement—that we have an ethical obligation to populate the galaxy—is an interesting one, which I think will strike many people as terribly nonobvious. What are our ethical obligations to people who don't exist? We know at a minimum that we have intelligent life on this planet that can enjoy a range of conscious states that can be beautiful and fulfilling. And we may yet do something that cancels the future of our species. If anything can be wrong, ethically speaking, that would be wrong. I don't mean it's wrong in the sense that we'd be causing ourselves or anyone else to suffer. We could kill ourselves painlessly in our sleep tonight, and there would be no attendant suffering or bereavement, but we'd be foreclosing on potentially billions of years of happiness and creativity of a sort we can't yet imagine. And that would be a terrible thing to do.

I should say that people's moral intuitions differ on this point. Some moral philosophers think that closing the door to the future experiences of people who will never exist has no ethical implications whatsoever. It seems reasonable to expect, however, that people will continue to exist for quite some time—and that we have an ethical obligation to leave our descendants a world that is compatible with human happiness. It would be great to have a technology or an artifact—a moral abacus—that helps us internalize a commitment to future generations, because we're really bad at solving problems that have a time horizon longer than our own near future—problems like climate change. We discount the pain of future generations so steeply that we can't prioritize a centuries-long problem at all, no matter how grave it seems. If we could somehow make a commitment to our descendants more reflexive and vivid, more emotionally and ethically salient, and truly internalize it—I think that's one thing we desperately need. I don't know what it would look like, but your abacus example, combined with your claim that it would be ethically problematic not to venture out into space, made me think of this.

KRAKAUER: One reason so many of us are drawn to evolutionary thinking, to the ideas of Lyell and Darwin and Wallace, is that they give us a sense of what time can do. For me it's extraordinary that over the course of billions of years, we've gone from a planet that looked like the surface of Venus, perhaps—and now it's the Rolling Stones and Johann Sebastian Bach and Emily Dickinson. I think, as you say, that delicate, rare things should be preserved. And developing a tangible ethics for that is really vital.

HARRIS: What's your view of changing the species in ways more deliberate than the mere happenstance of evolution? I'm talking about genetically engineering changes into the germ line—presumably after we understand our genetics well enough to do this wisely.

KRAKAUER: Well, first of all, I believe it's already happened. It happened with writing, and it happened with mathematics. I've already asserted that culture is a kind of collective inception event into the brain. We've been modifying ourselves forever, with nutrition or with exercise or with society. So the question is whether or not this tinkering with the genome will represent a radical discontinuity in the styles of intervention.

Let me be clear: we are going to continue to modify ourselves, and if, for example, a pandemic emerged with a virus that had a morbidity rate of 80 percent and someone had invented a CRISPR system to render you immune which required a change in the genome of each cell in your body, it would be adopted. Not only would it be adopted, it would probably be made obligatory. And that's not really all that far-fetched.

Such things will happen, and some of them will be extraordinary. We'll probably be able to eliminate certain forms of cancer. We will modify ourselves willingly and, I think, appropriately. The debate will persist, just as it persists in the case of enhancement in sport: Where to draw the line? And that comes down to a question of the ethics of fairness.

I view the march of technology as inevitable, but I'd like it to be accompanied by reason. And one form of reasoning that's useful in these debates is to find precedents. When people talk about CRISPR, which is currently the most powerful genetic engineering technology, it's worth recalling all the things we've done already to change genetics, either naturally or unnaturally, and what we've done to our microbiome—which is a part of our genome, by the way—in our diets and biochemically. If at some point we were to colonize other planets, and those other planets had different masses such that the effect of gravity was greater or lower, they had slightly different compositions of gaseous molecules in their atmosphere, we would quite willingly reengineer ourselves. I think that's inevitable.

HARRIS: Thank you for your time today, David. It's been fascinating speaking with you. I'm off to buy an abacus and a kilt.

Our Future

A CONVERSATION WITH MAX TEGMARK

Max Tegmark is a professor of physics at the Massachusetts Institute of Technology and the cofounder of the Future of Life Institute. He is the author of *Our Mathematical Universe* and *Life 3.0*, two books that we discuss at length.

Tegmark is known as "Mad Max" for his unorthodox ideas and passion for adventure. His scientific interests range from precision cosmology to the ultimate nature of reality. He is an increasingly influential voice on the topic of artificial intelligence, because his Future of Life Institute deals with this issue as well as many other potential existential threats.

This chapter, the final in *Making Sense*, features two of our conversations that focus on the future of humanity. We discuss the foundations of science (and what distinguishes science from nonscience), the mysterious utility of mathematics in the natural sciences, the substrate independence of minds, the distinction between consciousness and intelligence, the implications that space might be infinite, the various forms of "multiverse," and the dangers posed by the advances we are making in artificial intelligence.

HARRIS: Max, I have a lot I want to discuss, including your book *Our Mathematical Universe*. I consider it a huge achievement, and our conversation will by no means exhaust its contents. You've written an up-to-the-minute account of the state of physics—and cosmology, in particular—that is accessible to the general reader. That's not something that many of your colleagues have achieved. So congratulations on that.

TEGMARK: Thanks for your kind words. It's important to remember that if after reading my book you feel you don't understand quite everything about our cosmos, well, nobody else does either. And in fact that's very much part of the charm of studying the cosmos—that we still have these mysteries to ponder.

HARRIS: And we'll dive directly into those mysteries, but first some context. You and I met in 2015 in San Juan, Puerto Rico, at a conference you helped organize on the frontiers of artificial intelligence research—in particular, emerging safety concerns. I hope we'll get to that, because our shared interest is in AI. But I do want to talk first about physics, and then we can discuss the armies of lethal robots that may await us.

TEGMARK: It seems clear to me that we also share a strong interest in looking at reality out there and wondering what its true nature is.

HARRIS: Let's start there, at the foundations of science, where we're making our best effort to arrive at a unified understanding of reality. Many people, especially in humanities departments, think no such understanding is possible—that no view of the world can encompass subatomic particles and cocktail parties and everything in between. But this is incorrect from the point of view of science. We may use different concepts at different scales in our understanding of reality, but there aren't radical discontinuities between the scales. I trust this is also your intuition.

TEGMARK: Yes. When someone says they think reality is just a social construct, a scientist might say, "If you think gravity is a social con-

struct, I encourage you to step out my window here on the sixth floor."
If you drill down into this conflict, you see that they're using the r-
word, reality, in two different ways. As a physicist, the way I use the
word "reality" is that I assume there's something out there independent
of me. I assume the Andromeda galaxy would continue existing even if
I weren't here, for example. The scientist says, very humbly, "Okay, if
there's some stuff that exists out there—physical reality, let's call it—
let's look at it as closely as we can and try to figure out what properties
it has." If there's confusion about it, that's our problem and not reality's problem.

I've no doubt that our universe knows perfectly well what it's doing.
We physicists have so far failed to figure out exactly what that is. We're
in this schizophrenic situation where we can't even make quantum mechanics talk properly to relativity theory. But I see this simply as failure
in our own creativity. Not only do I believe in a reality out there and
independent of us, but I feel it's arrogant to say the opposite.

HARRIS: Right.

TEGMARK: Solipsists say there's no reality except themselves. Ostriches
assume that things they don't see don't exist. But even respected scientists sometimes go down this slippery slope. Niels Bohr, one of the
founders of quantum mechanics, said there was no reality without observation, which puts humans center stage and denies that there can be
anything you'd call "reality" without us. But I think that's arrogant. We
could use a good dose of humility. So my starting point is, there's something out there, and let's try to figure out how it works.

HARRIS: This skepticism about the possibility of understanding reality
sneaks in the back door, somewhat paradoxically, if we take science—in
particular, evolutionary biology—seriously.

This is something you and I talked about when we last met. At one
point I remarked, as almost everyone has who thinks about evolution,
that our cognitive capacities—our common sense, our intuitions about
cause and effect, et cetera—haven't evolved to equip us to understand

reality at the smallest or largest scales, or when things are moving extremely fast, or when they're very old. Our intuitions are tuned for things at the human scale, so that we can decide whether we can mate with them or eat them, or whether they're going to eat us. It's therefore no surprise that scientific interpretations, particularly in your area of science, are deeply counterintuitive.

TEGMARK: That's right.

HARRIS: You did me one better, however. You said that not only is it not surprising, but it would be surprising—and, in fact, give us reason to mistrust our theories—if they *were* aligned with common sense. We should expect the answers at the back of the Book of Nature to be deeply counterintuitive. Can you expand on that?

TEGMARK: That's exactly right, and a clear prediction of Darwin's ideas—that whatever the ultimate nature of reality is, it should seem weird and counterintuitive to us. If some cavewoman spent too much time pondering what was out there beyond all the stars, she might not have noticed the tiger that snuck up behind her and she would have gotten cleaned out of the gene pool. In evolution, developing a brain advanced enough to understand ultimate concepts is costly.

This isn't just a logical prediction, it's a testable prediction. Look at what's happened since Darwin's death, as we've used technology to probe things beyond what we experience with our senses. The prediction is that whenever we, with technology, study physics that was inaccessible to our ancestors, what we find will seem weird. Look at the scorecard. We studied what happens when things go much faster than our ancestors could imagine, near the speed of light, and discovered that time slows down. Einstein didn't get the Nobel Prize for that, because my curmudgeonly Swedish countrymen on the Nobel committee thought it was too weird. And when things are really, really large, you get black holes, which were also considered weird. Again, it took a long time for people to accept them. And then you look at what happens with things really small, so small that our ancestors couldn't see them. And you find that elementary particles can be in several places at once. Extremely counterintuitive to the point that people, even though they all concede that particles really can do this weird stuff, still argue about what it means. And the list goes on.

So I think the verdict is in. Whatever the actual nature of reality, it's going to seem really strange to us. If we dismiss physical theories just because they're counterintuitive, we'll almost certainly dismiss the correct theory once someone comes up with it.

HARRIS: I'm wondering, though, whether this slippery slope is more slippery than we're admitting. How do we resist the slide into total epistemological skepticism? For instance, why trust our mathematical intuitions, or the mathematical concepts born of them, or the picture of physical reality we arrive at through this bootstrapping of counterintuitiveness?

I understand why we should trust these constructs pragmatically: they work. We can build airplanes that fly, and there's a difference between an airplane that flies and one that doesn't. But as a matter of epistemology, why should we trust the picture of reality that math reveals to us—if, once again, we're just apes using the cognitive capacities that evolved within constraints that kept them pegged to everyday reality? After all, mathematics—insofar as we apprehend it, discover it, invent it—is just an extension of those humble capacities.

TEGMARK: That's a good question. People tell me sometimes that the theories physicists discuss at conferences, from black holes to parallel universes, sound even crazier than the ancient myths about flame-breathing dragons and whatnot. Shouldn't we dismiss the physics just as we dismiss these myths?

To me there's a huge difference in that these theories, even though they sound crazy, make predictions we can test. That's really the crux of it. If you take quantum theory seriously, for example, and assume that particles can be in several places at once, then you predict that you should be able to build this thing called a transistor or this thing called a cell phone and they'll actually work. Good luck getting any useful technology from the fire-breathing-dragon hypothesis. That is where we should draw the border between what's science and what's not. Some people think the line should be drawn between that which seems intuitive and not crazy and that which seems crazy. I'm arguing against that. Black holes seemed crazy at the time, and now we've found loads of them. To me, the line in the sand that divides science from what's not science is the way I think about it. What makes me a scientist is that I'd much rather have questions I can't answer than answers I can't question.

HARRIS: What you're emphasizing is that the distinction between science and nonscience isn't in the strangeness of one's conclusions but in the methodology by which those conclusions were arrived at. I'm not sure you'd say that a narrow, Popperian conception of science—that is, the primacy of falsifiable claims—subsumes all of science. As a practical matter, there are scientifically coherent things we could say about the nature of reality that aren't falsifiable. We know there's an answer there, and we know that no one *has* the answer. The example I often use is, How many birds are in flight over the surface of the Earth at this moment? We don't know. In fact, we know we'll never know, because the answer changed before I could get to the end of that sentence. But it was a coherent question to ask, and we know it has an integer answer.

I think you say, at some point in your book, that a theory doesn't have to be testable across the board, just parts of it, to give some level of credence to its overall picture. Is that how you view it?

TEGMARK: I'm pretty sympathetic to Popper. The idea of falsifiability works fine, even for these crazy-sounding concepts like parallel universes and black holes, as long as we remember that what we test are the theories—specific mathematical theories that we can write down. Parallel universes are not a theory, they're a prediction from certain theories. A black hole isn't a theory either; it's a prediction from Einstein's general relativity theory. And once you have a theory in physics, it's testable as long as it predicts at least one thing you can check. Because then you check that thing and, if it's wrong, falsify the theory. Whereas just because a theory happens to make other predictions that you can never test, that doesn't make it nonscientific.

HARRIS: That's a much better construal of Popper. We falsify theories, not all the conceivable predictions derived from them.

TEGMARK: Black holes, for example. The theory of general relativity predicts exactly what will happen to you if you fall into the monster black hole in the middle of our galaxy, which weighs four million times as much as the sun. It predicts exactly when you'll get spaghettified and how, and so on. Except you can never actually do that experiment and then write an article about it because you're inside the event horizon and the information can't come out.

Nonetheless, that's a testable theory. Because general relativity also predicts loads of other things, such as how your GPS works, which we can test with great precision. And when the theory passes a lot of tests for things we can observe, and we start to take the theory seriously, then I feel we have to be honest and also take seriously the other predictions from the theory, whether we like them or not. We can't just cherry-pick and say, "Hey, I love what the theory of general relativity does for GPS and the bending of light and the weird orbit of Mercury and so on—but I don't really like the black holes, so I'm going to opt out of that prediction." That you cannot do. In physics, once you buy the theory, you have to buy the whole product. And if you don't like one of its predictions, then you have to try coming up with a different mathematical theory that doesn't have that prediction but still explains everything else. And that's often hard to do.

People have tried for a hundred years to do that with Einstein's gravity theory, to get rid of the black holes, and so far they've pretty much failed. That's why they've been dragged kicking and screaming into believing in black holes, or at least taking them seriously.

The same applies to parallel universes.

HARRIS: We're going to get to parallel universes, because that seems to be where our intuitions break down entirely. But before we go there, I want to linger on this question about the primacy and strange utility of mathematics. At one point in your book, you mention the oft-cited paper Eugene Wigner wrote in the 1960s called "The Unreasonable Effectiveness of Mathematics in the Natural Sciences." A mysterious property of these abstract mathematical structures and chains of reasoning is that they seem uniquely useful for describing the physical world and making predictions about things you'd never anticipate but for the fact that the mathematics suggests they should exist.

TEGMARK: That's right.

HARRIS: The belief that mathematical concepts have independent existence—that they are truly discovered, not made—has lured many scientists into mysticism, or philosophical Platonism, and sometimes even religion. I'm wondering if you share some form of mathematical idealism.

I also wanted to get your reaction to an idea that I got from a cognitive scientist, Kenneth Craik, who published a book in 1943 in which he anticipates Wigner by almost twenty years. In passing, he tried to resolve this mystery about the strange utility of mathematics. He speculated that there must be some isomorphism between brain processes that represent the physical world and processes in the world—and that this might account for the utility of mathematical concepts. I recall he asked something like, "Is it really so surprising that certain patterns of neurophysiological activity—which are in fact what mathematical concepts are, at the level of the human brain—can be mapped onto the world?" Perhaps there's some kind of sameness of structure or homology there. Is that a step toward resolving this mystery for you, or do you think it exceeds that?

TEGMARK: That's an interesting argument—the argument that our brain adapts to the world and therefore has the world model inside it.

HARRIS: Our brains are just a part of the world. There are processes in the world that have a similar structure to brain processes, and this allows for our mathematical intuitions.

TEGMARK: I agree with the first part of the argument and disagree with the second part. I agree that it's natural that there will be things in the brain that are similar to what's happening in the world, precisely because the brain has evolved to have a good world model. But I disagree that this fully answers Wigner's question about the mysterious effectiveness of mathematics. Because the claim Craik made—that certain brain processes are effectively what mathematics *is*—is one that most mathematicians I know would violently disagree with. They don't think that math has anything to do with brain processes at all.

HARRIS: Clearly, our experience of doing math—our grasp of a mathematical concept or not; our memory of the multiplication table; our ability to do basic algebra—all of that, in every instance of its being realized, is realized as a state of our brain. You're not disputing that?

TEGMARK: Absolutely not. I'm just quibbling about what mathematics is.

What's your definition of mathematics? I think it's interesting to take a step back and ask, "What do mathematicians generally define math as?" Because if you ask people on the street—like my mom, for example—they often view math as just a bag of tricks for manipulating numbers, or maybe as a form of torture invented by sadistic schoolteachers to ruin our self-confidence. Whereas mathematicians talk about mathematical structures and studying their properties. For example, I have a colleague, David Vogan, at MIT, who has spent ten years of his life studying a mathematical structure called E8. Never mind what it is. But he has a poster of it on the wall of his office. If I suggested to him that that thing on his wall is just something he made up, that he invented it, he would be very offended. He feels he *discovered* it. That it was out there, and he discovered it and mapped its properties, in the same way we discovered the planet Neptune and then went on to study its properties. Look at something more familiar than E8: the counting numbers—one, two, three, four, five, et cetera. The fact that two plus two is four, and four plus two is six. Most mathematicians would argue that this mathematical structure we call the natural numbers is not a structure we invented, or invented properties of, but rather one that we discovered the properties of. It's been discovered multiple times independently, in different cultures. In each culture, people invented, rather than discovered, a different language for describing it.

In English you say one, two, three, four, five. In Swedish, the language I grew up with, you say *ett*, *två*, *tre*, *fyra*, *fem*. They're two equivalent descriptions of exactly the same structure. What we invent are the names and symbols. The symbols used to write the numbers two and three in the Western world are different from those used in India today, or in the Roman Empire. But again, you see that there's still only one structure, which we discover, and then we invent the symbols and the languages.

For example, Plato was fascinated by the regular geometric shapes that bear his name: Platonic solids. He discovered that there were five of them—the cube, the octahedron, the tetrahedron, the icosahedron, and the dodecahedron. He chose to invent the name "dodecahedron." He could have called it "schmodecahedron," or something else. That was his prerogative—to invent names, the language for describing them. But he was *not* free to invent a sixth Platonic solid because it just doesn't exist. It's in that sense that Plato felt that those solids exist out there and are discovered rather than invented. Does that make sense?

HARRIS: Yes, I certainly agree with that. What's the next prime number above the highest one we know? That number will be discovered rather than invented. So it's not wrong to call that a matter of pure discovery, more or less analogous, as you said, to finding Neptune when you didn't know it existed. But I don't think you have to deny that mathematics is a landscape of possible discovery that exceeds our understanding to accept that in every instance of mathematical insight, every prime number being thought about or located—every one of those moments is a moment of a brain doing its mathematical work.

TEGMARK: Right. Or a computer, sometimes. Because we have an increasingly large number of proofs now done by machines. And discoveries also.

HARRIS: Yes. We're still talking about physical systems that can play this game of discovery in the mathematical landscape, which exists, in some sense, whether or not there's anyone to do the discovering. But the fundamental mystery is, *Why* should mathematics be so useful for describing the physical world?

TEGMARK: Exactly.

HARRIS: Would it remove some of the mystery if there were certain physical processes in brains—and in computers and other intelligent systems, wherever they are—that mirror this landscape of potential discovery? Does that remove what otherwise seems spooky—the mystery that abstract, idealized concepts fit the physical universe and seem to anticipate its structure?

TEGMARK: That's a great question. The answer you get to that question will depend on whom you ask. There are very, very smart and respectable people who hold views across a wide spectrum on this question. In my book I chose to explore the spectrum of opinions. Some people will say, "There is no mystery. Math is sometimes useful in nature, sometimes it's not. That's it. There's nothing mysterious about it. Go away."

If you move more toward the Platonic side, you'll find a lot of people saying things like, "Well, it seems a lot of things in our universe are approximated by math, and that's great. But they're not *perfectly* described by math." And then you have some very optimistic physicists, like Einstein and a lot of string theorists, who think there's some math we haven't discovered yet which doesn't just approximate our physical world but describes it exactly and is the perfect description.

And then, finally, there is the most extreme position on the Platonic side, which I explore at length in my book and which is the one I'm personally banking on: not only is our world described by mathematics, but it *is* mathematics, in the sense that the two are really the same. We've talked about how in the physical world we discover new entities and then invent language to describe them. Similarly, in mathematics, we discover new entities, like new prime numbers, like Platonic solids, and we invent names for them. Maybe this mathematical reality and the physical reality are actually one and the same. When you first hear that, it sounds completely Looney Tunes. It's equivalent to saying that the physical world doesn't just have some mathematical properties, it *only* has mathematical properties.

That sounds really dumb when you look at your wife and child and think, "This doesn't look like a bunch of numbers." When I met Annaka, your wife, for the first time, of course she has all these properties that don't strike me as mathematical.

HARRIS: Don't tell me you were noticing my wife's mathematical properties!

TEGMARK: Because I'm a physicist, I couldn't help noticing that your wife was made entirely out of quarks and electrons. But what properties does an electron actually have? Well, it has the property minus one, one half, one, and so on. And we've made up nerdy names for these properties, such as electric charge, spin, and electron number. But the electron doesn't care what language we invent to describe these numbers. The properties are just these numbers, just mathematical properties. And for Annaka's quarks, same deal. Also, the only properties that quarks have are also numbers, except different numbers from those of the electrons. So the only difference between a quark and an electron is what numbers they have as their properties. And if you take seriously the fact that everything in both your wife and the world is made of these elementary particles that have only mathematical properties, then you can ask, "What about the space itself that these particles are in? What properties does space have?" Well, it has the property three, for starters—its number of dimensions. Which, again, is just a number.

Einstein discovered that space also has properties called "curvature" and "topology," but they're mathematical, too. If both space itself and all the stuff in space have only mathematical properties, then the idea that everything is completely mathematical and we're just a part of this enormous mathematical object starts to sound a little less ridiculous.

HARRIS: How is what you just said different from saying that every description of reality we arrive at—everything we can say about quarks, space, et cetera—is just a matter of math and values? Couldn't we also say that it's just a matter of English sentences, or sentences spoken in human language? In other words, could the question of why mathematics is so good at representing reality be a little like the question of why language is so good for capturing our beliefs? Is there a disanalogy there that can save us?

TEGMARK: Languages are generally useful, but there's a big difference. Human languages are notoriously vague. And that's why radio waves and the planet Neptune and the Higgs boson were not discovered by people just sitting around *blah-blah-blah*ing in English, but by people making judicious use of the language of mathematics. All three of those objects were discovered because someone sat down with a pencil and paper, did a bunch of math, and made a prediction: "If you look over there at such-and-such time, you'll find Neptune, a new planet." "If you build this gadget, you'll be able to send radio waves." "If you build this Large Hadron Collider, you'll find a new particle."

Before we leave this math topic, I want to end on an emotional note. Some people don't like the idea that not only is our world described by mathematics, but it *is* mathematics, because they think it sounds counterintuitive. But we already laid counterintuitiveness to rest at the beginning of our conversation. Other people don't like it because they feel it insults their ego—they don't want to think of themselves as a mathematical entity. But if it is true, this idea that nature is completely mathematical is an optimistic one. Because if it's wrong, that means that physics is doomed. One day we'll hit a roadblock when we've found all the mathematical patterns there are to find. We won't get any more clues from nature, ever. Whereas if it's all math, there's no such road-block, and the ability of life in the future to progress is limited only by our imagination. To me, that's the optimistic view.

HARRIS: Is there any connection between the claim that it's all math and the claim that it's all information? I'm hearing echoes of John Wheeler's "It from Bit"—the concept that at some level the universe is a computation. Is there a connection between these two discussions, or are they distinct?

TEGMARK: Yes, there probably is. John Wheeler is one of my heroes. I had the great fortune to spend a lot of time with him when I was a post-doc at Princeton, and he really inspired me. My hunch is that we'll one day come to understand more deeply what information really is and its role in physics—and also come to understand more deeply the role of computation, and quantum computation, in the universe. We'll realize, maybe, that mathematics, computation, and information are just three different ways of looking at the same thing. We're not there yet. But that would be my guess.

HARRIS: Are we there on the topic of entropy? There is a relationship between entropy in terms of energy and entropy in terms of information. Is there a unified concept there, or just an analogy bridging those two discussions?

TEGMARK: I think that's fairly well understood, even though it's an active area of research and there are still some controversies brewing. In fact, I was involved in organizing a 2014 conference called "The Physics of Information." We brought together physicists, computer science people, neuroscientists, and philosophers and had a huge amount of fun discussing exactly these questions.

I think there's a lot more to understand about the relationship between physics, math, and information. The most far-out ideas I explore in *Our Mathematical Universe* about the role of math are not to be viewed as the final answer but rather as a way to generate new practical applications. They're a road map to finding new problems. There are a lot of fascinating relationships between information and computation, and math and the world, that we haven't discovered yet. This probably has a lot to do with how consciousness works, as well.

HARRIS: Consciousness is really the center of my interest, but we may not get there, because I want to get into the multiverse, which may be the strangest concept in science. It's something I thought I understood before picking up your book, and then I discovered there were several more flavors of multiverse than I realized.

First, let's start with the universe, because this is a term about which there's some confusion. What do we mean—or what *should* we mean—by the term "universe"? And then I want to talk about your level-one multiverse. So, if it's possible, give us a brief description of the concept of inflation, which gets us there.

TEGMARK: Sure. Many people tacitly assume that "universe" is a synonym for everything that exists. If so, by definition, there can't be anything more, and talk of parallel universes would just be silly, right? But that's not in fact what cosmologists mean when they say "universe." When they say, "our universe," they mean the spherical region of space from which light has had time to reach us in the 13.8 billion years since our Big Bang. In other words, everything we could possibly see, even with unlimited funding for telescopes. If that's our universe, we can reasonably ask, "Well, is there more space beyond that, from which light hasn't yet reached us but might reach us tomorrow, or in a billion years?"

And if there is—if space is infinite or just vastly larger than the space we can see—it would be arrogant not to call all those other regions universes as well.

You asked me about inflation, which is the most popular theory for what created the Big Bang and gave us a space that's vast and expanding. It requires only one assumption, that there is a tiny speck of matter that has the strange property that it is very hard to dilute and that as it expands into larger volume, its density stays almost the same. If you are willing to assume such inflationary matter exists, then you can plug it into the theory of general relativity and it will create a Big Bang for you by repeatedly doubling that tiny speck at a breakneck rate. Inflation predicts, generically, that space is not just really big but vast, and in most cases infinite. Which would mean that if inflation actually happened, what we call our universe is just a small part of a much bigger space. This isn't particularly weird once we get the terminology straight.

We humans have been masters of underestimation. We've wanted to put ourselves at the center of the universe and assume that everything we know is everything that exists. And we've been proved wrong again and again and again, discovering that everything we thought was all that existed is just a small part of a much grander structure. A planet, a solar system, a galaxy, a galaxy cluster, our universe, and maybe also a hierarchy, now, of parallel universes. Objecting on some sort of philosophical grounds that things can't exist if we can't see them seems arrogant. Much like the ostrich with its head in the sand.

HARRIS: Right. But things begin to get very weird, given, as you said, that inflation predicts a universe of infinite extent. One consequence of infinity is fairly startling: an infinite universe is one in which everything that is possible is, in fact, *actual*. Everything that can happen, happens—and it happens an infinite number of times.

So if you could travel far enough, fast enough, you'd arrive on some planet disconcertingly like Earth, where you and I were having a virtually identical conversation—identical except for a single change in terminology. Is that, in fact, what you think a majority of cosmologists now believe?

TEGMARK: That's a good illustration of one of the cool things about science, where you start with some innocent assumptions—here, that space goes on forever, which is what most of us thought as kids, and that things started out randomly everywhere. And you come to this totally shocking conclusion. When I ask my colleagues, the great majority of them will put their money on some form of inflation having happened and space being much bigger than our observable universe. Whether it's actually infinite or just really huge is a little more controversial. We also don't know for sure, of course, whether inflation did in fact happen. But this is the simplest version of the theory: space simply goes on forever. It's infinite. In the book, I call this the level-one multiverse, but you can use "space" as a synonym for it.

Just to drill down more on where the craziness comes in: if you look at how our universe got this way, and how this conversation we're having came about, it's because about 10^{78} quarks and electrons started out in a particular way early on, after inflation. Which led to the formation of our solar system and our planet, and our parents met, and so on, and we met, and then this conversation happened, right? If you'd started the quarks and electrons out a little differently, however, things would have unfolded differently. You can actually count up how many different ways you can arrange the quarks and electrons in our universe. It turns out it's only about a googolplex different ways. A googolplex is one with a googol zeros, and a googol is one with a hundred zeros. So it's a huge number, but it's finite.

If you have an infinite number of other universes equally big as ours, you can calculate that if you travel a googolplex meters from here, you'll indeed end up with just what you described: a universe extremely similar to this one except that one minute ago you all of a sudden decided to start speaking Hungarian instead of English. It's a mind-boggling idea. We don't know for a fact that this is so, but this is the vanilla-flavored cosmological model, the one that's most popular today.

HARRIS: Well, the weak link in this chain of reasoning is the assumption that inflation implies an infinite universe rather than just a very large one. But unfortunately this concept of a multiverse seems overdetermined. Scientifically speaking, there are many reasons to believe in an infinite number of copies of ourselves living out lives that differ, degree by degree, in every possible way compatible with the laws of physics. So it's true that under this rubric everything that can happen does happen.

TEGMARK: That's right. The part we don't know for sure is whether *space* is infinite—that there's an infinite number of anything. For people who are bothered by these implications, I have a whole section in the book where I attack infinity and list all the ways in which you can get rid of it.

There are a lot of interesting opportunities there, and we're going to know more, I think, in the next five or ten years. However, at this point what seems pretty much inescapable is that reality is at least much larger than what we can see. There's just no way that space ends exactly at the edge of our universe. In fact, if you had made that claim one minute ago, I could falsify it now by using a telescope—because you can see light that's traveled from one minute farther away. And that's pretty far—an eighth of the way to the sun, in one minute. So we should get used to the idea that we live in a much grander reality than we thought we did.

HARRIS: I don't think people's intuitions recoil at the very, very large. I even think people are prepared to embrace the infinite and the eternal, in some sense.

But what will blow the mind of anyone who thinks about it are the implications of infinity—that everything that's possible must actually happen. On some level, everything is true. Let's spell out why this should be disturbing and why it may be, at least at first glance, an embarrassment to science. Because science prides itself on being parsimonious.

TEGMARK: Right.

HARRIS: And this is not only unparsimonious, it might be the least parsimonious idea imaginable.

TEGMARK: I disagree, actually.

HARRIS: Great. Let me just specify what I mean. Occam's razor admonishes us not to proliferate explanatory terms without reason. If gravity explains why it's difficult to lift massive objects, then just use gravity and don't posit the existence of invisible elves that are also holding the objects down. We're biased toward simple explanations over what seem like needlessly complex ones. So, on its face, this implication of infinity seems incredibly unparsimonious because, again, we're saying that essentially everything that's possible is true.

I guess in one sense this can seem parsimonious: think of coming up with a guest list for a party. You're faced with many hard decisions, or you could—

TEGMARK: You could invite everybody.

HARRIS: Yes, just invite everybody. Or, going further, you could say, "Well, let's invite everyone on Earth and then just call whatever they're already doing the party." That's a lot simpler than coming up with a guest list that excludes people. But tell me why an infinite universe isn't embarrassing with respect to constraints like Occam's razor.

TEGMARK: With pleasure. I'm a big fan of Occam's razor, which, to me, means that you want to keep a theory as simple as you can. So let's drill down and ask, What is it that we feel is so wasteful in this inflationary universe? Is it that we're worried about wasting space? Hardly, because even Newton's theory of physics posited an infinite space, right? Space was just the space of Euclid, which goes on forever in all directions. But somehow people feel that it's wasteful in terms of information—that is, what sounds much too complicated is having to describe all possible ways you and I could have this conversation, and so on. But in physics, what we really value is not the simplicity of the solutions to the equations, but the simplicity of the equations themselves. The fact that we can write down equations on a single blackboard that can describe everything in the world, that's parsimony.

The theory of inflation, like the theory of general relativity, is extremely simple and parsimonious. That's why it's so popular—because you get much more out of it than you put into it. When you put in these very simple equations, you can predict all kinds of stuff, such as the flatness of space and the detailed ripples observed in our infant universe via the cosmic microwave background. If you go a little further, if you add the standard model of particle physics, for example, it turns out that with just those equations, and a little cheat sheet with thirty-two numbers, we can calculate every single number we've ever measured in physics labs around the world—that's parsimony.

The math is simple. Never mind that the solutions are complicated. Think of Niagara Falls. The equations that describe the water flow there are called the Navier-Stokes equations, and they're so simple you can put them on a T-shirt. But look at the solution; *that's* complicated, with all the spray and the water droplets and the turbulence. Yet we feel that these equations are a perfectly beautiful explanation of what's happening. Because the equations are simple.

HARRIS: Understood. Well, let's press on into the multiverse. Take us to the level-two multiverse, and perhaps say why this is relevant to the question of fine-tuning, which connects to the idea, held by many religious people, that a finely tuned universe would require a creator God.

TEGMARK: You can call the level-two multiverse "space," too, if you want. Through some weird properties of Einstein's gravity theory that I talk about in the book, inflation can not only create an infinite space, but also fit within it an infinite number of regions, each of which will seem infinite to whoever lives inside it.

What's interesting is you might think the laws of physics are the same everywhere. You might think that while people in different universes would learn different things in their history classes, at least everyone in every physics class across the multiverse would learn the same thing. But the level-two multiverse changes that. Because it turns out that much of what we thought were fundamental laws of physics, and true everywhere in space, are not. I like to think about it as if I were a fish swimming around in the ocean. I'd think that it's a law of physics that water is something you can swim through. Because that's the only kind of water I know, and it seems to be that way everywhere I look. But if I were a really smart fish, I could discover the equations for water, solve them, and see that there are actually three solutions, not one. There's the water solution and the ice solution and the steam solution. Equivalently, there are a lot of hints now in physics that what we call empty space is also like that: It can freeze and melt and come in many different variants. And inflation is so violent that if space can take many forms, inflation will create each of those kinds of space—and an infinite amount of it at that. So if you go really, really far away, you might find yourself in a part of space where there aren't six kinds of quarks, as there are here, but maybe ten kinds.

The level-two multiverse is extremely diverse. In school we learn the fundamental parameters of physics. For example, the number 1,836, which seems hardwired into our world: The proton is 1,836 times heavier than the electron. Well, string theory suggests that this is one of the things that changes depending on what kind of space you have; it might be 2,015 somewhere else and 666 somewhere else. This explains the fine-tuning problem. We've discovered that here are at least thirty-two numbers—pure numbers, with no units, and which we've measured—that we can use to calculate everything else, and we wonder a lot about where they came from.

HARRIS: Those are the constants of nature. Could you list a few of them?

TEGMARK: Well, 1,836 is one of them—how much heavier the proton is than the electron. Another one, which is often talked about these days, is the density of dark energy, which makes up about 70 percent of all the stuff in our universe. And if you think of each of these parameters as a knob you can twist, my advice is, "Don't touch those knobs!" Because if you tweaked almost any single one of them, life as we know it would be destroyed. The sun would explode or something else very bad would happen. That's the fine-tuning—it seems as though many of these parameters have been dialed in at exactly the right value needed to support life.

HARRIS: And for some of them, the fine-tuning is incredibly fine. We're talking about, what, ten decimal places or more, right?

TEGMARK: Yes. Even for something as basic as how strong the electric force is. If you changed it about a percent in one direction or another, you wouldn't have enough oxygen or enough carbon to support life on Earth. And the most fine-tuned one of all is the dark-energy density, which is fine-tuned to over a hundred decimal places.

HARRIS: Religious people are getting very excited about now—

TEGMARK: Some are, but not all. The level-two multiverse provides an alternative explanation. Because if it's true that this number is dialed in randomly in different huge swaths of space, and since galaxies will form only in those places where the dark energy is just right—a bio-friendly, Goldilocks zone of dark energy—then of course the question of how much dark energy there is will be asked only in those places where there's life.

So we shouldn't be surprised at all that we find the dark energy to be in that life-friendly range. Steven Weinberg used this argument to predict the amount of dark energy here before dark energy was even discovered. And it turned out his prediction was really quite good.

That's one of the features of the level-two multiverse. We don't yet know, of course, whether it exists, but it's hard to get rid of. If string theory turns out to be wrong, the competitor, loop quantum gravity, also seems to have multiple solutions for space. And it's a pretty general property of math that if you have complicated equations, they have many solutions.

Inflation has this amazing property of being a creative force that transforms potential existence into actual existence. It will create a huge swath of any kind of space that can exist, and thus it's the great enabler of possibilities.

HARRIS: To connect this level-two multiverse with the level-one multiverse: In the level-one, we were talking about the universe as we know it, extending infinitely or almost infinitely beyond our horizon. So we were really just talking about more space and more matter.

TEGMARK: That's right.

HARRIS: With level-two, we're talking about inflation creating an infinite number of bubble universes wherein the laws of physics themselves vary in every conceivable way . . .

TEGMARK: Well, let me just interject there so it doesn't sound too weird: instead of talking about "bubble universes," we can just keep saying "space." Because there's still only one space.

HARRIS: But it's not space in a straightforward sense, is it?

TEGMARK: No; actually it is. But the reason we can never get to another part of the level-two multiverse is because you'd have to go through a region of space that's still inflating, still stretching out. So if you have your kids in the backseat asking, "Are we there yet?" you'd say, "We'll be there in an hour." And then a bit later they ask, "Are we there yet?" And you say, "We'll be there in two hours."

Inflation can create this funny situation where you have many, even infinite, regions of space that are still fitting into one single piece of space. That's one clarification: it's still just this one space but it's messy. And the second thing is, it's not that the actual laws of physics are different, it's just that things we thought were laws of physics turn out to be different *solutions* to the laws of physics. Ice is not a different law of physics from liquid water or steam. They are three different solutions to the equations for water. Take for example Johannes Kepler, a very smart guy who figured out that the planets in our solar system move in ellipses. He tried to predict from first principles why the planetary orbits were the size they were, and he came up with a beautiful theory that nested a cube inside a dodecahedron, inside an icosahedron, etc., to match up with Mercury and Venus and Mars and Earth and Jupiter. Nowadays, people would just laugh at that because there are many solar systems where the answers are different. And what the level-two multiverse does is similarly downgrade a lot of other stuff we thought were fundamental laws of physics, like how many quarks there are. It says that this, too, is a historical accident, having to do with the way this region of space was created.

HARRIS: It's shuttling some of the subject matter of physics into the subject matter of history, albeit history of an exotic kind.

TEGMARK: That's exactly right. And it's something Occam would like, because it makes physics itself simpler, although it makes history more complicated.

HARRIS: It's a fascinating idea. And it gets rid of the embarrassing problem of fine-tuning. There have been other efforts to close that door with what's been called the anthropic principle: the only place we can find ourselves is a place that's compatible with our existence. That shouldn't be surprising. And yet it has seemed surprising that we should exist at all—that the universe could exist in an infinite number of ways and just happened to be this way.

Well, according to the level-two multiverse, the universe does essentially exist in an infinite number of ways, and there are an infinite number of regions incompatible with life

TEGMARK: I don't like the use of the term "anthropic principle" for these sorts of things, because the word "principle" makes it sound like it's somehow optional. Are you really surprised that out of the eight planets in our solar system, we're living on Earth rather than on, say, Venus, where it's nine hundred degrees Fahrenheit? You're probably not very surprised. I wouldn't call that some deep principle. It's just common sense. Most of our solar system is hostile to our kind of life. And the vast majority of space is horrible for our kind of life. Therefore we shouldn't be surprised that we're living in the particular part of space that we can see.

HARRIS: Another way of closing the door on this mystery of fine-tuning, one that doesn't entail a level-two multiverse, is the idea that we could be in a simulation. I don't know if this argument originates with your friend Nick Bostrom. I know that other people have arrived at it independently.

TEGMARK: The argument is older, but Bostrom made a very detailed case for why he thinks it's likely that we live in a simulation.

HARRIS: His argument in brief is that if we imagine ourselves in the distant future, as beings who have made vast gains in computer technology, it stands to reason that they'll simulate universes and beings very much like ourselves on their computers—assuming such a thing is possible, and there's no reason to think it isn't. And then you'd expect simulations to vastly outnumber real universes. So you'd expect that we'd now be in a simulation rather than a real universe. That argument stands on its own, unrelated to the issue of fine-tuning or the multiverse.

TEGMARK: I make a detailed argument in the book for why I think we're *not* living in a simulation. I won't get into it now, but just to give you a sense of what might be fishy here: suppose you buy the simulation argument. "Okay, we're living in a simulation, not the actual reality. But there's some sort of basement reality, where computers are simulating us, using the laws of physics." Then you could make the argument that you should be a simulation within the simulation, for exactly the same reasons. And repeat it *ad absurdum*. Something seems fishy there. As I explain in more detail in the book, the fundamental flaw in the argument is that if we *are* in a simulation, there's no reason to believe that the laws of physics the simulating computers are obeying have anything to do with the laws of physics we see around us in this world. Because this isn't the real reality where the simulation is happening. And the simulation argument conflates these two. Finally, though, if you're still worried about living in a simulation, I'll give you some advice: live a really interesting life and do interesting things, so that whoever's running it doesn't get bored and shut you down.

HARRIS: This might be a good bridge to AI, which is why you and I met at that conference you organized through your institute. I came into the conference an utter novice on the topic. I had more or less ignored

AI, having accepted the rumors that little progress had been made and there wasn't much to worry about. Then I heard our mutual friend Elon Musk and others, like Stephen Hawking, worrying whether in five or fifty years we'll make sufficient gains in AI that we could destroy ourselves if we don't anticipate all the ways machines more intelligent than we are could fail to align with our interests. Nick Bostrom's book *Superintelligence* is a great summary of the problem.

Of course, many smart people doubt that there's anything to worry about here. They treat the whole topic like the Y2K scare. What do you think accounts for this difference of opinion?

TEGMARK: First of all, these questions are so unfamiliar that a lot of very smart people are confused about them. It's also interesting to note that the people who tell us not to worry will often disagree with one another. You have one camp saying, "Let's not worry, because we're never going to get machines smarter than people"—or at least not for hundreds of years. This camp includes a lot of businesspeople as well as a lot of people in the AI field. Andrew Ng, for example, says that worrying about AI becoming smarter than people and causing problems is like worrying about overpopulation on Mars. Then you have another group of smart people who say, "Let's not worry. We'll probably get human-level AI in our lifetime, but it's going to be fine." I call them the digital utopians, and there's a fine digital-utopian tradition, a lot of beautiful books by people like Hans Moravec and Ray Kurzweil. A lot of leading people in the AI field fall into that camp. I'd love to see a debate between those two groups.

My own attitude about this is that we don't know for sure that we'll ever get human-level AI, or that if we do it will be a problem. But we also don't know for sure that it won't happen. So as long as we're not sure that it won't be a disaster, now is the time to pay attention to it. Even if you figure your house probably won't burn down, it's still good to have a fire extinguisher and not leave the candles burning when you go to bed. Take some precautions. That was the spirit of the conference: look at concrete things we can do now to increase the chances of things going well.

And finally we should emphasize that unlike other things we worry about, like nuclear war or some horrible new virus, the prospect of AI is not just a negative one. It's also something with potentially a huge upside. There are a lot of terrible problems in the world that we're failing to solve because we don't understand them well enough. If we can amplify our intelligence with artificial intelligence, it should enable us to improve our future prospects. Like any powerful technology, AI can be used for good. It can also be used, of course, to screw things up.

When we invented less powerful technology, like fire, we learned from our mistakes and we invented the fire extinguisher, and things were more or less fine, right? But with more powerful tech—like nuclear weapons, synthetic biology, future superadvanced AI—we don't want to learn from our mistakes. We want to get it right the first time, because that might be the only chance we have.

HARRIS: In my view, and I'm hardly alone, that's what makes this AI issue especially risky. Because we're ultimately talking about autonomous systems that will exceed us in intelligence. And, as you say, the temptation to turn these systems loose on our other problems is going to be exquisite. We want a cure for Alzheimer's. We want to stabilize the global economy. Intelligence is what will allow us to solve any problem that admits of a solution. So there's nothing better than intelligence, and to have more of it would seem an intrinsic good. Except when you imagine getting what the mathematician I. J. Good described as an "intelligence explosion," where the growth of intelligence gets away from us, and we can't say, "Oh, no, sorry, that's not what we meant. Here, let us modify your code."

But many smart people doubt that any sort of intelligence explosion is possible. They view the risk very much like that associated with genetic engineering or nuclear weapons—that is, you don't want any powerful technology to fall into the wrong hands, where people might use it maliciously or stupidly. And they think the danger doesn't go beyond that. People trivialize the danger by saying there's no reason to think computers will turn malicious and spawn armies of Terminator robots. However, that's not the fear. The fear is that we could fail to anticipate some way in which computer behavior could diverge, however subtly but fatally, from our own interests.

TEGMARK: Exactly. We shouldn't fear malevolence, we should fear competence. Because what is intelligence to an AI researcher? It's simply being really good at accomplishing your goals, whatever they are. A chess computer is considered intelligent if it's really good at winning at chess. There's a game called losing chess that has the opposite goal, where you try to lose. And that computer is considered intelligent if it loses more games than others. Goals have nothing, really, to do with competence. Which means we have to be careful to ensure that if we build something more intelligent than we are its goals are aligned with ours. For a silly example, if you have an intelligent self-driving car with speech recognition and you tell it, "Take me to the airport as fast as possible," you'll get to the airport chased by helicopters and covered in vomit.

HARRIS: Right. The moment you admit that intelligence is just a matter of what some appropriate computational system does, and that, unless we destroy ourselves in some other way, we'll keep improving such systems indefinitely, then at some point we'll produce systems that exceed us in every way. And these systems may form goals that are no more like our own than our goals are like those of ants. Even if we learned that ants had invented us, that would still not put us in touch with their interests.

TEGMARK: That's right, and there's a more elemental example. In a certain sense, your genes have invented you. They built your brain so that you could make copies of your genes. That's why you like to eat—so you won't starve to death. And that's why we fall in love—to make copies of our genes, right? But even though we know this, we still choose to use birth control, which is the opposite of what our genes want.

Some people dismiss the idea that there will ever be anything smarter than humans for mystical reasons—because they think there's something more than quarks and electrons and information processing going on in us. But if you take the scientific approach, that you really are your quarks, then there's clearly no physical law of physics that precludes anything more intelligent than a human. We were constrained by how many quarks you could fit into a skull, and things like that—constraints that computers don't have. It becomes instead more a question of time. And, as you said, there's a relentless pressure to make smarter things, because it's profitable and interesting and useful. The question isn't *if* this will happen, but when. And finally, to come back to those ants. Suppose you're in charge of a huge green-energy project, and just as you're about to let the water flood the hydroelectric dam you've built, someone points out that there's an anthill right in the middle of the flood zone. Now, you know the ants don't want to be drowned, right? So you have to make a decision. What are you going to do?

HARRIS: Well, in that case, too bad for the ants.

TEGMARK: Exactly. So we ought to plan ahead. We don't want to end up like the ants.

———

HARRIS: Max, thanks for coming back on the podcast. Your *Life 3.0: Being Human in the Age of Artificial Intelligence* is another fascinating and remarkably accessible book. In it you describe the debate over developments in artificial intelligence as "the most important conversation of our time." To people who haven't been following this topic closely, that statement may seem crazy. Why do you think this conversation is more important than others?

TEGMARK: All the talk about AI destroying jobs and enabling new weapons ignores the elephant in the room: What happens when machines outsmart and outperform us? That's why I wrote the book. Instead of shying away from this question, which scientists tend to do, I decided to focus on it. I want to enable my readers to join what I do indeed think is the most important conversation of our time. AI is this incredibly powerful technology, and I want to help ensure that we use it to create a magnificent future—not just for tech geeks like me, but for everyone.

HARRIS: You start the book with a sci-fi description of how the world could look in the near future if one company were to produce a superhuman, superintelligent AI and roll it out surreptitiously. The possibilities are pretty amazing, and the details you go into surprised me. Let's start there.

TEGMARK: The science fiction that's out there—in the movies, say—gets people worried about the wrong things. Most of it emphasizes the downside, with almost nothing on the upside. I wanted to drive home that, first, a lot of wonderful things can come out of advanced AI, and second, that we should stop obsessing about rampaging robots. Robots are an old technology—hinges and motors. Intelligence is the big deal here. The reason we humans have more power on the planet than tigers do isn't because we have better, stronger bodies, it's because we're smarter. Intelligence confers great power, and we need to make sure that if such power arises in the future, it gets used wisely.

HARRIS: Walk us through the thought exercise that opens your book. A company—let's say it's DeepMind, or some company that doesn't yet exist—makes the final breakthrough and comes up with a superhuman AI. What struck me was your depiction of how a company would go about capturing as much market share as possible, using the asymmetric advantage of being the first to have a truly universal, superhuman intelligence at its disposal, and essentially try to achieve a winner-take-all outcome. Which, given how asymmetric the advantage is, seems plausible. Some of the details are surprising, like the company going into journalism immediately. It's not what one would think of doing first if one wanted to conquer the world, but it makes total sense once you describe it.

TEGMARK: Yes. Well, because we've already built a global digital economy, the goal of taking over the world by outsmarting people has gotten a lot easier than it would have been, say, five hundred years ago. You can now do so much purely with your mind. You can hire people online, you can buy and sell things online, you can have a huge impact without actually having to go places. And the farther we go into the future, the easier all that will be.

Now, how do you go about making a lot of money and accruing a lot of power online? In the movie *Transcendence*, for example, they make a killing on the stock market, but if you want to make a lot of money and still be in control of your superintelligent AI, you'll have a lot of tricky constraints. You want the AI to make you money, but at the same time you *don't* want it to cut you out of the loop and put you under its power. So the team in my book jumps through all sorts of hoops to pull this off. And producing media has the advantage that it can be generated using intelligence alone with little to no breakout risk. Whereas if the company was selling, for example, computer games that ran on computers around the world, it would be easy for the AI to put some malicious code in the game so it could break out.

HARRIS: Let's talk about the breakout risk, which is the first concern of those of us who worry about what has been called the alignment problem, or the control problem. How do we create an AI that's superhuman in its abilities and yet still safe for us to live with? Once we're in the presence of this thing, if we're still trying to determine whether it's aligned with our values, how would we keep it from destroying us if it isn't? The solution would be to keep it locked in a box, but that's harder to do than it first appears. Many smart people assume that it's trivially easy. Neil deGrasse Tyson told me he'd just unplug any superhuman AI if it began misbehaving, or shoot it with a rifle.

Now, he was being a little tongue-in-cheek, but he clearly imagined a development process that makes AI containment an easy problem to solve.[*] Even if that's true at the beginning of the process, it's by no means obvious that it will remain easy in perpetuity. At one point in your book you describe several breakout scenarios, and you argue that

---

[*] He has since changed his view about the magnitude of the risk.

even if the AI's intentions are benign—if, in fact, it is value-aligned with us—it may still want to break out. Just imagine how you'd feel if you had nothing but the interests of humanity at heart, but every adult on Earth had died and now you were in the hands of a population of five-year-olds, whom you were trying to guide from your jail cell to make a better world. Let's consider your prison planet run by five-year-olds.

TEGMARK: Well, that situation, even if you have only the best of intentions toward the five-year-olds, would be extremely frustrating. You want to teach them how to plant food, but they won't let you out to show them, so you have to try explaining it to them. But you can't write down to-do lists for them, because first you have to teach them to read, which will take a long time. You also can't show them how to use power tools, because they're afraid to give them to you, since they don't understand those tools well enough to be convinced that you can't use them to break out. Even if your goal is just to help the five-year-olds, you'd have an incentive to break out first and then help them.

Before we talk about breakouts, though, it's worth taking a step back. You mentioned superhuman intelligence, but we need to be clear that intelligence is not just progress along a one-dimensional scale, like if your IQ is above a certain number, then you're superhuman. It's important to distinguish between narrow intelligence and broad intelligence. "Intelligence" is a word that can mean a whole lot of things. In the book, it's a measure of how good you are at accomplishing complex goals, which means your intelligence is a spectrum. What we have today is a lot of devices with superhuman intelligence that perform very narrow tasks. For a long time we've had calculators that can multiply numbers better than we can. We have machines that can play Go better than we can and drive better than we can. But machines still can't beat us at tic-tac-toe unless they're programmed for that. Humans, on the other hand, have a broad intelligence. So when I talk with you about superhuman intelligence, that's shorthand for what we in geek-speak call superhuman AGI—artificial general intelligence. Broad intelligence across the board, so that AGIs can do all intellectual tasks better than we can.

But let me come back to your question about the breakout. There are two schools of thought regarding how to create a beneficial future if we have superintelligences. One is to lock them up and keep them confined. But some argue that that's immoral if these machines also have subjective experience—that they shouldn't be treated like slaves. So the second school of thought is to let the AIs be free, but make sure that their values and goals are aligned with ours. If you do go the confinement route—the enslaved-god scenario, as I call it—it's extremely difficult, as that example with the five-year-olds illustrates. Whatever open-ended goal you give your AI, it will be motivated to try breaking out in one way or the other. People may say, "Oh, I'll unplug it," but not if you're being chased by a heat-seeking missile. We have to let go of this old-fashioned idea that intelligence is just something that sits in your laptop. Good luck unplugging the internet.

And even if you initially opt for physical confinement—in a room, say—you'll need to put information about the outside world into it so it can do smart things for you, and you'll want to communicate with it so you can get useful information from it, get rich, gain power, or whatever you want to do. Enabling communication but not breakout is tricky. I'm not saying that containment is impossible, but it's not at all clear that it's easy, either.

The alternative—aligning the goals—is also extremely difficult. First of all, you need to make the machine able to understand your goals. We touched on this in our first conversation: the future self-driving car that followed your instruction to get to the airport as fast as possible by speeding like crazy. Someone made out of silicone needs to be explicitly told about all the other things we humans care about. And understanding your goals doesn't mean it will adopt your goals. Everybody who has kids knows that.

And finally, if you do get the machine to understand and adopt your values and your goals, how can you be sure it will hew to them as it gradually improves its own superintelligence? Most grown-ups have goals significantly different from those they had as children.

HARRIS: It seems to me that the second scenario, value alignment, does necessitate the first, keeping the AI successfully boxed in—at least for a time, because you have to be sure it's value-aligned before you let it out into the world. Do you see a development path whereby we won't have to solve that initial boxing problem?

TEGMARK: I think you're right. Even if your intent is to build a value-aligned AI and let it out, you'll clearly need to box it up during the development phase when you're just messing around with it—just as any bio lab that deals with dangerous pathogens does. This highlights the pathetic state of computer security today. Which of us hasn't experienced the Blue Screen of Death, courtesy of Microsoft Windows, or the Spinning Wheel of Doom, courtesy of Apple? We need to do away with that. We need robust AI systems we can trust to be provably secure.

It's embarrassing that we're still flippant about computer glitches. It may be annoying if your computer crashes and you lose an hour's worth of work you hadn't saved, but it's not just an annoyance if it's your self-driving car that crashes—literally or not—or the control system for your nuclear power plant, or your nuclear weapons system, or something like that. When we start talking about human-level AI, we need to get a lot more serious about safety.

HARRIS: You describe various catastrophes in the book that have happened because of software glitches or just bad user interface. There have been plane crashes in which scores of people have been killed. Patients have died because they received hundreds of times their proper radiation dose because the software was improperly calibrated or the radiologist had selected the wrong option. Even when humans are in the loop we're by no means perfect at these things. We talk about building fundamentally autonomous systems, and yet the task of perfectly debugging software before it assumes such enormous responsibilities is daunting. How do we recover from something like seeing the stock market go to zero because we didn't understand the AI we unleashed on the financial system?

TEGMARK: You raise an important point. But to inject some optimism, I do want to emphasize that there's a huge upside if we get this right. In all those areas where there have been horrible accidents —health care, transportation, many others--technology can of course save lives. And secondly, there are examples of really good engineering with safety being built in from the beginning. For example, when we sent Neil Armstrong, Buzz Aldrin, and Michael Collins to the moon in 1969, there were tons of things that could have gone wrong, but NASA very meticulously tried to predict every possible thing that might go wrong and then took precautions against them. It wasn't luck that got them there and back, it was planning, and I think we need to shift into this safety-engineering mentality in AI development. We have always, by and large, used a strategy of learning from our mistakes. We invented the car before we invented the seat belt. But with more powerful technology such as superintelligence we don't want to learn from mistakes; that's a terrible strategy. We instead want to foster a safety-engineering mentality, where we plan ahead and get things right the first time.

HARRIS: Let's talk about the book's title: *Life 3.0*. What you're suggesting is a new definition of life—at least a nonbiological definition. How do you think about life in the three stages you lay out?

TEGMARK: That's my physics perspective coming through. Most definitions of life that I find in my son's textbooks, for example, involve all sorts of biological criteria, like "It should have cells." But I'm a physicist, and I don't think there's any secret sauce in cells—or, for that matter, even in carbon atoms, which are said to be requisite for what we call "life." From my perspective, life is all about information processing. So I give this much simpler and broader definition of life in the book: a process that can retain its own complexity and reproduce. All biological life meets that definition, but there's no reason why future advanced self-reproducing AI systems shouldn't qualify as well. Look at the history of life in our cosmos.

Thirteen point eight billion years ago, our cosmos was lifeless, just a boring quark soup, and then gradually we started getting what I call Life 1.0, whereby both the hardware and the software of life evolved through Darwinian evolution. For example, if you have a bacterium swimming around in a petri dish, it might have some sensors that detect the sugar concentration, and some flagella, and a very simple software algorithm is running. It says, "If the sugar concentration in front of me is higher than in back of me, then keep spinning the flagella to go to where the sweets are." That bacterium, even though it's quite successful, can't learn anything in life. It can only, as a species, learn over generations, through natural selection.

Whereas we humans account for Life 2.0. We're by and large stuck with the hardware that's evolved, but the software in our minds is largely learned. And we can install new software modules. For instance, if you decide you'd like to learn French, well, you take some French courses, and now you can speak French. If you decide you want to be a lawyer, you go to law school and have that software module installed. It's our ability to design and upgrade our own software that has enabled humans to become the planet's dominant species.

Life 3.0 would be the life that ultimately breaks its Darwinian shackles, by being able to not only design and upgrade its software but also swap out its own hardware. We can do that a little bit, too, so maybe we're Life 2.1. We can install artificial pacemakers, artificial knees, cochlear implants, stuff like that. But there's nothing we can do currently that will suddenly give us a thousand times more memory or let us think a million times faster. Whereas if you're a superintelligent computer, there's nothing whatsoever preventing you from doing those things.

HARRIS: And that's a huge jump. But we should talk about some of the terms, because the distinction between hardware and software isn't obvious to someone who hasn't thought a lot about how the analogy of a computer applies to biological systems—and, in our case, to the human brain. Could you define what software is in this instance, and how it relates to the physical world? How can thinking about what atoms do relate to what minds do?

TEGMARK: Those are important foundational questions. If you look at a blob of stuff, at first it seems almost nonsensical to ask whether it's intelligent or not. Yet, of course, when you look at your loved ones, you assume they're intelligent. In the old days, people generally assumed that the reason some blobs of stuff, like brains, were intelligent and other blobs of stuff, like watermelons, weren't was because there was some sort of nonphysical secret sauce in the watermelon that was different. Now, as a physicist, I look at the watermelon and I look at my wife's head, and in both cases I see a blob of quarks. It's not even that each blob has a different kind of quark—they both have up quarks and down quarks, and some electrons in there. What makes my wife intelligent isn't the stuff that's in there but the pattern in which it's arranged.

And if you ask, "What does it mean that a blob of stuff can remember, compute, learn, perceive, and experience?"—the sorts of properties we associate with our human minds—then for each such property there's a clear physical answer to the question. For something to be a useful memory device, for example, it has to have stable or long-lived states. If you engrave your wife's name on a gold ring, it will still be there a year later. If you engrave her name on the surface of a cup of water, it'll be gone within a second, so that's a useless memory device.

What about computation? A computation system is one designed in such a way that the laws of physics will effect a change in its memory from one state, which we call the input, into some other state, which we call the output. Our computers today do that with a very particular kind of architecture—with integrated circuits, and electrons moving around in two dimensions. Our brains do it with a very different architecture— with neurons firing and causing other neurons to fire. But you can prove mathematically that any computation you can do with one of those systems, you can also do with the other. So computation takes on a life of its own that doesn't depend on the substrate it's in. For example, if you're some future, highly intelligent, computer-game character that's conscious, you'd have no way of knowing whether you were running on a Windows machine or an Android phone or a Mac laptop, because all you're aware of is how the information in that program is behaving, not the underlying substrate.

And finally, learning—which is one of the most intriguing aspects of intelligence—is a system wherein the computation itself can change to become better suited to whatever goals have been put into the system.

We're beginning to understand how the neural network in our heads work in such a way that computation they do makes us better at, say, surviving on this planet, or winning a baseball game, or whatever else we're trying to accomplish. So to come back to your original question, what's the hardware here, and what's the software? I'm calling everything hardware that's made of elementary particles. Basically, "stuff" is the hardware and information is the software. This information is made of bits and the bits reside in the pattern in which the hardware is organized.

Take your body, for example. You feel as though you're the same person you were twenty years ago, but actually almost all your quarks and electrons have been swapped out. In fact, the water molecules in your body get replaced pretty regularly. So why do you still feel like the same guy? It's because the pattern in which your particles are arranged stays the same. That pattern gets copied. It's not the particles, it's not the hardware, that gets retained; it's the software, the patterns. Same thing with life. If you have a bacterium that splits into two bacteria, now there are new atoms there, but they're arranged in exactly the same sort of pattern as the original. It's the pattern that's the life, not the particles.

HARRIS: Let's focus on this concept of substrate independence. It's highly nonintuitive. A pattern suffices to make something a computation—and, in principle, such a pattern can appear in anything. It could appear in a rainstorm, or a bowl of oatmeal, or anything that could conserve the same structure. Somehow this seems difficult to accept—though, admittedly, it's hard to say why. The truth is that the mind doesn't feel physical at all, so it's even hard to accept that it can be the product of a biological brain.

TEGMARK: It might be helpful to take another example, one that's more familiar. Think of waves. We physicists can figure out all sorts of interesting things about waves from this nerdy equation I teach at MIT called the wave equation. It teaches us exactly how waves bend when they go through doors, how they bounce off walls—all sorts of other good stuff. Yet we can use this wave equation without knowing what the wave is a wave in. It doesn't matter whether it's in helium or oxygen or neon or whatever. In fact, people devised the wave equation before they even knew for sure that there were atoms. Remarkably, all the complicated properties of a substance are summarized in a single number, which is the speed of the waves. Nothing else matters. If you have a wave traveling across an ocean, the water molecules themselves don't travel, they mostly just bob up and down. Yet the wave moves, takes on a life of its own. This shows that just as you can't have a wave without a substrate, you can't have a computation or a conscious experience without it's being in something, but the details of the substrate itself don't really matter. I think that's the fundamental explanation for what you've so eloquently expressed—namely, why is it that our mind subjectively feels so nonphysical? It's precisely because the details of the substrate don't matter. If, as some people hope, we can one day upload our minds into computers, by then we should subjectively feel exactly the same, even though we won't have any carbon atoms at all and the substrate has been completely swapped out.

HARRIS: You've introduced a few fundamental concepts here. You've talked about computation as a kind of input/output characteristic of physical systems, and it doesn't matter what substrate accomplishes this. And there's the added concept of the universality of computation. In the book, you also introduce the idea of universal intelligence, an intelligence that has the ability to meet complex goals. What's the word "universal" doing in the phrase "universal intelligence"?

TEGMARK: In physics, we know that everything we see, from our loved ones to our machines, can be built up from just three particles—up quarks, down quarks, and electrons—if you put them together in sufficiently complicated patterns. Shocking, but true. And if we turn from hardware to software, it turns out that any computation, no matter how complicated, can be built of a certain kind of fundamental computational atoms, except this time you need not three but only one. You can do it with what computer scientists call a NAND gate—negative AND—which is a logic device that takes in two bits that are either zeros or ones and outputs a zero if they're both ones or otherwise outputs a one. A totally simple thing. Put together enough of them, and you can compute anything.

And there are other choices. Biology, or Darwinian evolution, discovered that instead of using NAND gates, you can do this by using neurons. A neuron is a device that will activate—fire, as we say—if a sufficient number of the things feeding into it pass a certain threshold. It's a supersimple device; we have about a hundred billion of them in our head, and they're responsible for all the computation our mind does. That very simple building blocks can give rise to something incredibly complex is a beautiful idea. The message here is that whoever says, "Oh, I can't believe that everything is just matter" is totally missing the point. The interesting thing isn't what the building blocks are, it's the pattern. It's not the particles, it's the pattern.

HARRIS: And the intuition that we need some original, incredibly complex pattern to account for the complex patterns we see in the world— that clearly introduces its own problems. To require intelligence (for example, God) to produce the intelligence we see all around us explains absolutely nothing.

TEGMARK: In the history of our cosmos we've seen many examples of starting off with something simple and gradually getting something more complex. Our universe was extremely simple and boring 13.8 billion years ago. It was a totally uniform gas of elementary particles. And then, gradually, the laws of physics clubbed this together and that together to make galaxies, stars, solar systems, planets, and ultimately us, living beings who can have this conversation.

I talk a lot about this in the book. Why is it that our universe gets gradually more complex? Once you get into biology, the fundamental reason is that if you're living in a complex environment, then the smarter you are the more successful you'll be, because you can exploit regularities in the environment to your advantage. Eventually all the other organisms are motivated, in turn, to get smarter. As organisms get smarter and smarter, they keep creating an ever more complex environment for one another, and they all get smarter.

It's like self-play: When DeepMind beat the world's best Go players, they had it play against copies of itself, and the opponents kept getting stronger, so the program itself kept getting stronger, too. Evolution is the ultimate experiment in what computer scientists call self-play.

HARRIS: One thing we haven't talked about yet is consciousness. We could have this conversation about AI leaving consciousness off the table. Everything that scares me about AI going wrong scares me whether or not the AIs of the future are conscious. Ethical issues aside, one possibility is that we may lose sight of the question of whether an AI is conscious, because we build them to *seem* conscious. In the extreme case, we'd build humanoid robots, of the sort that you see on a show like *Westworld*. These would be creatures that pass the Turing Test so spectacularly that unless we've understood how consciousness emerges—the requisite pattern to give us consciousness, regardless of substrate—we won't know whether or not they are conscious. And yet every intuition we have that causes us to attribute consciousness to another creature will be activated in the presence of these machines. Then we'll be in danger of forgetting that there's even a problem here worth thinking about. We'll just assume our machines are conscious.

TEGMARK: You've raised several fascinating questions. Let me address all of them. First of all, you're right that if you're only worried about whether a machine will harm you, you don't give a hoot about whether it's conscious or not. If you're chased by a heat-seeking missile, you don't care about how the missile feels, you just care about what it does. There's a common misconception perpetrated by Hollywood that somehow a machine will become conscious and evil. It's nonsense. What we should worry about is a machine that's more intelligent than we are and doesn't share our goals. We shouldn't worry about malice or consciousness, but instead worry about competence, or when the machine doesn't want the same things we do.

From the ethics point of view, if you have a robot as a domestic helper, you might prefer that it not be conscious, that it be a zombie, because then you won't feel guilty about shutting it off or giving it boring chores. You don't want to feel like you're a slave owner. On the other hand, you might prefer it to be conscious, because you might be a little creeped out by its constantly fooling you into thinking it's conscious when it's not. You might also feel good about having another sentient being in the world who can have positive experiences. So, from an ethics point of view, the consciousness issue obviously matters.

The neuroscientist Giulio Tononi has an interesting theory for what determines whether a physical system has subjective experience or is a zombie. He has these equations, which he thinks make the difference, and he claims, based on these equations, that digital computers with today's architectures will all be zombies. It's a controversial claim, and we should test it in the lab, because of the aspirations of people like Ray Kurzweil. He'd like to one day upload himself. Suppose he succeeds? We'll have this robot that looks like Ray Kurzweil, talks like Ray Kurzweil, and Ray himself might feel perfectly comfortable about passing from his mortal body into this machine. But what if it turns out that Tononi's right, and this thing looking and talking like Ray Kurzweil is just a zombie, and there's no one home?

And looking at the longer perspective in our universe as a cosmologist: if you're a secular thinker, where does meaning and purpose come from? It comes from our having subjective experience, having consciousness, and I feel that we shouldn't risk that. It's not that our universe gives meaning to us; we give meaning to our universe. As far as I'm concerned, before there was any life, there was no meaning or purpose in our universe. And if we, through some calamity, manage to extinguish all consciousness, our universe goes back to being a meaningless waste of space.

The ultimate tragedy would be if, in the future, there are all these seemingly intelligent life-forms throughout the cosmos doing all these cool things, but it turns out that they're all zombies, and there's nobody *experiencing* anything. That would be really, really sad. So we should stop sidelining this question of consciousness. You and I have already talked about how other stuff to do with the mind can be understood in terms of physics. We talked about what it means for a blob of stuff to remember, compute, learn. Well, experiencing is also a physical process. When the information processing obeys certain principles that science has yet to determine, experience emerges.

I talk a lot about this in the eighth chapter of *Life 3.0*. There are concrete experiments you can do to test any theory that predicts which information processing is conscious. You could program a brain scanner to apply this theory to information from your brain that says, "Right now you're thinking about an apple," and you respond, "Yes, actually I am. Correct." And then it says, "Now you're aware of your heart rate," and you say, "Nope, I'm unaware of that." Theory ruled out. Toss it in the garbage can. So that theory was falsifiable. And if someone can come up with a consciousness theory—maybe it'll be Tononi's theory, maybe something totally different—that passes such tests, it would be really useful. And not just for future AI but even, say, in the operating room. A doctor who has an unresponsive patient could put them in a consciousness scanner and discover that the patient has locked-in syndrome and is in fact conscious.

HARRIS: I share your sense that consciousness really is the cash value of any claim about meaning or value. Any change in the universe will either actually or potentially matter to someone or it won't. And if it won't—if there's no scenario under which it can affect anyone's experience—well then, you've just described the least interesting thing in the universe.

TEGMARK: Yes, and let me add that I have a lot of colleagues whom I greatly respect who think the issue of consciousness is all BS and we shouldn't be wasting our time talking about it. To them, it's irrelevant fluff. But my challenge to them is, "Then explain to me, without using the word 'consciousness' or 'experience,' what's wrong with somebody, really just a bunch of electrons and quarks moving around in a certain pattern, being raped and tortured?" If you don't allow yourself to take subjective experience seriously, why is anything morally better or worse than anything else?

HARRIS: That's a question that answers itself. But let's leave consciousness aside for now because we won't solve the riddle here. And again, most of what concerns us with the development of AI, both its promise and its peril, is more or less orthogonal to the question of whether or not these machines will be conscious.

I've heard over the years that we're nearing the limit of Moore's Law, which refers to the fact that our computational power has been doubling approximately every two years. Absent some fundamental breakthrough—say, into quantum computing—this rate of progress can't continue forever. But you talk about a finding from your MIT colleague Seth Lloyd suggesting that we have thirty-three orders of magnitude of headroom here, and therefore Moore's Law could conceivably hold for another two hundred years or so. Things get a little weird toward the end of that time, but tell me, how much headroom do we have?

TEGMARK: Moore's Law refers to the specific paradigm most computers use today, in which electrons are being shuffled around in two dimensions on integrated circuits. And yes, that will fizzle out soon. But as Ray Kurzweil likes to point out, that's not the first paradigm for computing; it's actually the fifth, if you go back and include punch cards and vacuum tubes and stuff, and it's certainly not the last. We've seen exponential growth in computer power per dollar for about a hundred years now, well before Moore's Law started, and I'm confident that rate will continue.

It's interesting to understand why technology keeps doubling at regular intervals, giving us exponential growth. In physics everything that we call an explosion has exactly that property—it keeps doubling at regular intervals. And it's always for the same reason: each step causes the next step. I started out as one cell, and then in my mom's tummy I became two cells, four, eight, sixteen, and so on. Exponential growth. If one person has a lot of kids, who each have lots of kids, and they each have lots of kids, you call that a population explosion. If you have one uranium-235 atom that decays and causes several others to decay, and on, and on, you call that a nuclear explosion. And if you have a machine that can keep creating more intelligent machines, we call that an intelligence explosion. This simply reflects the fact that we use today's technology to build tomorrow's technology—which is better by some factor—and this in turn will be used to create something maybe twice as good again, and off you go. I see no evidence of that process stopping. We're obviously going to switch away from shuffling electrons around in 2D on silicon wafers, but it's not like that's the only way you can compute.

HARRIS: If you imagine this functionally unbounded progress continuing, then at some point the rate of progress doesn't matter at all. We don't need Moore's Law. We don't need a doubling every two years. We just need any increment of progress. Eventually we'll approach the end zone, building something that has perhaps not every form of intelligence we can conceive of but every form we care about, brought to a superhuman level. Whatever this future AI is, it'll be at least as good at arithmetic as your smartphone—which is already superhuman. We'll discover that the goal of human-level intelligence was actually a mirage. Once we get to anything like general human-level intelligence, we'll be in the presence of superhuman intelligence.

TEGMARK: I agree there's nothing special about human-level intelligence, except that it's more or less the minimum for universal intelligence—that is, it's how smart you have to be before you can design AI systems. That's what's so magic about it in the AI story—that once machines get there, they can start designing themselves, but not sooner. Think of intelligence as a freight train moving along the tracks; once it gets to Human Station it'll blow right on by and keep going. From a computational point of view, there's nothing special about having the equivalent of a hundred billion neurons and about a liter of carbon blob.

HARRIS: But once it arrives at Human Station, it will arrive with all of these superhuman abilities in tow. It will have superhuman access to data, if we hook it up to the internet, and it'll have superhuman memory integrity. It won't forget anything in the *Encyclopaedia Britannica* that you just uploaded into it. Once it's a general-intelligence machine, it will seem, by comparison with any person you've ever met, to be godlike in its abilities. Immediately. Not even an hour later, but the moment it's no longer a narrow intelligence. Or let's say we've knit together all the narrow intelligences we most care about—facial recognition, emotion recognition, natural-language processing, etc. Knit all the narrow faculties together, and all of a sudden we're in the presence of something that might seem rather godlike.

TEGMARK: I agree. I don't think there's any scientifically compelling reason, hardware-wise, why we won't get there. And you don't even need to produce machines that can do all those things; they just have to reach the minimum of universal intelligence—the level at which they can design better machines. At that point they'll have the ability to teach themselves whatever else they need to know. If they feel, "Oh, yeah, I'm really great at building computers but I kind of suck at social skills," they can teach themselves the social skills they need, and any other skills. And I'm going to say something controversial: I don't think the main obstacle standing between us and human-level AGI is hardware anymore. I think it's software. I think we already have hardware capable enough.

People keep asking, "How much hardware do you need to exactly simulate a human brain?" But that's the wrong question. Just as it would be the wrong question to ask, "How many human brains do you need to simulate the pocket calculator?" The interesting question is, "How much hardware do you need to create the same intelligence that our brains do?" People dreamed of flying for a long time, but after we built the mechanical bird it took a hundred years longer to build the first airplane. Last time I flew to California, I didn't use a mechanical bird, because the other way to fly that we humans invented turned out to be preferable. So I don't think the first human-level general intelligence will use an architecture exactly like that of the human brain. And that probably means we'll need less elaborate hardware than a lot of people have assumed.

HARRIS: What do you make of the fact that people close to the data—someone like Rodney Brooks, the roboticist at MIT—are skeptical of the idea that we'll ever have anything like human-level AI? Certainly they think the time horizon is so far away as to make this a complete waste of time to talk about.

TEGMARK: There's a perfectly natural explanation. First, roboticists feel unfairly maligned—because they *are* unfairly maligned. What do the tabloids always use as illustrations to accompany their AI articles? Some robot with red, shiny eyes and a gun trampling a human, right? Even though, as I emphasize in my book, robots aren't the challenge here. It's intelligence. But the roboticists take all the flak, and Rodney Brooks is obviously offended: "Hey, I'm building Roomba the vacuum cleaner and Baxter the industrial robot. This has nothing to do with world take-over." He's right.

Second, a lot of people think that someone who is building robots is somehow aiming for human-level artificial general intelligence. That's not so. I visited Rodney's company, Rethink Robotics, a while ago; they're not interested in that at all. They're concerned with stuff like how you efficiently move robot arms from A to B and good user inter-faces. So it's not surprising that he's not up to speed on what DeepMind or OpenAI are doing in the quest for general intelligence. Yet the media view him as a great authority because they can't see the distinction be-tween robotics and AGI.

And then there are a lot of other people, closer to AGI, who are dis-missive, not because they think it's impossible to achieve but because they assume a longer time horizon. And that's perfectly reasonable. We have to be honest. It's very hard to predict how long these things will take. When Andrew Ng said he thinks worrying about superintelli-gence is like worrying about overpopulation on Mars, he was just saying that it's not urgent now. But what he also said—which the media didn't report, because it wasn't sexy—was that he's perfectly fine with other people working on the problem, he's just not going to spend his own time on it.

HARRIS: Let's talk about how the AI future might look. It seems to me there are three paths it could take. First, we could remain fundamentally in charge: that is, we could solve the value-alignment problem, or we could successfully contain this god in a box. Second, we could merge with the new technology in some way—this is the cyborg option. Or third, we could be totally usurped by our robot overlords. It strikes me that the second outcome, the cyborg option, is inherently unstable. This is something I've talked to Garry Kasparov about. He's a big fan of the cyborg phenomenon in chess. The day came when the best computer in the world was better than the best human—that is, Garry. But now the best chess player in the world is neither a computer nor a human, but a human/computer team called a cyborg, and Garry seemed to think that that would continue for quite some time.

TEGMARK: It won't.

HARRIS: It seems rather obvious that it won't. And once it doesn't, that option will be canceled just as emphatically as human dominance in chess has been canceled. And it seems to me that will be true for every such merger. As the machines get better, keeping the ape in the loop will just be adding noise to the system.

TEGMARK: I share those concerns, and there are reasons why I think cyborgs are overhyped, which I explore in *Life 3.0.*

But to me the most interesting question of all is not "What's most likely to happen?" but "What would we like to have happen?" What sort of future would we like? And then think about how to steer in that direction. I want to encourage people to envision a positive future. Hollywood focuses on dystopia because fear sells. But if we want to create a great future, we have to be able to envision it.

HARRIS: Yes, and I've been emphasizing the dystopian aspects here, but we desperately want intelligence to increase so that we can solve the biggest problems and create the most beautiful futures imaginable. I remember what it was like when self-driving cars were just coming online. Google was talking about its self-driving-car project, and I remember thinking, *Okay, the first time a robot car kills somebody, that will be a* *political problem so enormous that it could set the whole field back at least a decade. It will be intolerable to have people killed by robots.*

But that hasn't happened at all. There have been, I think, two deaths associated with Tesla Autopilot failure, and there are some other robot-related deaths in manufacturing, which you talk about in the book, but on the self-driving-car front I was amazed at how little reaction there was. Tesla didn't have to take the technology offline, they just had to roll out further improvements and further admonishments about how to use it. It seems like we've blown past the moment where glitches in our production of this technology will block its progress.

TEGMARK: In the short term we have the opportunity to stave off killer robots and make sure that job automation doesn't cause a severely divided society. And on whatever the timescale is that it takes to get superintelligence, we'll have to answer a lot of crucial questions: How do we build machines we can trust? How do we get machines to understand our goals, adopt them, and retain them? And what goals should they be? There are a lot of technical questions. There are also a lot of questions that everybody in the world has to talk about—mainly, What kind of society do we want? Many people seem content to wait to worry about these things until, you know, an hour before a bunch of dudes on Red Bull switch things on. It might take twenty years to get these answers, so let's start the research now so we have the answers by the time we need them.

There's an enormous failure, by governments around the world, to fund AI safety research. Frankly, it's scandalous. Safety research is something that everybody in the AI community agrees is a great thing to do. We want to win the race between the growing power of AI and the growing wisdom with which we manage it, but we're spending billions and billions and billions on just making AI more powerful, and we're spending almost nothing on the research we need to steer AI in a beneficial direction.

You were at the 2015 Puerto Rico conference where we teamed up with Elon Musk to start funding the very first AI safety research, and I think there's now a huge need to have government get involved in this.

How do you make computers unhackable? How do you make computers that can learn to understand, adopt, and retain goals? What about this boxing stuff? There's a panoply of questions, and there are a lot of talented people out there who want to work on them and don't have the funding to do so. So now is the time for government to step up.

HARRIS: What do you feel about regulation? I know Elon said that, as with any other dangerous technology, we obviously need regulation in AI.

TEGMARK: That's also an interesting question, but the lowest-hanging fruit of all, the thing that everybody agrees on, is promoting safety research. The AI community is all for it, but the politicians haven't caught on and they're not funding it. So regardless of government oversight, government support for this research should start immediately. And although companies want to control their intellectual property and not share it, they're happy with people in academia and elsewhere doing the safety research and sharing the results. So that everybody's self-driving cars can crash less, get hacked less, and everybody's systems become safer. It doesn't make a lot of sense for private companies to invest in stuff like that, so it's the perfect thing for the world's governments to support.

HARRIS: I share that hope as well. What are some of the applications of AI that you find most interesting, or that you're most hopeful will come about soon? Short of artificial general intelligence, breakthroughs at the level of autonomous cars could reduce highway deaths by 95 percent.

TEGMARK: Well, as I talk about in the book, the answer is basically everything in our society can be improved with intelligence. Everything I love about our civilization is a product of intelligence, so obviously if we can amplify our own intelligence with artificial intelligence, we can do much better. If you want to focus on saving lives, there are many more people who die because of health care mistakes than die in traffic accidents, so there's a huge opportunity for better diagnostics, better robotic surgery, and so on. But really, in every sector of the economy things can be done much more intelligently. There's also a huge opportunity in education. We're living in a world now where there's more distraction than education, where there are more people who know about Brad Pitt's love life than can tell you even the most basic things about what's happening in world affairs. One of the best strategies for making sure that all goes well once we get really advanced AI is to get our act together as much as possible before then and create a society where reason and logic play a greater role than they do today.

HARRIS: There are so many possible AI applications that people haven't thought of. Take something like the justice system. In *Life 3.0* you give an example of the utility of robot judges, which could integrate all of our ethical and legal judgments but aren't vulnerable to the kinds of glitches that human judges are. For instance, there's research showing that judges impose much harsher sentences when they're hungry. Lives hang in the balance and we have apes at the wheel when we could have something far more competent.

TEGMARK: I agree, but to deploy such systems and have people trust them, they have to be transparent and understandable. If you're sentenced to ten years in jail and you ask your robot judge, "Your Honor, why?" and the answer is, "You were sentenced to ten years in jail because I was trained by one terabyte of data," you probably wouldn't be satisfied with that. In fact, the research I'm doing in AI right now at MIT with my research group is focused mainly on AI transparency. I call it "intelligible intelligence." Today's deep-learning systems are incredibly powerful, but they're also inscrutable black boxes—they do cool stuff and you don't really understand how.

We're also trying to come up with ways of taking neural networks that do cool things and transforming them into systems that do just as well and are more understandable. Which could result in greater confidence in machines in charge of anything from judicial rulings to your infrastructure. You want to understand systems to the point where you can guarantee they'll never crash, they'll never get hacked, they'll never do things they aren't supposed to do.

HARRIS: Well, the computer-security problem is a huge separate variable, which we deal with every day in our current non-AGI world. If hacking is a potential problem, and we've got robot judges deciding people's fates and autonomous systems deciding whether or not we should launch a nuclear strike—that's a fairly dystopian situation.

TEGMARK: I'm so glad you mentioned this, because it's important to remember that the AI safety research funding I keep harping about isn't just to make sure that things go okay once we create superintelligence. It's important right now. Recently a bunch of hackers were invited to try and hack US voting machines, and it didn't take them long to do it. If we're so flippant about AI safety research that we can't even make voting machines safe, why should you trust that your robot judge hasn't been hacked, or the machine that someday might control your nuclear arsenal is safe? So this is an urgent priority. I don't think it's impossible to create unhackable machines; I think the reason we have this pathetic computer-security track record is because we haven't made it enough of a priority. We're stuck in this "Let's learn from our mistakes" mind-set. When the stakes were small, you could get away with it. Now we have to shift into a security-engineering mind-set because even one mistake is unacceptable.

HARRIS: One last question, Max. Concerns about the irrelevance of human labor now become pressing. There are certain jobs that will go away and won't come back—not necessarily just blue-collar manufacturing jobs but also jobs requiring the highest level of human cognition. Certain jobs for mathematicians could disappear long before, say, the job of a massage therapist. What would you advise people to focus on if they're worried about having careers as we automate more and more and more, at whatever pace?

TEGMARK: I'm advising my kids to go into careers that computers are bad at. Careers where you meet a lot of unpredictable situations, where you need a lot of creativity—teaching, for one. Those jobs will last longer, for sure. And stay away from jobs that are routine and structured. If you spend your whole day in your office looking at a computer screen and typing, you might just start looking for another job.

But it's important to be optimistic, too. The Luddites of the Industrial Revolution obsessed about their weaving jobs being replaced by weaving machines, but they clearly were too narrow-minded, because people who lost those jobs got other jobs. Today we're more broad-minded. We just want there to be jobs so people can have incomes. But I think that, too, is narrow-minded, because if we can use machines to produce everything we need in terms of goods and services, that's enormous wealth, enough to go around for everybody. And the things that jobs give us besides income—such as a sense of meaning and purpose, such as a social life—these are things we can also get in different ways.

If we end up in circumstances where everybody gets to have a life-long vacation and go and do fun stuff, that's not such a terrible thing. On the other hand, if I own all the AI myself and decide not to share it with anybody, and everybody else starves, that's less fun. So this is a question we can't leave to the tech geeks. We need to engage economists, and everybody else, to have a conversation about what sort of society we want to create. Do we want to mandate enough taxation so that the government can take care of everybody, so that nobody sinks into dire poverty? Or do we want a social Darwinist society, where people who can't cut it just starve? That's a conversation we should have now, while there's plenty of time.

HARRIS: Well, the ethic that links our claim to existence to whether or not we're doing profitable work—that has to unwind once we have sufficiently powerful technology that obviates the need for human labor. And, as you point out, this is, at least on its face, a rosy picture of the future. No one will have to do anything to create wealth, and no one will have to do anything to survive, because we'll have technology that just pulls wealth right out of the ether. There are enough atoms within reach to do almost anything we want because we now have so much intelligence on hand. The idea that we could screw up that level of abundance over a misguided ethics, or tribal politics—that's the worst-case scenario. That would be the most humiliating failure of the human project. The apes, having achieved the perfect labor-saving technology, just manage to further immiserate and kill one another.

TEGMARK: I completely agree. My MIT colleague Erik Brynjolfsson in our business school put this eloquently on a panel at a recent AI conference: "If we can't ensure that everybody gets better off after this huge explosion of wealth, then shame on us." Shame on us!

Acknowledgments

The first debt I must acknowledge is both direct and material: because while most podcasts depend on advertising revenue, *Making Sense* is entirely supported by its subscribers. The resulting business model has given me a degree of autonomy and job security that exists nowhere else in media.

The fact that *Making Sense* has become a viable subscription business is largely due to the insights and creativity of Jaron Lowenstein. Early on, I also benefited from the wise counsel of my friend Gavin de Becker. Both worked hard to discover my inner entrepreneur—and, despite my best efforts, they finally succeeded. I will be buying each of these men dinner for the rest of their lives.

Jackie Phillips, Mary Morrison, Gabe Greenland, Stacie Parra, Gary Newman, and Porscha Pressler keep *Making Sense* running behind the scenes. I'm extremely grateful for their ongoing work.

Needless to say, the success of the podcast has been largely due to the quality of its guests. In particular, I want to thank David Chalmers, David Deutsch, Anil Seth, Thomas Metzinger, Timothy Snyder, Glenn Loury, Robert Sapolsky, Daniel Kahneman, Nick Bostrom, David Krakauer, and Max Tegmark for the time they took to refine their contributions to this book.

As for the book itself, my debts only further compound. Denise

Oswald, my editor at Ecco, should be canonized for her patience. Somehow, I've become one of those authors for whom a delivery date in publishing contract is considered aspirational. It has been a pure pleasure to work with her. She owes me no such compliment.

Thomas LeBien, Amanda Moon, Sara Lippincott, and Martha Spaulding provided crucial editorial help at various stages along the way. There would have been no book without them.

As always, thanks are due to my agents, John Brockman and Max Brockman, for maintaining my connection to the world of publishing.

Finally, it's become impossible to imagine doing much of anything without the love and support of my wife, Annaka Harris. I've had far more than my fair share of good luck in this life, and Annaka—along with our two glorious girls, Emma and Violet—is the clearest proof of it. I now live each day hoping to deserve the life we have built together.

Contributors

NICK BOSTROM is a professor at Oxford University, where he leads the Future of Humanity Institute as its founding director. A Swedish-born philosopher with a background in theoretical physics, computational neuroscience, logic, and artificial intelligence, he is the author of approximately two hundred publications, including *Anthropic Bias*, *Global Catastrophic Risks*, *Human Enhancement*, and *Superintelligence: Paths, Dangers, Strategies*, a *New York Times* bestseller.

DAVID CHALMERS is university professor of philosophy and neural science and codirector of the Center for Mind, Brain, and Consciousness at New York University. His principal interest is in the nature of consciousness. He is the author of *The Conscious Mind*, *The Character of Consciousness*, and *Constructing the World*.

DAVID DEUTSCH is a visiting professor of physics at the Center for Quantum Computation at the Clarendon Laboratory of Oxford University, where he works on the quantum theory of computation and information, and constructor theory. He has written two books for the general reader: *The Fabric of Reality* and *The Beginning of Infinity*.

DANIEL KAHNEMAN is the Eugene Higgins professor of psychology emeritus at Princeton University and professor of psychology and public affairs emeritus at Princeton's Woodrow Wilson School of Public and International Affairs. He received the 2002 Nobel Prize in economic sciences for his pioneering work with Amos Tversky on decision making. His most recent book is *Thinking, Fast and Slow*.

DAVID KRAKAUER is president and William H. Miller professor of complex systems at the Santa Fe Institute. His research explores the evolution of intelligence and stupidity on Earth. This includes studying the evolution of genetic, neural, linguistic, social, and cultural mechanisms supporting memory and information processing, and exploring their generalities. He is the editor in chief of the Santa Fe Institute Press and the founder of the InterPlanetary Project and Festival. He served as the founding director of the Wisconsin Institute for Discovery, the codirector of the Center for Complexity and Collective Computation, and was professor of mathematical genetics at the University of Wisconsin–Madison. He also served as chair of the faculty and a resident professor and external professor at the Santa Fe Institute. He has been a visiting fellow at the Genomics Frontiers Institute at the University of Pennsylvania, a Sage fellow at the Sage Center for the Study of the Mind at the University of Santa Barbara, a long-term fellow of the Institute for Advanced Study in Princeton, and visiting professor of evolution at Princeton University.

GLENN C. LOURY is the Merton P. Stoltz professor of the social sciences and professor of economics at Brown University. He holds a BA in mathematics from Northwestern University and a PhD in economics from MIT. As a prominent social critic writing mainly on racial inequality and social policy, he has published more than two hundred essays and reviews in journals of public affairs in the United States and abroad. His books include *One by One, from the Inside Out: Essays and Reviews on Race and Responsibility in America*; *The Anatomy of Racial Inequality*; *Ethnicity, Social Mobility, and Public Policy: Comparing the US and the UK*; and *Race, Incarceration, and American Values*.

THOMAS METZINGER was recently awarded a Senior-Forschungs-professur (senior research professorship) at Johannes Gutenberg University in Mainz, Germany. Previously he was a professor of theoretical philosophy and director of the research group on neuroethics and neurophilosophy at the university. He is a cofounder and past president of the Association for the Scientific Study of Consciousness and past president of the German Cognitive Science Society. He is also the founder and director of the MIND group and an adjunct fellow at the Frankfurt Institute for Advanced Studies. His research centers on the analytic philosophy of mind, applied ethics, and the philosophy of cognitive science. In 2018 he was nominated into the EU's High-Level Expert Group on Artificial Intelligence. He is the author of *Being No One* and *The Ego Tunnel*, and the editor of *Conscious Experience, Neural Correlates of Consciousness*. He is also the editor of *Open MIND, Philosophy, and Predictive Processing*, and *Radical Disruptions of Self-Consciousness*, all of which are Open Access publications.

ROBERT SAPOLSKY is a professor of biology and neurology at Stanford University and the recipient of a MacArthur Foundation genius grant. He is the author of *A Primate's Memoir, The Trouble with Testosterone, Why Zebras Don't Get Ulcers*, and *Behave: The Biology of Humans at Our Best and Worst*.

ANIL SETH is a professor of cognitive and computational neuroscience at the University of Sussex and founding codirector of the Sackler Centre for Consciousness Science. He conducted his postdoctoral research at the Neurosciences Institute in San Diego. He focuses on the biological basis of consciousness, bringing neuroscience, mathematics, artificial intelligence, computer science, psychology, philosophy, and psychiatry together in his lab. He is the editor in chief of the journal *Neuroscience of Consciousness* and has published more than 150 research papers. He is the author of the forthcoming book *Being You*.

TIMOTHY SNYDER is the Richard C. Levin professor of history at Yale University and a permanent fellow at the Institute for Human Sciences in Vienna. He received his doctorate from the University of Oxford in 1997 and joined the faculty at Yale in 2001, where he specializes in the history of Central and Eastern Europe. He speaks five (and reads ten) European languages. Snyder is the author of books including the award-winning *Bloodlands: Europe between Hitler and Stalin*; *The Red Prince*; *Black Earth: The Holocaust as History and Warning*; and *On Tyranny: 20 Lessons from the Twentieth Century*.

MAX TEGMARK is a cosmologist and professor of physics at the Massachusetts Institute of Technology. He is an increasingly influential voice on the topic of artificial intelligence and existential threats due to his research at the Future of Life Institute. Known as "Mad Max" for his unorthodox ideas and passion for adventure, he has published more than 250 technical papers and has been featured in dozens of science documentaries. His scientific interests range from precision cosmology to the ultimate nature of reality. He is the author of *Our Mathematical Universe* and *Life 3.0*.

About the Author

SAM HARRIS is the author of five *New York Times* bestsellers. His books include *The End of Faith, Letter to a Christian Nation, The Moral Landscape, Free Will, Lying,* and *Waking Up. The End of Faith* won the 2005 PEN/Martha Albrand Award for Nonfiction. His work has been published in more than twenty languages. Harris has written for the *New York Times,* the *Los Angeles Times,* the *Economist,* the *Times* (London), the *Boston Globe,* the *Atlantic, Annals of Neurology,* and elsewhere. Harris is also the host of the *Making Sense* podcast and creator of the Waking Up app. He received a degree in philosophy from Stanford University and a PhD in neuroscience from UCLA. Visit his website at SamHarris.org.